CO-AXA-954

CONFRONTING COMMUNISM

CONFRONTING COMMUNISM

U.S. and British Policies toward China

Victor S. Kaufman

University of Missouri Press

COLUMBIA AND LONDON

Kaufman, Victor S., 1969–
  Confronting Communism : U.S. and British policies toward China /
Victor S. Kaufman.
      p.   cm.
  Includes bibliographical references (p.   ) and index.
  1. United States—Foreign relations—China.   2. China—Foreign
relations—United States.   3. United States—Foreign relations—1945–
1989.   4. Great Britain—Foreign relations—China.   5. China—
Foreign relations—Great Britain.   6. United States—Foreign relations—
Great Britain.   7. Great Britain—Foreign relations—United States.
8. Communism—China—History.   I. Title.

E183.8.C5 K34   2001
327.73041—dc21   00-051222

⊗ This paper meets the requirements of the
American National Standard for Permanence of Paper
for Printed Library Materials, Z39.48, 1984.

Text design: Elizabeth K. Young
Jacket design: Vickie Kersey DuBois
Typesetter: The Composing Room of Michigan, Inc.
Printer and binder: Thomson-Shore, Inc.
Typefaces: Minion, Gill Sans, Sanvito

Portions of some chapters previously appeared in the *English Historical
Review,* Oxford University Press, and in the Journal of American-East
Asian Relations and are reprinted here with permission; materials from
the Chester Bowles Papers are used with the permission of Yale University;
materials from the Wellington Koo Papers are used with the permission
of Columbia University; materials from the George F. Kennan Papers are
used with the permission of George F. Kennan and Princeton University;
materials from the John Foster Dulles Papers are used with the permission
of Princeton University.

TO MY PARENTS

CONTENTS

PREFACE

Shortly after the Bolsheviks took power in Russia in 1917, British Prime Minister David Lloyd George told the American ambassador of his decision to try to improve relations with the new Russian government. When informed by the American ambassador that the United States would not shake hands with the new leaders in Moscow, Lloyd George responded, "I'll tell you what to do. If you don't want to shake hands with the Bolsheviks, you let us do it, and then you shake hands with us."[1]

These words are quite surprising, considering that after the Bolshevik Revolution, Lloyd George had stood alongside U.S. President Woodrow Wilson in condemning Russia's new leaders, and he had joined the Americans in sending soldiers to support the Bolsheviks' enemies. But by 1919, reality had begun to set in. It had become clear that the Communists were going to consolidate their power. Weakened by World War I and desirous to open new markets for the benefit of the British economy—if not the economy of Europe—Lloyd George decided it was best to accept the new Russian government and cease Britain's military intervention. Furthermore, contacts with the Bolsheviks would "demonstrate the vitality of liberal democracy," which might serve to moderate the attitude of the new Communist leadership toward the West, if not alter its character.[2]

Wilson found Lloyd George's arguments nonsensical. Granting recognition to the Bolsheviks, Wilson believed, "would encourage them and their followers in other lands." The president and his advisers hoped that this new ideology, which was anathema to the liberal capitalist values the president favored, would simply disappear.[3] The Bolshevik leadership, however, did not disappear, and finally, in 1933, the United States accorded recognition to the Russian leadership.

1. Lord Beaverbrook, *The Decline and Fall of Lloyd George*, 291.
2. Lloyd C. Gardner, *Safe for Democracy: The Anglo-American Response to Revolution, 1913–1923*, 264–65, 270; Edward M. Bennett, *Recognition of Russia: An American Foreign Policy Dilemma*, 48.
3. N. Gordon Levin, *Woodrow Wilson and World Politics: America's Response to War and Revolution*, 57–58, 70–71.

This brief story of the Anglo-American response to the revolution in Russia is most interesting, for there are parallels between it and the countries' response to the communist revolution that took place in China in 1949. If there was one difference, it was that the United States realized from almost the beginning that China's Communists would achieve victory. The similarities, however, are striking: whereas the British took the position that it was important to "shake hands" with the Chinese Communist leadership for the benefit of both British and Western interests, the United States rapidly traveled to the opposite pole: toughness was the best way to deal with China.

In short, at issue was how to properly contain China and the communist threat writ large. The British favored a policy of compromise and negotiation. Through contacts, argued Whitehall, the new Chinese leaders would come to see what the West could offer them, thereby moderating their attitude toward the West. In turn, they would be kept from turning completely to the Soviet Union, thus weakening the unity of the communist world. And, as a nice side benefit, contacts with the new People's Republic (PRC) would promote Sino-British commerce, which was vitally important to a United Kingdom weakened economically by World War II.

At first, the White House, at least on paper, agreed with Whitehall's position of negotiation and compromise. Rather quickly, however, it drifted to the opposite pole: a policy of pressure stood a better chance of success. While such a stance would push Beijing into Moscow's arms in the short run, in the long run it would create divisions because the Chinese Communists would come to realize that the Soviets could not fulfill their needs. In turn, the PRC would have no choice but to make concessions to the West so as to get the materials it required.

While other scholars have pointed out divisions between the United States and Britain over how to contain China and split the Sino-Soviet relationship, they tend to focus on the military initiatives involved, such as military assistance or actual or threatened war. Such efforts to contain the PRC included military aid to nations on China's periphery, the war in Korea, "United Action" in Indochina, and the offshore islands crises of 1954–1955 and 1958. Yet there was more to the policy of containment. It was not just military in nature, but also *economic* and *political*. The former consisted of policies designed to weaken the PRC's industrial, and hence its economic and military, power by denying Beijing a wide variety of raw materials and other goods. The latter revolved around the questions of recognizing the Communist government and admitting it to the United Nations. In comparison to the issue of military containment, the economic and political components of the containment of China have received far less attention.

What these scholars also tend to ignore is the sheer length of the disputes involved. Divisions between the United States and Britain over how best to deal with the PRC continued for over two decades. Unfortunately, most of the literature on American or British relations toward China focuses on the period from 1949 to 1960, and there is not a single work on Anglo-American policies toward China that traverses the year 1958.[4]

The purpose of this study, therefore, is to examine the divisions between the United States and Britain over how best to contain Communist China at the military, political, and economic levels from the year before the Chinese Communist Party (CCP) took power to the Sino-American rapprochement of 1972, and to assess how the Anglo-American alliance withstood the strains caused by those divisions. I make two conclusions. First, as noted, the goal of the allies was the same, but the methods differed. Britain favored a policy of negotiation and compromise; the United States preferred one of pressure. The White House would maintain this policy of pressure until the mid-1960s. When the Cultural Revolution began in 1966, Washington saw the opportunity for an improvement in Sino-American relations, culminating in Richard Nixon's trip to Beijing in 1972.

Second, despite this difference of opinion over how to approach Beijing, the Anglo-American alliance did not suffer a schism because, more often than not, the British adopted, in whole or in part, the U.S. position. Whether they wanted to accept it or not, U.K. officials could not escape the fact that their country was dependent upon the United States, both financially and militarily. Not wanting to present a divided front to the communist world, or to risk losing much-needed American military and economic aid, the British compromised most every time. Furthermore, when they did refuse to follow the U.S. lead, they generally did so in the most cautious manner.

Of course, in examining Anglo-American policy toward China, it is important not to ignore Beijing's views of its place in the world and of Western efforts to contain it. Since the 1980s, conditions for research in the PRC have improved. Scholars now have greater access to CCP documents and a clear-

---

4. There is a large body of literature on Sino-American and Sino-British relations. An abbreviated list of more recent monographs includes Nancy Bernkopf Tucker, *Taiwan, Hong Kong, and the United States, 1945–1992: Uncertain Friendships;* Rosemary Foot, *The Practice of Power: U.S. Relations with China since 1949;* David M. Finkelstein, *Washington's Taiwan Dilemma, 1949–1950: From Abandonment to Salvation;* David Clayton, *Imperialism Revisited: Political and Economic Relations between Britain and China, 1950–54;* and Zhong-ping Feng, *The British Government's China Policy, 1945–1950.*

For Anglo-American relations toward China, see Lanxin Xiang, *Recasting the Imperial Far East: Britain and America in China, 1945–1950;* Qiang Zhai, *The Dragon, the Lion, and the Eagle: Chinese-British-American Relations, 1949–1958;* and Edwin W. Martin, *Divided Counsel: The Anglo-American Response to Communist Victory in China.*

er view of the PRC's attitude during the Cold War. It is clear from these new materials that the Chinese, while ideologically bound to Marxism, also demonstrated a tactical flexibility in dealing with "imperialist" nations. By taking a harder line with the United States than with the United Kingdom, the CCP hoped to divide the Anglo-American alliance and weaken the non-communist world. China's leaders, moreover, were determined to protect the security of their nation from foreign attack and to prevent the division of China between the mainland and Taiwan.

Most of the Chinese personal and place names are given in *pinyin*. Because of their familiarity to readers, however, some Wade-Giles names, such as Taipei, Quemoy, Matsu, and Chiang Kai-shek, are used.

ACKNOWLEDGMENTS

Completing this work would not have been possible without the generosity and assistance of many people. My father, Burton Kaufman, read over portions of the manuscript and gave me both commentary and advice. I would also like to thank Drs. Alonzo Hamby, Donald Jordan, and Jie Li for their suggestions. Most of all, though, my appreciation goes to my adviser, Dr. Chester Pach, who carefully read over the manuscript, raised questions, suggested changes, and gave of his time to help me turn a mass of documents into a coherent manuscript.

The staff at the University of Missouri Press went out of their way to help me prepare the manuscript for publication: acquisitions editor Clair Willcox, managing editor Jane Lago, marketing manager Karen Caplinger, and director Beverly Jarrett. My gratitude also goes to the two anonymous readers for their comments and suggestions.

Financial support for this project came primarily from two sources. The Contemporary History Institute at Ohio University provided me a travel grant, as did the Lyndon B. Johnson Library.

There are numerous people I would like to thank for assisting me with researching this project and for opening their homes to me during my travels. Dennis Bilger, Randy Sowell, Liz Safly, and Sam Roche, who made me feel right at home, at the Harry S. Truman Library, David Haight at the Dwight D. Eisenhower Library, William Johnson of the John F. Kennedy Library, and John Wilson at the Lyndon B. Johnson Library all provided me much-needed assistance. I would also like to thank the staffs of those libraries, as well as the staffs and archivists at the National Archives (including the Richard Nixon Presidential Materials Project), the National Security Archive, the Marshall Foundation National Archives Project, Butler Library at Columbia University, Mudd Library at Princeton University, Yale University's Sterling Memorial Library, and the Public Record Office. During my work in Independence, Missouri, Heraldine Helm offered a warm, comfortable room. The Keithleys, longtime friends—and my adopted "second parents" —opened their doors to me and kept me well fed as I researched in Abilene, Kansas. My grandmother, Fanny Lazarus, took good care of me while I was in Texas, as did my aunt in Boston, Shirley Novack. The Cresswells treated me like family during my stay in London. Finally, I cannot express enough gratitude to my parents for their love and encouragement.

ABBREVIATIONS

The following abbreviations appear in the notes.

AWF	Ann Whitman File
BL	Butler Library, Columbia University, New York, New York
CAB	Cabinet Records, Public Record Office, Kew, London
DBPO	*Documents on British Policy Overseas*
DDEL	Dwight D. Eisenhower Library, Abilene, Kansas
FO	Foreign Office Records, Public Record Office, Kew, London
FRUS	*Foreign Relations of the United States*
HSTL	Harry S. Truman Library, Independence, Missouri
JFKL	John F. Kennedy Library, Boston, Massachusetts
LBJL	Lyndon B. Johnson Library, Austin, Texas
MFNAP	Marshall Foundation National Archives Project, Preston Library, Virginia Military Academy, Lexington, Virginia
ML	Mudd Library, Princeton University, Princeton New Jersey
NA	National Archives, College Park, Maryland
NPMP	Nixon Presidential Materials Project, National Archives, College Park, Maryland
NSA	National Security Archive, Gelman Library, George Washington University, Washington, D.C.
NSC	National Security Council
NSF	National Security File
POF	President's Office File
PREM	Prime Minister's Office Records, Public Record Office, Kew, London
PRO	Public Record Office, Kew, London
PSF	President's Secretary's File
RG	Record Group

SML   Sterling Memorial Library, Yale University, New Haven, Connecticut

VPSF   Vice Presidential Security File

WHCF   White House Central File

WHO   White House Office

WHSF   White House Special File

CONFRONTING COMMUNISM

I

FROM QUIESCENCE TO COMPLAINT,
1948–1950

The years 1948 and 1949 provided a stark contrast in terms of U.S. and British policies toward China. During 1948, the United Kingdom looked to the United States to take the lead in dealing with China. Whitehall had what it regarded as more important concerns elsewhere, and as its interests were not directly affected by America's attitude, there was no reason to challenge Washington.

The situation was completely different in 1949. Early on, it became obvious that a Communist victory was highly likely; moreover, the Communists took a variety of actions that angered the United States. Accordingly, U.S. policy on China hardened on all fronts: militarily, economically, and politically. When Washington pressured Whitehall to follow suit, the British found themselves trapped between a China policy they favored, and the demands of the United States, upon which they relied heavily.

China in 1948 was a nation torn. For twenty years, two groups had been fighting for control of the country: the Chinese Communist Party (CCP), led by Mao Zedong, and the Nationalist (or Kuomintang, KMT) government of Chiang Kai-shek. Although the KMT had held the upper hand throughout most of the civil war, after World War II, the Communists made significant gains. Nationalist corruption, Chiang's unwillingness to implement social and economic reforms, the Communists' effective economic program and propaganda machine in those areas of China they controlled—largely in the northeast—and Russian support for Mao and his lieutenants helped bolster the CCP's popularity, manpower, and military capabilities. By late 1948, the Communists had enough arms and men to break out of Manchuria; within a year, they had taken China and forced Chiang into exile on the island of Taiwan.

Both the United Kingdom and United States were aware of the situation in China, but the former was unwilling to involve itself in trying to resolve the crisis. That desire became evident in early 1945, when the head of the Foreign Office's Far Eastern Department, J. C. Sterndale-Bennett, argued that an

1

end to China's civil war would allow Britain to regain the influence there it had lost during World War II. Sterndale-Bennett's colleagues did not concur. For them, other areas of the world were more important. Primary concern was given to Europe, including the home islands. Great Britain itself had suffered damage to both its cities and its economy during the war and had emerged with a large debt.[1] Moreover, by 1948 Soviet communism had taken hold throughout much of Eastern Europe, and the British thought it vital to keep communism from spreading throughout the remainder of the continent.

Second to Europe was the Middle East. Not only did the United Kingdom have large investments in this part of the world, especially in oil, but British officials believed that withdrawing from the region would leave a power vacuum that the Soviet Union would fill. Additionally, Washington wanted London to continue to play a role in the area, thereby freeing up U.S. resources for use elsewhere.[2]

After Europe and the Middle East came East and Southeast Asia. Even here, China ranked below the colonies of Hong Kong and Malaya. In the latter the British colonial government was fighting a Communist insurgency. This is not to say that Whitehall totally ignored China. Indeed, Britain saw in China a potentially large market, as demonstrated by U.K. investments there, which were far greater than those of any other Western power. Yet it was clear to British officials by the end of World War II that Britain no longer had the power to play a predominant role in Chinese affairs. Hence, Whitehall looked to the United States to take the lead in China and devoted its attention to what it regarded as more vital interests.[3]

The United States was prepared to take that leading role. Officials in Washington shared London's concerns about the spread of communism. Creating a stable, pro-Western China would play an important part in America's larger worldwide effort to contain the Marxist threat.

Yet the policy adopted by the United States between 1945 and 1947 was contradictory. On the one hand, Washington continued to provide economic and military assistance to the Nationalists. Indeed, the U.S. military helped move KMT soldiers to Manchuria in an attempt to prevent the CCP from filling the vacuum left by the Japanese. On the other hand, the United States

1. Tang, *Britain's Encounter with Revolutionary China,* 15–16; D. Cameron Watt, "Britain and the Cold War in the Far East, 1945–58," in *The Origins of the Cold War in Asia,* ed. Yonosuke Nagai and Akira Iriye, 93–94.

2. Nagai and Iriye, eds., *Origins of the Cold War in Asia,* 94; C. J. Bartlett, *British Foreign Policy in the Twentieth Century,* 75

3. Nagai and Iriye, eds., *Origins of the Cold War in Asia,* 94–95, 98–99.

sought a cease-fire between the CCP and KMT followed by the formation of a stable, pro-Western, coalition government. Yet it proved impossible to overcome years of distrust between the Nationalists and the Communists. Continued U.S. aid to the KMT did not help matters: the CCP saw such assistance as proof that Washington was not an honest broker; the Nationalists saw it as a sign that the United States would not abandon them, even if they refused to make concessions to the Communists.

By early 1948, the White House had begun to reassess its position. Despite billions of dollars in aid to the Nationalists, the tide showed signs of turning in the favor of the Communists. The United States withdrew its military presence on the mainland and looked toward developing a defensive perimeter in the western Pacific.[4] At the same time, it had to assess how to handle a China that looked likely to come under Communist control. The Truman administration decided the best response was one of wait and see, an attitude shared by British Prime Minister Clement Attlee and his subordinates.

Truman, when he became president in 1945, had little experience in foreign affairs. As a senator, and later as vice president, Truman had devoted his time primarily to domestic issues. Becoming president required him to give more attention to foreign policy. He proved a fast learner, though he devoted much of his attention to Europe. He admitted in early 1946, "I know very little about Chinese politics." Yet what he did know disturbed him. After World War II, he had supported the continuation of aid to the Nationalists, but his attitude soon changed. He came to dislike Chiang Kai-shek, telling a friend in 1951 that the Nationalist leader was the head of "the most corrupt government in the history of the world." As for Nationalist officials in general, he privately mused in 1948 that they were "all thieves, every last one of them." Indeed, by mid-1947, he had effectively written off the Chinese leader.[5]

Attlee had far more experience in foreign policy than his American counterpart. In 1924, he was appointed secretary of war in Ramsay MacDonald's first government. Three years later, he became a member of the Simon Commission on India. In 1935, he was appointed head of the Parliamentary Labour Party; during his tenure, he met numerous foreign leaders, including Juan Negrín of Spain, Léon Blum of France, and Edward Benes of Czechoslovakia. In 1936 he also visited the Soviet Union, thereby acquiring knowl-

4. Marc S. Gallicchio, *The Cold War Begins in Asia: American East Asian Policy and the Fall of the Japanese Empire,* 143.

5. Zhai, *Dragon, the Lion, and the Eagle,* 35; Alonzo L. Hamby, *Man of the People: A Life of Harry S. Truman,* 398; James T. Patterson, *Grand Expectations: The United States, 1945–1974,* 170.

edge of Moscow's foreign policy concerns. In 1940, he became deputy prime minister in Winston Churchill's wartime coalition cabinet.[6]

Following his election to the prime ministership in July 1945, Attlee appointed Ernest Bevin foreign secretary. Bevin had much less experience in foreign policy than Attlee; he had spent much of his time prior to 1940 in the labor movement. In 1940, however, he had joined Churchill's wartime cabinet as minister of labor. Frank Roberts, the foreign secretary's private secretary, commented that Bevin's experience in the cabinet during the war gave "him experience of the problems of handling international affairs at the highest level in most crucial times." If Bevin had one major problem, it was that he spent too much time on politics and foreign policy and not enough attending to his health. His doctor stated that he had "no sound organ in his 18-stone body apart from his feet." The foreign secretary smoked heavily and suffered from numerous ailments, including angina, cardiac failure, sinusitis, an enlarged liver, and high blood pressure. (His health was so bad that in 1947 the British Broadcasting Corporation began planning his obituary.) Despite these ailments, he survived to age seventy, passing away in March 1951.[7]

Like Truman, Attlee and Bevin devoted much of their attention, at least until 1950, to Europe. Britain concentrated on rebuilding areas damaged in the war, meeting the threat posed by the Soviet Union, and in Asia, dealing with affairs in India, Hong Kong, and Malaya. China remained a secondary concern. Therefore, the two men largely left China policy in the hands of their subordinates.[8]

In 1948, Bevin's counterpart in Washington was George Marshall. Marshall had enjoyed a renowned military career, as well as substantial experience in China. He had served in China on three separate occasions in the 1920s and 1930s. In 1945, only a day after retiring as army chief of staff, Marshall acceded to Truman's request that he return to China to try to bring an end to the civil war. Although he called for both a cease-fire and a coalition government, continued U.S. assistance to the Nationalists served both to anger the CCP and to harden Chiang's unwillingness to make concessions to the Communists. Fed up with the intransigence of both sides, Marshall left China in early 1947. By then, he had developed strong doubts about the future of the Nationalists and their stability. In fact, he believed that Washington should not commit itself to the KMT and told the Senate Foreign Rela-

6. Raymond Smith and John Zametica, "The Cold Warrior: Clement Attlee Reconsidered," 238–39.

7. Tang, *Britain's Encounter with Revolutionary China*, 9; Robert D. Pearce, *Attlee's Labour Governments, 1945–51*, 20–21; Peter Weiler, *Ernest Bevin*, 146.

8. Robert Boardman, *Britain and the People's Republic of China, 1949–74*, 9; Tang, *Britain's Encounter with Revolutionary China*, 10.

tions Committee in February 1947 that such a commitment would drag the United States into the civil war. His views had a powerful influence upon Truman, who believed strongly in Marshall's judgment, and help explain in part the president's own changing attitude toward supporting Chiang.[9]

Marshall's resignation in January 1949, as a result of ill health, and the naming of Dean Acheson as his replacement did not represent a change in perceptions of China. If anything, Acheson devoted even less attention to China than had his predecessor. The son of a well-to-do family and the recipient of a law degree from Yale, Acheson had been involved in Washington politics for some fifteen years. In 1940, Franklin Roosevelt had appointed him to the State Department; under Truman, he became undersecretary of state. Acheson was a Europeanist, devoting much of his attention to the growing Cold War tensions in Europe. He had had some exposure to China, working with Marshall in trying to bring an end to the civil war and sharing his superior's frustrations with Chiang. But China was less important than Europe. "It could not provide the markets or commodities that other areas would supply. It was essentially insignificant, complicated—a morass better avoided." Therefore, like Attlee and Bevin, Acheson chose to leave China policy to his subordinates.[10]

The two men upon whom Acheson relied the most when it came to China policy were Ambassador-at-Large Philip Jessup and Undersecretary of State for Political Affairs Dean Rusk. A close friend of Acheson, Jessup acted as a sounding board, someone to whom the secretary could provide information and from whom he could receive advice. Rusk had experience in Asia, having fought in the China-Burma-India theater during World War II. Balancing Acheson's concentration on European affairs, Rusk devoted more time to East Asia. Though aware that the United States could not prevent the Communists' capture of the mainland, he looked for opportunities to spare the people of China from Communist rule.[11]

Three other officials who devoted attention to China were the director of

9. Mark A. Stoler, *George C. Marshall: Soldier-Statesman of the American Century,* 133; Ed Cray, *General of the Army: George C. Marshall, Soldier and Statesman,* 581; Warren I. Cohen, "Acheson, His Advisers, and China, 1949–1950," in *Uncertain Years: Chinese-American Relations, 1947–1950,* ed. Dorothy Borg and Waldo Heinrichs, 14; William Whitney Stueck, Jr., *The Road to Confrontation: American Policy toward China and Korea, 1947–1950,* 58; William P. Head, *America's China Sojourn: America's Foreign Policy and Its Effects on Sino-American Relations, 1942–1948,* 226–27.

10. Robert M. Blum, *Drawing the Line: The Origin of the American Containment Policy in East Asia,* 13–14; Borg and Heinrichs, *Uncertain Years,* 14; Nancy Bernkopf Tucker, "China's Place in the Cold War: The Acheson Plan," in *Dean Acheson and the Making of U.S. Foreign Policy,* ed. Douglas Brinkley, 111.

11. Borg and Heinrichs, *Uncertain Years,* 17–18.

the Office of Far Eastern Affairs—and later assistant secretary of state for Far Eastern Affairs—W. Walton Butterworth; the head of the Policy Planning Staff (PPS), George Kennan; and the PPS's China specialist, John Paton Davies. A foreign service officer with previous experience in China, Butterworth had developed a strong distaste for anyone with sentimental attachments to that country. He did not like the CCP, but he also questioned the value of furnishing aid to the Nationalists. His attitude earned him the enmity of Chiang and his advisers, who were pleased when Butterworth was reassigned in 1950.[12]

Kennan, the State Department's premier Soviet specialist, believed that Japan, not China, had the potential to play a major role in Asia. He considered ties with Chiang "to be both fateful and discreditable" and favored severing them "at once, at the cost, if need be, of a real domestic-political showdown." Moreover, he strongly questioned the susceptibility of the CCP to Soviet control and contended that a Communist victory would not necessarily prove disastrous for the United States.[13]

Kennan's ideas on China were greatly influenced by Davies. The son of missionary parents, Davies had been born in China. Even so, he was very detached when it came to China and the KMT. As early as 1943, he had warned against Washington tying itself too closely to Chiang. By 1947, he believed that nothing short of overt military action could save the Nationalists. He argued that to continue the policy of economic and military assistance to the KMT would only serve to push the Communists into Moscow's arms. Rather, he felt that the United States should prepare itself to deal with a Communist-led China. Such a situation, he added, would not prove detrimental to America's interests. The Kremlin would have difficulty dominating the CCP. In fact, he argued, America should develop relations with China against the Soviet Union.[14]

Bevin could also turn to several people for information on China, but his most influential adviser was Esler Dening. Dening had substantial experience in East Asia; he had served in the Japanese Consular Service and then as Lord Mountbatten's political adviser during World War II. Under Attlee, he became superintending undersecretary first of the Foreign Office's China De-

12. Ibid., 18–19; Blum, Drawing the Line, 14.

13. Borg and Heinrichs, Uncertain Years, 19–20; George Kennan, Memoirs: 1950–1963, 54–55; Minutes of the Meeting of the Secretary of State's Council, Jan. 14, 1948, Papers of George F. Kennan–Writing and Publications Collection, box 17, ML; John Lewis Gaddis, The Long Peace: Inquiries into the History of the Cold War, 163.

14. Borg and Heinrichs, Uncertain Years, 20–21; David Allan Mayers, George Kennan and the Dilemmas of U.S. Foreign Policy, 171–72; John Paton Davies, Dragon by the Tail: American, British, Japanese, and Russian Encounters with China and One Another, 299.

partment and later of the Far Eastern Department. Dening believed that the CCP would seek to establish working relations with other nations, including those in the West. Thus, he too favored a wait-and-see approach.[15]

The policies the United States and Britain adopted reflected the support within the Truman and Attlee governments for a watchful stance. Implementing those policies was another matter. Inconsistency continued to plague the U.S. attitude toward China. But as the United Kingdom and its interests were not directly affected, it had no reason for complaint.

By early 1948, it had become clear to officials in Washington that the Nationalists were unlikely to win the civil war. Accordingly, Kennan had the PPS prepare a comprehensive study of future U.S. policy on China. Presented to Marshall in September 1948, the document clearly reflected the influence of Kennan and Davies. Yet because it was the result of a collaborative effort of the various bureaus of the State Department, this study can be regarded as representing the view of that entire department.[16]

In its study, the PPS determined that Chiang's government could only be saved through large-scale aid. Repeating Marshall's warning of the year before, Kennan's group cautioned that such assistance would ultimately require overt U.S. intervention, which would serve to push the Chinese people into the arms of the Communists. Without American aid, the CCP was likely to win the war, but such an eventuality would not prove "catastrophic" for the United States. Indeed, a Chinese Communist victory could lead to a Sino-Soviet rift: the CCP would likely develop ties with the Kremlin but would want to keep them hidden because of strong nationalist and xenophobic sentiment among the Chinese people; yet the Soviets, intent on avoiding an experience similar to that they had faced with Yugoslavia's leader, Joseph Broz Tito—who openly broke with Moscow in 1948—would want to bring China's subservience out in the open. "The possibilities which such a situation would present us . . . need scarcely be spelled out."[17]

The PPS, accordingly, recommended for the first time what became known as the "wedge" strategy: policies designed to produce division in the Sino-Soviet relationship. Creating divisions would assist in the policy of containing communism by weakening the solidarity of the communist world. The PPS implied that the "wedge" strategy stood the best chance of success if the United States maintained a completely flexible position. While Washington for the time being should continue to recognize the Nationalist gov-

15. Tang, *Britain's Encounter with Revolutionary China*, 11.

16. Gaddis, *Long Peace*, 163; Yu-ming Shaw, *An American Missionary in China: John Leighton Stuart and Chinese-American Relations*, 235.

17. PPS 39, "United States Policy toward China," Sept. 7, 1949, *FRUS, 1949*, 8:146–55.

ernment, "[w]e must not become irrevocably committed to any one course of action or any one faction in China and we must be willing to cut our losses when it becomes evident that any involvement is likely to prove to be a losing proposition." Both Acheson and Truman liked the PPS's conclusions and made them official policy.[18] Flexibility was the keyword for the administration.

In late 1948, Dening took the first step in redefining the U.K. position. In November, he stated, "I do not think that any useful purpose will be served by bolstering up Chiang Kai-shek's regime, because it has grown too rotten. Nor do I believe that the American [sic] would have the [ability] even if such a course was feasible." Bevin found Dening's argument convincing and asked the Whitehall departments to prepare a paper for the cabinet examining the implications for Britain of a communist China. The following month, Dening presented the paper to the foreign secretary; it clearly reflected the influence of the Far Eastern Department head. Communist control of all of China, the paper noted, posed a number of dangers to Britain. It would increase the threat to Hong Kong, India, Pakistan, and Southeast Asia, including Malaya. Furthermore, the CCP might decide to expropriate Britain's holdings in China, which had totaled some £300 million in 1941. The Whitehall departments wanted the United States to continue to take the lead when it came to China, as only Washington had the "financial, material and military resources for counter action against the Chinese Communists." The problem was that there was no indication that the United States was prepared to act, and even if it was, there was no guarantee that such "counter action . . . will be effective." Thus, it was best for Britain to keep a foot in the door. Doing so would allow the United Kingdom to maintain trade contacts with China. Commerce with China would preserve the economic health of Hong Kong, and Britain's postwar economic problems demanded that it too look for places to export goods. Furthermore, contacts with the Chinese Communists offered the possibility of driving a wedge between them and the Soviet Union. Like the PPS, the Whitehall departments believed that a weak, divided communist world would be easier to contain than a strong, united one. Bevin found his subordinates' recommendations persuasive and submitted the memo to the cabinet without changes. Later that month it became the official policy of the Attlee government.[19]

18. Ibid.; Gaddis, *Long Peace,* 163; Shaw, *American Missionary in China,* 236; NSC 34/2, "U.S. Policy toward China" and memorandum to NSC from Lay, Mar. 3, 1949, *FRUS, 1949,* 9:491–95, 499.

19. Feng, *British Government's China Policy,* 100–101, 104; memorandum by Dening, "China," Dec. 4, 1948, FO 371/69546. Dening's memorandum was submitted on Dec. 13 to the cabinet by Bevin as C.P. (48) 299, entitled, "Recent Developments in the Civil War

Maintaining this policy of flexibility proved far more difficult for Truman than for Attlee. First, there was a long-standing U.S. commitment to Chiang Kai-shek. Prior to and during World War II, the United States had provided him with military and economic aid. After the war, and despite calls by the PPS to avoid tying Washington to Chiang's government, this assistance continued. Stopping aid to the Nationalists was like trying to give up on a friend who was untrustworthy, but a friend nevertheless.

Additionally, there was the "domestic-political showdown" to which Kennan referred. As Acheson wrote some friends in early 1950, "Formosa is the subject which seems to draw out the boys like a red haired girl on the beach." In the United States, these "boys" came in the form of the so-called "China bloc" and its backers. Such support for China can be traced back to the late 1800s, when American missionaries arrived in China in large numbers. Influenced by their reports, Americans adopted a sentimental image of China. The Chinese people, it was believed, wanted to adopt American ways of life and government and would do so if given proper education and guidance.[20]

Such a sentimental, paternalistic stance toward China continued beyond the late 1800s. Americans praised Chiang Kai-shek's decision in 1930 to convert to Christianity and his claims of supporting democracy in China. But they could identify even more with his second wife, Soong Mei-ling, or Madame Chiang. The child of a U.S. missionary, Mei-ling had been raised in an Americanized environment. She had traveled to the United States in 1908, where she had attended Wellesley College; by the time she graduated she was thoroughly Americanized. She reportedly said at one point, "The only thing Oriental about me is my face." In November 1942, she returned to the United States, captivating Americans during her seven-month stay. Her talk of Sino-American unity and China's desire for a stable democratic government appealed to a wide audience. As one scholar noted, "Madame Chiang symbolized the message American missionaries had propagated for decades: a democratic, Christian China appeared on the verge of realization." While many Americans saw in Chiang Kai-shek a strong, democratically oriented

---

in China," CAB 129/31; Minutes of Cabinet Meeting, C.M. 80 (48), Dec. 13, 1948, CAB 128/13, PRO.

20. Acheson quote in David S. McLellan and David C. Anderson, *Among Friends: Personal Letters of Dean Acheson,* 68. For background on American interest in China and the Chinese people, see Jane Hunter, *The Gospel of Gentility: American Women Missionaries in Turn-of-the-Century China;* Michael Schaller, *The United States and China in the Twentieth Century;* Michael H. Hunt, *The Making of a Special Relationship: The United States and China to 1914;* Patricia Neils, ed., *United States Attitudes and Policies toward China: The Impact of American Missionaries.*

leader, "he could not match his wife in many fundamentally important ways. Because she managed to appear both Chinese and American at the same time, Americans long interested in China could not have asked for a better symbol to express their hopes than Madame Chiang Kai-shek."[21]

World War II reinforced the perception that the Chiangs were great leaders who supported democracy and that the Chinese people were much like Americans. Charles Edison, the chairman of United China Relief, and the son of inventor Thomas Edison, explained during a National Broadcasting Corporation radio broadcast that China was America's "sister democracy across the Pacific." Likewise in one installment of his *Why We Fight* series, Hollywood director Frank Capra depicted the Japanese as destructive barbarians and the Chinese as dignified and heroic.[22]

The end of the war only strengthened these perceptions, which were strongly reinforced by the efforts of *Time-Life* tycoon Henry Luce. The son of a missionary who worked in China, Luce had developed a close affinity for the Chinese people and a belief that Chiang Kai-shek was China's savior. Using not only his magazines *Time, Life,* and *Fortune,* but also newsreels and radio, Luce sold his views to millions of Americans. *Life* alone by 1947 was reaching nearly 4.7 million readers; indeed, a United Service to China study conducted in early 1947 found that more people listed *Life* as their source of information than any other magazine or newspaper.[23]

Such advocacy for aiding the Chiang government helped to dispel any idea of returning to isolationism after World War II ended, both among the public at large and among those working on Capitol Hill. Although there were individuals in Congress who favored isolationism, they realized that taking such a stand would make them look foolish. They, like the internationalists, feared communism. Yet they felt that Truman's method of fighting communism everywhere would cost too much. Hence, they found a way to adhere—at least to some extent—to their isolationist views while attacking Truman and the Democrats: they charged that the president was centering too much

---

21. Howard L. Boorman, *Biographical Dictionary of Republican China,* 3:146–48. For the influence of Madame Chiang on Americans, see T. Christopher Jespersen, *American Images of China, 1931–1949,* chap. 5. For more on Mei-ling herself, see Emily Hahn, *The Soong Sisters;* and Sterling Seagrave, *The Soong Dynasty.*

22. Jespersen, *American Images of China,* 72; John Dower, *War without Mercy: Race and Power in the Pacific War,* 17–18.

23. For more on Luce's support of the Nationalists and his influence on the U.S. public, see Jespersen, *American Images of China;* Robert E. Herzstein, *Henry R. Luce: A Political Portrait of the Man Who Created the American Century;* and Patricia Neils, *China Images in the Life and Times of Henry Luce.* For statistics on *Life* and the USC study, see Jespersen, *American Images of China,* 131, 144.

attention on Europe and not enough on Asia. But they were not prepared to spend large amounts of money to fight communism, be it in Asia or anywhere else. For their hypocritical stance toward Asia, Lewis McCarroll Purifoy labeled them "new isolationists" or "Asialationists."[24]

Led by two Republicans, John Taber of New York in the House and Robert Taft of Ohio in the Senate, the Asialationists found support from another group, the so-called China bloc. Like the Asialationists, China bloc members felt that the Truman administration was not devoting enough resources to Asia. Unlike the Asialationists, though, they had a sincere interest in China and a firm belief that the Chiangs needed large-scale U.S. assistance.[25]

The leader of the China bloc was Representative Walter Judd (R-Minnesota). Of Judd, one of Luce's biographers wrote, "No one, not even Harry Luce, could exceed him in loyalty to the China of Chiang Kai-shek." A former missionary in China, Judd was known for his strong, if not fanatical, support of the Chiangs. Like Luce, he saw the Chiangs as the saviors of China to whom the United States needed to give its full support.[26]

Judd found a number of allies, the most vocal of whom was Senator William Knowland (R-California). Knowland became interested in China from letters he received during the fall of 1948 from Col. Robert Griffin, an administrator of the U.S. economic aid program in China. He was also a determined opponent of Truman's Europe-first attitude. Because of his strong support for Chiang, his critics dubbed him the "senator from Formosa." Other members of the China bloc—largely made up of Republicans—included Senators H. Alexander Smith (R-New Jersey), Pat McCarran (D-Nevada), Owen Brewster (R-Maine), and Styles Bridges (R-New Hampshire); and Representatives Robert Chiperfield (R-Illinois), John Vorys (R-Ohio), and James Fulton (R-Pennsylvania).[27]

Though the China bloc itself was not large, it held substantial power. A number of its members sat in key positions in Congress. Bridges was chairman of the Appropriations Committee; Smith was a key member of the For-

24. Lewis McCarroll Purifoy, *Harry Truman's China Policy: McCarthyism and the Diplomacy of Hysteria, 1947–1951*, 49–50.

25. Ibid., 58 n 15, 59–60.

26. Quote from Herzstein, *Henry R. Luce*, 290. For more on Judd's background and his commitment to China, see Lee Edwards, *Missionary for Freedom: The Life and Times of Walter Judd*.

27. Chester J. Pach, Jr., *Arming the Free World: The Origins of the United States Military Assistance Program, 1945–1950*, 224–25. For more on the ACPA and the formation of the "China bloc" in Congress, see Stanley D. Bachrack, *The Committee of One Million: "China Lobby" Politics, 1953–1971*, chaps. 1–2. See also Ross Y. Koen, *The China Lobby in American Politics*. A source that suggests that domestic politics alone drove U.S. China policy is Purifoy, *Harry Truman's China Policy*.

eign Relations Committee; and Judd and Vorys sat on the Foreign Affairs Committee. Additionally, they had the support of the powerful chairman of the Senate Foreign Relations Committee, Arthur H. Vandenberg (R-Michigan), because he felt it was vital to make concessions to them to guarantee passage of legislation aimed at areas other than China. Finally, there was the impact of the 1948 presidential election. Truman's amazing come-from-behind victory infuriated many Republicans, who "decided that the 1952 contest would have to be ruthless and that China offered a vulnerable area for attack."[28] The 1948 elections thus gave the China bloc reinforcements from the Republican Party.

Unlike the Asialationists, most China bloc members agreed with their fellow lawmakers and the White House that priority had to be given to Europe. But when Marshall in 1947 proposed his European Recovery Program (ERP, or Marshall Plan) to aid Europe, the China bloc threatened to withhold its support if provision was not made for China. Marshall did not want to be responsible for bringing down the Nationalist government by not providing additional aid and therefore proposed $570 million in economic assistance. Simultaneously, he warned the House Foreign Affairs and Senate Foreign Relations Committees against giving additional military assistance to the KMT, lest the United States get dragged further into the civil war. Though he found some support for his views, particularly on the Foreign Relations Committee, the House proved less sympathetic. Here, Judd and his supporters succeeded in altering Marshall's proposal to include $150 million in military aid. Vandenberg did not favor such a large commitment to China, but he believed that the China bloc could successfully prevent passage of the ERP and undermine his efforts at maintaining a bipartisan foreign policy; accordingly, he called for $338 million in economic aid and $125 million to be used "on such terms as the president may determine." Realizing that priority had to be given to Europe, and that they had received at least part of what they wanted, the China bloc agreed to the legislation.[29]

But the fight was not over. When the question arose in the House of appropriating the funds of the now-named China Aid Act, the China bloc and its allies again made their voice heard by calling for supervision of the $125 million in military aid. The White House, with the help of Vandenberg, defeated the proposal. In its final form, the appropriations bill, signed by Truman in late June 1948, provided a total of $400 million (including the $125

28. Blum, *Drawing the Line,* 44; Koen, *China Lobby,* 90; Pach, *Arming the Free World,* 183; Nancy Bernkopf Tucker, *Patterns in the Dust: Chinese-American Relations and the Recognition Controversy, 1949–1950,* 163.

29. For more on passage of the China Aid Act, see Stueck, *Road to Confrontation,* 58–60; and Pach, *Arming the Free World,* 179–83.

million in unsupervised military aid).[30] The administration had succeeded in defeating the China bloc's efforts, but the debate over the China Aid Act and the subsequent appropriations bill demonstrated the difficulties the China bloc and its allies could and would create for Truman and his advisers.

The Attlee government did not face such difficulties. Domestic opinion in Britain, if anything, sought an improvement in relations with the Chinese Communists. Leading the way were U.K. businesses, particularly those in Hong Kong, which favored continuing or increasing their trade with the CCP.[31]

Whitehall realized that the White House faced greater problems than it did in maintaining a truly flexible policy. Yet it said little publicly about it during 1948. To make comments would drag Britain into the volatile American electoral climate. Dening pointed out that this concern "must condition any references to the Chinese situation which His Majesty's Government may feel obliged to make in Parliament." Moreover, there was no evidence that the administration intended to close the door completely to possible relations with the Chinese Communists. Indeed, Britain seemed content to let the United States take the lead when it came to China, a fact not lost on the White House.[32] Unless or until U.S. and British policy toward China came into conflict, Whitehall would stay quiet.

That conflict began to make itself felt in 1949. The Chinese Communists' breakout from Manchuria and the Nationalists' inability to stop them made it clear on both sides of the Atlantic that a communist China was even more likely than before. The Truman administration began to shift even further away from its stated position of flexibility. Already concerned about its troubles with the China bloc, the White House now had to take into consideration CCP harassment of U.S. personnel and requisitioning of U.S. property in China, as well as the need to contain the communist threat to China itself. It therefore implemented a series of economic, military, and political measures. Economically, Washington imposed controls on goods it believed had military value and looked for allied help to make this policy effective. Militarily, it continued its program of building a defensive perimeter in the Pa-

30. Pach, *Arming the Free World,* 184.

31. Indeed, *U.S. News,* quoting the *Far Eastern Economic Review,* said in December 1949 that British businesses in Hong Kong were very upset with London's indecisiveness over recognizing Mao's government. See *U.S. News and World Report* (Dec. 16, 1949): 23. See also Karl Lott Rankin, *China Assignment,* 22–23; and Tang, *Britain's Encounter with Revolutionary China,* 49–52.

32. Memorandum by Dening, "China," Dec. 4, 1948, Department of State Policy Statement, "Great Britain," June 11, 1948, *FRUS, 1948,* 3:1101; telegram, no. 5717, Franks to Foreign Office, Nov. 11, 1948, FO 371/69586.

cific, including the continuation of aid to Taiwan, and pressured Britain not to turn over to the CCP some Nationalist-owned planes at Hong Kong. Politically, the White House refused to accord early recognition to the Communist government and urged Whitehall to follow suit.

In considering the American requests, Bevin looked at what he saw as "three interlocking circles: the Atlantic circle, the Commonwealth, and Western Europe." Britain, believed the foreign secretary, stood within these three circles. He explained to the House of Commons in November 1949 that these "three great sectors of the free world" were interconnected and that London "not only now but always will have to reconcile its responsibilities to all three; we cannot isolate ourselves from any one of them."[33]

This view of its position in the world created severe problems for Whitehall. One difficulty posed was that of the so-called special relationship between the United States and Great Britain. The United Kingdom believed that it, of all America's allies, deserved special treatment. With the exception of the United States, Britain was the only major noncommunist power to have emerged from World War II undefeated. (This does not include China, which London felt was not a major power.) Germany, Japan, and France had all surrendered. Additionally, Britain believed that it was still a great power. Bevin stated in mid-1947: "His Majesty's Government do not accept the view . . . that we have ceased to be a Great Power, or the contention that we have ceased to play that role. We regard ourselves as one of the Powers most vital to the peace of the world and we still have our historic part to play."[34]

By late 1948 the United Kingdom had removed its military forces from Greece and Palestine; it still, however, maintained a presence in Germany, the Middle East, Africa, and Southeast Asia. As a great power, Britain merited appropriate treatment. To some extent, the United States conceded Whitehall's desire for preferential treatment, as evidenced by regular but informal discussions between Acheson and British Ambassador to the United States Sir Oliver Franks. British officials hoped to use this relationship to play the role of "'elder statesman' and adviser to the newly emerged United States that was still inexperienced in the ways of power politics."[35] Actually exerting that influence was another issue.

First, the United Kingdom was in economic trouble after World War II.

33. Avi Shlaim, Peter Jones, and Keith Sainsbury, *British Foreign Secretaries since 1945,* 50–51.

34. Ibid., 38.

35. Peter Jones, *America and the British Labour Party: The "Special Relationship" at Work,* 52; Geoffrey Warner, "The Anglo-American Special Relationship," 483. In fact, Acheson met with Franks more than with all other ambassadors combined. See Alex Danchev, *Oliver Franks: Founding Father,* 118–19.

The war had left Britain with some 470,000 homes destroyed, depleted financial reserves, and a £3.5 billion debt. The severe winter of 1946–1947 only added to the nation's woes. The economy was in such a bad shape that the nation's economic experts argued that Britain's exports would have to be raised to 175 percent of their prewar total for the country to achieve a full economic recovery. The influential British economist John Maynard Keynes warned that without U.S. financial assistance, Britain faced a "financial Dunkirk." Washington agreed to help, providing a $3.75 billion loan in 1946, followed by Marshall Plan assistance. But the U.K. economy remained vulnerable, as was illustrated by the devaluation of the pound from $4.02 to $2.80 in 1949, the Suez crisis of 1956, and further devaluation of the pound in 1967.[36]

London also depended on Washington militarily. Attlee and Bevin believed that only the United States had the power to deter the threat posed by the Soviet Union, and for this reason Washington could not remain indifferent to Europe's plight.[37] To strengthen these military bonds Bevin proposed the formation of an organization that became the North Atlantic Treaty Organization (NATO).

Of course, Washington did not hold all the cards. As recent literature suggests, the Truman administration greatly worried about the United States becoming isolated. Isolation would force the country to become a "garrison state." Americans would have no choice but to husband their resources and give up the capitalist-democratic values they so cherished. Only by helping its allies and standing together with them could America prevent this bleak future.[38]

In sum, both the United States and Britain had reason to cooperate. Both realized the importance of containing communism and presenting a common front. Even so, Washington held the upper hand, both economically and militarily; hence, it played an important role in two of the three circles: the Atlantic alliance and Western Europe. Consequently, the United Kingdom had to act very cautiously whenever it attempted to guide U.S. China policy.

Yet there was a third circle, the Commonwealth. As leader of the Commonwealth, the United Kingdom could not ignore the feelings of its members, especially those with direct interests in East Asia: India, Australia, and New Zealand. Australia and New Zealand could, and did, influence decision

36. David Childs, *Britain since 1939: Progress and Decline,* 75, 89–90; Pearce, *Attlee's Labour Governments,* 34.

37. Alan Bullock, *Ernest Bevin: Foreign Secretary, 1945–1951,* 235; Jerry H. Brookshire, *Clement Attlee,* 216–17.

38. Melvyn P. Leffler, *A Preponderance of Power: National Security, the Truman Administration, and the Cold War,* 13.

making in London, but India was of special importance. To Whitehall, the decision in 1947 to grant independence to India served two purposes. First, it transformed the Commonwealth "from an organization of British settler states into a truly multiracial community." Second, it gained favor among the nations of Asia.[39] To Whitehall, New Delhi's position on China was important, in that it either reflected a wider feeling in Asia or could influence the attitude of other Asian countries. It would be the collective view of the Commonwealth circle and, more specifically, the stance taken by India, that proved decisive in Britain's decision to recognize the People's Republic (PRC).

Conflict between the United States and Britain first erupted over the subject of trade. The White House in early 1949 decided that it would continue to trade with China, as that would keep the CCP from turning to Moscow for all its economic needs and possibly create a split between them.[40] But such ties could also endanger containment. With the breakout of the People's Liberation Army (PLA) from Manchuria, it only seemed a matter of time before the Communists took control of all China. If the United States traded with China in strategic goods, it would enhance the ability of the CCP to wage aggression beyond China's borders. Such a concern appeared in February 1949, when the National Security Council (NSC) put together its first major study on commerce with China. The NSC noted, "The economic aspects of the situation . . . are of major strategic importance, and it is in the field of economic relations with China that the United States has available its most effective weapons vis-à-vis a Chinese Communist regime."[41]

How was America to limit China's war-making capability while using trade as a wedge? The NSC examined two possible answers: an extensive program of severe restrictions or a limited one involving controls only on strategic goods. The White House rejected the former, arguing that it would create difficulties for Japan—which needed trade for the revitalization of its economy—and drive China into the arms of the Soviet Union. The latter, however, would allow for the maintenance of contacts with China. At the same time, Washington would make clear that if the Communists engaged in actions inimical to American interests, the United States, in conjunction with other nations, had the power to create trouble for the Chinese economy.[42] In short, limited trade would achieve the same goal as unfettered trade with China.

The administration understood that one of the difficulties in implement-

39. Nagai and Iriye, eds., *Origins of the Cold War in Asia*, 97.

40. June M. Grasso, *Truman's Two-China Policy, 1948–1950*, 59.

41. NSC 41, "To Determine United States Policy Regarding Trade with China," Feb. 28, 1949, *FRUS, 1949*, 9:826–34.

42. Ibid.

ing this program concerned allied cooperation. "Other western nations, particularly the United Kingdom, have investments much larger than those of the United States"—Britain by this time had approximately $840 million in investments in China versus no more than $200 million for the United States—"and the economic position of Hong Kong is dependent on an active entrepôt trade with the Chinese mainland." Despite such obstacles, the NSC recommended the imposition of controls based upon the second possible course of action. Under this limited program, the United States would embargo all items classed as "List 1A" and place restrictions on those that were "List 1B." The former list included goods of high military significance; the latter, vital transportation, industrial, and communications equipment. On March 3, Truman approved the proposed controls.[43]

As the administration had predicted, the Attlee government strongly opposed the U.S. proposal on trade controls. Bevin agreed on the importance of containing the communist threat in East Asia. But economic weapons, he explained, "should be held in reserve as long as the Communists are prepared to tolerate the functioning of British concerns." The CCP would retaliate against such controls by putting pressure on Western businesses, followed by "some form of expropriation." Bevin, in short, was alluding to two concerns that guided, and would continue to guide, U.K. China policy: first, that while the United Kingdom would support or even assist U.S. efforts to contain China, it had serious qualms about taking action that might hurt the British economy; second, that while Whitehall agreed with the White House in dividing the Sino-Soviet alliance as a means of containing the communist threat, it felt the best way to drive wedges was not through more pressure, but by maintaining contacts with the new CCP government, once established. As Bevin told his ambassador in China, Sir Ralph Stevenson, in early 1949, "[W]e must bear in mind the possibility of [Mao's] wanting to develop independence of policy at a later stage and the desirability of our not discouraging such a development."[44]

Bevin's argument fell on deaf ears. Indeed, beginning in the middle of the year, the U.S. position on trade hardened. When Senator Knowland found out that the Truman administration had not stopped petroleum shipments to China, he openly condemned the White House. Public opinion supported him, with 46 percent of Americans opposed to trade with China, versus 37

43. Ibid.; memoranda of conversation, Feb. 10 and Mar. 22, 1949, *FRUS, 1949,* 823–26, 836; memorandum to the president from Souers, Mar. 3, 1949, PSF, NSF-Meetings, box 205, HSTL.

44. Memorandum by the Secretary of State for Foreign Affairs, "The Situation in China," C.P. (49) 39, Mar. 4, 1949, CAB 129/32, PRO; telegram, no. 134, Bevin to Nanking, Jan. 28, 1949, FO 1110/194, PRO.

percent in favor.[45] The final straw, however, was the CCP's refusal to release the U.S. consul in Shenyang (Mukden), Angus Ward. In November 1948, the CCP had put Ward under house arrest for refusing to turn over the consulate's radio transmitter. The Chinese Communists ignored Acheson's repeated calls for Ward's release.[46] Therefore, in June, the Commerce and State Departments recommended extending the controls to cover a wide variety of List 1B items. Acheson explained to Bevin that this extension would not only further limit the Communists' military capabilities, but would also "permit the Western Powers to demonstrate their bargaining strength *vis-à-vis* the Chinese Communist régime, to influence the orientation of that régime." Bevin balked. The British did not face such difficulties with the Chinese. Indeed, the only major incident between Whitehall and the Chinese Communists occurred in April 1949, when the PLA bombarded the U.K. frigate *Amethyst*. The incident upset many members of Parliament, but their anger was tempered by a belief that the CCP still hoped to develop trade relations with the West. Not until October 1949, and only after continual U.S. approaches, did London agree to place restrictions on strategic goods on the 1A list, but the foreign secretary rejected additional measures. He argued that they would not achieve the desired results and would undermine British efforts to keep a foot in the door and protect U.K. business interests in China.[47]

Additional efforts by the United States to obtain agreement on List 1B got nowhere. London regarded trade with China as vital. Meanwhile, the United States was not willing to press the United Kingdom so hard that it might strain the Anglo-American alliance. When the Communists in October announced a government, the Truman administration could wait no longer. It unilaterally extended the controls, adding some one hundred items to the restricted list, including certain types of oil and machine tools, as well as a variety of iron and steel products.[48] While not a complete embargo, it represented another step in that direction.

45. David Allan Mayers, *Cracking the Monolith: U.S. Policy against the Sino-Soviet Alliance, 1949–1955*, 50.

46. For a fine study of the Ward case, see Jian Chen, "The Ward Case and the Emergence of Sino-American Confrontation, 1948–1950."

47. Aide mémoire, "Control of Trade with China," Aug. 3, 1949, attached as annex "d" to memorandum by the Secretary of State for Foreign Affairs, C.P. (49) 180, "China," Aug. 23, 1949, CAB 129/36, PRO; telegram, no. 2156, Acheson to London, June 22, 1949; memorandum of conversation, June 3, 1949; aide mémoire, "Control of Trade with China," Sept. 12, 1949; memorandum to Sawyer from Webb, Oct. 4, 1949; circular telegram, unnumbered, Acheson to Certain Diplomatic and Consular Officers, Oct. 11, 1949, *FRUS, 1949*, 9:849–50, 856–59, 875–84; David C. Wolf, "'To Secure a Convenience': Britain Recognizes China—1950," 309.

48. "History of COCOM/CHINCOM," undated, RG 59, Records of the Bureau of Far Eastern Affairs, 1957, box 3, NA.

The two allies also had differences over how to contain China militarily. This divergence led to two separate disputes, the first of which centered on military assistance to Taiwan. Publicly, Truman administration officials avoided making any commitment to Taiwan. For instance, the president stated on January 5, 1950, that the United States had "no desire to obtain special rights or privileges, or to establish military bases on Formosa at this time." A week later, in his famous speech before the National Press Club, Acheson omitted Taiwan from the American defense perimeter. Accordingly, it seemed as though the United States was not prepared to defend Taiwan if the Communists attacked it.[49]

Again, however, stated policy contradicted action. In April 1949, the Truman administration had extended the life of the China Aid Act until mid-February 1950. In part, extension of the act would allow for the transmission of economic aid to those parts of mainland China still under Nationalist control, as well as to Taiwan. But domestic politics also came into play. The White House was preparing a framework for Western European defense and did not want to face a battle with the China bloc and its allies over it.[50] Yet later in the year, Chiang's congressional supporters influenced debate over the Military Assistance Program (MAP). MAP would provide military aid to various parts of the world, including Europe, as part of the containment policy, but it quickly ran into trouble. Members of both parties in both houses of Congress had difficulty with the proposed program because of its cost. The China bloc joined the opposition because of MAP's omission of aid for the Nationalists and enlisted the help of Gen. Claire Chennault, who had headed the famous "Flying Tigers" in China during World War II. Lobbying before Congress and through Luce's magazine *Life*, the general called for providing $150 to $200 million in military aid for Chiang. Neither Butterworth nor Acheson favored giving so much money to the Nationalists, the former arguing that such aid would only help the Communists since they would gain access to the new U.S. supplies. The secretary of state, however, realized he would have to find some means to satisfy the China bloc so as to get the votes he needed for the MAP's passage. He therefore agreed to a proposal to devote $75 million to the "general area" of China. The KMT's congressional supporters voted in favor, believing that this assistance would be used to conduct covert operations in China against the CCP. (Eventually, most of this money went not to China but to Indochina, which the Truman administration considered much more important to the United States.)[51]

49. Harry S. Truman, *Public Papers of the Presidents of the United States: Harry S. Truman, 1945–1953*, 1950, 11; *Department of State Bulletin* (Jan. 23, 1950): 111–18.

50. Stueck, *Road to Confrontation*, 120.

51. Pach, *Arming the Free World*, esp. 224–25; Blum, *Drawing the Line*, 73–75.

The Nationalist government used the military assistance it received from Washington to procure from the United States materials ranging from spare parts to guns and tanks. Bevin protested the continued shipment of arms, arguing that it "will not be used effectively and will ultimately fall into the hands of the Communists." The augmentation of the CCP's military strength "will then constitute an additional potential threat to Hong Kong." The administration, fearful of another run-in with the China bloc, could only promise "to keep 'careful watch over heavy armaments and aircraft supplies.'"[52] Not wanting to increase the administration's difficulties by pressing the issue—and unwilling to get dragged into American politics—the British backed off.

The same considerations did not apply to another military-related argument between the two allies, this one over some seventy Nationalist planes stationed at Hong Kong. Both China and the United States laid claim to the aircraft. Unlike in the dispute over Taiwan, Whitehall now found itself stuck in the middle. Rejecting the CCP's claim to ownership would threaten U.K. interests in and around China; rejecting the American claim would strain Whitehall's relations with Washington. This heated quarrel over ownership of the planes, which had erupted in early 1950, was not resolved until the Korean War. The conflict surrounded two airline companies: the China National Aviation Corporation (CNAC), based in Hong Kong, with majority control in the hands of the Nationalists; and the Central Air Transport Corporation (CATC), an official organization run by the Nationalist government. Following the fall of Shanghai in May 1949, CATC also stationed its planes at the British colony.[53]

In November, the general managers of both airlines defected to the Communists, along with twelve fully manned planes (although one returned to Hong Kong). This left seventy-one aircraft—Convair 440s, C-46s, DC-4s and DC-3s—at Hong Kong, to which the CCP laid claim. Chennault and Whiting Willauer, two associates of another aircraft company in China, Civil Air Transport (CAT), reacted to the defections with astonishment and concern. There were reports that the Communists intended to parachute troops into Taiwan, and if they got the other seventy-one planes, they could easily take the island. Willauer commented, "considering the chaos which existed

52. Memorandum, "Formosa," Dec. 6, 1949, Papers of Dean Acheson, box 65, HSTL; telegram, no. 22, Foreign Office to Tokyo, Jan. 8, 1950, FO 371/83279, PRO; memoranda of conversation, Dec. 6 and 8, 1949, and memorandum to Acheson from Butterworth, Dec. 7, 1949, *FRUS, 1949*, 9:435–37, 438–41, 442–43.

53. For more on the history of CNAC and CATC, and their status as of late 1949, see William M. Leary, *Perilous Missions: Civil Air Transport and CIA Covert Operations in Asia*, 1–91.

on Formosa at that time, it would have been a pushover for the Reds to have taken Formosa." Moreover, by this time, Britain was moving in favor of recognizing China; U.K. recognition of Beijing would automatically pass title of the planes to the CCP. Realizing the danger, Willauer talked with Chiang about using CAT as an agent for the KMT, with full authority to take over title to the planes. The plan failed. Sir Alexander Grantham, the governor of Hong Kong, refused to take any action that might upset the new Chinese government. With that, Willauer and Chennault decided the only hope was for CAT to purchase the airlines. By the end of December, they had accomplished this goal.[54]

The planes, though, remained in Hong Kong. In late November, the Hong Kong courts granted injunctions to CNAC, CATC, and the National Resources Commission to keep the Communists from taking the planes. The courts also granted an injunction to employees of a company with reported ties to the CCP, thus keeping the issue of ownership tied up.[55]

The Truman administration strongly supported CAT. Clark Clifford, a close adviser to the president, wrote that if the planes fell into Mao Zedong's hands, "it will solve his air transportation problem," allowing him "to consolidate his economic and military gains of the past year." It would also threaten Taiwan and the U.S. effort to contain China. The British shared American concerns about the aircraft falling into communist hands, but they refused to interfere in the colonial judicial process.[56]

On February 23, 1950, the Hong Kong Supreme Court voted in favor of the CCP. The American response was quick and strong. Acheson told reporters the following day of his protests to authorities in London and Hong Kong. Senator Knowland called the decision "one of the greatest blows to the non-Communist world that has been delivered in that part of the world." Livingston Merchant, the deputy assistant secretary of state for Far Eastern Affairs, warned Franks that the court's action had angered lawmakers in both political parties, thus threatening future Marshall Plan and MAP appropriations.[57]

54. Ibid., 91–96; memorandum of conversation, Nov. 15, 1949, *FRUS, 1949*, 8:598; Felix Smith, *China Pilot: Flying for Chiang and Chennault*, 161; Nancy Allison Wright, "Claire Chennault and China's 'Airline Affair,'" 304

55. Memorandum by Montagu-Pollock, "Chinese Civil Aircraft at Hong Kong," Jan. 3, 1950, FO 371/84782, PRO.

56. Memorandum by Clifford, Jan. 4, 1950, Papers of Clark Clifford, Subject File, box 2, HSTL; FO Minute by Strang, Jan. 3, 1950, FO 371/84782, PRO.

57. Memorandum by the Secretary of State for the Colonies and the Minister of State, C.P. (50) 61, "Chinese Civil Aircraft at Hong Kong," Apr. 3, 1950, FO 371/84788; telegram, no. 1051, Franks to Foreign Office, Apr. 1, 1950, FO 371/84787, PRO; Leary, *Perilous Missions*, 97.

Merchant was not joking. Britain's decision to recognize Beijing the month before—to be discussed further momentarily—had infuriated the China bloc. Knowland had told an audience in October 1949 at a celebration in New York City, "[N]either this Government nor the British should recognize a Communist regime in China." Recognition, he continued, would enhance the CCP's "prestige and weaken opposition to communism in all of the Far East." Worried that Britain's action might open the door to China's admission to the United Nations, during debate over MAP, Knowland considered adding amendments to limit the program to seven months rather than a year "so that Congress might see whether other nations seat Red China in the United Nations before granting the countries aid." Britain relied heavily on the ERP and American military aid and took threats of cuts in assistance very seriously.[58]

On top of U.S. pressure, Attlee had to consider his own Chiefs of Staff, who argued that the planes might be used in Indochina. Yet Whitehall could not overlook its relationship with the new Communist government. To give the planes to the United States would jeopardize the process begun following Britain's recognition of China in January 1950 to achieve full diplomatic relations with Beijing.[59]

Whitehall also looked at the possibility of China retaliating against Hong Kong if the aircraft were turned over to Washington. British policymakers knew that the PRC could create troubles for Hong Kong, if not take it by force, but there was no evidence that Beijing planned to take action against the colony. Indeed, CCP officials in Hong Kong told their British counterparts that the colony was safe. Furthermore, Chinese troop levels in bordering Kwangtung Province were small, and propaganda against the colony was muted.[60]

The Chinese Communists had a couple of reasons not to threaten Hong Kong. For one, the United Kingdom was not as threatening as the United States. Britain was an "imperialist" power, but its strength had been weakened by World War II, while that of the United States had increased. America was thus more dangerous. As an old imperialist nation, commented Mao, Britain was sophisticated, but "the United States as a new imperialist power is much less predictable."[61] Seeing Britain as relatively unthreatening, the Communists had no reason to take Hong Kong by force. A second reason concerned the Anglo-American alliance. Zhang Wentien, the CCP's theo-

58. "Communist Flags Fly in Chinatown," *New York Times,* Oct. 11, 1949; *Congressional Quarterly Almanac,* 81st Cong., 2d Sess., 1950, 220–23; Clayton, *Imperialism Revisited,* 29–30.

59. Memorandum, "Chinese Civil Aircraft at Hong Kong."

60. Clayton, *Imperialism Revisited,* 99–100.

61. Zhang, *Deterrence and Strategic Culture,* 27; Zhai, *Dragon, the Lion, and the Eagle,* 13.

retician, argued in 1940 for the importance of dividing the enemy. It is thus not surprising that the Communists treated British officials in China with less derision than they did their American counterparts. The CCP also expressed a desire to trade with Britain, reflecting not only the realization that the United Kingdom had enormous trading interests in China, but also the hope that it could split the United States and Britain over the trade issue.[62]

In short, notes historian Michael Sheng, the CCP's leaders were not "tactless doctrinarians whose policy was determined by a few cut-and-dried ideological principles," but "flexible tacticians who were ready to make compromises and take detours to reach their ultimate goal, if the situation necessitated such undertakings."[63] By avoiding pressure on Hong Kong and sending other positive signals to the British, the Chinese hoped to divide the two Western allies.

Whatever concerns they might have had regarding China's attitude, the British were not prepared to challenge the United States. The Truman administration appealed the Hong Kong Supreme Court's decision. Not wanting the planes to leave, and believing the United States had a right to an appeal, Whitehall ordered Grantham to do everything possible to keep the aircraft in the colony. Yet questions emerged as to what the governor could do under the law. Therefore, in April, the British cabinet decided in favor of issuing an Order-in-Council. Pronounced on May 10, the order altered the existing law; now, Grantham was told to keep the planes in Hong Kong pending determination of ownership. The new statute guaranteed a long litigation process, with the right to a final appeal in London. Beijing attacked the order, calling it "a demonstration of a most unfriendly attitude toward the Chinese People's Republic."[64] But for the British, angering China was less hazardous than creating strong tensions in its relationship with the United States. Here matters stood until after the Korean War erupted.

These disputes over trade with China, military aid to Taiwan, or the aircraft at Hong Kong likely would have occurred even without the Ward case or the China bloc, for containment policy made it absolutely imperative that U.S. officials do nothing to augment communist military power. (Of course, it is just as clear that the Ward case and the China bloc moved Acheson to impose trade controls more stringent than he initially favored.) There remained, however, the possibility of political contacts between the United

62. Zhai, *Dragon, the Lion, and the Eagle*, 15.

63. Michael Sheng, *Battling Western Imperialism: Mao, Stalin, and the United States*, 7–8.

64. Telegram, no. 361, Grantham to Secretary of State for the Colonies, Apr. 5, 1950, FO 371/84788; Minutes of Cabinet Meeting, C.M. 24 (50), Apr., 24, 1950, CAB 128/17, PRO; Zhai, *Dragon, the Lion, and the Eagle*, 107; Clayton, *Imperialism Revisited*, 100–101.

States and the CCP. On this score, the Truman administration attempted to maintain some measure of flexibility, but again, communist actions and domestic constraints placed limits on what it could or would do.

Recognizing the new Communist government was a possibility. In May 1949, Acheson told his ambassador to China, John Leighton Stuart, that recognition should "not be withheld as [a] political weapon except in extreme cases" and only if it would serve Washington's national interests. Putting this view into practice was another matter. A July Gallup poll found that Americans opposed recognizing the Communists by a two-to-one margin. There was also the strong reaction to the China White Paper. Released in August 1949, the White Paper represented an attempt by the Truman administration to undermine charges by the China bloc and its Republican allies that the president gave too much attention to Europe and not enough to China. In just over one thousand pages of narrative and supporting documents, the paper laid the blame for the Nationalists' troubles squarely at the feet of the KMT government. Despite billions of dollars in aid, Chiang and his subordinates had failed to enact measures that could have prevented communist military and political success. The White Paper did not have the intended effect. Past sentimental images of China and fears of communism fueled an outraged response to the report. Senators Knowland, McCarran, Bridges, and Kenneth Wherry (R-Nebraska) called it a "whitewash of a wishful, do-nothing policy" that opened the door to Soviet conquest of Asia. Judd attacked it on similar lines. Through *Time* magazine, Luce said the White House had "filed a petition in bankruptcy, [and] seemed desperate to be seeking solvency in platitudes and recriminations." The *Wall Street Journal* and *Chicago Daily Tribune* also weighed in against the White Paper. Such a powerful outburst made clear that the administration had to proceed cautiously. Finally, there was the Ward case. Acheson later wrote, "My view was that the treatment of Angus Ward, our Consul General in Mukden, by the Chinese Communists and their attitude toward our rights and Chinese obligations were precluding recognition."[65]

How to proceed? Acheson clearly was upset with the treatment of Ward and faced pressure from both Congress and the general public. At the same time, though, his advisers were divided, with Rusk and Jessup calling for him to remove all U.S. officials from the mainland, and Butterworth opposing

65. Telegram, no. 589, Acheson to Nanking, May 13, 1949, *FRUS, 1949,* 9:22; memorandum, "Popular Opinion on U.S. Policy toward China," July 7, 1949, *Confidential U.S. State Department Central Files, United States-Chinese Relations, 1940–1949;* Bachrack, *Committee of One Million,* 41–42; Jespersen, *American Images of China,* 176–78; Zhai, *Dragon, the Lion, and the Eagle,* 43; Dean Acheson, *Present at the Creation: My Years in the State Department,* 340.

quick action. Putting these various considerations together, the secretary of state split the difference: he cut most, but not all, lines of communication with the Communists. Indeed, he ordered Stuart to remain at Nanjing so the ambassador could establish contact with the CCP. Stuart eventually got in touch with Huang Hua, the director of the CCP's Alien Affairs Office, but after two months of talks, they still had not achieved a breakthrough. Infuriated, Acheson ordered the ambassador to return to the United States and began to close various American consulates, starting with Shenyang in May, followed by Urumqi (Tihwa), Wuhan (Hankow), Dalian (Dairen), Qingdao (Tsingtao), Kunming, Chongqing (Chungking), and Guangzhou (Canton). By late August, the only U.S. diplomatic personnel in China were in Beijing.[66] The United States had cut its possible lines of communication with the CCP from at least eight to one.

While Acheson was reducing the American diplomatic presence in China, he was also endeavoring to develop a common front with U.S. allies so as to place additional pressure on the CCP. But with the Communists clearly approaching victory, the British wavered. In August, the Foreign Office explained to Washington that it was "legally objectionable" not to recognize a government that had "effective control of a large part of China." Additionally, any "delay in proceeding with recognition might seriously prejudice Western interests in China without any compensating advantages being obtained." Yet there was more involved than the CCP's control over China or Western interests there. The policy of containment was also at issue. Here, the United Kingdom made two points. One was related to Hong Kong. In May, Attlee told the cabinet that if Whitehall could not meet the threat to the colony posed by a communist China, Britain's prestige throughout East Asia would be seriously damaged. At the same time, the United Kingdom realized that the Communists probably could take the colony if they wished. If London could get the CCP to acquiesce to a continued U.K. presence in Hong Kong, not only would it safeguard Britain's trading presence in the region—thus helping the U.K. economy—but it also would "strengthen the anti-Communist front throughout South-East Asia." The second point concerned the Sino-Soviet relationship. Like maintaining trade contacts, recognition stood a chance of dividing the CCP and the Soviet Union, thereby weaken-

---

66. Telegrams, nos. 103, 510, 775, and 819, Acheson to Nanking, Jan. 26, Apr. 22, July 1, and July 12, 1949; no. 1410, Stuart to Secretary of State, June 30, 1949; no. 1475, Stuart to Secretary of State, July 11, 1949; Acheson to Peiping, no. 299, May 17, 1949; no. 101, Acheson to Tihwa, July 29, 1949; and no. 56, Acheson to Hankow, Aug. 15, 1949, *FRUS, 1949*, 8:667–68, 682–83, 766–67, 769, 781, 957, 1138, 1305–6; Blum, *Drawing the Line*, 91, 95–96; Shaw, *American Missionary in China*, 250; Chen, "The Ward Case and the Emergence of Sino-American Confrontation," 162.

ing the communist world and assisting efforts to contain communism. The Chinese communists, London argued, favored close ties to Moscow, but—and in an allusion to Tito's split with the Kremlin in 1948—there was "the possibility that the pattern will eventually develop along the lines of our present relationship with Jugoslavia." Hence, "the Western Powers should be careful not to prejudice future possibilities by developing an openly hostile attitude towards a communist régime from the outset."[67]

On October 1, the Chinese Communist foreign minister, Zhou Enlai, declared the founding of the People's Republic of China (PRC). Eager to maintain a foothold in China, Whitehall decided to establish informal relations with the new government but postponed a move toward recognition while consulting its allies and the Commonwealth. The United States urged Britain to delay action. Not only had the Communists yet to control all of China, but U.K. recognition might influence members of the United Nations to vote to expel the Nationalist representative from the Security Council in favor of one sent by the Communists. France wanted Whitehall to delay action until it had ratified its agreement with Bao Dai over Indochina; the Netherlands wanted time to transfer sovereignty to Indonesia. Likewise, Australia and New Zealand wanted to wait until after their national elections were over. Pakistan and Ceylon supported the United Kingdom while Canada supported the United States. Bevin believed that waiting until after the New Year would provide enough of a delay to eliminate the concerns of those favoring postponement and would allow Britain to avoid creating divisions within the Commonwealth as well as with its allies.[68]

India, however, pushed Whitehall into action. According to Krishna Menon, the Indian foreign secretary, Bevin, for the sake of Commonwealth unity, had urged New Delhi more than once not to accord early recognition to the new PRC government. "Ultimately, I had to tell him," stated Menon, "'We cannot wait any longer and we are going to recognize China.'"[69] Bevin decided to follow suit. India was a powerful Asian nation, and its position on

67. Circular telegrams, nos. 921 and unnumbered, Acheson to Certain Diplomatic and Consular Officers, May 3 and 6, 1949, *FRUS, 1949,* 9:14–15, 15 n 27, and 17; memorandum by Minister of Defence, C.P. (49) 118, "Defence of Hong Kong," May 24, 1949, CAB 129/35; Minutes of Cabinet Meeting, C.M. 38 (49), May 26, 1949, CAB 128/15; memorandum by the Secretary of State for Foreign Affairs, C.P. (49) 180, "China," Aug. 23, 1949, CAB 129/36, PRO.

68. Memorandum by the Secretary of State for Foreign Affairs, C.P. (49) 248, "Recognition of the Chinese Communist Government," Dec. 12, 1949, CAB 129/37, PRO; memorandum of conversation, Sept. 17, 1949; document transmitted by the French Embassy to the Department of State, Oct. 6, 1949; and memorandum to the Department of State from the British Embassy, Nov. 28, 1949, *FRUS, 1949,* 9:88, 90, 103, 200–201; R. Ovendale, "Britain, the United States, and the Recognition of Communist China," 145.

69. Quoted in Michael Brecher, *India and World Politics: Krishna Menon's View of the World,* 137.

recognition could influence that of other Asian countries, including those of the Commonwealth. "Since United Kingdom interests in China are far greater than those of any other Commonwealth country," the British foreign secretary wrote, " . . . it seems clear that a firm decision should be taken without delay." On December 15, the cabinet decided in favor of according recognition to the new Communist government. Whitehall also determined to withdraw recognition from the Nationalist government, though it intended to maintain de facto relations with Taiwan. The U.S. response was muted. The State Department declared that Whitehall's decision did not imply a disagreement with Washington over "the ultimate objective of a stable, independent China free of foreign domination." The China bloc, as noted, was not nearly as calm. Democrats in Congress, though not terribly pleased with Britain's decision, took a more moderate tone. Senate Foreign Relations Committee Chairman Tom Connally (D-Texas) declared that London had the right to recognize Beijing. His House counterpart, John Kee of West Virginia, stated that he did not like Britain's decision but realized it was part of Whitehall's "life and death struggle" to recover economically.[70]

In November 1949, the Communists released Ward and his staff and expelled them from China. Ward's release, however, did not alter the American position. Angry at the Truman administration for not having done more to help the Nationalist government, and longing to get revenge against Truman for his 1948 election victory, the China lobby and its Republican supporters charged the White House with "losing" China to the Communists. The president and his advisers could not afford the political fallout that would result from recognition of the new Communist government. Moreover, in January 1950, the CCP requisitioned the U.S. consular premises in Beijing. An angry Truman administration ordered the withdrawal of the remainder of its representatives in China. Franks reported back to Bevin that the Communists' action had "checked the growth" of London's perceived movement in favor of recognition. Bevin agreed, commenting, "As regards the United States, it must be accepted that China is now an issue of internal politics and is likely to remain so until after the November elections." Thus, "it would now in our view be extremely difficult for the United States to make any overtly friendly gesture toward the People's Government."[71]

70. Memorandum, "Recognition of the Chinese Communist Government"; Minutes of Cabinet Meeting, C.N. 72 (49), Dec. 15, 1949, CAB 128/16, PRO; telegram, no. 11751, Foreign Office to Washington, Dec. 23, 1949, FO 371/75828, PRO; Clifton Daniel, "London Drops Chiang Envoy in Move to Recognize Reds," *New York Times*, Jan. 6, 1950; William H. White, "Congress Divided on British Action," *New York Times*, Jan. 7, 1950; Shlaim, Jones, and Sainsbury, *British Foreign Secretaries*, 63; Lanxin Xiang, "The Recognition Controversy: Anglo-American Relations in China, 1949" 339.

71. Telegram, no. 164, Franks to Foreign Office, Jan. 16, 1950, FO 371/83282; telegram,

Maybe recognition was out of the question, but one possible arena for friendly political contact remained: the United Nations. In November 1949, Zhou Enlai, speaking for the new Chinese government, laid claim to China's seat in the United Nations, then held by the Nationalists. Having decided to recognize the Communist government, Whitehall took the position that the CCP deserved the seat. The Truman administration, still seeking to avoid a total commitment to Chiang, but also not wanting to anger the China bloc, stated that it would fight for the Nationalist representative—a determination made clear by its concerns over British recognition of the Communist government; however, in an important concession, it added that if a majority of UN members voted in favor of the Communists, the United States would not use its veto power to prevent a change in representation.[72] The administration was not counting out the possibility of contacts with the CCP through the UN.

Still, the White House could not end its support of the Nationalist claim to the China seat; since the United States had powerful leverage in the United Nations, the British considered it best to abstain on any votes on representation. Only when enough UN members supported the PRC did Whitehall plan to vote in favor of the Beijing government. When Jakob Malik, the Soviet representative to the Security Council, introduced a resolution in January 1950 to expel the Nationalist and seat the Communist representative, he lost, by a six-to-three vote (with Britain and Norway abstaining). As a result, Malik walked out of the UN, beginning a six-month period of self-exile that ended which only after the Korean War erupted.[73]

By 1948, U.S. and British policies toward China were similar on paper, but there was clear dissimilarity when it came to actual implementation. Not facing the difficulties of the Truman administration, particularly that posed by a strong legislative bloc that favored assistance to the Nationalists, the Attlee government found it relatively easy to maintain a truly flexible, hands-off stance. Whitehall realized the troubles the White House faced in terms of giving up on the Nationalists, yet there was little reason to complain. U.S. China policy did not affect the United Kingdom in any direct way, and making

no. 286, Foreign Office to Nanking, Feb. 9, 1950, FO 371/83285, PRO; McLellan and Anderson, *Among Friends*, 122.

72. Telegram, no. Delga 233, Austin to Secretary of State, Nov. 20, 1949, *FRUS, 1949*, 9:195; memorandum, "Recognition of the Chinese Communist Government"; telegram, no. 4, Acheson to New York, Jan. 5, 1950, *FRUS, 1950*, 2:186–87; telegram, no. 782, Franks to Foreign Office, Mar. 8, 1950, FO 371/88504, PRO.

73. FO Minute (no author given), May 30, 1950, FO 371/88418, PRO; Thomas J. Hamilton, "Malik Again Quits Council as Chinese Ouster Is Beaten," *New York Times*, Jan. 14, 1950.

complaints would unnecessarily drag London into the volatile electoral climate of 1948.

Whitehall's attitude began to change in 1949. Not only was American policy growing increasingly hostile toward the Communists—despite a stated desire for a flexible position—but, more important, America was pushing Britain to alter its policy. With its interests directly affected, Whitehall now had reason for complaint. Moreover, this divergence in the Anglo-American attitude provided indications of many of the elements that would condition their future respective China policies and the relationship between the two allies.

First, Whitehall proved least willing to bow to U.S. pressure if it endangered Britain itself, particularly its economic health. In the name of Anglo-American unity, and under considerable pressure, it agreed to some controls on trade with China. Still, it refused to follow completely the stringent program of the United States. Not wanting to threaten Western unity, the Truman administration did not press the matter further. In 1951, however, the White House *would* press the question of trade controls, forcing Britain to make some difficult decisions.

Tied in with the question of trade controls was the issue of the Sino-Soviet relationship. Britain agreed with the United States on containing communism and dividing the CCP and Kremlin. But the two allies disagreed on how to achieve the latter goal. The United Kingdom favored a policy of contacts. Trade and diplomatic ties would benefit Britain financially while helping to prevent China from becoming isolated and, thus, willing to turn completely to the Soviet Union for its needs. Using its leverage, Britain might be able to drive wedges between the two communist countries, increase the size of subsequent rifts within the Sino-Soviet relationship, and weaken the communist world. The United States concurred with Britain's arguments, on paper, yet its actions during 1949 and into 1950 demonstrated a markedly dissimilar policy. Washington placed controls on trade, eventually eliminated all diplomatic links with the CCP, and refused to recognize the Communist government. And though willing to accept a Communist representative in the United Nations, it was not about to allow such an eventuality without a fight. Such a hardened stance was a precursor to the argument that Washington would soon express: that a policy of pressure, not concessions, on all fronts would succeed in driving wedges. In short, the United States was well on its way to justifying any change in its China policy as in accordance with the achievement of a Sino-Soviet split.

On top of the Sino-Soviet relationship, Britain had to consider its relationships with China and the Commonwealth. As Bevin pointed out during discussion over trade sanctions, the imposition of stringent controls on commerce with Beijing would lead the PRC to take actions inimical to U.K. interests on the mainland. Similarly, when considering the status of the planes at Hong Kong, Whitehall could not ignore the possible reaction of the CCP. The Commonwealth's members, for their part, had clearly swayed Whitehall on the question of recognition and would, in the future, have an impact on U.K. China policy.

Finally, there was the Anglo-American alliance. The very fact that the United States desired to maintain Western unity before the communist threat gave Britain some leeway. It could accordingly adopt a policy on recognition and trade controls that did not follow completely the American line. But this did not mean that the United Kingdom had full freedom of action. It was a junior partner in the relationship with the United States. And, like Washington, London did not want to create a schism in the Western alliance. Therefore, it reluctantly agreed to some controls on trade, did not press the United States over aid to Taiwan, and, when faced with intense pressure, gave in to the American desire to keep the CNAC/CATC aircraft at Hong Kong pending appeal. Such reliance on the United States and the impact that reliance had on U.K.-China policy became even more apparent after war broke out on the Korean peninsula.

2

CONFLICT IN KOREA, 1950–1953

On the evening of June 24, 1950, President Harry S. Truman was sitting in the library of his family home in Independence, Missouri, when Secretary of State Dean Acheson phoned him. "Mr. President," Acheson said, "I have very serious news. The North Koreans have invaded South Korea."[1]

The eruption of war on the Korean peninsula greatly increased Anglo-American concerns about the communist threat. Both Washington and London considered it vital to stop the North Koreans and to demonstrate Western unity in the face of the new danger to world peace. Maintaining this unity, however, was not easy, particularly following the People's Republic of China's intervention in the war in November 1950. U.S. China policy fully hardened militarily, economically, and politically. The White House increased its military commitment to Taiwan and Southeast Asia, signed a peace treaty with Japan, imposed a full-scale economic embargo against China, and determined to keep Beijing out of the United Nations. Once again, Washington sought London's support for these measures. And, once again, Britain found itself having to make some difficult decisions. The fact that the United States desired British support and wanted to maintain Western unity gave Whitehall some maneuvering room, but the United States still held the upper hand. The result was that, more often than not, London did the compromising.

In his memoirs, former Soviet Premier Nikita S. Khrushchev contended that North Korea's leader, Kim Il-sung, planned the invasion of the South and requested Moscow's support for his proposal. It is now clear from Soviet and Chinese archival materials that Khrushchev's recollection was accurate. As early as December 1949, Kim had asked the Soviets to endorse his proposed offensive. Arguing that the United States would not intervene and that he could win a quick victory, Kim eventually persuaded the Soviet leader, Josef Stalin, to go along. Yet Stalin made no commitment about Russian support

---

1. Harry S. Truman, *Memoirs*, vol. 2, *Years of Trial and Hope*, 332.

to Pyongyang. He also urged Kim to get the backing of China's leader, Mao Zedong. After much consideration, Mao also assented to Kim's plan.[2]

The attack, when it came on June 25, 1950 (Korean time), was a complete surprise to both the British and the Americans. The Western powers regarded it as the work of the Soviet Union, designed to divert their attention to East Asia so as to give Moscow a freer hand in Europe or the Middle East. The Truman administration responded during the next several months by implementing a massive military buildup, increasing its defense commitment to the North Atlantic Treaty Organization (NATO), and seeking the rearmament of Germany. European nations also built up their military forces.

Korea, of course, was the most immediate concern. Truman and his advisers were keenly aware of Korea's proximity to Japan and worried that if communists won control of the peninsula, they would try to expand their reach through continued aggression (with the potential of isolating the United States). Furthermore, "losing" Korea on top of China carried political ramifications. Consequently, upon his return to Washington, Truman consulted with his advisers and decided on a plan of action. The United States guided the passage on June 27 of a UN resolution calling upon all its members to help South Korea. Simultaneously, the administration boosted U.S. military assistance to the Philippines and Indochina, sent the Seventh Fleet to the Taiwan Strait to protect Taiwan from an attack by Communist China, and asked the Nationalist government of Chiang Kai-shek to cease air and naval attacks on the mainland.[3]

The British government of Prime Minister Clement Attlee agreed about

2. For more on this topic, see Nikita Khrushchev, *Khrushchev Remembers*, trans. and ed. Strobe Talbott, 367–69; Nikita Khrushchev, *Khrushchev Remembers: The Glastnost Tapes*, trans. and ed. Jerrold L. Schecter with Vyacheslav V. Luchkow, 144–46; Sergei N. Goncharov, John W. Lewis, and Xue Litai, *Uncertain Partners: Stalin, Mao, and the Korean War*, 136–54; Kathryn Weathersby, "New Findings on the Korean War," 1, 14–18 and "The Soviet Role in the Early Phase of the Korean War: New Documentary Evidence," 425–58; Burton Kaufman, *The Korean War: Challenges in Crisis, Credibility, and Command*, 19–21; Zhihua Shen, "China Sends Troops to Korea: Beijing's Policy-Making Process," in *China and the United States: A New Cold War History*, ed. Xiaobing Li and Hongshan Li, 13–21; and John Lewis Gaddis, *We Now Know: Rethinking Cold War History*, 71–75.

3. Memorandum, "President Truman's Conversations with George M. Elsey," June 26, 1950, Papers of George Elsey, box 71, HSTL; memorandum of conversation, June 25, 1950; "Editorial Note"; telegram, no. JCS 84681, Joint Chiefs of Staff to MacArthur, June 29, 1950; telegram, no. C-56942, MacArthur to Secretary of State and telegram, no. JCS 84718, Joint Chiefs of Staff to MacArthur, June 30, 1950, *FRUS, 1950*, 7:157–61, 240–41, 248–50, 263; For more on the domestic pressures Truman and Acheson faced, see Stephen Pelz, "U.S. Decisions on Korean Policy, 1943–1950: Some Hypotheses," in *Child of Conflict: The Korean-American Relationship, 1943–1953*, ed. Bruce Cumings.

the need to protect South Korea. Losing it, believed Attlee and his subordi-nates, would encourage the Soviet Union to take action in other parts of the world, hurt Western prestige, and raise the morale of communist guerrillas fighting the British in Malaya. Therefore, Whitehall supported the June 27 UN resolution and placed its Far Eastern fleet at the disposal of the UN com-mander in Korea, Gen. Douglas MacArthur.[4]

But the two allies did not see completely eye-to-eye. The U.S. decision to send the Seventh Fleet to the Taiwan Strait worried the British, who feared that Washington had altered its noncommittal stance toward Taiwan. Addi-tionally, Whitehall could not ignore the Commonwealth, especially India. If China decided to attack the island, the result would be an expansion of the war "over an issue on which the United States had little Asian support." The administration assured Whitehall that it had not changed its position and even for a time supported a U.K. resolution in the UN calling for the estab-lishment of a commission to determine Taiwan's status. Only with the PRC's intervention in Korea did Acheson quash debate of the British resolution.[5] Acheson's action demonstrated that American policy toward the island was changing further. From 1948 to 1950, it had become clear that the United States was committed to supporting Taiwan, despite claims to the contrary. Now, with America engaged in a war against communist aggression in East Asia, it was even less willing to give up the island.

That unwillingness to abandon Taiwan was even more evident in the U.S. response to British and Indian efforts to end the war. In July, Bevin instruct-ed his ambassador in Moscow, Sir David Kelly, to ask Soviet Foreign Minis-ter Andrei Gromyko to use the Kremlin's influence to resolve the Korean con-flict. Simultaneously, Bevin made it clear to Acheson that such a resolution might require the White House to be more accommodating on the questions of Taiwan and China's representation in the United Nations. Meanwhile, New Delhi proposed a formula by which the United States would champion China's admission; in return, the Security Council (which would include

4. Minutes of Cabinet Meeting, C.M. 39 (50), June 27, 1950, CAB 128/17, PRO; Min-utes of Meeting of the Defence Committee of the Cabinet, D.O. (50) 11th Meeting, June 28, 1950, *DBPO*, ser 2, 4:7–8; memorandum of conversation and telegram, no. 3183, Acheson to London, June 28, 1950, *FRUS, 1950*, 7:214, 223; Zhai, *Dragon, the Lion, and the Eagle*, 82.

5. "United States Delegation Minutes of the Fourth Meeting of the Foreign Ministers of France, the United Kingdom, and the United States," Sept. 14. 1950; telegram, no. Del-ga 106, Austin to Secretary of State, Oct. 11, 1950; and telegram, no. Gael 162, Acheson to New York, Dec. 5, 1950, *FRUS, 1950*, 6:500–501, 528–29 589; telegram, no. 2188, Franks to Foreign Office, Aug. 10, 1950, FO 371/83320; Minutes of Cabinet Meeting, C.M. 55 (50), Sept. 4, 1950, CAB 128/18, PRO; William W. Stueck, "The Limits of Influ-ence: British Policy and American Expansion of the War in Korea," 89.

representatives of China and the Soviet Union), would "support [an] immediate cease fire in Korea and withdrawal of North Korean troops to [the] 38th parallel."[6]

The Truman administration rejected both proposals. Neither Truman nor Acheson would agree to trade for peace in Korea. The secretary of state believed in negotiating from a position of strength, something the current state of the conflict in Korea did not provide him. Given its apparently weak state, the administration could not risk the political consequences of accepting either peace proposal. Acheson therefore told Truman of the need to get "the British and the Indians straightened out so they would not be attempting to mediate in the Korean situation." The secretary of state prepared a response to Bevin's message, which Truman approved. The president added that he wanted the U.S. ambassador to India, Loy Henderson, "to receive the same material and use it the best way possible to get these ideas into [Indian Prime Minister Jawaharlal] Nehru's mind." In his response, Acheson told the British foreign secretary that the United States would not agree at the present time to give up Taiwan or alter its position on representation. If the Communists could "extort concessions for desisting from unlawful conduct, the ability of the free world to prevent aggression would be totally lost." The secretary of state's strong response surprised Bevin and upset his subordinates. Bevin tried to explain to Acheson that he was not suggesting a trade. He could not, however, risk angering the United States by pressing the issue. Therefore, he said he would not make another move on a peace proposal without first consulting Washington.[7]

Ironically, the British joined the Americans in opposing the Indian initiative. Whitehall did not believe its own suggestion for ending the war required a trade. But it saw in Nehru's proposal such a prerequisite. The British prime minister explained to his Indian counterpart that China did not have the votes for admission to the UN, which would make the Soviet Union even less willing to get North Korea to stop the war. Acheson made clear to Nehru that he would not accept any idea of trading Chinese representation for an end to the war. Under such pressure, Nehru relented.[8]

6. Telegrams, nos. 54 and 83, Kirk to Secretary of State, July 6 and 10, 1950, and "Extract from telegram from the Foreign Office to the British Embassy, Washington, Dated July 6th, 1950," *FRUS, 1950,* 7:312–14, 340–41; telegram, no. 3092, Foreign Office to Washington, July 7, 1950, PREM 8/1405, PRO.

7. Memoranda of conversation, July 10, 1950, Papers of Dean Acheson, box 75, HSTL; telegram, no. 132, Acheson to London, July 10, 1950; annex to memorandum of conversation, July 15, 1950; and telegram, no. 398, Douglas to Secretary of State, July 18, 1950, in *FRUS, 1950,* 7:347–51, 396–99, 421–22; M. L. Dockrill, "The Foreign Office, Anglo-American Relations and the Korean War, June 1950–June 1951," 462; Rosemary Foot, *A Substitute for Victory: The Politics of Peacemaking at the Korean Armistice Talks,* 22–23.

8. Telegram, no. 106, Acheson to New Delhi, July 22, 1950 *FRUS, 1950,* 7:447–49; Gye-Dong Kim, *Foreign Intervention in Korea,* 218–19.

In the meantime, the United States looked to other members of the UN coalition to increase their commitment to Korea. Attlee already had offered ships, but Washington favored a greater British presence. On June 30 and again on July 20, the chairman of the Joint Chiefs of Staff (JCS), Gen. Omar Bradley, asked the British to provide at least a token land force to Korea, but they turned him down, arguing London already had responsibilities abroad, particularly in Hong Kong and Malaya, and thought it best to keep Britain's forces where they were.[9]

Whitehall soon changed its mind. Had the Chinese demonstrated any threat to Hong Kong, Attlee and his advisers might have been less willing to compromise. But there was no evidence that Beijing planned to take aggressive action against the colony. Indeed, in the hopes of splitting the Anglo-American alliance, the Chinese Communist government did not increase its criticism of Britain, despite London's decision to offer naval support to the U.S. effort in Korea. Chinese officials, reported the U.K. chargé in Beijing, John Hutchison, continued to treat their British counterparts courteously and talked with him about the establishment of full diplomatic relations. Meanwhile, Washington stepped up its pressure for a commitment of British ground troops. In mid-August, Acheson warned that Congress was growing restless over Britain's foot-dragging: "You will readily appreciate," he told Bevin, "[the] possible effect of this growing opinion on our current plans for invigorating NATO and voting funds to assist our allies to build up their defensive strength." Washington, in short, was threatening a possible Anglo-American schism if London did not cooperate. Not wanting to jeopardize Britain's alliance with the United States, and believing China was not a danger to Hong Kong, the chiefs of staff decided to send two battalions of troops to Korea. British forces remained in Malaya to contend with communist guerrillas in the colony.[10]

As the growing UN force gradually moved up the Korean peninsula, the Chinese Communist government became increasingly concerned. Mao Zedong and his subordinates strongly distrusted Washington. To them, the United States had committed aggression against China since the mid-1800s. While most members of the CCP's hierarchy had little experience in dealing with Americans—or with most any other nation—"from those few occasions where contacts had taken place, they felt cheated and humiliated." By

9. "Summary of Bilateral Conversations with the British on the World Situation," July 20, 1950, Selected Records Relating to the Korean War, box 4, HSTL; Kim, *Foreign Intervention in Korea*, 159.

10. Telegrams, nos. 401 and 788, Acheson to London, July 21, 1950, and Aug. 11, 1950, *FRUS, 1950*, 7:447 n 1 and 560 n 1; Circular telegram, no. 24, Attlee to Prime Ministers of Canada, New Zealand, South Africa, and Australia, Aug. 19, 1950, PREM 8/1405, PRO; Tang, *Britain's Encounter with Revolutionary China*, 89.

early 1949, Mao and his lieutenants had come to regard U.S. policy toward the CCP as clearly unfriendly; they saw as evidence the American effort to revitalize Japan, continued aid to the Chinese Nationalists on Taiwan, and U.S. military activities in China, such as reconnaissance flights over Communist-held territory.[11]

Such mistrust was supported by the CCP's favorable opinion of and relations with the Soviet Union. Although Mao himself did not travel outside of China until his visit to Moscow in December 1949, he sought to strengthen ties with the Kremlin during the civil war. He attempted to move the CCP's troops closer to the Sino-Soviet border so he would have access to Russian assistance and accepted orders on strategy from Stalin via radio. In mid-1948, Mao gave his famous "lean to one side" speech, designed to alleviate any suspicions Stalin might have that he would betray him as Tito had. The CCP leader clearly wanted to maintain the favor of the country he saw as the "father of socialism."[12]

Mao's subordinates also had close ties with Russia. Of the other twelve members of the politburo elected in June 1945, only four—Peng Dehuai, Peng Zhen, Gao Gang, and Zhou Enlai—had not studied in the Soviet Union. Only a few had experience in nations other than Russia. Dong Biwu and Lin Baiqu had studied in Japan, and Dong had traveled to the United States as the CCP representative in China's delegation to the 1945 San Francisco Conference. Zhang Wentien had also spent some time in the United States. The only member of the Politburo who had studied in Western Europe was Zhou Enlai. Given their backgrounds and ideology, Mao's lieutenants shared his positive view of the Soviet Union. To them, the Soviets were "comrades fighting in the same trench."[13]

The Soviet Union used its influence to encourage the CCP's distrust of the United States. Through Gao Gang, Stalin warned Mao several times during the Chinese civil war that if the Communists advanced south of the Yangtze River, Washington might send in military forces. He added that if the Unit-

11. Zhai, *Dragon, the Lion, and the Eagle,* 9; Zhang, *Deterrence and Strategic Culture,* 18, 20.

12. C. Martin Wilbur and Julie Lien-ying How, *Missionaries of Revolution: Soviet Advisers and Nationalist China, 1920–1927,* 22–23; Bevin Alexander, *The Strange Connection: U.S. Intervention in China, 1944–1972,* 33; Steven I. Levine, *Anvil of Victory: The Communist Revolution in Manchuria, 1945–1948,* 31–33, 41–42; Sheng, *Battling Western Imperialism,* 17–20; Gaddis, *We Now Know,* 59–62; Zhai, *Dragon, the Lion, and the Eagle,* 27.

13. Tang, *Britain's Encounter with Revolutionary China,* 20–21; Zhai, *Dragon, the Lion, and the Eagle,* 7–8; Chen, "The Ward Case and the Emergence of Sino-American Confrontation, 1948–1950," 159.

ed States used force, Moscow could not provide assistance for fear of provoking a U.S.-Soviet war in East Asia.[14]

The close relationship with the Soviet Union did not preclude CCP cooperation with the United States. But by 1949, only with a complete withdrawal of the U.S. presence in East Asia could Washington hope to foster closer Sino-American relations, and that was unacceptable.[15] Moreover, the PRC's leadership believed, following Chiang's self-exile in Taiwan, that the United States would intervene in China's affairs and try to return the Nationalists to power. It is therefore not surprising that Mao sought and signed in early 1950 a defensive alliance with the Kremlin.[16]

The stationing of the Seventh Fleet in the Taiwan Strait and the growing presence of U.S. troops in Korea all seemed to confirm the fear of Mao and his subordinates that Washington was preparing for action against the mainland. On July 7, therefore, Chinese Premier Zhou Enlai ordered the nation's top military commanders to prepare for war with Korea; accordingly, the CCP had to delay a plan for an invasion of Taiwan. Following MacArthur's trip to Taiwan later that same month, China sped up these preparations.[17]

Two months after MacArthur traveled to Taiwan, UN troops landed at Inchon, near Seoul. They rapidly overwhelmed the North Korean army and began moving toward the thirty-eighth parallel. The PRC's anxiety reached new heights. UN forces had not directly threatened Chinese soil; the Seventh Fleet had yet to show any intention of landing troops on the mainland; and the fighting in Korea was in the South. But now there was nothing to stop the Americans, who made up the bulk of the UN forces—and possibly their Na-

14. Zhang, *Deterrence and Strategic Culture*, 28–33.

15. See Jian Chen, "The Myth of America's 'Lost Chance' in China: A Chinese Perspective in Light of New Evidence"; John W. Garver, "Little Chance"; Michael Sheng, "The Triumph of Internationalism: CCP-Moscow Relations before 1949"; Odd Arne Wested, "Losses, Chances, and Myths: The United States and the Creation of the Sino-Soviet Alliance, 1945–1950"; Russell D. Buhite, "Missed Opportunities? American Policy and the Chinese Communists, 1949"; and Thomas J. Christensen, *Useful Adversaries: Grand Strategy, Domestic Mobilization, and Sino-American Conflict, 1949–1958*, chap. 5. For a counterargument, see Donald S. Zagoria, "Choices in the Postwar World: Containment and China," in *Caging the Bear: Containment and the Cold War*, ed. Charles Gati.

16. Zhang, *Deterrence and Strategic Culture*, 28–33, and *Mao's Military Romanticism: China and the Korean War, 1950–1953*, 34–35, 46–52. See also Chen Xiaolu, "China's Policy toward the United States, 1949–1955," in *Sino-American Relations, 1945–1955: A Joint Reassessment of a Critical Decade*, ed. Harry Harding and Yuan Ming, 185–87 and Michael H. Hunt, *The Genesis of Chinese Communist Foreign Policy*, 197–98.

17. Jian Chen, *China's Road to the Korean War: The Making of the Sino-American Confrontation*, 127, 142; Zhai, *Dragon, the Lion, and the Eagle*, 66–67; China also made preparations in the event Taiwan decided to attack the mainland. See Zhang, *Mao's Military Romanticism*, 58, 63–67.

tionalist allies—from moving into North Korea and, ultimately, into China itself.

These security concerns were interwoven with ideological and domestic military ones. Mao and his lieutenants saw a need to save fellow revolutionaries, if not the revolutionary movement. During the Chinese civil war, North Korea had been a refuge for Chinese Communists. It was now the CCP's turn to help those who had assisted it earlier. Moreover, total victory for the United Nations would undermine the communist movement altogether. Expressing what one might consider a Chinese version of the "domino theory," Zhou argued, "If Korea fell down, breaches in other places would be opened one by one. If the enemy were allowed to break down the gate of the Eastern Front and make his way into our house, how could we devote ourselves to construction?"[18] Additionally, the government in September 1950 was less than a year old. It still faced problems with KMT guerrillas on the mainland and the existence of a rival government on Taiwan. If the UN succeeded in Korea, Nationalist guerrillas and individuals opposed to the Communists might rebel. Meanwhile, Chiang might try to stage attacks along the coast or join up with the UN forces.[19]

Still, not all of Mao's lieutenants favored intervention. At an October 2 Politburo meeting, Gao Gang, who commanded the army in northeast China, and Gen. Lin Biao expressed their opposition to war with the United States. They pointed to America's economic and atomic power and the need for China to continue with economic reforms and to destroy the KMT guerrillas. Mao, Zhou, and Gen. Peng Dehuai disagreed. Mao and Peng argued that the United States was overextended with its worldwide commitments, that atomic bombs would not hurt China because of its large size and dispersed population, and that Korea's geography would limit the ability of the UN to successfully maneuver. Accordingly, Mao made the final decision to intervene.[20] Simultaneously, Zhou and Acting Chief of Staff Nie Rongzhen sent warnings, via the Indian ambassador in Beijing, K. M. Panikkar, that China would intervene if UN forces crossed the parallel. On October 10, Beijing publicly warned that it would not "stand idly by" while U.S. troops invaded North Korea.[21]

18. Bruce Cumings, *Origins of the Korean War*, vol. 2, *The Roaring of the Cataract, 1947–1950*, 364, 733–34, 738–39; Chen, *China's Road to the Korean War*, 159.

19. Chen, *China's Road to the Korean War*, 160.

20. For more on this meeting, ibid., 173–75; Hao Yufan and Zhai Zhihai, "China's Decision to Enter the Korean War: History Revisited," 104–8; Zhang, *Mao's Military Romanticism*, 80–82; and Li and Li, eds., *China and the United States*, 28–29.

21. K. M. Panikkar, *In Two Chinas: Memoirs of a Diplomat*, 108, 110; telegrams, no. 792, Kirk to Secretary of State, Sept. 29, 1950 and no. 1934, Holmes to Secretary of State, Oct. 3, 1950; and "Editorial Note," *FRUS, 1950*, 7:821–22, 839, 914.

There were voices in both Washington and London that opposed travers-
ing the South Korea–North Korea border. George Kennan, on leave from the
State Department; Paul Nitze, Kennan's successor at the Policy Planning Staff
(PPS); and U.S. Ambassador to Moscow Charles Bohlen all argued against it,
as it risked expanding the war. In Britain, Sir John Slessor, speaking for the
Chiefs of Staff, contended that "the military disadvantages of crossing the
38th parallel outweighed the political advantages." Rather than crossing into
North Korea, he preferred seeking a political solution to the Korean problem
in the UN.[22]

The dissenters were in the minority. John Allison, the director of the State
Department's Office of Northeast Asian Affairs; MacArthur; Assistant Secretary of State for Far Eastern Affairs Dean Rusk; Ambassador-at-Large Philip
Jessup; and the China specialist on the PPS, John Paton Davies, all favored
crossing the parallel, arguing that it was necessary to unite Korea under non-
communist rule and that Beijing would never risk war with Washington. Truman and Acheson agreed, and in London, Attlee and Bevin both supported
unifying Korea. Attlee persuasively explained to the cabinet, "The United Nations had always desired that the artificial distinction between North and
South Korea should be abolished, and world opinion was likely to accept unification as a desirable objective." Furthermore, if Britain succeeded in persuading the United States to stop at the North-South border, "and military
problems arose later on, the British would take the blame."[23]

The two allies were aware of China's warnings to stop at the thirty-eighth
parallel but for various reasons rejected them. Aside from supporting the
idea of a united, pro-Western Korea, Truman could not ignore the fact that
the congressional elections were less than two months away: the White
House could not risk Republican accusations that it did not roll back communism when given the opportunity, and he doubted China's seriousness.
As Acheson later wrote, Zhou's "words were a warning not to be disregard-
ed, but, on the other hand, not an authoritative statement of policy."[24] Along
similar lines, the Chiefs of Staff's own Joint Intelligence Committee argued
that China would not intervene in Korea because to do so would risk a war

22. James I. Matray, "Truman's Plan for Victory: National Self-Determination and the
Thirty-Eighth Parallel Decision in Korea," 323; Charles Bohlen, *Witness to History, 1929–
1969,* 292–93; Peter N. Farrar, "Britain's Proposal for a Buffer Zone South of the Yalu in
November 1950: Was It a Neglected Opportunity to End the Fighting in Korea?" 330.

23. Memoranda, to Rusk from Allison, July 1, 1950, to Nitze from Allison, July 24,
1950, and to Jessup from McConaughy, Aug. 25, 1950, and draft memorandum by Davies,
Sept. 22, 1950, *FRUS, 1950,* 7:272, 458–61, 649–52, 753–55; Minutes of Cabinet Meeting, C.M. 61 (50), Sept. 26, 1950. *DBPO,* ser. 2, 4:153; Bullock, *Ernest Bevin,* 85; Matray,
"Truman's Plan for Victory," 318, 319, 329.

24. Matray, "Truman's Plan for Victory," 314–15; Kaufman, *Korean War,* 56; Donald
R. McCoy, *The Presidency of Harry S. Truman,* 241; Acheson, *Present at the Creation,* 452.

with the United States. Bevin similarly noted that Zhou Enlai "must surely appreciate the consequences of an attack upon the United Nations forces in Korean territory."[25]

Judging that China would not intervene, the UN on October 7 approved troops crossing the border, and action began less than two days later. The same day the UN sanctioned the unification of Korea, Mao sent a formal order to intervene in the war, only to delay it shortly thereafter. The reason for Mao's hesitation concerned the Soviet Union. When informed of Beijing's decision, Stalin at first expressed support; Chinese intervention, he felt, posed less of a risk of world war than similar Russian action. But he soon changed his mind. The American response to the war had been much faster and more tenacious than he had anticipated. If the United States upped the ante and used nuclear weapons against China, the Soviet Union, under the Sino-Soviet alliance signed earlier that year, would have to intervene. The Russian leader therefore reneged on his offer. Mao spent sixty sleepless hours trying to decide whether to go ahead. On October 13, he determined to press on, even without Soviet help. (Following the PRC's intervention, Stalin sent two air force divisions to defend northeast China. But Mao never forgave the Soviet leader for hesitating.)[26]

The first Chinese troops crossed the Yalu River into North Korea on October 19. Six days later, they surprised the UN forces. Two South Korean divisions were destroyed, a third crippled, and the U.S. Eighth Cavalry Regiment suffered heavy losses. On November 5, short of food and munitions, the PRC stopped its assault.[27]

The short Communist offensive separately led Acheson and the Australian representative at the UN General Assembly, Sir Keith Officer, to recommend the establishment of a demilitarized buffer zone (DMZ) between the Korean peninsula and China. Bevin turned them both down, arguing that China would never agree to a DMZ. Yet the foreign secretary changed his mind in the middle of November, when his Chiefs of Staff warned that the United Nations could not win the war without running a serious risk of its extension

25. Chiefs of Staff Joint Intelligence Committee memorandum, J.I.C. (50) 88, "Chinese Communist Intentions and Capabilities—1950/51," Oct. 11, 1950, CAB 158/11; telegrams, no. 2765, U.K. High Commissioner in India to U.K. Delegation, New York, Sept. 28, 1950, and no. 1258, Jebb to Foreign Office, Sept. 29, 1950, FO 371/ 84098, PRO.

26. Hao and Zhai, "China's Decision," 109–11; Goncharov, Lewis, and Xue, *Uncertain Partners*, 191. For Mao's anger with Stalin over lack of Soviet support, see Zhisui Li, *The Private Life of Chairman Mao*, 117–18.

27. Roy E. Appleman, *Disaster in Korea: The Chinese Confront MacArthur*, 20–21; Zhang, *Mao's Military Romanticism*, 106.

beyond the peninsula. To limit the conflict to Korea, the chiefs supported the creation of a DMZ. Bevin now endorsed the proposal; following cabinet approval, the foreign secretary forwarded the plan to Acheson.[28]

Despite Acheson's earlier suggestion of the zone, the United States now gave the idea a chilly reception. He told Bevin on November 21 that proposing a DMZ would confuse the situation prior to MacArthur's offensive. Additionally, it would lock the United Nations into a commitment, which China would use to demand further concessions. Bevin backed down. Once again, London did not want to press the United States too hard on an issue it did not enthusiastically support and risk harm to the Anglo-American relationship.[29]

In the meantime, the Chinese prepared for another offensive. Peng Dehuai correctly assumed that the short October action would not prevent another UN drive north. He also felt that the UN had underestimated China's strength. On November 25, the PRC began a full-scale offensive, involving nineteen divisions totaling 150,000 soldiers.[30] Ironically, the Chinese ran head-on into MacArthur's "final offensive," which he launched that same morning. Taking advantage of MacArthur's division of his forces, the Chinese struck between them, driving the UN into full retreat. Within two months, they had pushed the allied coalition nearly one-third of the way into South Korea.

The PRC's intervention had a powerful impact upon Anglo-American relations toward both the war in Korea and China itself. Up to November 25, U.S. and British policy in Korea largely coincided. The Truman and Attlee governments agreed the war was the work of the Soviet Union, designed to divert Western attention from Europe, and that a strong response was required. And, despite some misgivings within their administrations, Truman and Attlee agreed to send troops across the thirty-eighth parallel in an effort to unify Korea. There were some differences of opinion, of course. But realizing they could not threaten their relationship with the United States, the British backed down each time. They gave up their effort to achieve an early cease-fire, sent troops to Korea, and refused to press strongly for a DMZ.

The situation changed dramatically in November 1950. Washington fully adopted a policy of pressure against China. The administration repeated its

28. Farrar, "Britain's Proposal for a Buffer Zone South of the Yalu in November 1950," 332–34; message to Franks from Bevin, Nov. 13, 1950, *FRUS, 1950,* 7:1138–40.

29. Memorandum of conversation, Nov. 21, 1950; message to Franks from Bevin, Nov. 21, 1950; and telegrams, no. 2673, Acheson to London, Nov. 21, 1950, and no. 3012, Holmes to Secretary of State, Nov. 22, 1950, *FRUS, 1950,* 7:1210–1213, and 1213 n 3; Zhai, *Dragon, the Lion, and the Eagle,* 83–84.

30. Zhang, *Mao's Military Romanticism,* 107; Appleman, *Disaster in Korea,* 44–45.

desire to split the Sino-Soviet alliance and to keep the war in Korea confined to the peninsula. But other policies underwent important changes. The Truman administration formally repudiated its stated no-commitment policy toward Taiwan. It declared its intent to persuade Britain to join the full-scale embargo on trade with China, to "continue to oppose seating Communist China in the UN, [and to] intensify efforts to persuade other nations to adopt similar positions." It decided to speed up efforts to conclude a peace treaty with Japan and to build up Japan's military. Finally, it resolved to increase military aid to French Indochina.[31]

Did this hardened policy, particularly those initiatives involving China and Taiwan, not threaten to do what the administration most feared—drive China into the arms of the Soviet Union? Washington recognized the danger. Yet as the National Security Council (NSC) noted in January 1951 with regard to trade controls, lack of access to Western goods "probably will lead to some degree of disillusionment on the part of the Chinese Communists when they find Russia either unwilling or unable to meet their requirements."[32]

What is significant about the NSC's comment is that the United States had once again changed policy but found a way to make the new rules compatible with the wedge strategy. In 1948, Washington had favored trade contacts with China as a means of drawing the Chinese Communists away from the Soviet Union. In 1949, the White House had placed limits on trade with the CCP but justified them as part of the wedge strategy. Now, in 1951, it was altering policy once again, cutting all trade with the PRC. Each time, the United States argued that its newest initiatives would succeed in creating rifts between the Kremlin and the CCP.

To make its policies effective, the United States increased the pressure on Britain to concur. In 1949, Washington had accepted some divergence in Anglo-American policy toward China, but now it wanted to bring the British in line. Of course, Washington needed to avoid putting too much pressure on London. The Truman administration, for example, desired the continuation of Britain's military presence in the Middle East and supported London's proposal for the establishment of a Middle East Command for the region.[33] In East Asia, the White House believed that Whitehall's attitude could influence that of other countries, both in the Commonwealth and throughout Europe. Attlee thus had some maneuvering room, which he used to make

31. NSC 48/5, "United States Objectives, Policies and Courses of Action in Asia," May 17, 1951, *FRUS, 1951,* 6:33–39.

32. Untitled memorandum (no author given), Jan. 17, 1951, PSF-NSF, Meetings, box 211, HSTL.

33. Burton I. Kaufman, *The Arab Middle East and the United States: Inter-Arab Rivalry and Superpower Diplomacy,* 13.

clear his opposition to the use of nuclear weapons or to the imposition of a full-scale embargo against the PRC.

Yet again, Washington held the upper hand. Whitehall's resources were already strained. Not only had it expanded its military spending because of the Korean crisis, but it also had military commitments in Europe, the Middle East, Hong Kong, and Malaya. Even without these commitments, London did not have the military capability to resist the Soviet Union, which now seemed to pose a greater threat than ever before. The British had neither the long-range bomber force nor the nuclear capability of the Americans.[34] Given these considerations, it was vital that Whitehall not anger Washington or present any indication to the Communists that the Anglo-American alliance was divided. Thus constrained, Britain more often than not followed the U.S. lead on China policy.

Such became clear with regard to Taiwan. Following the PRC's intervention, the Truman administration renounced its previously declared unwillingness to commit itself to Taipei. U.S. military and economic aid to Taiwan skyrocketed. In February 1951, Truman authorized $50 million for Chiang's army; a month later, the State Department accepted a Defense Department recommendation to provide $237 million in military aid "to Taiwan for the upcoming fiscal year, somewhat more than 40 percent of the entire Mutual Defense Assistance program appropriation for the Far East." Economic aid increased from $40 million for fiscal year 1951 to $80 million for fiscal year 1952.[35]

There were conditions attached to this assistance. Most important among them, Taiwan could not stage unauthorized attacks on the mainland. But the administration did not prevent Chiang from staging raids along the Chinese coast, nor did it stop Nationalist interference with ships heading to China, including those owned by British companies. In late 1952, Britain asked the United States to use its influence over Taiwan to end these infringements. The British consul in Taiwan, E. H. Jacobs-Larkcom, broached the issue with Karl Rankin, the American ambassador in Taipei. When Rankin told Jacobs-Larkcom that Britain could expect little U.S. sympathy, the consul informed Charles H. Johnston, the head of the Foreign Office's China and Korea Department, that "it would pay us better to reserve our appeals for assistance for more worthy causes."[36] The Foreign Office apparently followed Jacobs-

34. William [Whitney] Stueck, [Jr.], *The Korean War: An International History,* 72; David Reynolds, *Britannia Overruled: British Policy and World Peace in the Twentieth Century,* 181.

35. Robert Accinelli, *Crisis and Commitment: United States Policy toward Taiwan, 1950–1955,* 67.

36. Ibid., 98; letter to Johnston from Jacobs-Larkcom, Nov. 19, 1952, FO 371/99329, PRO.

Larkcom's advice, for London did not raise the matter again until after the war ended.

The Truman administration also bolstered its assistance to Indochina, where the French faced problems against the Communist Vietminh. Behind Korea, Indochina was the most important concern of the administration, even more so than Western Europe. In this case, the British supported the American effort, for it helped London defend its interests in Southeast Asia, particularly in Malaya.[37]

Finally, Washington augmented efforts to achieve a peace treaty with Japan. MacArthur had raised the idea of such a treaty in 1947, but he found little support for it within the Truman administration. As communism spread in China, though, Washington began to reconsider. In 1950, Truman appointed John Foster Dulles as special ambassador to Japan, with the job of concluding a peace and military agreement with Tokyo. Dulles believed it vital to sign such a pact as soon as possible. "Japan is, with Germany, one of the two great assets that the Soviet power seeks for exploitation in aid of its aggressive policies," he wrote in December 1950. Without a treaty, Japan might choose not to commit itself to the West.[38]

The British wanted Japan free to choose sides; they believed that if Japan wanted to establish relations with China, it had the right to do so. Indeed, London wanted Tokyo to form ties with Beijing as well as Taipei (a position Japan favored as well). Politically, Sino-Japanese relations would buttress the British policy of maintaining contacts with the PRC as part of its wedge strategy. Economically, China offered Japan a sizeable market; British exports could continue to flow to Southeast Asia without being undercut by cheaper Japanese products. Whitehall also wanted the PRC to be able to attend the peace treaty conference, something Washington opposed.[39]

The British quickly realized the Americans would not agree to Beijing's attendance at the treaty conference; the Americans believed the British position on the treaty could influence those of other nations. Thus, they offered a compromise. Dulles suggested that neither China nor Taiwan be invited, to which British Foreign Secretary Herbert Morrison—who had replaced an

37. Leffler, *Preponderance of Power*, 382; Steven Hugh Lee, *Outposts of Empire: Korea, Vietnam, and the Origins of the Cold War in Asia, 1949–1954*, 129.

38. Michael Schaller, *The American Occupation of Japan: The Origins of the Cold War in Asia*, 94–97; Howard B. Schonberger, *Aftermath of War: Americans and the Remaking of Japan, 1945–1952*, 151; Dulles quote from Ronald W. Pruessen, *John Foster Dulles: The Road to Power*, 467–68.

39. Chihiro Hosoya, "Japan, China, the United States, and the United Kingdom, 1951–2: The Case of the 'Yoshida Letter,'" 250; Zhai, *Dragon, the Lion, and the Eagle*, 110; Howard Schonberger, "Peacemaking in Asia: The United States, Great Britain, and the Japanese Decision to Recognize Nationalist China, 1951–52," 62–63.

ailing Bevin in March 1951—agreed. Additionally, Dulles accepted Morrison's request to let Tokyo decide with which China it would establish relations. Following this agreement between the two foreign secretaries, Dulles completed work on the treaty, which forty-nine nations signed in September 1951.[40] But the harmony between the White House and Whitehall over Japan would not last long.

Bolstering the ability of Taiwan, Indochina, and Japan to resist communism was, of course, secondary to the conflict in Korea. Both the Americans and the British intended to keep the war confined to the peninsula. Yet the United States seemed to move in the opposite direction when, in an off-the-cuff response to a reporter's question at a November 30, 1950, news conference, Truman said that Washington had "always been" actively considering the use of nuclear weapons and that any decision to use them would be up to the "military commander in the field." Interestingly, his statement not only contradicted his own opposition to the use of nuclear weapons, but neither the State Department nor the JCS had recommended their use. Understandably, his comment created a sensation throughout Europe. Roy Jenkins, a Member of Parliament (MP) from the Labour Party, pointed out that Truman's remark came "at a particularly sensitive time," for the House of Commons was then holding a debate on foreign affairs. Seventy-six Labour MPs condemned the president's comment and announced they would withdraw their support from Attlee if Whitehall backed a U.S. effort to expand the war to China, which could lead to another world war. Attlee decided to travel to Washington in hopes of calming the British public's concerns.[41]

Bevin was too ill to make the long trip to Washington, leaving Attlee to assume the foreign secretary's role at the talks. The prime minister attempted to convince Truman and Acheson that Titoism was still very much a possibility in China and again raised the Taiwan question. Acheson pointed to domestic opposition in the United States to Washington having relations with Beijing or to giving up Taiwan; while he did not deny the possibility of an eventual Sino-Soviet split, current circumstances required strong measures.[42] The secretary of state's comment reflected the new belief in Washington that driving the PRC and the Soviets closer together actually could pose benefits in the long run.

40. Schonberger, "Peacemaking in Asia," 64–66.

41. Minutes of Cabinet Meeting, C.M. 80 (50), Nov. 30, 1950, CAB 128/18, PRO; Truman, *Public Papers,* 1950, 727; Hamby, *Man of the People,* 552; Kaufman, *Korean War,* 70; Roy Jenkins, *Truman,* 178; Rosemary Foot, "Anglo-American Relations in the Korean Crisis: The British Effort to Avert an Expanded War, Dec. 1950–Jan. 1951," 45.

42. Bullock, *Ernest Bevin,* 821; memorandum of conversation, Dec. 4 and 5, 1950, *FRUS, 1950,* 7:1397–98, 1401–2.

The three men also discussed the question of using nuclear weapons. The president acted upon Bradley's insistence to avoid any commitment that might restrict their use. Rather, he promised not to use them without first consulting London. When the prime minister asked whether this should be put in writing, Truman responded, "If a man's word wasn't any good it can't be made any better by writing it down."[43] Attlee was not pleased by Truman's rebuff. But as Acheson told one of Attlee's biographers, "I had to tell [the prime minister] that [Truman] had always said in public that nothing could limit his power to use the bomb if he believed the use of it was necessary . . . and that if he made that statement, there could be an uproar." While Attlee came away with less than he hoped, the discussions served as a reminder to the administration that its allies did not approve of any talk of expanding the war beyond Korea.[44]

Britain also had concerns about MacArthur's inclination to expand the war. A World War II hero and Supreme Commander of the Allied Powers (SCAP) in Japan, MacArthur opposed what he regarded as the Eurocentric attitude of the Truman administration. In particular, he advocated closer ties between the White House and Chiang's Nationalist government. As early as June 1950, he told Washington that it was vital that the island not fall to the Communists; Taiwan's loss, he contended, would endanger the security of U.S. interests throughout the region.[45]

The British considered MacArthur the best choice for the job in Korea, but they had strong misgivings about him. Not only did he have a history of mistreating U.K. officials and correspondents, but also he had on several occasions questioned allied policy in Korea and even issued orders without Washington's approval. For instance, in October, MacArthur ordered the bombing of bridges across the Yalu River. Only by chance did the Defense Department learn of the UN commander's plan; Truman promptly instructed MacArthur to postpone any bombing within five miles of the Chinese border. Given MacArthur's behavior, Attlee recommended the establishment of a commission to direct the war effort; Bradley rejected the idea, arguing, "A war cannot be run by committee." Again, unwilling to create unwanted tensions in the Anglo-American alliance, the British relented.[46]

43. Memorandum for the Record by Jessup, Dec. 7, 1950, *FRUS, 1950,* 1462. On Dec. 4, Bradley told Marshall he had no objection to Truman discussing the use of the atomic bomb, but wanted him to avoid any commitment restricting its use. See memorandum to Secretary of Defense from Bradley, Dec. 4, 1950, Xerox 2569 (box 2), MFNAP.

44. Acheson quote from Kenneth Harris, *Attlee,* 464; Foot, "Anglo-American Relations in the Korean Crisis," 50.

45. Douglas MacArthur, *Reminiscences,* 337; memorandum on Formosa by MacArthur, June 14, 1950, *FRUS, 1950,* 7:161–64.

46. Memorandum by Battle, Dec. 6, 1950, *FRUS, 1950,* 7:1431; Francis Williams, *Twilight of Empire: Memoirs of Prime Minister Clement Attlee,* 236; Laura Belmonte, "Anglo-

Truman's eventual decision in April 1951 to fire MacArthur brought relief in Britain. Realizing that open applause would incite anger in the United States, Foreign Secretary Morrison urged members of Parliament to keep their elation under wraps.[47] In the United States, MacArthur's firing created an enormous uproar. Hearings in the Senate gave the general an opportunity to express his views. Witnesses for the administration, most notably Bradley, took MacArthur to task, arguing that the general risked putting the United States "in the wrong war, at the wrong place, at the wrong time and with the wrong enemy." By mid-1951, controversy over the firing had died down, though Truman's approval rating remained very low.

If London did not press the MacArthur issue, the same could not be said about economic sanctions against China, which directly affected Britain's financial health. In 1949, the Attlee government had agreed to place restrictions on List 1A goods destined for China. But this covered only the shipment of materials from the United Kingdom to China; Hong Kong and Singapore remained free to ship materials to the PRC. In October of that year, Whitehall declared that it would place restrictions on List 1A items shipped from its East Asian colonies only if Belgium, France, and Holland did the same regarding their colonies in the region. (Even if such agreement was reached, London remained unwilling to extend controls to List 1B.) Yet Britain did agree to restrict the shipment of oil to levels necessary for civilian Chinese consumption.[48]

With the beginning of the war in Korea, the United States imposed an oil embargo against Pyongyang and Beijing and asked that Britain impose similar controls on shipments between Hong Kong and Singapore and China. Whitehall balked, arguing that such action would involve "a reversal of United Kingdom policy towards China." Moreover, Britain's supply of oil to the PRC was "negligible." Whitehall's attitude prompted Deputy Assistant Secretary of State for Far Eastern Affairs Livingston Merchant to warn Graves that Americans would be furious if China intervened in Korea with equipment powered by British oil. Finally, by July 1, Belgium, France, and Holland

---

American Relations and the Dismissal of MacArthur," 654; Kaufman, *Korean War,* 64–65; Dockrill, "The Foreign Office," 465.

47. Belmonte, "Anglo-American Relations and the Dismissal of MacArthur," 662.

48. Yoko Yasuhara, "Japan, Communist China, and Export Controls in Asia, 1948–52," 80; Minutes of meeting of the China and South-East Asia Committee of the Cabinet, S.A.C.(49) 6th Meeting, July 22, 1949, CAB 134/669, PRO. There is no indication from the meeting exactly how much oil would meet civilian requirements. It is clear, however, that the Foreign Office had indications of how much oil it would allow for sale to the PRC. For instance, Whitehall ordered Shell Oil to sell only 26,000 tons of oil products to China, amounting to 5 percent of Beijing's total demand for 1950. See Clayton, *Imperialism Revisited,* 57.

had agreed to impose controls on trade with North Korea and the PRC. In light of the American response and Britain's promise regarding the other European powers, Bevin now urged London to join with the United States. "All that was needed," he argued, "was to add China to the confidential list of countries to which export licenses were in practice refused." The cabinet concurred, but the problem remained of how to impose controls without angering the CCP government. London solved the problem in the middle of July: the admiralty requisitioned all oil in Hong Kong, on the grounds that the British military needed it for its own purposes.[49]

Despite the increased restriction of goods, the Truman administration still intended to continue its policy of maintaining contact with China through at least some trade. The PRC's November offensive changed all that. On November 29, Secretary of Commerce Charles Sawyer informed Acheson that "he was giving serious thought to putting an embargo, or at least controls on everything going to China." The secretary of state supported the idea. On December 3, the administration unilaterally imposed a complete embargo on all exports to the PRC. Additionally, because of "the close proximity of Hong Kong and Macao to Communist China, and the fact that those areas are traditional funnels for trade with China," the United States levied controls on exports destined for those colonies. Two weeks later, Washington froze Beijing's assets in the United States.[50] As noted earlier, the United States realized that these actions might strengthen ties between China and the Soviet Union but believed in the long run they would actually serve to divide the two communist powers.

On January 20, the administration went a step further, when the permanent U.S. representative to the UN, Warren Austin, introduced a resolution attacking China's unwillingness to hold peace talks, branding China an aggressor, and calling upon the United Nations "to consider additional mea-

49. Memoranda of conversation, July 4, 1950, 7:298–99; memorandum to Sawyer from Acheson, June 8, 1950; "Editorial Note"; telegram, no. 5, Douglas to Secretary of State, July 1, 1950; and memorandum of conversation, July 18, 1950, *FRUS, 1950,* 6:638–40, 642, 651–54; telegram, no. 3686, Douglas to Secretary of State, June 28, 1950, RG 59, Central Decimal File, 1950–54, box 2204, NA; Minutes of Cabinet Meeting, C.M. 42 (50), July 4, 1950, CAB 128/18; Minutes of Cabinet Meetings, C.M. 44 (50), July 10, 1950, and C.M. 46 (50), July 17, 1950, CAB 128/18, PRO.

50. Memorandum of telephone conversation, Nov. 19, 1950; memorandum by Lucius Battle, Nov. 30, 1950; and Circular telegram, no. 278, Acheson to various consular and diplomatic officers, Dec. 16, 1950, *FRUS, 1950,* 7:666–67, 668, 682–83; memorandum by Popper, Apr. 12, 1951, *FRUS, 1951,* 7:1956; memorandum, "History of COCOM/CHINCOM," undated, RG 59, Records of the Bureau of Far Eastern Affairs, 1957, box 3, and memorandum of conversation, Dec. 14, 1950, RG 59, Records of the Policy Planning Staff Relating to State Department Participation in the National Security Council, 1935–1962, box 7, NA.

sures to be employed to meet this aggression." Once again, London had a difficult decision to make. First, the Commonwealth was divided over the resolution. India opposed it, believing it would make China even less willing to talk peace. New Zealand and Australia, which wanted U.S. support for a Pacific defense pact, supported it. Second, Britain had to consider its own economy. In 1951, the United Kingdom had between £200–250 million in assets in China. During that year, London directly exported £2.7 million to the PRC; it exported an additional £36 million to Hong Kong, much of which made its way into China. While these numbers made up only a small portion of Britain's overall exports, given the U.K. financial situation, they were significant. And there was always the possibility that trade, if unencumbered, might grow. It is not surprising, therefore, that Bevin contended that the resolution would hurt London more than Beijing. Third, given past statements, Bevin probably believed that continued contacts with the Chinese government via trade offered the best means of splitting the Sino-Soviet alliance and containing the communist threat. (In fact, a cabinet paper in late 1953 expressed this very intent: it was vital, stated the paper, for the United Kingdom "to keep a toe in the door in case divergences between China and Russia develop and can be exploited.") Fourth, there was the possible Chinese response. British officials contended that voting for additional measures might preclude further progress toward the establishment of full Sino-British diplomatic relations. Finally, there was the United States. The permanent British representative to the United Nations, Sir Gladwyn Jebb, told Bevin that if London voted against the resolution, other nations would follow suit. "I cannot help feeling that the resulting mood in the country and in Congress might be the reverse of helpful so far as the defence of Western Europe is concerned," he warned. Seeking a middle ground, Bevin urged the Truman administration to postpone a vote on the resolution so as to test once more China's willingness to talk peace; needing British support to move ahead on the resolution, the White House agreed. Acheson believed that if the CCP government once again rejected a peace proposal, it would facilitate passage of the condemnatory resolution.[51]

Britain still had to decide what to do if the Chinese rejected the latest peace

51. "Editorial Note"; telegram, no. 4071, Gifford to Secretary of State, Jan. 23, 1951, *FRUS, 1951,* 7:115–16, 119–20; telegram, no. 32, Foreign Office to Ankara, Jan. 19, 1951, FO 371/92776; telegram, no. 117, Jebb to Foreign Office, Jan. 20, 1951, FO 371/92769; telegram, no. 145, Foreign Office to New York, Jan. 24, 1951, FO 371/92270; telegram, no. 272, Hutchison to Foreign Office, Feb. 2, 1951, FO 371/92233; telegram, no. 129, GHQ, Far East Land Forces to Ministry of Defence, Mar. 22, 1951, FO 371/92195, PRO; "The Present China," *London Times,* July 16, 1952; Stueck, *Korean War,* 153; Acheson, *Present at the Creation,* 513; Tang, *Britain's Encounter with Revolutionary China,* 117. For statistics on Sino-British and U.K.-Hong Kong trade during the Korean War years, see Clayton, *Imperialism Revisited,* 141–43.

offer. Bevin's illness greatly hindered his ability to lead; Minister of State Kenneth Younger took over the Foreign Office's day-to-day affairs. When the cabinet met on January 25, the foreign secretary was absent. Younger, who strongly disliked what he regarded as Bevin's inclination to follow consistently the American line, got the cabinet to agree to vote against the resolution if the United States did not support another mediation effort. Deputy Undersecretary of State for Foreign Affairs Roger Makins and Chancellor of the Exchequer Hugh Gaitskell deplored the decision, Gaitskell commenting that a "no" vote could threaten future U.S. financial assistance to Britain. Attlee supported his treasury secretary. The cost of rearmament, an inability to meet rising consumer demand because of the rearmament program, and a negative balance of payments led Britain to face a £400 million debt by the end of 1951. Accordingly, it was important to maintain America's favor and its much-needed financial support. As one of the prime minister's biographers noted, "[T]he economic situation was now so dire that it was important to lose no more American goodwill than was necessary." In fact, the matter resolved itself. Realizing London's vote would influence those of other nations and expose to the Communists a schism in the Western ranks, the United States agreed to incorporate the British cabinet's amendment favoring another approach to the Chinese. The resolution's modification, plus China's refusal to consider a cease-fire, led to easy passage of the U.S. resolution on February 1.[52]

Declaring China an aggressor was one thing; imposing additional measures was another. The United States now took the position that imposition of additional sanctions eventually would divide the Sino-Soviet alliance, but the British maintained that the best way to achieve this goal was through continued contacts with Beijing, including trade. Hence, Whitehall adamantly opposed any idea of accepting a full embargo. Acheson agreed to compromise. The State Department believed the embargo, as it stood, covered approximately 90 percent of strategic material heading for China; a selective embargo would cover the remainder. C. A. Gerald Meade and R. Burns of the British embassy reacted favorably to selective controls, with Burns commenting that "such a program would not cause insuperable difficulties [for Britain] from the economic point of view." Acheson also pressured White-

52. "Resolution 498 (V), adopted by the United Nations General Assembly, Feb. 1, 1951," *FRUS, 1951,* 7:150–51; see also 150 n 1, *FRUS, 1951;* Bullock, *Ernest Bevin,* 826–27; Dockrill, "The Foreign Office," 470–71; Peter Lowe, "The Significance of the Korean War in Anglo-American Relations, 1950–53" in *British Foreign Policy, 1945–56,* ed. Michael Dockrill and John W. Young, 132; Kaufman, *Korean War,* 133; Foot, "Anglo-American Relations in the Korean Crisis," 55–56; Harris, *Attlee,* 469; C. J. Bartlett, *A History of Postwar Britain, 1945–1974,* 87, 89.

hall to prevent reexport of goods from Hong Kong to China, which London agreed to do in March. In April, following another Chinese offensive, the secretary of state pressed for the passage of a UN resolution calling for a selective embargo. In light of Beijing's action, U.S. pressure, the fact that Washington was not seeking a full embargo, and possibly out of a desire to get American help in dealing with the government of Iran—which had recently nationalized Britain's oil facilities there—Whitehall agreed to support the resolution. On May 18, the United Nations passed a resolution calling for selective trade controls. The United Kingdom followed up by putting under embargo over four hundred items. Chinese Vice Foreign Minister Zhang Hanfu responded angrily to the British decision but made no threats against Hong Kong; Beijing clearly wanted to continue its contacts with Britain, both to obtain materials it could not get from Moscow and to drive a wedge into the Anglo-American alliance. The following year approximately fifteen nations formed the China Committee (CHINCOM) to oversee the multilateral trade controls.[53]

U.S. policy also stiffened on the questions of recognition and China's representation in the United Nations. China's intervention made it clear to U.K. officials that there was no chance in the near future of the United States according recognition the CCP government.[54] But Washington determined to go a step further and prevent Beijing from achieving admission to the UN, thereby precipitating another dispute with London.

Prior to June 1950, the Truman administration had adopted the position that it would oppose Beijing's admission but would accept a majority vote in the General Assembly in favor of the Communists. The administration augmented efforts to keep China out once the war began but maintained its willingness to abide by a pro-Beijing decision in the UN.[55] The possibility of

53. Memorandum, "History of COCOM/CHINCOM"; telegram, no. 818 Saving, Foreign Office to Washington, Feb. 17, 1951, PREM 8/1405; telegram, no. 355 Saving, Franks to Foreign Office, Apr. 21, 1951, CAB 21/1949; Minutes of Cabinet Meeting, C.M. 34 (51), May 7, 1951, CAB 128/19; FO Minute by Wilson, Sept. 16, 1954, FO 371/110292, PRO; memorandum to Bonbright from Allen, Feb. 15, 1951; memorandum of conversation, Feb. 21, 1951; memorandum by Popper, Mar. 26, 1951; telegram, no. 881, Acheson to New York, Apr. 26, 1951; telegram, no. 6138, Gifford to Secretary of State, May 24, 1951, *FRUS, 1951,* 7:1914–15, 1923–28, 1953–63, 1974–75, 1989; "U.N. Asks All Bar Arms to Red China," *New York Times,* May 19, 1951; Clayton, *Imperialism Revisited,* 91–92;; Stueck, *Korean War,* 192 and 409 n 158; Foot, *Practice of Power,* 5.

54. Ovendale, "Britain, the United States, and the Recognition of Communist China," 157–58; Kaufman, *Korean War,* 65; Charles Dobbs, *The United States and East Asia since 1945,* 73.

55. Message to Bevin from Acheson, Aug. 4, 1950, *FRUS, 1950,* 2:257–58; memorandum, "Review of United States Position on the Question of Chinese Representation in the United Nations," Apr. 16, 1951, RG 59, Bureau of Far Eastern Affairs, 1953, Miscellaneous Subject Files for the Year 1953, box 4, NA.

such a decision increased in August, when the Soviet Union's representative returned to the United Nations after boycotting the international body because of the UN's refusal to admit China. Realizing that Russia's return meant the PRC stood a better chance of a hearing in the UN, Whitehall decided to stop abstaining on the question of representation and began to vote in favor of Beijing.[56]

Following China's intervention, the United States altered its position on representation and pressured Britain not to support the PRC's admission. The White House now argued that allowing China into the UN would be tantamount to rewarding aggression and would enhance the prestige of the CCP government; moreover, it could not risk inflaming congressional or public opinion by letting in Beijing. As with the issue of trade controls, the United States saw London's support as vital. The State Department's Office of Chinese Affairs noted that "a number of the European states which recognize the Chinese Communists tend to follow the lead of the UK on the Chinese representation issue." The problem was that Britain itself seemed unwilling to follow suit. Bevin explained to Acheson that not only was there strong support in Britain to vote in favor of China, but that it made sense to vote for Beijing given Britain's recognition of the PRC. Additionally, voting against admission would only serve to strengthen communist unity, to the detriment of the containment policy: "If China continues to be excluded from the United Nations, and if the attitude of the West continues to be coldly hostile, must she not come to the conclusion, even when the moment arrives when she would like to move away from Moscow, that she has no other course but to maintain her association?" Acheson saw things differently. Not only would admitting Beijing enhance the PRC's prestige, but—in a reference to the new American attitude regarding driving wedges—it would not have an impact upon the Sino-Soviet relationship.[57]

In an effort to bridge the gap between their respective positions, Acheson suggested in April 1951 the idea of a moratorium. Morrison was not sure at first what Acheson meant by "moratorium," but further discussion made clear that the secretary of state wanted to postpone discussion of the repre-

56. Memorandum by the Secretary of State for Foreign Affairs, C.P. 50 (195), "Chinese Representation at the General Assembly," Sept. 1, 1950, CAB 129/41; "Brief for Lord Henderson for the I.P.U. Conference in Washington: The Background of the Question of Recognition of the Central People's Government of China," Sept. 11, 1953, FO 371/105225, PRO.

57. Negotiating Paper on China for Truman-Churchill Meetings, Jan. 2, 1952, PSF-General File, box 116, HSTL; Foot, *Practice of Power*, 30; letter to Franks from Acheson, Aug. 4, 1950, and message to Franks from Bevin, Aug. 11, 1950, FRUS, 1950, 2:257–62; memorandum by the Office of Chinese Affairs, "Question of Chinese Representation in United Nations and Specialized Agency Bodies," Mar. 20, 1952, FRUS, 1952–54, 3:620.

sentation question while the war in Korea continued. Following further consideration, Morrison reluctantly agreed to Acheson's proposal. He noted that Beijing had refused to bring an end to the war in Korea, and there was still no indication that Beijing would take action against Hong Kong or British interests in China if the United Kingdom supported the moratorium. Morrison agreed to postponement, but he made sure to tell Acheson that his decision did not imply support for the Nationalist claim to China's seat.[58]

Thus, by the time the belligerents in Korea began peace talks in July 1951, Britain had substantially hardened its position toward China. The United States wanted to demonstrate Anglo-American unity before the Communists and believed Britain's position could influence those of other nations. These facts allowed the Attlee government to make its influence felt on some policies or even to alter them to fit Britain's interests. Hence, Truman listened to the prime minister's concerns about expansion of the war—which reinforced his own qualms—and agreed not to force Whitehall to adopt a full-scale embargo against China. Even so, Washington remained the senior partner in the "special relationship." The United States had the power Whitehall needed, particularly in the present crisis. Britain accordingly did not strongly press the United States on the issue of increased American aid to Taiwan, Nationalist infringements on U.K. shipping, or MacArthur's leadership. It implemented additional controls on trade with Beijing and agreed to postpone discussion of China's representation. The Chinese protested London's actions, but in hopes of splitting the Anglo-American alliance, they maintained their contacts with British officials.

Why the Chinese were willing to talk with the United Nations by mid-1951 remains a subject of contention. Heavy losses, a lack of Soviet assistance, a need to regroup, troubles financing the war, and the fact that UN forces had been pushed behind the thirty-eighth parallel have been put forward as reasons for Beijing's flexibility. The UN coalition, meanwhile, had conducted a successful counteroffensive and defeated Communist attacks in April and May. Moreover, the United States faced growing pressure from its European allies, who did not want to leave themselves vulnerable to Soviet aggression by becoming indefinitely mired in a conflict in the Far East.[59]

58. Telegram, no. 5480, Acheson to London, May 25, 1951, and memorandum of conversation, June 1, 1951, *FRUS, 1952–1954*, 2:245–48, 251–52; memorandum to McConaughy from Bacon, *FRUS, 1952–1954*, 3:645; telegram, no. 129, G.H.Q. Far East Land Forces to Ministry of Defence, Mar. 22, 1951, FO 371/92195; telegram, no. 114, Hutchison to Foreign Office, July 25, 1950, FO 371/83293, PRO; letter to Scott from Hutchison, Aug. 8, 1950, RG 59, Central Decimal File, 1950–1954, box 2917, NA; Pearce, *Attlee's Labour Governments*, 34.

59. See Harding and Yuan, eds., *Sino-American Relations*, 229; Zhang, *Mao's Military*

The result was the opening of talks on July 8 at the village of Kaesong. (Britain did not play a role in these talks. It seemed content to enjoy special access to daily reports on the talks and largely supported the American position.) The negotiations quickly ran into trouble as each side accused the other of undermining the neutrality zone established around town. On August 23, the Communists suspended the negotiations, contending that a UN plane had strafed the area.[60] The two sides did not resume discussions until October.

The same month the talks recommenced, Britain held elections. The Labour Party, already divided over the war, grew even more so when Aneurin Bevan, the leader of the left wing of the party, resigned in protest against the Attlee government's rearmament program. Labour actually received more votes than the Conservative Party, but the inability of the Liberal Party to put up a large number of candidates allowed the Tories to win more seats in Parliament. After six years out of office, the Conservative Party, led by Winston Churchill, returned to power.

Churchill, now seventy-seven, was not the same man who had led Britain during World War II, at least in terms of his health. He had suffered a mild stroke in August 1949 and was told the following year that he was going deaf. (Indeed, increasingly, he had to have statements repeated to him.) Yet his health by no means reduced his desire to maintain, if not strengthen, the bonds linking Great Britain and the United States. Of the "three circles" London had to consider in making its foreign policy—the Commonwealth, Western Europe, and the Atlantic Alliance—he placed the last first. For instance, in December 1951, Fourth Sea Lord Mountbatten argued that the prime minister should not tie Britain's fortunes to those of the United States, especially if doing so could lead to war. Churchill responded by accusing Mountbatten of having "Left-wing views" and warned that as a military man, the sea lord should "avoid expressing any political opinions."[61]

In strengthening these ties, Churchill planned to avoid creating troubles with the United States over China. As early as May 1950, he accused the Labour Party of holding pro-Chinese and anti-American sentiments. In January 1951, he told the foreign secretary of his wartime administration, Anthony Eden, that London had to avoid a split with Washington on China,

---

Romanticism, 217–18, and Deterrence and Strategic Culture, 130–31; Kaufman, Korean War, 117, 118–29.

60. Telegram, no. HNC-258, Joy to Ridgway, June 23, 1951, FRUS, 1951, 7: 848–50; Dockrill, "The Foreign Office," 473–74; Stueck, Korean War, 239; Foot, Substitute for Victory, 48.

61. Shlaim, Jones, and Sainsbury, British Foreign Secretaries, 50; Martin Gilbert, Winston S. Churchill, vol. 8, "Never Despair," 1945–1965, 672–73.

even if the United States decided to impose a blockade against Beijing, and even if such a blockade hurt Hong Kong. The following year, he told Eden, "Don't let us fall out with the United States for the sake of China." In fact, the prime minister held a very low regard for China and the Chinese people. "I do not regard Communist China a formidable adversary," he wrote in August 1952. The Chinese people "cannot swim, they are not much good at flying and the Trans-Siberian railway is already overloaded." He concluded, "In the late war I never believed in the power of China. I doubt whether Communist China is going to be the monster some people imagine."[62]

Eden, for his part, had enjoyed a long career in foreign policy even before he served with Churchill. In 1931, he had been undersecretary for foreign affairs; in 1934, minister for the League of Nations. The next year, Prime Minister Neville Chamberlain had named him foreign secretary; Eden had resigned three years later in protest of Chamberlain's policy of appeasement toward Germany. Two years later, though, following Churchill's election to the prime ministership, Eden returned as foreign secretary.

Although Eden had served with Churchill before, he was experiencing increasing trouble with his superior. Eden too believed in the "three circles," but he put Britain and the Commonwealth first, even if it meant upsetting the United States. Moreover, he believed he could conduct world affairs better than his American counterparts.[63] Then there was a personal issue: Churchill's unwillingness to retire. The prime minister might be more famous, but, just as with his ability to conduct foreign policy, Eden felt he could do a better job in leading Great Britain. Eden wanted to be prime minister, but Churchill would not retire until April 1955. During the three-and-a-half-year wait, Eden's frustrations boiled to the surface on more than one occasion.[64]

Despite their differences, Churchill and Eden agreed that no matter what their relationship with the United States, they had to "restrain the extremes in American foreign policy." This meant keeping the war in Korea restricted

62. FO Minute by Johnston, Sept. 5, 1952, FO 371/99584; Minute by Churchill, Aug. 26, 1952, FO 371/99584, PRO; Shlaim, Jones, and Sainsbury, *British Foreign Secretaries*, 50; Gilbert, *Winston S. Churchill*, 8:582–83, 894.

63. Shlaim, Jones, and Sainsbury, *British Foreign Secretaries*, 91; John Charmley, *Churchill's Grand Alliance: The Anglo-American Special Relationship, 1940–57*, 244–45; Sir Robin Renwick, *Fighting with Allies: America and Britain in Peace and at War*, 194–95.

64. Eden's memoirs give no hint of the foreign secretary's feelings on this score. The best inside source regarding Eden's questions about Churchill's ability to serve Britain— as well as the foreign secretary's interest in becoming prime minister in his own right— is the memoirs of Evelyn Shuckburgh, Eden's principal private secretary. See Evelyn Shuckburgh, *Descent to Suez: Diaries, 1951–56*.

to the peninsula. Such a concern surfaced the month after the British elections. The resumption of the cease-fire talks raised the question of how to deal with China if the belligerents agreed to an armistice and the communists broke it by renewing their aggression. Washington therefore came up with the idea of a statement warning of "greater sanctions" against Beijing. As Acheson explained to Eden in late November, the statement would serve to reduce the risk posed to the UN forces following the war's end. Eden replied he could not give any answer until after talking with Churchill.[65]

Two days later, Churchill discussed the matter with his defense ministers and the Chiefs of Staff. They agreed that any statement should be issued "in general terms." Eden transmitted the decision to Acheson.[66] A vague declaration would keep the Communists guessing and deter them from future action, a tactic later used by the administration of Dwight D. Eisenhower during crises in Indochina and the offshore islands. It also would avoid committing Britain publicly to any particular type of response.

In January 1952, Churchill and Eden visited the United States for talks with Truman and Acheson. The allies again debated the question of Titoism in China (though Churchill was much less willing than Attlee to press the subject) and discussed the warning statement. It is also possible that Truman used the talks to raise his concerns about the status of planes owned by the China National Aviation Corporation and the Central Air Transport Corporation. A Hong Kong court in early 1950 had awarded the planes to China, but the Attlee government had bowed to U.S. pressure for a legal appeal. Even if Truman did not raise the issue directly with Churchill, the White House was putting pressure on Whitehall through its first secretary at the U.S. embassy in London, Arthur Ringwalt, who later recalled holding "almost daily" talks with the Foreign Office about the aircraft. In June 1952 the Privy Council awarded the planes to Washington. Though Whitehall denied politics played a role in the council's judgment, that is clearly untrue. Angered by the decision, China requisitioned British dockyards and public utilities in Shanghai.[67]

65. Position Papers, SD/A/C.1/367, "United Nations Action against Aggression in Korea (Alternative I—If There is No Armistice") and SD/A/C.1/368, "United Nations Action in Korea (Alternative II—If an Armistice is Achieved)," Oct. 12, 1951, and memorandum of conversation, Nov. 28, 1951, *FRUS, 1951,* 7:1016–26, 1189–93; Peter Boyle, "The 'Special Relationship' with Washington," in *The Foreign Policy of Churchill's Peacetime Administration, 1951–1955,* ed. John W. Young, 37.

66. Telegram, unnumbered, British Secretary of State for Foreign Affairs to the British Embassy in Rome, Dec. 3, 1951, *FRUS, 1951,* 7:1221–23; Peter Lowe, "The Settlement of the Korean War," in *Foreign Policy of Churchill's Peacetime Administration,* ed. John W. Young, 210.

67. There is no mention of these aircraft in either the British or American minutes of the talks. However, a negotiating paper prepared before the talks suggested Truman raise

Upon returning home, Churchill announced that if the Communists broke the truce, the UN "response would be prompt, resolute, and effective." Sir John Colville, the prime minister's private secretary, commented that "these words [had] no special significance except to declare that the Allies would react strongly to such an attack." Yet Churchill's statement created an uproar in London. Members of the Labour opposition believed he had in mind nuclear war. Ten Labour MPs, led by Sydney Silverman and Harold Davies, issued a motion in the House of Commons declaring their opposition to expanding the war beyond Korea and calling for China's admission to the United Nations. Members of the opposition also accused the prime minister of accepting new commitments in the conflict and moved for a vote to censure the Conservative government. Furious with the charges leveled against him, and cognizant of the divisions within the Labour Party over the war, Churchill announced that "greater sanctions" did not represent a change in policy; indeed, he continued, the Attlee government secretly had made a similar commitment the year before. Churchill felt he had dealt a heavy blow to his political opponents: "It was a great day," he exclaimed to a friend, "a great triumph, and I am glad that you joined us in time to witness it."[68]

Churchill was right, on both counts. In May 1951, Morrison told Acheson that if the Chinese assaulted the UN forces, "there will be no alternative but to meet this new threat by the most effective military means at our disposal, namely by bombing the bases in China from which the attacks have been launched." The prime minister's announcement of this previously secret decision widened the rift within the Labour Party. Attlee had no choice but to acknowledge the accuracy of Churchill's statement. Labour's left wing, led by Bevan, condemned Washington: "Behind the guise and facade of the United Nations," Bevan stated, "the Americans are waging an ideological war with weapons against the Soviet Union."[69]

Churchill's support for Washington, however, did not carry over to the U.S. decision to alter its earlier arrangement with London regarding the Jap-

---

the issue with Churchill. See Negotiating Paper on China from Truman-Churchill-Meetings, Jan. 2, 1952, PSF-General File, box 116; Arthur Ringwalt Oral History, Truman Library Oral History Project, HSTL; dispatch, no. 72, Lamb to Foreign Office, Feb. 18, 1953, FO 371/105188, PRO.

68. "Mr. Churchill on Britain's Enduring Strength," *London Times*, Jan. 18, 1952; "Labour M.P.s' Motion on Korea," *London Times*, Jan. 31, 1952; "Britain's Attitude to Korean Conflict," *London Times*, Feb. 6, 1952; "Anglo-American Policy in Korea," *London Times*, Feb. 27, 1952; Randy Rowan, "A Foreign Policy in Opposition: The British Labour Party and the Far East, 1951–1964," 42–43; Sir John R. Colville, *The Fringes of Power: 10 Downing Street Diaries, 1939–1955*, 640; Gilbert, *Winston S. Churchill*, 8:707.

69. "Text of a Message from Mr. Morrison to Mr. Acheson, Dated 10th May, 1951," *FRUS, 1951*, 7:427; "Labour Policy on Korea," *London Times*, Feb. 29, 1952; Bevan quote in Kaufman, *Korean War*, 149.

anese peace treaty. The Dulles-Morrison agreement did not please Congress, where fifty-six senators declared their opposition to relations between Tokyo and Beijing. With ratification of the treaty threatened, Dulles traveled to Britain in hopes of getting the Churchill government to accept a revision regarding Japan's relationship with China; Eden refused to accept anything that would subvert the Dulles-Morrison understanding. Unmoved, Dulles traveled to Tokyo at the end of 1951 and made clear to Prime Minister Yoshida Shigeru that Japan had to commit itself to Taiwan. Sir Esler Dening, the British ambassador in Tokyo, kept Eden informed of Dulles's maneuvering. Eden resented the special ambassador's actions, but Dening proved unable to convince the U.S. representative to change course. Yoshida also resisted, but the pressure proved too much; he finally relented in the famous December 1951 "Yoshida letter" that required Japan to normalize relations with Taiwan. Infuriated, Eden wrote Dwight D. Eisenhower, a possible presidential candidate for the upcoming U.S. elections, asking him not to appoint Dulles secretary of state if the Republicans won. Whitehall's reaction failed to move the Senate, which ratified the treaty in March 1952.[70]

A month after the ratification of the Japanese peace treaty, the negotiations to end the war—which had stalled several times over issues such as rehabilitation of airfields, and which were now being held at Panmunjom—ground to a halt once again, this time over the question of repatriation. Here the belligerents had two serious disagreements. First, the Communists pointed to the 1949 Geneva Convention, which called for forcible repatriation of prisoners of war (POWs). Second, the UN reported that only 70,000 Communist prisoners wanted to return home. The Chinese and North Koreans considered this number too low, and the talks deadlocked.[71]

Without consulting Britain, Truman and the UN Command agreed that it would be both immoral and inhumane to force POWs to return to their countries against their will. The president declared in May 1952 that forced repatriation "would be repugnant to the fundamental moral and humanitarian principles which underlie our action in Korea." John Addis of the Foreign Office disputed this line of reasoning, believing that demanding voluntary repatriation would prevent a settlement of the war. Churchill and Eden, however, stood behind Washington, not only for the purpose of Anglo-American unity, but also for moral reasons.[72]

70. Schonberger, *Aftermath of War*, 272–77; Hosoya, "Japan, China, the United States and the United Kingdom," 254–57.

71. Kaufman, *Korean War*, 156–57.

72. Minute by Churchill May 28, 1952, FO 800/781; Minute by Churchill, July 8, 1952, FO 800/782, PRO; Dockrill and Young, eds., *British Foreign Policy*, 135–36; *Foreign Policy of Churchill's Peacetime Administration*, ed. John W. Young, 212; Truman, *Memoirs*, 2:460–61.

With the POW question preventing movement forward at the talks, the United States decided to step up the pressure in June by bombing power plants on the Korean side of the Yalu River. One attack, on Supung Dam, blacked out North Korea for over two weeks and eliminated 90 percent of the country's power. It also cut the power supply within Manchuria by 23 percent. Washington did not consult Whitehall before the attack, thus angering the British public and members of Parliament. The timing of the American action was also poor, for India was in the middle of another effort to broker an armistice. Acheson explained to Eden that the circumstances had required complete secrecy and pointed to the fact that not a single plane had been lost. Furthermore, the attack did not represent a change in the U.S. policy of confining the war to Korea. Eden responded "that it seemed clear that United States policy had not changed but, so far as [London] was concerned at any rate, it was important that there be no more surprises like the Yalu River bombing." Despite the uproar in Britain, the United States escalated the air raids, and even made one on an oil refinery only eight miles from the Soviet Union.[73]

Further discord within the Anglo-American alliance occurred later in the year when the Indian foreign minister, Krishna Menon, introduced a resolution designed to settle the POW issue. Throughout the conflict the Indian government had been in contact with Beijing and believed that China was becoming more flexible with regard to settling repatriation. Menon's resolution called for the establishment of a commission of neutral nations to deal with the question of repatriation; the political conference that would take place following an armistice would decide what happened to those prisoners resisting repatriation. Britain liked the resolution and found support from members of the Commonwealth, including Australia, Canada, and New Zealand. The resolution might finally break the deadlock on repatriation and end the war. Acheson, though, opposed Menon's proposal, arguing that it was too vague on the subject of voluntary repatriation. The secretary of state's attitude frustrated Eden. "Acheson himself could not have been more rigid, legalistic and difficult," commented the British foreign secretary. "At times it almost seems as if [the] United States Government were afraid of agreement at this time." Eden tried to make the resolution more amenable to Washington. But with the Commonwealth united behind Menon's pro-

---

73. Telegram, no. Tosec 14, Bruce to London, June 25, 1952, *FRUS, 1952–1954*, 15:352–53; memorandum of conversation, June 27, 1952. Papers of Dean Acheson, box 71, HSTL; Daniel T. Kuehl, "Airpower vs. Electricity: Electric Power as a Target for Strategic Air Operations," 246–47; Kaufman, *Korean War*, 161–62; Young, ed., *Foreign Policy of Churchill's Peacetime Administration*, 217.

posal, he had additional reason not to undermine his Indian counterpart's efforts.[74]

On November 26, the Soviet ambassador to the UN, Andrei Vishinsky, blasted the Menon resolution, arguing that it would perpetuate rather than end the war. Not wanting to be seen as siding with the Soviets, the United States back-pedaled and declared its support for the resolution. Following some minor changes, on December 1 the General Assembly, with Washington's approval, overwhelmingly approved the Indian proposal.[75]

Several weeks before the passage of the Indian resolution, Dwight Eisenhower had won the presidential election by a landslide. Churchill and Eden knew the new president very well from World War II and Eisenhower's tenure as commander of NATO. They could therefore identify with the new president on a personal level.

The same could not be said for his new secretary of state, John Foster Dulles. (Clearly Eden's pleading with Eisenhower not to select Dulles had had no effect.) Growing up, Dulles had been surrounded by foreign policy, politics, and religion. His grandfather, John Watson Foster, had been secretary of state during the short presidency of Benjamin Harrison. His uncle, Robert Lansing, had served at the same post under Woodrow Wilson. His father, Allen Macy Dulles, was a minister. Dulles had been a member of the U.S. delegation at the Versailles Conference, had written the peace treaty with Japan, and had been a leading Republican spokesperson on foreign policy for a decade.

Although Dulles was well qualified for the job, neither Churchill nor Eden liked him. He had a penchant for sermonizing, and he liked to monopolize conversations and to speak of political issues in moral terms. Eden had hoped that Eisenhower would appoint New York Governor Thomas E. Dewey as secretary of state "because," he told Eisenhower in mid-1952, "I do not think I would be able to work with [Dulles]." Eden's difficulties with Dulles continued, not only during the former's tenure as foreign secretary but also during his short prime ministership. His hatred for Dulles was made clear in 1958, after he resigned as Britain's head of state, when he mused that it had been "easier to deal with Ribbentrop or Laval" than Eisenhower's secretary of state.[76]

74. Telegrams, nos. Delga 149, 150, and 151, Acheson to Department of State, Nov. 8, 1952, *FRUS, 1952–1954,* 15: 585–89; telegram, no. 797, Jebb to Foreign Office, Nov. 13, 1952, FO 371/99589, PRO; Eden quote in Young, ed., *Foreign Policy of Churchill's Peacetime Administration,* 221.

75. Kaufman, *Korean War,* 175; Thomas J. Hamilton, "India's Truce Plan is approved in U.N. by Vote of 53 to 5," *New York Times,* Dec. 2, 1953.

76. Stephen E. Ambrose, *Eisenhower,* vol. 2, *The President, 1952–1969,* 21; Peter Boyle, "The 'Special Relationship' with Washington," in *Foreign Policy of Churchill's Peacetime Administration,* ed. John W. Young, 32; David Dutton, *Anthony Eden: A Life and Reputation,* 142.

Churchill shared Eden's dislike for Dulles. The prime minister, stated Aldrich, "referred to him as 'Dullith,' hissing through his teeth. He thought [Dulles] was a stupid man. He could hardly bear the sight of him." The prime minister also noted Dulles' need to talk and take over conversations, commenting that "Mr. Dulles makes a speech every day, holds a press conference every other day, and preaches on Sundays. All this tends to rob his utterances of real significance."[77]

Dulles knew the British did not care for him, and the feeling was mutual; he even went so far as to claim privately that the British had kept him from becoming secretary of state the year before. Through his meetings with Churchill and Eden, he reached that conclusion that the latter was a sloppy administrator or failed to do necessary homework on issues of importance. In fact, later commented his assistant, Johnny Hanes, the secretary of state "had absolutely no regard for [the British] internationally. He felt that they were clumsy and inept, as opposed to their carefully nurtured reputation of being the opposite, and he really literally had no admiration for them."[78]

Upon taking office, Eisenhower and Dulles determined to increase the pressure upon the Communists so that they would make concessions at Panmunjom. One means was through offensives on the peninsula. During the presidential campaign, Eisenhower promised to go to Korea if elected; he did so following his victory. He concluded while there that "[s]mall attacks on small hills would not end the war." Rather, he intended to engage in a major aerial assault, striking areas hitherto off limits (such as hydroelectric plants on the Yalu River) and ordered the new UN commander, Gen. Mark Clark, to make preparations along these lines.[79]

Second, he "unleashed" Chiang. Dulles had favored such a move as early as March 1952. While he realized the need privately to restrain Chiang, publicly "unleashing" him "may recreate in Chinese Communist minds a theoretical risk of attack on the mainland," thereby deterring them from increasing "their commitments at the two flanks of Korea and Indo-China." Eisenhower also had reason to end neutralization of the Taiwan Strait: the Republican right wing, incensed by the death of American soldiers at the hands of PRC troops, wanted to turn up the heat on Beijing. "Unleashing" Chiang would serve this purpose. Moreover, in combination with efforts to work more closely with the Democrats, "unleashing" the Nationalists would

77. Winthrop Aldrich Oral History, Oct. 16, 1972, Eisenhower Oral History Project, DDEL; Townsend Hoopes, *The Devil and John Foster Dulles*, 149.

78. Hoopes, *Devil and John Foster Dulles*, 169–70; Leonard Mosley, *Dulles: A Biography of Eleanor, Allen, and John Foster Dulles and Their Family Network*, 353.

79. Dwight D. Eisenhower, *The White House Years: Mandate for Change, 1953–1956*, 95; Piers Brendon, *Ike: His Life and Times*, 236.

depoliticize U.S. China policy by pleasing the far Right. Consequently, on February 2, Eisenhower announced that he was rescinding Truman's June 1950 order. Once again, Bevan and the Labour Party's left wing led the attack. "It is necessary not merely to say to the United States that she will not get the cooperation of the British people in backing up Chiang Kai-shek's military adventures," Bevan said, "but that the time has come to withdraw recognition from Chiang's regime even if it means an empty seat on the Security Council of the United Nations." Fearing that the Eisenhower administration's decision could lead to an expansion of the conflict, the Churchill government agreed on the need for a protest. Eden stated that the U.S. action would intensify the Chinese civil war, raise fears over a general war in East Asia, and make a settlement in the region more difficult. Eisenhower immediately sent Dulles to London to reassure Whitehall that the United States would not actually "unleash" the Nationalists. (Indeed, while the White House did not stop small KMT raids on the mainland, it demanded consultation before Chiang engaged in any type of large attack.)[80]

Washington's reassurances did not completely calm London. Hoping to find a solution to the war, Eden in January 1953 endorsed an International Red Cross proposal to exchange sick and wounded POWs. The next month, Clark put the suggestion on the table at Panmunjom. Mao found the proposal intriguing and asked for the opinion of the Soviet Union and North Korea. During this period of consultation, Stalin died. His replacement, Georgi Malenkov, argued in favor of settling outstanding East-West issues peacefully. Whether Stalin's death or something else—such as Eisenhower's veiled threat to use nuclear weapons if the Chinese did not agree to end the war—made the Communists more flexible is not clear.[81] However, on March

---

80. Memorandum by Dulles, Mar. 31, 1952, Correspondence Series, Papers of John F. Dulles, box 60, ML; Dwight D. Eisenhower, *Public Papers of the Presidents of the United States: Dwight D. Eisenhower, 1953–1961,* 1953, 17; Raymond Daniell, "Dulles Due to Find London is Critical," *New York Times,* Feb. 2, 1953; Raymond Daniell, "Dulles in London as Clamor Mounts on Formosa Policy," *New York Times,* Feb. 4, 1953; Callum MacDonald, *Britain and the Korean War,* 86; Accinelli, *Crisis and Commitment,* 114–15, 117–18.

81. For the various explanations regarding the Communists' sudden willingness to make concessions, see Kaufman, *Korean War,* 179, 187–88; Daniel Calingaert, "Nuclear Weapons and the Korean War"; Roger Dingman, "Atomic Diplomacy during the Korean War"; Zhang, *Deterrence and Strategic Culture,* 150; Stueck, *Korean War,* 326–29; Gaddis, *Long Peace,* 126; Rosemary Foot, *The Wrong War: American Policy and the Dimensions of the Korean Conflict, 1950–1953,* 230, and "Nuclear Coercion and the Ending of the Korean Conflict"; Mark A. Ryan, *Chinese Attitudes toward Nuclear Weapons: China and the United States during the Korean War,* 161; Zhai, *Dragon, the Lion, and the Eagle,* 131.

28, to Clark's surprise, the Communists accepted. Two days later, they went further, announcing their willingness to turn all nonrepatriates over to a neutral state. This was a major concession, for the Communists no longer were demanding compliance with the Geneva Convention.[82]

The movement toward resolving the war made Churchill less willing to issue the warning statement agreed upon the year before. The Eisenhower administration found the prime minister's lack of resolve disturbing; it adhered to its predecessor's position that an armistice did not guarantee peace on the peninsula, thus requiring a warning. Additionally, failure to convey the warning would upset South Korean President Syngman Rhee. In the name of Anglo-American unity, London finally gave up its resistance, and in August 1953 the allies issued the statement.[83]

Rhee was another matter. The South Korean head of state wanted to unify Korea under his rule and thus sought to sabotage the armistice talks. He continually expressed his opposition to a settlement that left Korea divided, thus leading Washington to discuss for a time the possibility of forcibly removing him from office. Rhee put words into action on June 18, when he released 25,000 North Korean POWs. Both Churchill and Eisenhower were incensed. "If I were an American," minuted the prime minister, "I would vote for Rhee going to hell and taking Korea with him." Eisenhower wrote the South Korean president, "It is you who invoked the principle of unity and asked us to pay the price. We have paid it in blood and suffering. Can you now honorably reject the principle which, in your hour of need, you asked us to defend at so high a price?"[84] Such a strong response, plus the offer of a U.S.–South Korean mutual defense treaty, removed the Rhee factor from the remainder of the talks. Further discussion over repatriation resolved the issue on July 8. On July 27, the belligerents signed the armistice, ending the war.

After three years and 140,000 U.S. casualties, the war in Korea was over. The conflict completed the growing divergence of U.S. and British China policy. Up to November 1950, Washington continued to argue in favor of maintaining some contact with Beijing in the hopes of splitting the Sino-

82. MacDonald, *Britain and the Korean War,* 86; Kaufman, *Korean War,* 179; Zhai, *Dragon, the Lion, and the Eagle,* 129.

83. Memoranda of conversation, May 4 and July 21, 1953, *FRUS, 1952–1954,* 15:968–69, 1409–11; Lowe, "The Significance of the Korean War in Anglo-American Relations," in *British Foreign Policy,* ed. Michael Dockrill and John W. Young, 141, 145.

84. Churchill quote in Young, ed., *Foreign Policy of Churchill's Peacetime Administration,* 227; letter to Rhee from Eisenhower, June 22, 1953, AWF-International Series, box 35, DDEL.

Soviet alliance. Following China's intervention that month, U.S. policy toward the PRC solidified. Even so, the United States was still able to justify its change of position as being in accordance with the wedge strategy. Moreover, it sought British support to make these policies effective.

In formulating its response, the United Kingdom again had to look at a wide range of considerations: China's possible reaction; driving wedges; and the "three circles" of Europe, the Commonwealth, and the Anglo-American alliance. In formulating its position, Whitehall had some leeway. The United States wanted to maintain Anglo-American unity before the communist threat. Furthermore, at times, London found united support from the Commonwealth, such as during discussion of the Menon resolution.

Britain used what freedom of action it had to center primarily on two concerns. The first was its own economic health. During 1949, the United Kingdom made clear that it was not going to follow completely the American lead on trade with the PRC. Given the heightened possibility of war and its need for U.S. financial and military support, Whitehall during the Korean conflict made additional concessions on the trade issue. Yet it clearly saw commerce with China as not only beneficial to Britain, but as a means of dividing the Sino-Soviet alliance and containing communism. Hence, while it levied additional controls on trade with Beijing, it refused to impose a complete embargo.

The Korean War brought forth another concern, one which, like the question of trade, would guide future British policy. This was the fear of getting not only into another Korean-style conflict, but into one that risked expansion into something much larger. Hence, Attlee expressed his anxiety over Truman's statement on nuclear weapons and MacArthur's leadership, while Eden told Acheson of his opposition to the bombings near the Yalu River and refused to undermine Menon's efforts to end the war.

Yet it was Britain that did most of the compromising. A divided Commonwealth and the absence of a Chinese threat to Hong Kong played their parts in Whitehall's decision to send troops to Korea. Needing American support in Europe, and not willing to create tensions in its relationship with Washington, London also backed off from pressing the White House on the questions of U.S. aid to Taiwan, MacArthur's leadership, or a written agreement on the use of nuclear weapons; branded China an aggressor; and agreed to a moratorium on UN representation. In short, Korea demonstrated that as long as the United Kingdom in the future did not risk getting dragged into another such war, and as long as Britain's financial health was not placed in serious jeopardy, it was more willing than not to make the concessions the United States desired on China policy.

3

NO MORE KOREAS

Indochina and "Those Damned Little Islands,"
1954–1955

War with China in Korea had a powerful impact on Great Britain. Whitehall wanted to maintain Western unity but feared another fight with the PRC. This worry governed the British response to a crisis in Indochina in early 1954 and another in the Taiwan Strait later that year. In both cases, the White House argued that its response was the best way to contain the communist, particularly the Chinese Communist, threat, but Whitehall strongly resisted American initiatives, contending that they would open the door to another Korea. What made these two crises different from Korea was that Britain had a freer hand. There was not strong public support in the United States for military action in Indochina or the Taiwan Strait as there had been in Korea, and Washington needed London's aid in implementing the various plans it considered for resolving these two crises. As a result, Britain had increased leverage and used its influence to move the United States in directions favorable to U.K. interests.

The United States assigned a great deal of importance to Southeast Asia. That was emphasized in 1949 when the Truman administration redefined America's interests in the region. In March, the Policy Planning Staff (PPS) completed a study, and the report's conclusions became official U.S. policy. In its study, the PPS explained that "Southeast Asia represents a vital segment on the line of containment, stretching from Japan southward to the Indian peninsula." If Southeast Asia fell to communism, then so might India, Japan, and Australia. Using this line of reasoning, the Truman administration, with British support, increased economic and military assistance to the region. Of particular importance was Indochina, where the French were fighting against the Vietminh.[1]

1. Gary R. Hess, "The American Search for Stability in Southeast Asia: The SEATO Structure of Containment," in *The Great Powers in East Asia, 1953–1960*, ed. Warren I. Cohen and Akira Iriye, 273.

Despite enormous sums of assistance—by the end of 1953, Washington was covering approximately two-thirds of France's costs for the war—Paris could not win in Indochina. When the French garrison at Dienbienphu came under siege by the Vietminh, Paris turned to Washington for help. Eisenhower was ambivalent: he had no intention of sending U.S. ground troops into another Korea, but he refused to sit back and do nothing. Accordingly, he and Dulles decided upon a plan that became known as "United Action." By this they meant joining the United States, United Kingdom, Australia, New Zealand, the Philippines, and the nations of Southeast Asia against the communist threat. These countries would first use political measures to combat communism, followed, if necessary, by military force, with the United States providing air, naval, and logistical support. By only providing support, Washington would avoid getting bogged down in another ground war while bolstering French morale.[2]

United Action was also intended to deter Beijing from becoming involved. The secretary of state told British officials, "If the Chinese Communists could be made to see that stepped-up activities on their part in Southeast Asia could lead to disastrous retaliation on our part by sea and air, perhaps they could be persuaded to refrain from adventures in that area." Warning of attack, the White House believed, had frightened the Chinese Communists in Korea and could work again. As Dulles explained to French Ambassador to the United States Henri Bonnet, Washington "obtained an armistice in Korea primarily because the Chinese feared that we would knock out their industrial area north of the Yalu."[3]

United Action would serve one other long-established strategic goal: to split the Sino-Soviet alliance. The Truman administration implemented this policy. For instance, in 1951, it had pointed out that economic pressure would force the PRC to turn to the Soviet Union for assistance; eventually, the Chinese would discover they could not get all they wanted from Moscow, and they would be forced to make concessions to get materials from the West. There was as yet no solid evidence of success, but from the beginning, U.S. officials had realized that achieving this goal could take upwards of a decade. Accordingly, Dulles intended to continue this policy, using political, economic, "and, to the extent possible without war, military pressure."[4]

---

2. Memorandum of conversation, Apr. 5, 1954, *FRUS, 1952–1954,* 12:366–81; Chester J. Pach, Jr., and Elmo Richardson, *The Presidency of Dwight D. Eisenhower,* 94–95; Ambrose, *Eisenhower,* 173–74.

3. Memoranda of conversation, Apr. 2 and 3, 1954, *FRUS, 1952–1954,* 13:1217, 1227.

4. John Lewis Gaddis, *The United States and the End of the Cold War: Implications, Reconsiderations, Provocations,* 74–75; John Lewis Gaddis, *Stategies of Containment: A Critical Appraisal of Postwar American National Security Policy,* 116–17.

If United Action had any chance of moving forward, congressional and allied support were essential. Widespread opposition among the general public and Congress to unilateral U.S. action led Eisenhower to pledge that he would make no moves without Capitol Hill's approval. Congressional leaders, though, told Dulles on April 5 that they would not agree to unassisted action in Indochina. They opposed the idea of another Korea, "with the United States furnishing 90% of the manpower." Help from Britain, stated Dulles, was of "crucial importance." First, London's support, argued the secretary of state, would build up the will of the Associated States—Laos, Cambodia, and Indochina—and the nations of Southeast Asia to resist communism. Second, believed Eisenhower, France would be more willing to follow the American lead if it faced pressure from both the United States and the United Kingdom. Finally, U.S. lawmakers refused to endorse possible military action unless Whitehall also supported it. As the president later wrote, "[I]t seemed clear that Congress would not act favorably unless I could give assurances that the British would be by our side." The National Security Council (NSC) therefore called for obtaining the United Kingdom's "support for U.S. objectives in the Far East, in order to strengthen U.S. policies in the area."[5]

The NSC, however, also agreed to another goal: "[o]rganizing a regional grouping, including initially the U.S., the U.K., France, the Associated States, Australia, New Zealand, Thailand, and the Philippines," which would help defend Southeast Asia from communism, particularly the threat posed by China. Again, Washington needed London's support to guarantee cooperation from the Commonwealth.[6]

Great Britain objected to United Action. There was strong domestic opposition to the idea of using military force in Indochina. As Churchill ex-

5. Memorandum for the File of the Secretary of State, Apr. 5, 1954, Minutes of 192d Meeting of the NSC, Apr. 6, 1954, *FRUS, 1952–1954*, 13:1224, 1255–56, 1264; *The Gallup Poll: Public Opinion, 1935–1971*, 1236; Leonard A. Kusnitz, *Public Opinion and Foreign Policy: America's China Policy, 1949–1979*, 65–66; Waldo Heinrichs, "Eisenhower and Sino-American Confrontation," in *Great Powers in East Asia*, ed. Warren I. Cohen and Akira Iriye, 93; Eisenhower, *The White House Years: Mandate for Change, 1953–1956*, 347; George C. Herring and Richard H. Immerman, "Eisenhower, Dulles, and Dien Bien Phu: 'The Day We Didn't Go to War' Revisited," in *Dien Bien Phu and the Crisis of Franco-American Relations, 1954–1955*, ed. Lawrence S. Kaplan, Denise Artaud, and Mark Rubin, 87.

6. Minutes of 192d Meeting of the NSC; telegram, no. 3482, Dulles to Paris, Apr. 5, 1954, *FRUS, 1952–1954*, 13:1242; New Zealand's ambassador to the United States, Leslie Munro, told Dulles that for Wellington, "the attitude of the United Kingdom would be of the greatest significance." See memorandum of conversation, Apr. 4, 1954, *FRUS, 1952–1954*, 1234; Lee, *Outposts of Empire*, 233. See also Thomas J. Hamilton, "President's View Perturbs Geneva," *New York Times*, May 20, 1954.

plained to U.S. Adm. Arthur Radford, "The British people would not be easily influenced by what happened in the distant jungles of SE Asia; but they did know that there was a powerful American base in East Anglia and that war with China, who would invoke the Sino-Russian Pact, might mean an assault by Hydrogen bombs on these islands." Rather than using military force, both the Foreign Office and the Chiefs of Staff favored partitioning Vietnam. The chiefs, for instance, believed that dividing Vietnam not only would prevent an escalation of the crisis, but also would allow France to devote more attention to Europe's defense. With the support of his military leaders, Eden suggested to the cabinet that Britain do nothing with regard to United Action prior to the upcoming Geneva Conference. It was best to wait, he argued, and see what the Communists had to offer. With the cabinet's approval, the foreign secretary explained to Dulles his unwillingness to engage in any type of military response for the time being.[7]

Commonwealth opinion matched that of the United Kingdom. To try to force Britain into agreeing to United Action, Dulles put pressure on Australia, New Zealand, and Canada, arguing that unless there were a rapid response, the United States might be less willing to help defend Southeast Asia. Whitehall, aware of the American approach, countered with arguments pointing to the danger of United Action. These three countries no doubt did not appreciate finding themselves pulled in different directions by two of their closest allies. Wellington and Canberra in particular were very sensitive to the situation in Indochina and desired to resolve it. Yet all three had serious concerns about the U.S. strategy. The Australian government of Prime Minister Robert Menzies, for example, favored partition and feared that United Action could lead to Chinese military intervention. Canberra's situation was further complicated by the fact that 1954 was an election year: Menzies did not want to make any rapid decisions that could hurt his political ambitions. Meanwhile, Canadian Secretary of State for External Affairs Lester Pearson suggested that he would not support a military strike unless the United Nations requested one.[8] With the Commonwealth united against United Action, Eden could more easily reject a military strike.

7. Memorandum of conversation, Apr. 2, 1954, *FRUS, 1952–1954*, 13: 1216; Minutes of Cabinet Meeting, C.C. 26 (54), Apr. 7, 1954, CAB 128/27, PRO; Gilbert, *Winston S. Churchill*, 8:973; Geoffrey Warner, "Britain and the Crisis over Dien Bien Phu, April 1954: The Failure of United Action," in *Dien Bien Phu*, ed. Lawrence S. Kaplan, Denise Artaud, and Mark Rubin, 63, 65; Lee, *Outposts of Empire*, 226; Anthony Eden, *Full Circle*, 107–8.

8. Memoranda of conversation, Apr. 4 and 7, 1954, *FRUS, 1952–1954*, 13:1231–35, 1275–78; memorandum of conversation, Apr. 4, 1954; "Canada Not Involved," *London Times*, Apr. 4, 1954; Gregory James Pemberton, "Australia, the United States, and the Indochina Crisis of 1954," 54–57; Malcolm McKinnon, *Independence and Foreign Policy:*

Commonwealth opinion was not similarly unanimous on a Southeast Asia defense pact, and so the United Kingdom waffled. Ultimately, however, the Churchill government found a middle ground: it would agree to *talk* about establishing such an organization but would move no further pending the outcome of the upcoming Geneva Conference.

When first told of the proposal for a defense pact, Eden appeared accommodating. He told the British cabinet that it would remove the anomaly of the United Kingdom's exclusion from the Australia-New Zealand-United States defense grouping (ANZUS) and help assure the security of Hong Kong, Malaya, and the rest of Southeast Asia. As a result, on April 13, Dulles and he issued a communiqué declaring their willingness to look into the formation of a Southeast Asia defense organization.[9]

Difficulties quickly appeared. Based upon his understanding of the communiqué, Dulles requested that the ambassadors from those nations he foresaw involved in the pact meet in Washington. Eden refused to let his representative in the United States, Sir Roger Makins, attend. "According to my understanding," said the foreign secretary, "we reached no definite agreement in London on either (i) the procedure for the 'examination of the possibility of establishing a collective defence' or (ii) a definite list of states to be approached." Dulles was furious, for Eden was preventing the establishment of an organization he saw as vital to containing China. He told his sister, Eleanor, "Eden reversed himself and gone back [*sic*] on our agreement."[10]

Eden was more at fault than Dulles for this misunderstanding. The foreign secretary expected the development of a group similar to the North Atlantic Treaty Organization (NATO), the formation of which would take place sometime down the road, depending on what happened at Geneva. Dulles wanted a smaller, ad hoc group, to be constructed immediately. Denis Allen, the Foreign Office official in charge of Far Eastern affairs, told Evelyn Shuckburgh, Eden's principal private secretary, that "when Dulles was in London [Eden] *did* indicate that we should be willing to start such talks at once, provided we were not committed to any action in Indochina. The American

---

New Zealand in the World since 1935, 124; Trevor R. Reese, *Australia, New Zealand, and the United States: A Survey of International Relations, 1941–1968*, 171; Eisenhower, *Mandate for Change*, 352; Lee, *Outposts of Empire*, 226.

9. *Department of State Bulletin* (Apr. 26, 1954): 622; Minutes of Cabinet Meeting, C.C. 26 (54), Apr. 7, 1954, CAB 128/27, PRO. In 1951, the United States formed ANZUS. Washington purposely left out Britain for fear that allowing Britain into ANZUS would require the United States to have to help defend the United Kingdom's Far Eastern colonies.

10. Kaplan, Artaud, and Rubin, eds., *Dien Bien Phu*, 69–70; Hoopes, *Devil and John Foster Dulles*, 216.

record showed that, but ours was obscure on the point and A.E. has always denied it." One of Eden's biographers added that "this would not have been the first time Eden had found it easier to use the vocabulary of diplomacy to slur over an important difference rather than confront it head on." Dulles's attempts to change Eden's mind only irritated the foreign secretary.[11]

Within a few days, however, the United Kingdom had shifted its position slightly. On April 25, the British cabinet approved a memorandum in which it declared its willingness to "to join with the United States Government now in studying measures to ensure the defence of [Southeast Asia]." Two days later, before the House of Commons, Churchill announced his willingness to move forward: he called for talks between the United States, the United Kingdom, France, Australia, and New Zealand to examine the military, economic, and political situation in Indochina.[12] U.S. Undersecretary of State Walter Bedell Smith regarded Churchill's statement as a "considerable compromise" on Britain's part. He believed London's revised stance resulted from pressure from the United States, Australia, and New Zealand, as well as Whitehall's fear of an Anglo-American rift.[13]

Smith was right on both counts. During discussion in early April over the U.S. plan for a Southeast Asia defense pact, Churchill had told Eden that while he shared the latter's concerns about America's policy toward Indochina, he saw merit in any proposal that could improve Anglo-American cooperation. Moreover, Dulles had warned Eden that Congress would be furious if no movement occurred on a defense grouping. Australia and New Zealand, meanwhile, though opposed to United Action, wanted for strategic reasons to discuss a Southeast Asia defense organization as soon as possible, rather than wait until after the summit.[14] These various considerations, especially his desire for Anglo-American unity, probably moved Churchill to lean on Eden to begin the talks promised in the April 13 communiqué.[15]

11. Dispatch, no. 266, Godley to Department of State, Apr. 21, 1954, and Minutes of 194th Meeting of the NSC, Apr. 29, 1954, *FRUS, 1954–1954*, 13:1331, 1432–33; Dutton, *Anthony Eden*, 343; Shuckburgh, *Descent to Suez*, 189.

12. Eden, *Full Circle*, 118–19; telegram, no. Dulte 51, Smith to Department of State, May 5, 1954, *FRUS, 1952–1954*, 16:450–51.

13. Telegrams, no. Dulte 51, Smith to Department of State, no. Dulte 53, May 5, 1954, Smith to Department of State, May 7, 1954, *FRUS, 1952–1954*, 710–12.

14. Memorandum of conversation, Apr. 30, 1954, *FRUS, 1952–1954*, 623; Minutes of Cabinet Meeting, C.C. 26 (54), Apr. 7, 1954, CAB 128/27, PRO; Pemberton, "Australia, the United States, and the Indochina Crisis of 1954," 61–62; "Vietnam Hedges on Defense Pact," *New York Times*, May 18, 1954.

15. According to Geoffrey Warner, Eden's proposal for Five-Power talks was largely "the result of pressure from his officials who were deeply concerned over the continuing rift in Anglo-American relations." Warner does not say which officials these were, but giv-

Talking, however, did not mean action. Here Britain had to keep in mind another Commonwealth member, India. Prime Minister Jawarhalal Nehru strongly opposed any suggestion of a Southeast Asia defense arrangement, contending that the United States was out to "hem in India." Nehru also feared failure at Geneva could lead to any number of dangerous consequences, "from large scale Western intervention in Indochina (involving another 'Korean' campaign with every risk that this time the conflict could not be localized) to abandonment of Indochina." For New Delhi, therefore, the conference's success was "all important." Nehru clearly had an impact upon Whitehall. In a veiled reference to India, Eden explained to Smith that forming a Southeast Asia defense pact "before the results of the Conference are known would destroy any prospect of bringing along the Asian powers who really matter."[16] Putting these considerations together, the British prime minister's April 27 statement was designed to please not only the Americans, but also the Australians, the New Zealanders, and the Indians: it would demonstrate that Britain was willing to *talk* about Indochina's defense—thus satisfying Washington, Canberra, and Wellington—but, prior to the outcome at Geneva, not to commit itself to anything—which would please New Delhi.

Thus, when the Indochina portion of the Geneva Conference opened on May 8, it was clear that there had not been a meeting of minds between the United States and Britain. Dulles wanted a demonstration of Western unity before the summit; he believed it would bolster the French and deter the Chinese. The British, however, were unwilling to take any major steps. They opposed United Action, and while they were willing to talk about the formation of a Southeast Asia defense organization, they refused to move further. Additional steps, Churchill and Eden believed, would undermine any hope of a negotiated settlement in Indochina, tear apart the Commonwealth, and open the door to another Korean-style conflict. Eisenhower shared Dulles's frustration with London's intransigence: "I believe," the president wrote, "that the British government is showing a woeful unawareness of the risks we run in that region."[17]

---

en Churchill's past actions and comments, it would not be surprising if he was one of them. See Geoffrey Warner, "From Geneva to Manila: British Policy toward Indochina and SEATO, May-Sept. 1954," in *Dien Bien Phu*, ed. Lawrence S. Kaplan, Denise Artaud, and Mark Rubin, 150.

16. Telegram, no. Dulte 113, Smith to Department of State, May 25, 1954, and letter to Smith from Eden, May 11, 1954, *FRUS, 1952–1954*, 16:775, 930–31; Lee, *Outposts of Empire*, 229.

17. Memorandum for the Files by the president, Apr. 27, 1954, *FRUS, 1952–1954*, 13:1422–23.

Despite their frustration with Whitehall, Eisenhower and Dulles did not intend to sit around and see what came out of Geneva. Instead, the secretary of state pursued two courses of actions. On the one hand, he continued to seek forward movement on both United Action and the Southeast Asia defense pact. On the other, he used the conference to try to obtain the release of American nationals held by the Chinese. He made little headway toward either goal prior to the summit's conclusion.

Eden, for his part, went to the conference determined to succeed. He did manage to improve relations with China to some extent, but the Communists' intransigence on a settlement of the Indochina war made him decide to leave Geneva early. Fearful his departure could lead to a breakdown of the conference, the Russians and Chinese suddenly became more cooperative. As a result, in mid-July, the attendees finally reached an agreement designed to resolve the Indochina crisis.

The idea for a summit in Geneva had arisen at a four-power meeting earlier in the year in Berlin, when Soviet Foreign Minister Vyacheslav Molotov proposed a five-power conference, including China, to discuss Far Eastern issues. Dulles strongly condemned the proposal, but Molotov continued to press it. The foreign minister's insistence changed the secretary of state's mind. As he explained to Eisenhower after the Berlin meeting, "It seems quite possible that the Soviet Union is worried over the possibility of new aggression by the Chinese Communists." He also reported that he told Molotov that China's belligerence might lead to a clash with the United States; he hoped that the Soviets would take this warning to heart and put pressure on the Chinese Communist government.[18] In short, U.S. participation at a conference that included the Soviet Union and China offered the opportunity to turn Moscow against Beijing.

It is important to keep in mind that while Dulles agreed to attend the Geneva summit, neither he, nor Eisenhower, intended to use the meeting to improve relations with China. The American public and the White House were still furious with the Chinese for the deaths of tens of thousands of Americans in Korea.[19] Moreover, there was strong pressure on the administration from the China bloc not to soften U.S. policy toward the PRC at the conference. Finally, it is possible that the White House did not want to take any action on China at Geneva because of Chiang Kai-shek. At the time, the

18. "Editorial Note," *FRUS, 1952–1954,* 14:366; see also Chang, *Friends and Enemies,* 98–100.

19. For public and congressional opinion toward Beijing, see Kusnitz, *Public Opinion and Foreign Policy,* 69, and David Mayers, "Eisenhower and Communism: Later Findings," in *Reevaluating Eisenhower: American Foreign Policy in the 1950s,* ed. Richard Melanson and David Mayers, 97.

Nationalist leader was pressuring Washington for a U.S.-Taiwan defense treaty; Dulles and most of his subordinates opposed moving forward on this proposal for fear that it would undermine the Geneva Conference and anger America's other allies. To follow a refusal to discuss a U.S.-Taiwan defense pact with a meeting between high-ranking U.S. and Chinese Communist Party (CCP) officials could give Chiang the impression that Washington was abandoning him, leaving him no choice but to take drastic measures in an attempt to return to the mainland. It would also serve to confirm to members of the China bloc that U.S. policy toward Beijing was softening. For these reasons, both Eisenhower and Dulles made it clear that America's presence at Geneva did not imply diplomatic recognition of China. Similarly, Dulles told reporters that there was no chance of his personally meeting representatives from the PRC "unless our automobiles collide." Indeed, when the leader of the Chinese delegation, Premier Zhou Enlai, approached Dulles at Geneva, the secretary of state refused to shake hands with him. Dulles also refused to sit at the same table as the Chinese premier, which created numerous difficulties when it came to seating arrangements.[20]

Eden was more enthusiastic about the conference than his American counterpart. The British foreign secretary saw Geneva as offering the opportunity to prevent Indochina "from being the first in a chain of events leading to another catastrophe"—"catastrophe" referring to the war in Korea.[21] The conference also would allow him to demonstrate what he regarded as his diplomatic prowess. Finally, he could not disregard the Commonwealth (especially India) nor the British public. Most important among the latter was the U.K. business community, which saw an improvement in relations with China as a way to foster trade between the two nations (a subject that will receive fuller attention in the next chapter). Whitehall could not risk the political ramifications of failure at Geneva.

China also had a strong interest in the Geneva meeting. Following Moscow's lead, the PRC's leader, Mao Zedong, began to talk of "peaceful coexis-

20. Memoranda, to Dulles from Robertson, Feb. 25, 1954, and to Dulles from Merchant, Feb. 26, 1954, and memorandum for the file, "Remarks of the Secretary Regarding Proposed U.S.-Chinese Security Pact," Mar. 1, 1954, RG 59, Records of the Bureau of Far Eastern Affairs Relating to Southeast Asia and the Geneva Conference, 1954, box 2, NA; telegram, no. 823, Dulles to Taipei, Apr. 8, 1954, *FRUS, 1952–1954*, 14:407–8; telegram, no. Secto 6, Dulles to Department of State, Apr. 25, 1954, *FRUS, 1952–54,* 16:564; Dwight D. Eisenhower, *Public Papers of the Presidents of the United States, Dwight D. Eisenhower, 1953–1961,* 1954, 451; *Department of State Bulletin* (Mar. 8, 1954): 345; *Department of State Bulletin* (May 3, 1954): 699; Stanley D. Bachrack, *Committee of One Million,* 86–90; U. Alexis Johnson, *The Right Hand of Power,* 204.

21. Eden, *Full Circle,* 120.

tence"; settling disputes diplomatically, believed the CCP, would help improve China's diplomatic standing. Talks offered other benefits as well. They might prevent another Korea, thereby protecting China's security. If they could contact U.S. officials, CCP officials might persuade the United States to end its trade embargo with the PRC. The Communists also were well aware of the differences among Western nations over Indochina. Discussions at Geneva offered the opportunity to drive wedges within the anticommunist alliance.[22]

There were two parts to the Geneva Conference, which for a time ran concurrently. The first, concerning Korea, began on April 25. It ultimately achieved little. Negotiators deadlocked over the question of elections designed to reunify Korea and the role of the United Nations in the those elections. Yet neither side wanted to see renewed war on the peninsula. Thus, they left the question of the reunification of Korea unresolved.[23]

Dulles had not planned to stay at Geneva through the end of the conference and departed on May 3. He left Undersecretary Smith to lead the American delegation. The change pleased the British. Dulles and Eden had not gotten along well at the summit. The secretary of state was especially upset with what he viewed as the unwillingness of his British counterpart to defend the United States from communist polemics. On May 1, Shuckburgh wrote that "Dulles and A. E. have got thoroughly on each other's nerves," and that Eden was "hoping Dulles will go away as soon as possible." Eden, however, was close to Smith. The foreign secretary wrote that Smith's arrival on May 1 to lead the American delegation "did something to lift the pall which was beginning to descend on the discussions between the three Western allies."[24]

Six days after Smith's arrival, Dienbienphu fell; the following day, the Indochina phase of the Geneva Conference began. Dulles still wanted to move forward on United Action and a Southeast Asia defense grouping. With Menzies' reelection, the secretary of state again tried using Australia against Britain. The Australian prime minister remained uncooperative, leaving Dulles to return to his previous position of doing nothing about a military strike without London's concurrence.[25]

22. Qiang Zhai, "China and the Geneva Conference of 1954," 107–8; Zhai, *Dragon, the Lion, and the Eagle,* 140; Zhang, *Deterrence and Strategic Culture,* 183–84.

23. For more on this subject, see Robert F. Randle, *Geneva 1954: The Settlement of the Indochinese War,* 157–68.

24. Letter to Bidault from Dulles, May 3, 1954, *FRUS, 1952–1954,* 16:677; memorandum of conversation, May 5, 1954, *FRUS, 1952–1954,* 13:1467–68; Shuckburgh, *Descent to Suez,* 186; Eden, *Full Circle,* 124.

25. Telegram, no. Dulte 3, Dulles to Department of State, Apr. 25, 1954, *FRUS, 1952–1954,* 13:1404; Pemberton, "Australia, the United States, and the Indochina Crisis of 1954," 61–65; George C. Herring, "'A Good Stout Effort': John Foster Dulles and the In-

The secretary of state found similar problems with a Southeast Asia defense pact. Inspired by reports that Australia and New Zealand favored movement on a defense grouping, and that they disliked Britain's stance of waiting indefinitely, Dulles continued to hope for success. India's steadfastness, though, stayed Eden. Dulles and Eisenhower knew that Eden had Nehru in the back of his mind, but they still found Whitehall's refusal to move more quickly annoying. The secretary of state told the president in mid-May that he believed "the dilatory tactics being pursued by the U.K." would permit the communists "to prevent any action on our part until they had in effect consolidated their position throughout Indochina." Similarly, Eisenhower commented that he found Whitehall's stance "incomprehensible." Dulles feared that "Mr. Eden was trying to do what Chamberlain had done, bringing back from Geneva 'peace in our time,' and get elected Prime Minister."[26]

Eden did indeed want to become prime minister, but his immediate goal was to achieve peace and avoid another Korean conflict. He met on several occasions with Chinese Premier Zhou Enlai. Zhou also met with other British officials, including Humphrey Trevelyan, the British chargé in Beijing, as well as a number of members of the Labour Party. Huan Xiang, a member of the Chinese delegation, reported that the CCP delegates "had been very pleasantly surprised with the attitude of the British Delegation" and "were charmed by [Eden's] attitude." The relationship between the Chinese and British improved to the point that the CCP government offered to increase Trevelyan's status and to station a chargé in London. The U.K. and PRC representatives also discussed ways to improve Sino-British trade.[27]

While the Chinese and British tried to woo each other, the Russian delegates attempted to make the United States more conciliatory toward China. Molotov, the head of the Soviet delegation, told Smith that "China was a very young country": "only five years old and she needed time to devote her attention and resources to her internal problems." By "young," noted one scholar, Molotov meant China was "inexperienced and rash in international politics." Over time, however, Beijing "would become more restrained." Washington simply had to be patient with the CCP.[28]

dochina Crisis, 1954–1955," in *John Foster Dulles and the Diplomacy of the Cold War: A Reappraisal,* ed. Richard H. Immerman, 221.

26. Telegram, no. Dulte 113, Smith to Department of State, May 25, 1954; telegram, no. Tosec 406, Dulles to Geneva, June 12, 1954, *FRUS, 1952–1954,* 16:1125; memoranda of conversation, May 28 and July 9, 1954, *FRUS, 1952–1954,* 12:526, 612 n 3; memorandum of conversation, May 19, 1954, *FRUS, 1952–1954,* 13:1584.

27. Zhai, *Dragon, the Lion, and the Eagle,* 146–47; FO Minute by Nutting, May 7, 1954, FO 371/110245, PRO.

28. Telegram, no. Dulte 101, Smith to Department of State, May 23, 1954, *FRUS, 1952–1954,* 16:897–98; Zhai, *Dragon, the Lion, and the Eagle,* 144–45.

Though Dulles had no intention of improving relations with China, he did agree to use the conference to try to obtain the release of American nationals held by the Chinese. Unwilling to let Smith make direct contact with Chinese Communist officials for fear that it might imply recognition of the PRC, Dulles used Trevelyan as a middle man. Unable to make any headway with the Chinese, the British chargé concluded that he could do no more and requested that an American delegate accompany him to the next meeting with Huan. Deputy Assistant Secretary of State for Far Eastern Affairs Everett F. Drumright strongly opposed any idea of a meeting between U.S. and CCP representatives, declaring it would amount to de facto recognition of the PRC. Dulles felt otherwise: there was strong domestic sentiment in favor of using the Geneva talks to get American prisoners out. For the task, the secretary of state chose the ambassador to Czechoslovakia, U. Alexis Johnson.[29] Johnson and Wang Bingnan, representing the PRC, held several talks, with little progress. Yet their preliminary contacts led to the United States and China agreeing in mid-1955 to start holding ambassadorial discussions at Geneva.

Despite the headway in Sino-British relations, and the willingness of the United States to hold talks with Chinese officials, the main purpose of the conference, to solve the crisis in Indochina, remained unsettled. On May 27 Zhou proposed a formula to end the war that called for a supervisory commission of "neutral" nations to oversee an armistice in Indochina. His proposal led to a dispute over which nations were "neutral." Furthermore, he failed to address the American concern for a withdrawal of Vietminh forces from Laos and Cambodia. Meanwhile, Washington continued to press for a Southeast Asia defense organization. Believing in his superior diplomatic abilities, Eden decided he had no choice but to "undertake much of the exploratory personal diplomacy which had to be done if we were to make any progress." On May 28, he presented a proposal for bringing an end to hostilities in Indochina. Its provisions included a meeting of the French and Vietminh commands and a report of their findings and recommendations to Geneva. Dulles disliked the proposal, which he felt would lead to a partitioning of Vietnam, and suggested revisions. Smith stated that when informed of the American position, Eden and the U.K. minister of state, Lord Reading, "staged a demonstration of petulance and annoyance, the like of

29. Telegrams, nos. Secto 242, 249, 324, 330, and 350, Smith to Department of State, May 17, 18, 27, 28, and 30, 1954; Tosec 151 and 284, Dulles to Geneva, May 13 and 28, 1954; and Tedul 152, Dulles to Geneva, June 3, 1954; memorandum to Dulles from Drumright, May 31, 1954, FRUS, 1952–1954, 14:416–18, 421, 434–37, 438–41, 443; Kusnitz, Public Opinion and Foreign Policy, 64.

which I have never seen before at an international conference." Acting Secretary of State Robert Murphy told Dulles that it was becoming clear that the United States was trapped between Britain's "determination to see some form, almost any, of settlement" and France's desire to push Washington "into some form of military participation."[30]

By the end of the following week, though, it seemed that Eden might not achieve a settlement, as the Communists on June 9 suddenly became uncompromising. Both Zhou and Molotov demanded that political and military issues regarding Indochina be considered concurrently. Molotov further called for equal representation of communist and noncommunist nations on a committee that would oversee the armistice. Finally, the Vietminh refused to withdraw their "volunteers" from Laos and Cambodia.[31]

The Communists' sudden change of attitude was due to the fact that the Soviets wanted to bring down the French government of Joseph Laniel. In 1952, France, West Germany, Italy, and the Benelux nations had signed the European Defense Community (EDC) treaty, which would help bring a rearmed Germany into the Western military alliance system. The French parliament had yet to ratify the EDC at the time of the Geneva Conference. And Laniel's government was hanging on by a thread, having won a vote of confidence in May 1954 by only two votes. If the Laniel administration collapsed because of its inability to get out of Indochina, its successor might prove less willing to support the EDC. Indeed, argued Joseph Nogee and Robert Donaldson, "[T]he opportunity to derail the movement for German rearmament was more precious to Moscow than the prospect of a continuing war in Indochina that just *might* result in total communist victory." The Chinese, seeking to maintain unity with the Soviets, followed Moscow's line and adopted a similarly tough attitude.[32]

Eden concluded that, with the Communists intransigent, he should bring

---

30. Telegrams, no. Secto 366, Smith to Department of State, May 28, 1954; no. Tosec 307, Murphy to U.S. Delegation, May 29, 1954; and unnumbered, Smith to Secretary of State, May 30, 1954; and memorandum to Dulles from Murphy, May 31, 1954, *FRUS, 1952–1954,* 16: 965–66, 976–77, 977–78, 991; Ronald C. Keith, *The Diplomacy of Zhou Enlai,* 72–73; Eden, *Full Circle,* 135.

31. Randle, *Geneva 1954,* p. 271; Hoopes, *Devil and John Foster Dulles,* 232.

32. Hoopes, *Devil and John Foster Dulles,* 232; Joseph L. Nogee and Robert H. Donaldson, *Soviet Foreign Policy since World War II,* 92; Richard H. Immerman, "The United States and the Geneva Conference of 1954: A New Look," 60; There is general agreement that the Soviets' desire to bring down the EDC drove Moscow to take a harder position. See Randle, *Geneva 1954,* 271–72; Richard W. Stevenson, *The Rise and Fall of Détente: Relaxations of Tension in U.S.-Soviet Relations, 1953–84,* 31–32; Qiang Zhai, *China and the Vietnam Wars, 1950–1975,* 51–52; and Jian Chen, "China and the First Indo-China War, 1950–54," 106.

the conference to an end. On June 14, Smith reported that Eden apparently planned to leave Geneva and take most of the U.K. delegation with him. He suggested that if Eden left, so should he; Dulles agreed. Two days later, the foreign secretary announced his intention to return to London; Smith followed suit. Additionally, on June 15, the White House announced that Eden and Churchill planned to travel to Washington.[33]

Eden's sudden announcement and the plan for a U.S.-U.K. meeting likely played a part in making the Communists more conciliatory. They probably feared that the upcoming Anglo-American talks could lead to agreement to defend Laos and Cambodia, as well as southern Vietnam, with all the risks that entailed. More important, on June 12, the Laniel government collapsed. Pierre Mendès-France, the new premier, was strongly opposed to the EDC. There was no longer reason for a hard-line stance. As Zhou told Mao Zedong and China's head of state, Liu Shaoqi, on June 16, rapid agreement to a cease-fire would "encourage the new French government to resist American intervention and delay the issue of the European army." Accordingly, that same day, he told Eden that "he thought he could persuade the Vietminh to withdraw from [Laos and Cambodia]." He further declared his willingness to recognize Cambodia and Laos as independent states as long as the United States did not put military bases in Indochina and that the Communist delegations would separate military and political issues. The same day Molotov said that the Communists would accept a minority role on an international commission that would oversee the armistice. On June 21, Zhou met with Pham Van Dong, head of the Vietnamese delegation. He told Pham to accept a partition of Vietnam. "After the French withdrawal," the Chinese premier said, "the whole of Vietnam will be yours." Pham agreed to remove Vietminh troops from Laos and Cambodia, but Vietnamese acceptance of partition required some more work on Zhou's part.[34]

On June 25, Eden and Churchill arrived in Washington. They found Dulles much more responsive than before. The secretary of state said that the time frame for internationalizing the war had passed and that he would now

33. Telegrams, no. Dulte 180, Smith to Department of State, June 14, 1954; no. Tedul 200, Dulles to U.S. Delegation, June 14, 1954; no. Dulte 186, Smith to Department of State; and no. Tedul 204, Dulles to U.S. Delegation, June 16, 1954, *FRUS, 1952–1954,* 16:1136–37, 1137 n 2, 1165–66, 1166 n 2; James Reston, "Churchill and Eden Coming to See Eisenhower June 25; Korea Talks End at Geneva," *New York Times,* June 16, 1954.

34. Memorandum to Johnson from Keppel, June 17, 1954, *FRUS, 1952–1954,* 16:1169; Zhai, *Dragon, the Lion, and the Eagle,* 142–43, and *China and the Vietnam Wars,* 57–58; Eden, *Full Circle,* 145; Keith, *Diplomacy of Zhou Enlai,* 74–75; Hoopes, *Devil and John Foster Dulles,* 233, 235.

accept the partitioning of Vietnam. The British, for their part, agreed that no matter what happened at Geneva, they would press ahead for a plan for the collective defense of Southeast Asia. At the end of their talks, the two sides adopted a seven-point declaration, providing the terms the United Kingdom and United States could accept as part of an agreement in Indochina. It included the preservation of "the integrity and independence of Laos and Cambodia" and the southern half of Vietnam, the withdrawal of Vietminh forces from Laos and Cambodia, and a guarantee of "effective machinery for international supervision of the agreement."[35]

In mid-July, France agreed to the declaration. By this time, Zhou had returned from the city of Liuzhou, near the Chinese-Vietnamese border, where he had met with the Vietminh leader, Ho Chi Minh. Ho reluctantly agreed to abide by the proposed Geneva agreement. He did not want to threaten future assistance from his Chinese and Soviet allies by refusing to accept any settlement reached at the summit. He also believed that the elections proposed for 1956 would allow him to take control of Vietnam.[36]

On July 21, the delegations at Geneva signed a series of accords designed to bring a peaceful resolution to the conflict in Indochina. Vietminh forces would leave Laos and Cambodia. Vietnam would temporarily be divided at the seventeenth parallel, with elections to be held in two years to reunite the country. Vietnam itself would become neutral. Washington did not sign the accords but promised to abide by them. The following month, the United States, Britain, and six other nations signed the Southeast Asia Collective Defense Treaty, which formed the Southeast Asia Treaty Organization (SEATO).

Thus, the Geneva Conference had ended without the United States having achieved either of its goals, both of which the Eisenhower administration tied to its effort to contain China: a quick multilateral military response to save the garrison at Dienbienphu or the rapid formation of a multinational defense organization for Southeast Asia. Both required British approval, but the United Kingdom refused to agree to either prior to Geneva. Ultimately, an agreement, no matter how distasteful to the White House, was achieved. It did not, though, mean a lasting peace in East Asia, as another crisis soon erupted, this one in the Taiwan Strait.

The crisis in the Taiwan Strait involved some small islands off the Chinese coast, Quemoy (Jinmen) and Matsu (Mazu). The former, the larger of the

35. Memorandum of conversation, June 26, 1954, *FRUS, 1952–1954*, 6:1086–94; telegram, no. 4853, Dulles to Paris, June 28, 1954, *FRUS, 1952–1954*, 13:1757–58.
36. Memorandum of conversation, July 14, 1954, *FRUS, 1952–1954*, 13:1829–30; Zhai, *Dragon, the Lion, and the Eagle*, 142–43.

two, actually incorporated six islands (the largest of which was Big Quemoy), which totaled some seventy square miles and sat near the Chinese port of Xiamen (Amoy). The latter, further north, was a group of some thirteen small islands located near the port of Fuzhou (Foochow). Quemoy and Matsu had been under Nationalist control when Chiang Kai-shek was China's leader; after he fled to Taiwan, he kept troops on the islands. Chiang had several reasons for holding onto the islands: they served as bases for KMT vessels involved in the harassment of shipping along the Chinese coast, were used as radar posts to gather intelligence, provided protection from a potential Chinese Communist attack on Taiwan, and offered jumping-off points for his long-desired return to the mainland.[37]

In late 1949, the Chinese Communist People's Liberation Army tried but failed to capture Quemoy. The beginning of the Korean War delayed further consideration of an attack upon Taiwan, including the offshore islands. But in 1952, Beijing began to look again to Quemoy and Matsu. The proposed strategy was to take "one island at a time, from north to south, and from weak to strong." The PLA planned first to attack the Tachen (Dachen) Islands, located north of Matsu. Nationalist forces on the Tachens were weak; furthermore, the islands posed a threat to Zhejiang, one of the more developed provinces in the PRC.[38]

Following the Korean War, the CCP government emphasized peaceful coexistence, yet it believed the United States was not prepared to follow suit, given its apparent approval of Taiwan's harassment of the mainland. Even so, Beijing no longer considered appropriate its proposal of taking all the offshore islands and then Taiwan. The CCP leadership was concerned that the Nationalist and American governments might sign a defense treaty, which could permanently separate Taiwan from the mainland. Taking Quemoy and Matsu following such a defense pact would cut all links to the mainland and destroy the PRC's claim to Taiwan. Thus, the PLA revised its plans. Now, it would seek only the liberation of the Tachens. It would, however, shell Quemoy. This operation would serve several functions. Militarily, it would stop the Nationalists' harassment of shipping along the PRC coast and provide training for the PLA. Domestically, it "would help rekindle the enthusiasm of the Chinese people for New China after the conclusion of the Korean and Vietnam conflicts." Politically, it would demonstrate the determination of the PRC to take Taiwan. Diplomatically, it would test America's declared

37. Nancy Bernkopf Tucker, "Cold War Contacts: America and China, 1952–1956," in *Sino-American Relations,* ed. Harry Harding and Yuan Ming, 248.

38. He Di, "The Evolution of the People's Republic of China's Policy toward the Offshore Islands," in *Great Powers in East Asia,* ed. Warren I. Cohen and Akira Iriye, 223–24.

willingness to reduce tensions with socialist nations and possibly drive wedges not only between Washington and Taipei, but also between the United States and its other allies. In July 1954, Beijing completed its plans for the bombardment.[39]

It was clear to both the United States and Britain that tensions in the area were brewing even before the first shells fell on Quemoy. As early as May, Washington had received reports of a buildup opposite the Tachens.[40] Two months later, Beijing began a major propaganda campaign, calling for the liberation of Taiwan. Therefore, the bombardment of the offshore islands, when it began on September 3, did not come as a complete surprise.[41]

While the crisis may not have surprised the White House, it still created serious problems. Eisenhower did not want to get into another fight with the PRC. He told his advisers, "If we get into a general war, the logical enemy will be Russia, not China, and we'll have to strike there." At the same time, the administration had to act. The president told the NSC on September 12 that "Quemoy was not really important except psychologically," but that, in itself, made its retention essential. Dulles argued that inaction would only make the Communists more aggressive and prevent peace. Moreover, the loss of the islands "would have disastrous consequences in Korea, Japan, Formosa, and the Philippines." Yet if the United States went to war with the PRC over Quemoy and Matsu, "outside of [South Korean President Syngman] Rhee and Chiang, the rest of the world would condemn us, as well as a substantial part of the U.S. people." The administration consequently employed a two-track response. First, it adopted what Dulles later called deterrence "by un-

39. Ibid., 224–25; Tucker, "Cold War Contacts," in *Sino-American Relations,* ed. Harry Harding and Yuan Ming, 248–49; Zhai, *Dragon, the Lion, and the Eagle,* 153–54; Thomas E. Stolper, *China, Taiwan, and the Offshore Islands: Together with an Implication for Outer Mongolia and Sino-Soviet Relations,* 84; Gordon H. Chang and He Di, "The Absence of War in the U.S.-China Confrontation over Quemoy and Matsu in 1954–1955: Contingency, Luck, Deterrence?" 1508–9; Zhang, *Deterrence and Strategic Culture,* 198–99.

40. For reports and discussion regarding the Chinese buildup opposite the Tachens, see telegram, no. 633, Rankin to Department of State, May 20, 1954; memorandum of conversation, May 22, 1954; and Minutes of the 199th Meeting of the NSC, May 27, 1954, *FRUS, 1952–1954,* 14:425–27, 428–30, 433–34.

41. Cohen and Iriye, eds., *Great Powers in East Asia,* 225; Yi Sun, "John Foster Dulles and the 1958 Taiwan Strait Crisis," in *China and the United States,* ed. Xiaobing Li and Hongshan Li, 80. For specific examples of statements by the CCP regarding the capture of Taiwan, see "Peiping, Apologizing, Calls Downing of Plane an Accident," *New York Times,* July 26, 1954; William J. Jorden, "Formosa Capture Is Urged by Chou," *New York Times,* Aug. 14, 1954; and "Peiping Reiterates Threat to Formosa," *New York Times,* Aug. 21, 1954.

certainty." This involved publicly supporting the Nationalist government but making unclear whether this commitment extended to the offshore islands. By so doing, the United States hoped to deter China from attacking Quemoy and Matsu and thus prevent another Sino-American war. The strategy also served as an example of Dulles's plan to use military pressure to split the Sino-Soviet alliance. Second, the White House proposed bringing the issue before the United Nations Security Council. Such action, Dulles explained, would put the burden on the shoulders of the Soviet Union and PRC. "If they vetoed it, then Communist China would be taking action against the will of the majority of the UN. Under those conditions there would be a totally different atmosphere regarding our allies and the American people." If, though, the Soviet Union supported such an effort, it could represent "the beginning of a series of steps to stabilize the situation in the Far East." Dulles understood the Nationalists "might not be happy at such an injunction, [but] thought they would like it better than being left alone to take a defeat."[42]

Dulles explained at the September 12 meeting that a successful effort at the UN would require other nations, "particularly the UK" to support the United States. Accordingly, the following week, he raised his proposal with Eden in London. The foreign secretary was pleased that Washington was seeking a way out that did not involve military action. He also believed, incorrectly, that a cease-fire in the strait might lead Washington to reexamine its policy toward the PRC. When Dulles asked for a suggestion as to who should introduce a resolution to the Security Council, Eden suggested New Zealand, as it was "not closely identified" with the offshore crisis, but had a "legitimate interest" in the matter. Dulles and Eisenhower approved, and Wellington agreed to help.[43] The plan became known as "Operation Oracle."

42. Eisenhower, *Mandate for Change*, 464; Minutes of 214th Meeting of the NSC, Sept. 12, 1954, *FRUS, 1952–1954*, 14:616–17, 619–20, 623; memorandum of conversation, Jan. 20, 1955, *FRUS, 1955–1957*, 2:60; Gaddis, *United States and the End of the Cold War*, 75–76. In September, representatives of forty-six organizations, including labor, women's, and Jewish groups, called for a peaceful resolution to the offshore islands crisis. Early the following month, Americans for Democratic Action made a similar demand. See Kathleen McLaughlin, "Cease-Fire Urged in Formosa Area," *New York Times*, Sept. 20, 1954, and "Refer Formosa War Issue to U.N., A.D.A. Asks in Assailing U.S.," *New York Times*, Oct. 4, 1954. For examples early in the crisis of the United States declaring its commitment to defend Taiwan, see "Dulles in Formosa," *New York Times*, Sept. 9, 1954; Henry R. Lieberman, "Formosa Assured by Dulles That It Does Not Stand Alone," *New York Times*, Sept. 1, 1954; and Joseph A. Loftus, "Reds Cannot Take Formosa Bastion, Dulles Declares," *New York Times*, Sept. 13, 1954.

43. Minutes of 214th Meeting of the NSC; memoranda of conversation, Sept. 17 and 22, 1955; telegrams, no. Dulte 2, Dulles to Department of State, Sept. 27, 1954; no. Tedul 4, Smith to Secretary of State, Sept. 28, 1954; and no. 201, Smith to Taipei, Oct. 1, 1954, *FRUS, 1952–1954*, 14:621, 651, 653–54, 664, 672; memorandum to Dulles from Acting

Anglo-American unity soon began to break down. The first problem concerned a draft minute written up by the Eisenhower administration designed to clarify the obligations of the United States, United Kingdom, and New Zealand under Oracle. The British representative to the UN, Sir Pierson Dixon, complained that the minute said nothing about demilitarizing the islands; furthermore, there was no mention of using discussions in the Security Council as "a first step towards a general settlement." He continued, "I am afraid that I dislike this operation more and more as it develops. It seems to be getting further away all the time from what we had in mind when we discussed it in London." Obviously fearful of another Indochina or even a Korea, he suspected that if China and the Soviet Union rejected Oracle, the United States would "turn the Security Council proceedings into a call for 'United Action' in defence of Chiang Kai Shek. This could not fail to result in a public exposure of Anglo-American differences in the Far East on the most serious scale yet." Eden agreed and had his minister in Washington, Sir Robert Scott, explain that the U.S. minute was "unduly restrictive." What had attracted Britain to Oracle in the first place, he said, "was that it looked to a wider settlement." Dulles and his assistant secretary for Far Eastern Affairs, Walter Robertson, quashed such a suggestion, the secretary of state commenting that he "had never intended to suggest that if this particular situation were settled we would move right on from there to a general settlement of the Formosa problem."[44]

Dulles refused to agree to discuss the larger question of Taiwan because of the potential domestic political repercussions. During the crisis, China bloc members, including Senators William Knowland (R-California) and William Jenner (R-Indiana), wanted the United States to defend the islands, or even to provide assistance to the Nationalists so they could return to the mainland. Moreover, 1954 was an election year, and the White House did not want the GOP to become divided by severe disagreements over East Asian policy. Eden realized Dulles's problems, but he could not let his American counterpart push him into a corner. Australia and New Zealand opposed any actions in the Taiwan Strait, as they had with United Action in Indochina, that might lead to war. Indochina was also on Eden's mind. In language much like that of Dixon, the foreign secretary told Churchill that it was vital to "make sure that the United States do not turn proceedings in the Security Council into

High Commissioner of New Zealand, Sept. 29, 1954, FO 371/110232, PRO; Michael Dockrill, "Britain and the First Chinese Off-Shore Islands Crisis, 1949–55," in *British Foreign Policy, 1945–56*, ed. Michael Dockrill and John W. Young, 178.

44. Telegrams, nos. 960 and 961, Dixon to Foreign Office, Oct. 8, 1954, FO 371/ 110233, PRO; memoranda of conversation, Oct. 8 and 9, 1954, *FRUS, 1952–54*, 14:710– 13, 717–19.

a call for united action to defend Quemoy." Despite his interest in Anglo-American unity, the prime minister felt similarly. Using a World War II analogy, he told Eden that he understood the U.S. need to defend Taiwan, but "the loss of Quemoy really does not affect the defence of Formosa. Vide, the Channel Islands in our war."[45] Clearly, Churchill would stand with the United States, but not if it meant another war with China.

Eden found himself unable to convince Dulles. Additionally, New Zealand's ambassador to the United States, Leslie Munro, said that Wellington believed things were moving in the right direction. Outvoted two to one, and fearing the result of inaction, Eden agreed to proceed along the lines of the American minute. The three countries also harmonized upon the timing by which they would inform Taiwan, China, and the Soviet Union of Oracle, with Taipei to be advised immediately, followed the next day by Beijing and Moscow.[46]

Taiwan was key to the operation's success. When told of Oracle in early October, the U.S. ambassador in Taipei, Karl Rankin, warned that the Nationalist reaction would be adverse. Taiwan, he said, would consider the operation "another Yalta by which free China, this time at British behest, is to be sold down [the] river as [a] result of [a] secret deal made behind Chinese backs." Furthermore, Chiang would conclude that the United States had decided there was no hope of the Nationalists returning to the mainland. "In sum, [Taiwan] probably would see as [the] primary US motive appeasement to [the] UK and hence of [the] Communists, with all but disastrous and perhaps military results to free China and corresponding benefits to [the] Reds." Yet with Washington determined to press on, he recommended informing Taiwan as soon as possible to avoid Chiang learning of Oracle through a leak.[47]

It is most interesting that Rankin argued Chiang would regard Oracle as the result of British pressure upon the United States. From early on, the Nationalist leader viewed Washington much more favorably than London. Fol-

45. Letters to Churchill from Eden and to Eden from Churchill, Oct. 10, 1954, PREM 11/867, PRO; Zhai, *Dragon, the Lion, and the Eagle*, 163; Accinelli, *Crisis and Commitment*, 164. For the positions of Australia and New Zealand, David Lee, "Australia and Anglo-American Disagreement over the Quemoy-Matsu Crisis, 1954–55"; Gary Woodard, "Australian Foreign Policy on the Offshore Islands Crisis of 1954–5 and Recognition of China"; and McKinnon, *Independence and Foreign Policy*, 125.

46. Dulles to Robertson, Oct. 11, 1954, *FRUS, 1952–1954*, 14:725–26 and 728 n 3; telegram, no. 2173, Makins to Foreign Office, Oct. 11, 1954, FO 371/110233, PRO; Rosemary Foot, "The Search for a *Modus Vivendi*: Anglo-American Relations and China Policy," in *Great Powers in East Asia*, ed. Warren I. Cohen and Akira Iriye, 152.

47. Telegram, no. 244, Rankin to Department of State, Oct. 5, 1954, *FRUS, 1952–1954*, 14:682–83.

lowing his break with the Communists in 1927, Chiang had turned not to Whitehall but to the White House for help. Furthermore, like his wife, many of Chiang's advisers, including Wellington Koo, who became the Chinese ambassador to Washington in 1946; Quo Tai-chi, the minister of foreign affairs during most of 1941; T. V. Soong, Quo's replacement and Chiang's brother-in-law; and George Yeh, who received the head position at the Foreign Ministry in 1950, had all lived and studied in the United States.[48] Surrounded by so many people with ties to the United States, Chiang's own leanings in favor of Washington were reinforced.

The Nationalist leader had a more hostile attitude toward the British. He regarded Britain as the first nation to break down the walls that had isolated China from the world and as the main architect of China's humiliation during the 1800s. London's steadfastly correct attitude toward Japan's encroachments in the 1930s, its largely neutral stance during the civil war in China, and its decision to recognize the People's Republic did little to endear Whitehall to Chiang and his advisers.[49] Indeed, during the islands crisis, more than once the KMT leader contended that Britain was behind U.S. actions that seemed inimical to Taiwan's interests.

To try to convince Chiang not to oppose Oracle, Eisenhower and Dulles sent Robertson to Taiwan with authority to offer a mutual defense treaty in return for the Nationalist leader's agreement not to undermine Oracle. Though previously Washington had opposed the idea of signing a defense pact with Taipei, it now saw advantages to doing so. It would strengthen U.S. policy in East Asia and make clear to the Soviet Union and China that the United States had no intention of giving up on Taiwan. It would continue the policy of military pressure designed to split the Sino-Soviet alliance. Most important, it would allow Washington to gain more control over the Nationalist leader. This would be achieved through a provision that stated that Taiwan would not use force against the mainland without prior approval from the United States.[50]

Robertson made his presentation on October 13. Chiang did not like Oracle, arguing that it would undermine his nation's morale and represent a

---

48. Roderick MacFarquhar, "The China Problem in Anglo-American Relations," in *The "Special Relationship": Anglo-American Relations since 1945*, ed. William Roger Louis and Hedley Bull, 311–12; Boorman, *Biographical Dictionary of Republican China*, 2:255–59, 278–80; 3:149–53; and 4:29–31.

49. Louis and Bull, eds., *The "Special Relationship,"* 311–12; Boardman, *Britain and the People's Republic of China*, 7, 10- 11; Feng, *British Government's China Policy*, 106.

50. Bennett C. Rushkoff, "Eisenhower, Dulles and the Quemoy-Matsu Crisis, 1954–1955," 469; Accinelli, *Crisis and Commitment*, 167; *Sino-American Relations*, ed. Harry Harding and Yuan Ming, 251; Gaddis, *United States and the End of the Cold War*, 76.

first step toward Communist conquest of Taiwan. Robertson replied that as a member of the United Nations, the United States had to take some kind of action. Otherwise, it would seem "that we want to bring on war." He then pulled out the treaty card. Chiang saw benefits to accepting the proposal. He would get the treaty he had wanted for over a year. And, while the pact would not permit him to stage an attack on China without U.S. approval, it did not say that he would never be able to return to the mainland. After considering the pros and cons, he gave his nod to the U.S. proposal.[51]

Washington's decision to couple a U.S.-Taiwan defense pact with Oracle created a division among British officials. British Ambassador to the United States Sir Roger Makins, who tended to sympathize with the American position during the crisis, told Eden that Dulles had no intention of allowing Chiang to turn Taiwan into a "privileged sanctuary" from which he could stage attacks upon the mainland. Instead, it seemed the United States wanted to try to neutralize Taiwan and the nearby Pescadores Islands chain. In sum, while the defense pact complicated things, he felt it best to press ahead with Oracle. Dixon took the opposite stance. The defense treaty, he said, "would surely put off United States recognition of Peking and the seating of Peking in the United Nations . . . and freeze existing Anglo-American differences." Furthermore, the pact would undermine any possibility of "a general settlement in the Far East . . . [and] provide Chiang with a shield behind which he could renew attacks on the mainland of China." Eden felt similarly; at the foreign secretary's behest, the cabinet decided to hold off proceeding with Oracle pending more information about the scope and nature of the U.S.-Taiwan defense arrangement. New Zealand, while frustrated by the British attitude, would not take any action without the United Kingdom's support.[52]

Eden's concerns about proceeding with Oracle increased in early November. Assistant Secretary of State for European Affairs Livingston Merchant told Scott on November 3 that during the past thirty-six hours the Chinese Communists had increased the intensity of their attacks against Quemoy-Matsu and the Tachen Islands. U.S. intelligence believed this was a prelude to a full-scale assault by China against the islands. The deteriorating situation in East Asia led Eden to worry that the United States would not guarantee in its defense treaty that Taiwan would not be used as a sanctuary for attacks against the mainland. Without such a guarantee, Oracle would fail.[53]

51. Memorandum of conversation, Oct. 13, 1954, *FRUS, 1952–54*, 14:728–45.

52. Telegrams, no. 2200, Makins to Foreign Office, Oct. 14, 1954, no. 1020, Dixon to Foreign Office, Oct. 17, 1954, and no. 387, U.K. High Commissioner in New Zealand to Commonwealth Relations Office, Oct. 19, 1954, FO 371/110234; Minutes of Cabinet Meeting, C.C. 66 (54), Oct. 15, 1954, CAB 128/27, PRO.

53. Telegram, no. 5515, Foreign Office to Washington, Nov. 4, 1954, FO 371/110237,

Dulles was uncompromising. He wanted to proceed with Oracle, but he would not allow the treaty to state explicitly that it did not cover the offshore islands. Keeping the text vague might deter China from attacking the islands while discouraging Taiwan from using them to assault the mainland. Makins urged Eden to be lenient, stating that despite its "face-saving language," the treaty would be "quite clear" with regard to the islands. The foreign secretary refused to follow his ambassador's advice. He convinced the cabinet to postpone action, arguing that with the ambiguity of the treaty, presenting Oracle to the UN could expose Anglo-American differences on the offshore islands question.[54]

On December 2, the United States and Taiwan signed their defense pact. Reaction to the treaty was relatively muted, prompting Dulles to call for moving ahead on Oracle. The secretary of state, however, quickly changed his mind. At the end of November, to register its opposition to the U.S.-Taiwan defense treaty, Beijing imprisoned thirteen Americans, including eleven airmen, for espionage. The administration issued a strong protest, while Senator Knowland went so far as to call for a blockade of the PRC. The secretary of state and Eden considered it best to postpone further action on Oracle until the furor over the prisoners died down, unless an invasion of Quemoy and Matsu seemed imminent.[55]

Not only had the mutual defense treaty upset China, but it had failed to have the intended deterrent effect. Dulles and Eisenhower had believed the defense pact would forestall Beijing from attacking the offshore islands by leaving vague which islands the United States would help defend. Mao in-

---

PRO; memorandum of conversation, Nov. 3, 1954, *FRUS, 1952–1954,* 14:852. Merchant referred to "our intelligence personnel" as giving him this information regarding a Chinese attack against the islands, but did not say who exactly provided it. To which source he was referring is not clear, and it is likely still classified.

54. Telegram, no. 2518, Makins to Foreign Office, Nov. 23, 1954, FO371/110238; Minutes of Cabinet Meetings, C.C. 79 (54), Nov. 24, 1954 and C.C. 80 (54), Nov. 29, 1954, CAB 128/27; memorandum by the Secretary of State for Foreign Affairs, "Formosa and the Coastal Islands," C.(54) 367, Nov. 29, 1954, CAB 129/72, PRO; Zhai, *Dragon, the Lion, and the Eagle,* 165.

55. Telegrams, no. 423, Dulles to Geneva, Nov. 23, 1954, and no. Dulte 5, Dulles to Department of State, Dec. 17, 1954; memorandum to Robertson from Murphy, Nov. 24, 1954; memorandum by Bowie, Nov. 26, 1954; SNIE 100-6-54, "World Reactions to Certain Possible U.S. Courses of Action against Communist China," Nov. 28, 1954; memoranda of conversation, Nov. 30 and Dec. 1, 1954, *FRUS, 1952–1954,* 14:945, 949, 950–56, 961–63, 966, 1035; memoranda to Murphy from Cowles, Nov. 26 and 29, 1954, *Confidential U.S. State Department Central Files, China: Foreign Affairs, 1950–1954;* Stolper, *China, Taiwan, and the Offshore Islands,* 52; Foster Rhea Dulles, *American Policy toward Communist China: The Historical Record, 1949–1969,* 153.

stead reached the conclusion that because the pact did not specifically mention Quemoy and Matsu, he would proceed with a plan to attack the island of Yijiangshan (Ichang), located about ten miles from the Tachens. Word of the attack reached Washington on January 18. The increased tension in the Taiwan Strait reminded Americans of the potential for war, turning congressional and general opinion away from their imprisoned comrades and back to the offshore islands. With China apparently readying itself for an attack on Quemoy and Matsu, the White House moved quickly. First, Dulles and Eisenhower decided to get the Nationalists to evacuate all of the offshore islands, with the exception of Quemoy. (Quemoy, unlike the Tachens and Matsu, was within easy reach of Nationalist airbases and also could prove useful in the event the Communists attempted to attack Taiwan.) Second, Washington tried to revive Oracle. Finally, the administration sought congressional approval to defend Quemoy.[56]

During the next two days, Dulles held meetings with Taiwan's foreign minister, George Yeh, Ambassador Makins, and congressional leaders. Yeh strongly opposed evacuation of the Tachens, wanted to add Matsu to any guarantee the United States gave to defend Quemoy, and asked for "a positive interest" on America's part "in the retention of the off-shore islands . . . following up a public statement with 'suggestive action.'" Dulles was reluctant to include Matsu, and he refused to make any public statement: "We cannot indicate that we may intervene unless we are in fact prepared to do so," he said. "It would be disastrous if we made statements and then failed to follow through." Makins worried that a U.S. guarantee to help defend Quemoy represented a permanent extension of the U.S.-Taiwan defense treaty beyond Taiwan and the Pescadores; Dulles assured him this was not the case. He also said he wanted to revive Oracle. As for Congress, the secretary of state made clear that if the administration were to move forward, it would have to have congressional authority "to use the armed forces of the United States in the area for the protection and security of Formosa and the Pescadores." Dulles believed such a resolution would deter China from an assault against the offshore islands.[57]

On January 22, Chiang indicated his acceptance, however reluctant, of the U.S. proposal. He believed the decision to revive Oracle was part of a British plan to achieve a two-Chinas solution and that the White House's request to Congress was designed "to pigeonhole the mutual defense treaty." The day

56. Memorandum of telephone conversation, Jan. 18, 1955, and memorandum of conversation, Jan. 19, 1955, *FRUS, 1955–57*, 2:37, 50–51; see also ibid., 37 nn 2, 3; Chang and He, "The Absence of War in the U.S.-China Confrontation over Quemoy and Matsu," 1512–13; Accinelli, *Crisis and Commitment*, 186–88.

57. Memoranda of conversation, Jan. 19 and 20, 1955, *FRUS, 1955–1957*, 2:38–41, 44–46, 55–68.

before, however, the United States, in an effort to achieve Nationalist support, had agreed to add Matsu to those islands it would help defend; Chiang realized he could not afford to reject this reversal in U.S. policy. Moreover, no matter how much he wanted to hold the Tachens, he realized that doing so would prove most difficult. It was best to accept evacuation of the Tachens in return for protection of Quemoy and Matsu.[58]

The British proved more difficult. Eden disapproved of the American decision to defend Quemoy. The foreign secretary recalled Dulles telling him that the island could only be defended with nuclear weapons. Only if the White House agreed not to make a guarantee to safeguard the island would he support reviving Oracle. "If the Americans cannot defer the guarantee," he told Makins, "then once again the whole basis on which we originally agreed to Oracle has been changed and we should have to look at the whole situation very carefully once more."[59]

With the British set against a public guarantee, the Eisenhower administration reexamined its position. Dulles told the NSC that he felt Britain would not oppose the White House's request to Congress asking to use America's armed forces to defend the offshore islands as long as the United States did not identify "those offshore islands which [it] would help to defend." Makins informed Eden of Dulles's willingness to compromise and suggested that Britain now move forward on Oracle. Eden agreed.[60]

Now it was Chiang's turn to create difficulties for the United States. Between January 25 and 28, both houses of Congress passed the so-called Formosa Resolution, giving the president the right to use America's armed forces to protect Taiwan, the Pescadores, and "related positions and territories of that area in friendly hands." The president signed the resolution on January 29. Chiang told Rankin that he did not like the fact that the resolution did not explicitly mention Quemoy and Matsu. He added that he believed Britain was trying "to sabotage any extension of US support for [the] offshore islands." The U.S. ambassador tried to assure the Nationalist leader that the resolution did not have to name the islands to make America's intentions clear, but Chiang remained unconvinced.[61]

58. Minutes of 233d Meeting of the NSC, Jan. 21, 1955, *FRUS, 1955–1957*, 95–96; Accinelli, *Crisis and Commitment*, 191.

59. Memorandum of conversation, Jan. 20, 1955; telegram, no. 291, Foreign Office to Washington, Jan. 20, 1955, PREM 11/867, PRO.

60. Minutes of 233d Meeting of the NSC; memorandum of conversation, Jan. 21, 1955, *FRUS, 1955–1957*, 2:96–99; telegrams, no. 165, Makins to Foreign Office, Jan. 21, 1955, and no. 337, Foreign Office to Washington, Jan. 22, 1955, PREM 11/867, PRO.

61. Telegram, no. 496, Rankin to Department of State, Jan. 29, 1955, *FRUS, 1955–1957*, 2:166–67; William S. White, "House Votes 409–3 to Back Eisenhower on Formosa; Senate Hears Joint Chiefs," *New York Times*, Jan. 26, 1955; Elie Abel, "Senate Votes For-

The White House refused to let Chiang push it into a corner. The Formosa Resolution did not specifically include the offshore islands; to take the additional step of making a public commitment to defend Quemoy and Matsu would anger Britain, create an Anglo-American rift over East Asian policy, destroy Oracle—thus allowing the Communists to claim that it was the United States, not them, who threatened peace in the region—and potentially prevent any peaceful resolution to the crisis. It would also have a severe impact domestically. A majority of Americans opposed making a clear commitment to defend Quemoy and Matsu; indeed, a sizeable plurality wanted to see the Tachen Islands evacuated, a clear indicator that they wanted to avoid war if at all possible. Furthermore, the Democrats had won the 1954 congressional elections; as one historian pointed out, "the administration had reason to avoid precipitous actions in the strait, because this might unduly strain its cooperation with the opposition party in foreign affairs," such as Senate passage of the U.S.-Taiwan defense pact. Finally, differences with the British would jeopardize London's support for the West European Union, a proposed organization that would bring a rearmed Germany into the European defense system. Therefore, the administration let the Nationalist leader know privately that Washington would help defend the islands, but it refused to make any public statement. Yeh added his own voice, telling Chiang that any insistence on a statement making clear which islands the United States would defend would only delay the evacuation of the Tachens. "[It] seems necessary," he said, "to decide comparative priority of what we want most." Chiang backed down: on February 5, the administration received word that the Nationalist president had decided to begin evacuation of the Tachens, which was completed within a week.[62]

On February 16, Dulles declared that the United States would protect Taiwan and the Pescadores but left unclear what additional areas it might help defend. Now London began to put the pressure on Washington. Eden told Makins that the British public understood the need not to hand over Taiwan and the Pescadores to China. Yet the people of Britain were "troubled by the lack of clarity in the United States Government's intentions, as expressed in their public statements, both concerning the Matsus and Quemoy in regard

---

mosa Plan, 85–3; U.N. to Act, May Invite Red China; British Bid Soviet Curb Peiping," *New York Times,* Jan. 29, 1955; Elie Abel, "President Signs Formosa Measure; Sees Peace Guard," *New York Times,* Jan. 30, 1955.

62. Memoranda of conversation, Jan. 30 and Feb. 5, 1955; telegram, no. 421, Hoover to Taipei, Jan. 31, 1955, *FRUS, 1955–1957,* 2:170–71, 173–76, 182–84, 222; telegram, no. 518, Yeh to Taipei, Feb. 4, 1955, Papers of Wellington Koo, box 145, BL; Kusnitz, *Public Opinion and Foreign Policy,* 73; Accinelli, *Crisis and Commitment,* 164, 198; Frederick W. Marks III, *Power and Peace: The Diplomacy of John Foster Dulles,* 84–85.

to the use of Formosa as a base of operation against the mainland." He felt it best to evacuate Quemoy and Matsu at the same time as the Tachens. He urged Makins to push the Eisenhower administration into publicly declaring that they would "encourage and assist Chiang Kai-shek to evacuate all the coastal islands" and that they would confine him "to Formosa and the Pescadores and . . . prevent [him] from using [them] as a base for hostile activities of any kind against the mainland."[63]

On top of British public opinion, Whitehall had to consider the views of the Commonwealth. On January 28, New Zealand presented Oracle to the United Nations. Zhou Enlai quickly rejected the proposal, declaring it intervened in China's internal affairs. Prime Ministers Menzies and Sir John Kotelawala of Ceylon informed Eden that the Commonwealth prime ministers believed it a bad idea to continue with action in the United Nations. There was also serious concern about the ambiguity of the U.S. stance on Quemoy and Matsu. Menzies and Canadian Secretary of State for External Affairs Pearson supported a private approach to Washington, urging the Eisenhower administration to persuade Chiang to evacuate all of the off-shore islands.[64]

Having taken into account the consensus of opinion, Eden had Makins inform Dulles that while Britain understood America's problems with regard to the islands, "[I]f hostilities should occur over Quemoy or Matsu the great weight of opinion in the UK, and probably other free countries, would not support U.S. intervention in the off-shore islands." Dulles refused to budge. If the Chinese Communists provided assurances that they would not use Quemoy and Matsu for an attack upon Taiwan, he said, "that would of course alter our attitude regarding the off-shore islands. . . . We cannot take a different view of the off-shore islands so long as it seems that an attack on the off-shore islands would be a stepping stone or a prelude to an attack upon Formosa." Dulles recognized the difficult position the United Kingdom faced, but "[a]ny assumption that the Chinese Communists might now follow a more moderate course would fly in the face of threatening Chinese Communist words and deeds of the most formidable character."[65]

---

63. Telegram, no. 497, Foreign Office to Washington, Feb. 1, 1955, PREM 11/867, PRO; Russell Porter, "Dulles Sees Peace Talks if Reds Renounce Force; Repeats China Warning," *New York Times*, Feb. 17, 1955.

64. Telegram, no. 3458, Aldrich to Department of State, Feb. 4, 1955, *FRUS, 1955–57*, 2:212; Minutes of Commonwealth Prime Ministers Conference, P.M.M. (55) 9th Meeting, Feb. 8, 1955, PREM 11/867, PRO; Lindesay Parrott, "Peiping Rejects U.N. Bid to Debate; Ready to Discuss U.S. 'Aggression' Only if Council Ousts Nationalists," *New York Times*, Feb. 4, 1955.

65. Memorandum of conversation, Feb. 9, 1955, *FRUS, 1955–1957*, 2:244–46.

Eisenhower joined the debate. On February 10, he wrote Churchill, thanking the prime minister for doing everything possible to avoid a rift over the crisis in the Taiwan Strait but adding that he could not accept forcing Chiang to give up the islands. If the Nationalists surrendered Quemoy and Matsu, they would no longer have any hope for a return to the mainland. It would, in short, "destroy the reason for the existence of the Nationalist forces on Formosa." The psychological impact would undermine Chiang's government and allow the Communists to take over Taiwan. Churchill replied that he understood Eisenhower's position, but the president had to understand that Britain could not support a war with China over Quemoy and Matsu. He felt it was important for the United States to tell Chiang that there was no hope he could return to the mainland. "He deserves the protection of your shield but not the use of your sword." He asked that Eisenhower maintain the public declaration to defend Taiwan and the Pescadores but announce that he would seek evacuation of the remainder of the offshore islands.[66]

Eisenhower clearly felt the pressure. One of his allies, Taiwan, wanted U.S. help to defend the offshore islands, if not to return to the mainland. Yet if Washington got into a war over the islands, it could not expect much backing from its own citizens or those of its allies. Not only would Great Britain not support a Sino-American war over Quemoy and Matsu, it wanted the United States to get the Nationalists off the islands altogether. But pressuring Chiang to give up the islands threatened to undermine the morale of the KMT, which could lead to the loss of Taiwan with all the attendant repercussions. The president found the situation extremely frustrating. "Those damned little offshore islands," he told Senator Knowland. "Sometimes I wish they'd sink."[67]

Since the offshore islands were unlikely to slip beneath the ocean's surface any time soon, the United States still needed to find a way to resolve the crisis without getting into a war with China. Eden adamantly opposed moving forward on Oracle. With a conference of Asian and African nations about to open at Bandung, Indonesia, it was best, he argued, to avoid any action that might alienate "the Indians, Burmese and others whose views may not be without influence in Peking." The foreign secretary's resistance finally had its effect. On March 26, Makins informed the foreign secretary that Dulles believed that without Oracle, China might successfully use the Bandung Conference to garner support for its plan to take the offshore islands. He con-

66. Letter to Churchill from Eisenhower, Feb. 10, 1955, *FRUS, 1955–1957*, 259–61; letter to Eisenhower from Churchill, Feb. 15, 1955, AWF-International Series, box 19, DDEL.
67. Hagerty Diary Entry, Feb. 16, 1955, Papers of James C. Hagerty, box 1a, DDEL.

sented, however, to postpone the UN operation. Both Eden and Dulles sent messages to their representatives in nations attending the summit, urging them to ask the governments to which they were assigned to push Beijing into seeking a peaceful resolution to the crisis.[68]

With Oracle no longer an option, Dulles looked into alternatives. One possibility was the use of nuclear weapons. Earlier in March, Dulles had stopped off in Taiwan on his return from a SEATO conference in Thailand. His talks with Chiang had left the secretary of state with the impression that the conditions in the strait were far more serious than he had originally believed. Upon his return, he told the NSC of the importance of creating "a better public climate for the use of atomic weapons by the United States." Privately, Eisenhower wanted to avoid using such weapons unless absolutely necessary. But a public statement threatening their use had worked in Korea and might work again. Furthermore, if the United States refused publicly to consider the nuclear option, then the New Look would be seen as nothing more than rhetoric, thereby undermining America's credibility. Eisenhower himself explained that if America's adversaries did not believe Washington was prepared to use nuclear weapons, "'our entire military program would have to be drastically revised' to include conventional as well as nuclear weapons." As a result, in mid-March, the president told reporters that he believed atomic weapons should be used "just exactly as you would use a bullet or anything else." His comment created an uproar in Europe, especially in the United Kingdom, which felt that the United States was coming very close to war.[69]

The administration also looked into a solution they previously had seemed to reject: the evacuation of Quemoy and Matsu. Eisenhower and Dulles decided to send Robertson, as well as Radford, back to Taiwan, believing the two had Chiang's confidence and therefore stood the best chance of getting him off the islands. The two men were unable to convince the Nationalist president. Chiang and Yeh told them that evacuating Quemoy and Matsu would anger the people of Taiwan and destroy their morale. It was also clear

68. Telegram, no. 4858, Dulles to London, Mar. 23, 1955; Message to Dulles from Eden, Mar. 25, 1955; and telegrams, no. 4929, Dulles to London, Mar. 26, 1955, and no. 1295, Dulles to Ankara, Apr. 8, 1955, *FRUS, 1955–1957,* 2:387–88, 397–98, 404–5, 466–67; telegram, no. 668, Makins to Foreign Office, Mar. 26, 1955, FO 371/115043; Circular telegram, no. 126 Saving, from Foreign Office, Mar. 26, 1955, FO 371/115044, PRO.

69. Telegram, no. Dulte 29, Dulles to Department of State, Mar. 4, 1955; Minutes of the 240th Meeting of the NSC, Mar. 10, 1955; memorandum for the record by Cutler, Mar. 11, 1955, *FRUS, 1955–1957,* 2:320–28, 347, 358–59; Pach and Richardson, *Presidency of Dwight D. Eisenhower,* 103–4; Eisenhower, *Public Papers,* 1955, 332; H. W. Brands, Jr., "Testing Massive Retaliation: Credibility and Crisis in the Taiwan Strait," 142.

that the private U.S. guarantee to help defend the islands made the KMT president unwilling to budge. Chiang told the two Americans that "he had been given positive assurance by President Eisenhower that [the] US would participate in their defense under conditions such as now existed." The president had no intention of pushing Chiang any harder. As he explained to Churchill, as long as the Nationalist government felt its morale would be threatened by a withdrawal from the offshore islands, then "we must be careful of the pressure we attempt to apply to Chiang to bring about such a result."[70]

It seemed the White House might find itself indefinitely trapped between China, Britain, and Taiwan. Luckily for Washington, Beijing began to defuse the crisis. By the end of April, the PRC had liberated the Tachens and demonstrated to the world the dangers posed by trying to divide Taiwan from the mainland. It had also come under pressure from the Soviet Union and the Third World, neither of which wanted the crisis to escalate into a larger, potentially nuclear, conflict. Accordingly, during the Bandung Conference, Zhou Enlai declared that the "Chinese people are friendly to the American people" and that Beijing was "willing to sit down and enter into negotiations with the United States Government to discuss the question of relaxing tensions in the Far East, and especially the question of relaxing tension in the Taiwan Strait."[71]

Zhou's announcement pleased many Americans, who wanted an end to the conflict. The official response was more cautious. Dulles told reporters on April 26 that he was not sure Beijing's proposal was "sincere," but the United States planned "to try to find out." Eden told Trevelyan that it was important to exploit the new situation and asked the chargé to find out if Zhou was serious.[72]

Zhou was serious. On May 13, he repeated his desire to settle outstanding

70. Memoranda of conversation, Apr. 1 and 4, 1955; "Editorial Note"; and Message to Secretary of State from Robertson, Apr. 25, 1955, *FRUS, 1955–57*, 2:439–41, 444–45, 476–77, 510–17; letter to Churchill from Eisenhower, Mar. 22, 1955, AWF-DDE Diary Series, box 10, DDEL.

71. Telegrams, nos. 483 and 522, Bohlen to Department of State, 2 and 9 Oct., 1954, *FRUS, 1952–1954*, 14:674–75, 720–21; telegrams, nos. 1185 and 1345, Jan. 27 and Feb. 18, 1955, *FRUS, 1955–1957*, 2:147–49, 289–91; Tillman Durdin, "Chou Asks for U.S. Talks on Easing of Formosa Crisis; Washington Sees Terms," *New York Times*, Apr. 24, 1955; Zhai, *Dragon, the Lion, and the Eagle*, 170, 173–74; Cohen and Iriye, eds., *Great Powers in East Asia*, 228–29; Zhang, *Deterrence and Strategic Culture*, 220–22.

72. Telegram, no. 740, Foreign Office to Peking, Apr. 27, 1955, PREM 11/879, PRO; *Department of State Bulletin* (May 9, 1955): 754; Kusnitz, *Public Opinion and Foreign Policy*, 73.

differences between the United States and the PRC peacefully. Later that month, he told Trevelyan he wanted the Sino-American talks to center on a reduction of tensions in the Taiwan Strait. He refused to include a Nationalist representative in the discussions, stating he wanted to hold separate talks with the KMT. In July, Eisenhower and Dulles sent messages through Great Britain stating that the United States was prepared to hold negotiations with China at Geneva at the ambassadorial level. Zhou replied positively, and the talks began the following month.[73]

The crisis in the Taiwan Strait thus ended without a Sino-American war. Even so, as with Indochina, the Eisenhower administration was unable to act without the support of its allies, particularly the United Kingdom and Taiwan, which had opposite feelings about the offshore islands. America's attempt to resolve the crisis via Oracle did not please Taiwan; its defense treaty with Taipei did not please Britain; its initiative of "deterrence by uncertainty" pleased neither; and throughout, the threat to Quemoy and Matsu remained. Luckily for the United States, the PRC began to deescalate the crisis, freeing the United States from having to choose between going to war or forcing Chiang to evacuate the islands.

It was clear that the United Kingdom did not want another Korean-style conflict with China. Time and again during the Indochina and Taiwan Strait crises, British officials had pointed to their concern of another war with the PRC. The United States clearly did not want renewed hostilities either, but Eisenhower and Dulles believed United Action would prevent a replay of Korea while helping the French and deterring Beijing. Similarly, "deterrence by uncertainty" would leave the PRC guessing as to how the United States would respond to an attack upon Quemoy and Matsu. U.S. officials felt, however, that a united Anglo-American front would enhance Washington's efforts. The fact that Britain refused to follow completely the American lead created serious strains in the Anglo-American alliance. Whereas in Korea the United Kingdom had faced serious pressure to support U.S. policy, it did not face such pressure to do so in Indochina or the Taiwan Strait. The strong congressional and public support for a tough response that had existed in the United States in 1950 did not exist in 1954 or 1955. In addition, during these

73. Letter to Eisenhower from Dulles, May 18, 1955, *FRUS, 1955–1957,* 2:566; telegram, no. 239, Johnson to Department of State, Aug. 1, 1955, *FRUS, 1955–1957,* 3:1–3; telegrams, no. 80, Dulles to New Delhi, July 12, 1955 and no. Dulte 5, Dulles to Secretary of State, July 15, 1955, *Confidential U.S. State Department Central Files. China: Foreign Affairs, 1955–1959;* Zhai, *Dragon, the Lion, and the Eagle,* 175.

two crises, the United Kingdom usually found a Commonwealth bound together in opposition to United Action or precipitous measures in or around
the offshore islands. Consequently Whitehall had a much freer hand than it
had had during the Korean War.

Greater flexibility, however, was not complete freedom of action. Whitehall, and especially Churchill, wanted to avoid a serious schism with its closest
ally. Moreover, when it came to the question of a Southeast Asia defense organization, the United Kingdom confronted a divided Commonwealth, with
New Zealand and Australia in support and India opposed. To try to please all
of the interested parties, London, after some waffling, agreed to *talk* about
the formation of such a pact but refused to move further pending the outcome of the Geneva Conference.

Still, the British used their greater freedom of action to push the United
States in directions they considered favorable or, at the very least, to keep
Washington from adopting policies they regarded as potentially dangerous.
They succeeded in preventing United Action from becoming a reality and
kept forward movement on a Southeast Asia defense pact bottled up pending the discussions at Geneva. Great Britain encountered somewhat more
difficulty budging America when it came to Quemoy and Matsu, for here it
had to contend with another American ally, Taiwan. "Deterrence by uncertainty" might have been designed to deter China, but it also made the British
uncertain just how far the United States might go in helping Chiang.
Churchill and Eden proved unable to prevent the United States from signing
a defense pact with Taiwan, to persuade it to state publicly that Taiwan would
not be used as a "priveleged sanctuary" for attacks on the mainland, or to
convince Eisenhower and Dulles to put heavy pressure upon Chiang Kai-
shek to evacuate the two islands. But they did make it very clear that Great
Britain would not support a war over Quemoy and Matsu. They no doubt
reinforced the White House's opposition to making a commitment to defend
the offshore islands. And they used their influence to get Dulles to end consideration of Oracle when the United States did not meet the prerequisites
they sought.

4

A SCHISM IN THE WIND, 1953–1956

In October 1956, a serious rift developed in the Anglo-American alliance, but it was not over China. That month, British, French, and Israeli troops attacked Egypt in response to its harassment of Israel and its seizure of the Suez Canal. The United States feared that the attack would turn the Arab world against the West and, in a rare case of unity, joined with the Soviet Union in demanding a cease-fire and the withdrawal of foreign troops from Egypt. To put teeth into its demand, Washington used its veto power in the International Monetary Fund to prevent Britain from obtaining loans it needed to help offset a run on London's reserves caused by the crisis. U.S. pressure proved too much for the United Kingdom. In November, Britain and France agreed to end hostilities and remove their troops. Ill health, aggravated no doubt by the stress of the crisis, forced Prime Minister Anthony Eden to resign after less than two years in office.

Although Eisenhower administration officials had not relished taking such strong action against the United Kingdom, many of them breathed a sigh of relief that Eden was gone. Dulles had no love for the prime minister, and Eisenhower had become frustrated with Eden (to the point, contends one scholar, that he hoped to bring down the British head of state's government).[1] While Suez was the last straw for the U.S. government, its relationship with Britain had already become seriously strained because of their respective China policies. Eden and his predecessor, Winston Churchill, might have agreed on the need to avoid another Korean-style conflict, but their cooperation with the Americans did not extend to joining efforts to contain China economically or politically. Still, Churchill was unwilling to challenge the United States. He did succeed in getting U.S. help to end Nationalist harassment of British shipping, but he refused to answer domestic calls for an expansion of trade with the PRC or to bow to pressure from both inside and outside his government to support Beijing's admission to the United Nations. Eden, for his part, cooperated with Washington in trying to obtain the release of U.S. nationals being held in China. Yet he was far more willing than

---

1. Steven Z. Freiberger, *Dawn over Suez: The Rise of American Power in the Middle East, 1953–1957*, 199, 212.

Churchill to challenge the United States on UN representation and trade. As a result, prior to Suez, the two allies appeared headed for a schism on both of these subjects.

During the Korean War, the United Kingdom had supported the moratorium on Chinese representation in the United Nations, by which the UN agreed to postpone discussion of the subject. The Churchill government had seen no reason to alter its stance so long as the war continued and China refused to consider ending hostilities. As the conflict neared an end, however, the United States had begun to wonder if Whitehall would maintain this position.[2]

There had been pressure upon Churchill to admit China even before the armistice, both from members of the opposition and from some within the government. Leading the way among the latter was Sir H. M. Gladwyn Jebb, the permanent British representative at the UN. Jebb found the American position on Chinese representation bewildering and explained as much to his American counterpart, Henry Cabot Lodge. In June he told Lodge that he could not understand why the United States did not oppose the Soviet Union's membership in the United Nations but did oppose that of China. "There is just this difference," Lodge replied. "In the Korean war, the Chinese Communists inflicted more than 130,000 casualties on us and the Soviets haven't. To us this is quite a difference." Jebb remained unconvinced and the following day wrote Churchill supporting the PRC's admission. Admitting Beijing to the United Nations, he said, would make China less likely to represent to the people of India and Southwest Asia "a powerful and mysterious, and possibly irresistible, force." Asians would come to realize that the PRC was subject "to the frailties that affect all governments." Moreover, they would see that Beijing cared more about its own interests than, as Mao Zedong claimed, the interests "of the dependent peoples of the world."[3]

The end of the war brought Jebb a supporter: Eden. Up until the Korean armistice, the foreign secretary had seemed to agree with Churchill on the need to avoid a schism with the United States over the representation ques-

---

2. Draft aide mémoire, untitled, Feb. 27, 1953, FO 371/105225, PRO; memoranda, to Robertson and Johnson from Bacon, May 25, 1953, and to McConaughy from Bacon, May 26, 1953, *FRUS, 1952–1954,* 3:638–39, 641–51; memorandum, "Chinese Representation in the United Nations," June 10, 1953, RG 59, Bureau of Far Eastern Affairs, Miscellaneous Subject Files for the Year 1953, box 4, NA.

3. Telegram, no. 781, Lodge to Department of State, June 9, 1953, *FRUS, 1952–1954,* 3:660; letter to Churchill from Jebb, June 10, 1953, PREM 11/789, PRO. For parliamentary pressure to admit China to the UN, see *Hansard Parliamentary Debates,* 5th ser., vol. 514 (1952–53), col. 651; vol. 515, cols. 901–2, 914–15, 1003; vol. 517, col. 2247.

tion. The war's resolution, however, brought signs of potential trouble. As Eden explained a month after the armistice to the British chargé d'affaires in Beijing, Humphrey Trevelyan, if the situation in East Asia improved, "Her Majesty's Government will consider themselves entirely free to raise again [the] question of some change in the present policy."[4]

Eisenhower and Dulles favored continuation of the moratorium and wanted to make sure that they had British support. Like their predecessors, Eisenhower administration officials believed that a policy of pressure on all fronts would serve to divide the Sino-Soviet alliance and weaken the communist world. Secretary of State-designate Dulles argued in early 1952, for instance, that "the best way to get a separation between the Soviet Union and Communist China is to keep pressure on Communist China and make its way difficult as long as it is in partnership with Soviet Russia." Furthermore, Eisenhower administration officials argued that U.K. backing was vital to bringing the nations of Western Europe and the Commonwealth into line. Dulles therefore asked the ambassador in London, Winthrop Aldrich, to discuss the situation with Churchill. He repeated Secretary of State Dean Acheson's contention that admitting the Communists would reward aggression. It would also anger U.S. congressional and public opinion, "with probable unfortunate results," such as prejudicing American financial aid to the UN.[5]

Churchill had no intention of challenging the United States on UN representation. As he told the House of Commons in July 1954:

> I am very sure that to choose such a moment as this to try to force the entry of Communist China into the United Nations would be to complicate altogether the very grave affairs we have to deal with in so many other areas and would be regarded as a most harsh and uncalled-for act of unfriendliness by the mighty people of the United States, to whom we all owe much and from whom no Government ever received more than the Government of the party opposite.[6]

Churchill's unwillingness to anger the United States had been made clear when he and Eden visited Washington in late June 1954. "I told [Churchill]," Eisenhower informed his press secretary, James Hagerty, "that it was politically immoral and impossible for the United States to favor the admission of Red China in the United Nations." To the president's surprise, the prime minister agreed, noting that a state of war still existed between China and Britain

4. Telegram, no. 426, Foreign Office to Peking, Aug. 20, 1953, FO 371/105225, PRO.

5. Memoranda, to McConaughy from Bacon, May 6, 1953, to McConaughy from Bacon, May 26, 1953, and to Dulles from Hickerson, June 4, 1953, and telegram, Dulles to London, no. 7916 and Paris, no. 5985, June 12, 1953, in *FRUS, 1952–1954*, 3:638, 659, 644, 670; Gaddis, *United States and the End of the Cold War*, 74–75.

6. *Hansard Parliamentary Debates*, 5th ser., vol. 530 (1953–54), col. 492.

as a result of the conflict in Korea. "That was that," noted Eisenhower, "and we never discussed the situation again."[7]

Eden was less accommodating. He told Dulles that it would be difficult for Britain to support the United States on the representation question, largely because British public opinion held that Beijing deserved the China seat. Repeating his earlier warning, Dulles stated that if the Communists were admitted to the international body, Congress would demand that the United States withdraw from the UN. Noting the contradictory views, Eisenhower told Hagerty that Churchill's stance "did not reflect Eden's attitude and that Eden was more inclined to favor the admission of Red China."[8]

The disagreement between Churchill and Eden over China's representation exploded on their return to London. During the trip, the prime minister learned that Republican Senator Knowland had suggested that if the PRC entered the United Nations, the United States should leave. Churchill recommended to Eden that he state publicly that Britain would never agree to Beijing's admission as long as a state of war existed with the United Nations. The prime minister's private secretary, Sir John Colville, explained what happened next:

> Eden said that if we made any such statement it would destroy all chance of success at [the Geneva Conference]: we ought to keep our entry into UNO [the United Nations] as a reward for China if she were good. The PM looked grave; he had not realised, he said, that what Knowland said was in fact the truth— Eden *did* contemplate the admission of China into UNO while a state of war still existed.
>
> Eden got red in the face and there was a disagreeable scene.

Colville added that the two men "went to bed in a combination of sorrow and anger, the PM saying that Anthony was totally incapable of differentiating great points and small points."[9]

With British support, the moratorium again passed in 1954.[10] It was the last time the United Kingdom backed postponement under Churchill. In April 1955, under pressure from most of his cabinet to retire, the prime minister resigned. Eden took his place.

The Eisenhower administration wanted to make sure that it could expect Eden's support for the moratorium; as the 1955 vote approached, Lodge

7. Hagerty Diary entry for June 29, 1954, Papers of James C. Hagerty, box 1, DDEL.

8. Hagerty Diary entry for July 6, 1954, Papers of James C. Hagerty, box 1, DDEL; memorandum of conversation, July 2, 1954, *FRUS, 1952–54,* 3:733–34.

9. William S. White, "Knowland to Quit Party Post if U.N. Admits Red Chinese," *New York Times,* July 2, 1954 (see also "Text of Knowland's Statement"); Colville, *Fringes of Power,* 699–700.

10. Memorandum to Robertson from Bacon, Sept. 21, 1954, *FRUS, 1952–1954,* 3:795.

asked where he stood. Although the new prime minister agreed to go along, he asked his ambassador in Washington, Sir Roger Makins, to explain to the White House that his backing was reluctant. "It is a sense of comradeship, not real agreement, that impels us."[11]

Eden's reluctance to defer to the Americans on the moratorium became more evident in 1956. In January he informed Eisenhower and Dulles that he was having increasing difficulty supporting postponement. The president rejoined that he could not budge on the issue. Eisenhower noted that American public and congressional opinion still strongly opposed Beijing obtaining a seat in the international body. He believed "a Resolution would be passed by Congress recommending U.S. withdrawal within thirty minutes of China's admission." He shared lawmakers' sentiment, pointing out that "the Red Chinese are opposing the UN in Korea, that they are still holding U.S. citizens as prisoners, that they are threatening military action in Formosa, etc." As long as "conditions of this kind continue, any thought of Red Chinese entrance into the UN would be completely unacceptable to this country." Dulles asked Eden to support the moratorium through the whole of the upcoming UN session, which stood the chance of carrying into 1957, rather than simply through the end of 1956, but Eden was noncommittal.[12]

When Eden failed to give a prompt response, the Eisenhower administration, during May and June, had Acting Secretary of State Herbert Hoover, Jr., Assistant Secretary for Far Eastern Affairs Walter Robertson, and Assistant Secretary for United Nations Affairs Robert Murphy sound out Whitehall.[13] This pressure forced the Eden government to decide how it would vote. Makins argued that the U.S. midterm elections were approaching, and to vote for China's admission would anger the United States. (Indeed, both the Democrats and Republicans were running on platforms that included statements opposing the seating of the PRC in the international body.) Similarly, Foreign Secretary Selwyn Lloyd argued that there was no reason for Britain to threaten the Anglo-American relationship by adopting a controversial position on Chinese representation. He favored supporting the moratorium

11. Telegram, no. 690, Dixon to Foreign Office, Sept. 6, 1955, FO 371/115213; telegram, no. 4139, Foreign Office to Washington, Sept. 8, 1955, PREM 11/4673, PRO.

12. Memorandum of conversation, Jan. 31, 1956, AWF-DDE Diary Series, box 12, DDEL. Public opinion polls during this entire period (1953–56) showed a large majority opposed admitting China to the United Nations. See Kusnitz, *Public Opinion and Foreign Policy,* 162. Congressional opinion matched that of the general public. See *Congressional Quarterly Almanac,* 83d Cong., 1st sess., 1953, 162; 83d Cong., 2d sess., 1954, 272–73; 84th Cong., 1st sess., 1955; 84th Cong., 2d sess., 1956, 496–97.

13. Telegram, no. 7212, Hoover to London, May 26, 1956, *FRUS, 1955–1957,* 11:471; telegram, no. 1404, Makins to Foreign Office, June 21, 1956, FO 371/121023, PRO.

through the upcoming session, including 1957, while making clear that there should be full discussion of the issue in 1957.[14]

Eden continued to resist accommodating Washington, arguing that supporting the moratorium through the whole of the upcoming session would tie Britain's hands. Lloyd urged Eden to reconsider. The foreign secretary received support from the head of the Foreign Office's Far Eastern Department, C. T. Crowe, who contended that there were issues of more importance to Britain, such as the Middle East, than Chinese representation. Eden gave in to his advisers, but he emphasized that Whitehall expected the subject to receive thorough exploration in 1957.[15] The allies, in short, appeared headed for a battle over representation.

The issue of commerce with China remained contentious as well. As Makins wrote in February 1954, "During the first half of 1953, criticism [in the United States] of British trade with Communist China was widespread and bitter, and was more dangerous for Anglo-American relations than any single subject since the default on the World War I debts."[16] One reason was the emergence of a new China bloc ally by the name of Joseph McCarthy. A Republican senator from Wisconsin, McCarthy achieved national fame in early 1950, when he declared he had information about communists in the U.S. government. He continued to make charges concerning the existence of communists in influential positions in Washington. While his accusations went unproven, the public, inflamed by the postwar Red Scare, found much in the senator's statements to support.

At first, London largely ignored McCarthy. During the Korean War, British officials tended to focus their attention on the UN commander, Gen. Douglas MacArthur, whom they regarded as a much more serious danger. They also believed that McCarthy, with his unsubstantiated allegations, would only end up making a fool of himself and his party.[17]

Following MacArthur's dismissal in April 1951, Whitehall began to take more interest in the Wisconsin senator. British officials were especially ap-

14. Letter to Allen from Makins, June 6, 1956, FO 371/121023; memorandum by the Secretary of State for Foreign Affairs, C.P. (56) 175, "Chinese Representation in the United Nations," July 12, 1956, CAB 129/82, PRO; Rosemary Foot, "The Search for a *Modus Vivendi:* Anglo-American Relations and China Policy in the Eisenhower Era," in *Great Powers in East Asia,* ed. Warren I. Cohen and Akira Iriye, 145.

15. Memorandum to Eden from Lloyd, Aug. 27, 1956, PREM 11/4673; draft memorandum on Formosa by Crowe, Sept. 28, 1956, and letter to O'Neill from Morland, Oct. 15, 1957, FO 371/120914; memorandum of conversation, Oct. 7, 1956, FO 371/121025, PRO.

16. Dispatch, no. 73, Makins to Foreign Office, Feb. 23, 1954, FO 371/109099, PRO.

17. John P. Rossi, "The British Reaction to McCarthyism, 1950–54," 6–7.

palled by McCarthy's accusations that Secretary of State (and later Defense) George Marshall had played a role in the "loss" of China; they greatly respected Marshall, particularly for his role in the formation of the European Recovery Program. Those watching from London again hoped that the senator would destroy himself with such charges, but he only grew stronger. Eisenhower, following his election in 1952, did not seem prepared to help. It was true that Eisenhower did not care for McCarthy; as he told a friend, "I just won't get into a pissing contest with that skunk." Yet he felt that coming out publicly against the senator "would greatly enhance his publicity value without achieving any constructive purpose." The president thus limited his criticism to the senator's actions.[18]

The British did not like Eisenhower's refusal to put McCarthy in his place, but they realized that the administration's ability to maneuver was limited. As early as July 1952, McCarthy had accused the White House of preventing the Taiwanese navy from stopping and searching ships heading to mainland ports. The following year, he began a major campaign against trade with China, particularly between Britain and the mainland. In May, he urged Eisenhower to force Whitehall to end all commerce with the PRC. Realizing that pushing the Churchill government into a corner could hurt Anglo-American relations, Dulles told the senator that while he wanted to end all trade with China, such an effort was not feasible. The British, informed of the McCarthy-Dulles correspondence, understood that the White House was in a bind. Makins told Eden that many Americans, including many lawmakers, supported McCarthy's position on trade. The Eisenhower administration was thus faced with the choice of exposing "itself to criticism by McCarthy and others in Congress"—"others in Congress" no doubt referring to members of the China bloc—or trying "to coerce other governments into acceptance of United States policies." The British ambassador added that "all this represents a disturbing situation," one "which threatens to cover East West trade as a whole."[19]

McCarthy's tirade against the British calmed somewhat after the Korean armistice, but it did not end. In December 1953, Crowe pointed to the problems the British were having with Nationalist Chinese interference with U.K. shipping (a subject that will receive further attention shortly). He took note

18. Ibid., 8; Ambrose, *Eisenhower,* 57; Eisenhower, *The White House Years: Mandate for Change, 1953–56,* 320–21.

19. Memorandum, Allison to Dulles, July 17, 1952, RG 59, Bureau of Far Eastern Affairs, 1953, Miscellaneous Subject Files for the Year 1953, box 2, NA; letters to McCarthy from Dulles and to Dulles from McCarthy, May 6 and 7, 1953, Papers of John Foster Dulles, box 2, DDEL; telegram, no. 1000, Makins to Foreign Office, May 9, 1953, FO 371/105249, PRO; Rossi, "The British Reaction to McCarthyism," 12–13.

that Undersecretary of State for Foreign Affairs Anthony Nutting had suggested a formal approach to Washington about the matter. Crowe advised against it for a number of reasons, including "McCarthy's renewed campaign about British trade with China," which made an approach to the United States infeasible.[20]

McCarthy's self-destruction during his campaign to ferret communists out of the U.S. Army brought pleasure to Great Britain.[21] Yet his disappearance from the political spotlight did not mean that the White House would now agree to a reduction of the controls on trade with China—quite the opposite. Instead the dispute grew increasingly tense over the next several years.

The controversy surrounded the so-called differential. In January 1950, a number of nations established a joint coordinating committee, or COCOM, to oversee controls on trade with the Soviet Union and Eastern Europe. In September 1952, the members of COCOM set up a subsidiary body, the China Committee, or CHINCOM. Because of China's role in Korea at the time, the controls imposed against the PRC were more stringent than those aimed at the Soviet Union. This difference in the level of controls became known appropriately as the "differential."[22]

With the end of the Korean conflict, there seemed less justification in Great Britain for maintaining controls on trade with communist countries, including China. In fact, more than ever, expansion of that trade appeared vital for the United Kingdom. During the war, Britain's military spending had absorbed about 10 percent of the nation's gross national product. Such spending put intense pressure on London's resources; the Treasury warned that the United Kingdom must either cut its commitments abroad or increase its exports by 20 percent to keep its economy healthy. The nation's dollar reserves declined so far that in 1955 the governor of the Bank of England "warned that [they] were just above the danger mark." Added to this was pressure from the U.K. business community, which pointed to the benefits trade with China would provide to Hong Kong and Britain and argued that inaction would only help other countries. The Federation of British Industries, for instance, stated that the potential for more trade with Beijing, "if neglected by the United Kingdom, will be seized by our competitors." Members of both parties in Parliament added their voices to those of British firms,

20. F.O. Minute by Crowe, Dec. 7, 1953, FO 371/105286, PRO.
21. Rossi, "The British Reaction to McCarthyism," 16–17.
22. Memorandum, "History of COCOM/CHINCOM," undated, RG 59, Records of the Bureau of Far Eastern Affairs, 1957, box 3, NA; Jing-dong Yuan, "Between Economic Warfare and Strategic Embargo: U.S.–U.K. Conflicts over Export Controls on the PRC, 1949–57," 86.

pointing out that the China market would "help to maintain the not too certain chances of employment in this country."[23]

There was, of course, no guarantee that a relaxation of the controls on commerce with the PRC would lead to a rapid expansion of Sino-British trade. Indeed, in early 1954, Humphrey Trevelyan, the British chargé d'affaires in Beijing, noted that the PRC did not have a lot of sterling with which to buy U.K. goods. (In 1955, one U.S. estimate held that China could not buy more than $420 million a year in materials from the West.) Even so, Trevelyan added, "China has a great potential market."[24] In short, relaxing the controls offered possibilities the U.K. business community (and at least some U.K. officials) could not ignore.

Facing such pressure, Churchill in February 1954 called for increased trade with the communist bloc, but the wording of his statement is significant: "The more trade there is through the Iron Curtain and between *Great Britain and Russia* and her satellites the better and better will be the chances of our living together in increasing comfort [emphasis added]." He continued, "I am speaking so far, of course, only of trade with Russia. We cannot relax restrictions of trade with China until the Korean, or perhaps a wider Far Eastern peace, has been established."[25]

Why the distinction? As one scholar of the trade controls points out, "By 1954, the strategic, economic, and political conditions that had led West European governments to adopt economic warfare no longer obtained." Josef Stalin's death, the Korean armistice, and a thaw in East-West relations reduced the fear of war between the Soviet Union and Western Europe. "Without out the threat of imminent war, the justification for denying the Soviet exports that contributed to their 'war potential' was severely weakened." Furthermore, Western Europe's economies showed clear signs of recovery. "Recovery signaled the need for export outlets, and the traditional East Eu-

23. "Trade with Communist China," *London Times,* Sept. 16, 1954; Bartlett, *British Foreign Policy in the Twentieth Century,* 93; Qing Simei, "The Eisenhower Administration and Changes in Western Embargo Policy against China, 1954–1958," in *Great Powers in East Asia,* ed. Warren I. Cohen and Akira Iriye, 128–29. For specific examples of members of Parliament attacking the embargo, see *Hansard Parliamentary Debates,* 5th ser., vol. 515 (1952–53), col. 1002; vol. 520 (1953–54), cols. 1124–25; vol. 521, cols. 915–19; vol. 525, cols. 888–902; vol. 528, cols. 2254–56; vol. 529, cols. 1958–66; vol. 532, cols. 1030–31; and vol. 533, cols. 190–91. See also Clement R. Attlee, "Britain and America: Common Aims, Different Opinions," 193–95.

24. Dispatch, no. 9, Trevelyan to Foreign Office, Jan. 12, 1954, FO 371/110194, PRO.

25. "Excerpts from Churchill's Speech to the House of Commons," *New York Times,* Feb. 26, 1954, p. 4; memorandum, "East West Trade," May 26, 1955, WHO-NSC Staff Papers, Executive Secretary's Subject File Series, box 10, DDEL

ropean markets were a primary target."[26] Churchill, however, argued that Beijing still represented a potential threat to peace. And, given previous statements, he intended to do everything possible to avoid challenging Washington's strong views on China policy.

If Britain—or at least Churchill—was unwilling to take on the United States over trade controls, other nations were not so hesitant. West Germany and Japan strongly pushed for expansion of commerce with the PRC. The U.S.-Japan relationship was especially difficult. Japan's economy had long relied on trade with China and other East Asian countries. Without that commerce, it had to turn to the United States for a market; the American business community resented the competition it faced from cheap Japanese products. Additionally, Eisenhower regarded a strong Japanese economy as assisting the overall economic development of East Asia. If Tokyo could not trade with its traditional East Asian markets—and found its access to the American market limited by domestic U.S. opposition—then the security of Japan and the rest of East Asia would be imperiled.[27]

It was clear to the Eisenhower administration that America's allies were becoming restless on the trade issue, but its members were divided on how to respond. The leading advocate of a reduction of controls was Clarence Randall. Randall was a longtime supporter of free trade and the head of the Council on Foreign Economic Policy (CFEP), a group established by Eisenhower in 1953. After the Korean War, Randall pointed out that Western Europeans resented any talk of increasing, or even maintaining, restrictions on trade. He stated that Washington had to adopt a more flexible position on foreign commerce. The United States, he contended, had to "lend an understanding ear when other countries argue issues of economic defense in terms of general economic, political, employment or psychological factors rather than merely in terms of trade security considerations." Secretary of the Treasury George Humphrey agreed. Humphrey believed that it did not make sense to restrict trade, as it would hurt the economic recovery of America's allies. Furthermore, allowing Japan in particular to trade with China would benefit American companies, for it would divert cheap Japanese products into markets other than that of the United States. Hence, he contended, any "attempt to maintain elaborate trade controls on East-West trade over the long haul was as foolish as trying to hold back Niagara Falls." At the oppo-

26. Michael Mastanduno, "Trade as a Strategic Weapon: American and Alliance Export Control Policy in the Early Postwar Period," 145–46.

27. Foot, *Practice of Power,* 60; Cohen and Iriye, eds., *Great Powers in East Asia,* 126–27; Burton I. Kaufman, "Eisenhower's Foreign Economic Policy with Respect to East Asia," in *Great Powers in East Asia,* ed. Warren I. Cohen and Akira Iriye, 107; Michael Schaller, *Altered States: The United States and Japan since the Occupation,* 77–82.

site end of the spectrum were Dulles, Assistant Secretary Robertson, and Secretary of Defense Charles Wilson. For Dulles, as noted, controls on trade offered a means of putting pressure on the PRC and, ultimately, creating divisions in the Sino-Soviet alliance. Testifying before the CFEP in November 1953, Robertson argued that the embargo was wreaking havoc on the Chinese economy and that all trade with Beijing was strategic: the Chinese "don't use their precious resources for luxuries. The very fact that they make an importation into China is because they need that item." Because all trade with the PRC was strategic, all commerce with Beijing had to be cut off. Wilson similarly opposed expanding trade, even in nonstrategic items, with the communist bloc. There was also strong opposition in Congress, led by Democratic Senator John McClellan of Arkansas, who, following the 1954 midterm elections, became chairman of the Government Operations' Permanent Investigations Subcommittee. He believed that the United States should cut all aid to any nation that traded with the communist bloc.[28]

Eisenhower agreed with Randall and Humphrey, at least to some extent. The president saw trade controls as problematic for two interrelated reasons. First, they increased the economic difficulties of U.S. allies by limiting their ability to trade with other nations, even if those other countries included the Soviet Union and China. Second, too much government spending would weaken, if not destroy, the U.S. economy, Eisenhower believed, and he wanted to cut expenditures. Yet if America's friends could not trade with other nations, the United States would have to pour more money into its own military and foreign economic assistance programs.[29]

Eisenhower tended to avoid imposing his ideas about trade controls upon his cabinet, yet he was prepared to do so, particularly when an opportunity presented itself. Given his personal views, the president had no aversion to relaxing controls on commerce with the communist world. Permitting countries such as Britain to expand trade with the Soviet Union would allow Eastern Europeans to see what the West could offer them and possibly create divisions within the Soviet bloc. Letting Japan trade with China offered similar

---

28. Memorandum, "A Birdseye View of Current Issues Respecting East-West Trade Controls," undated, U.S. President's Commission on Foreign Economic Policy [Randall Committee], Studies of U.S. Foreign Economic Policy Series, box 66; Testimony of Walter Robertson before CFEP, Nov. 19, 1953, U.S. President's Commission on Foreign Economy Policy: Records, 1953–1954, box 9, DDEL; *Congressional Quarterly Almanac*, 84th Cong., 2d sess., 1956, 496–97; Tor Egil Førland, "'Selling Firearms to the Indians': Eisenhower's Export Control Policy, 1953–54," 236, 242; Cohen and Iriye, eds., *Great Powers in East Asia*, 53, 110–11; Walter LaFeber, *The Clash: A History of U.S.-Japan Relations*, 306.

29. Cohen and Iriye, eds., *Great Powers in East Asia*, 122–23, 124.

benefits. As he explained in an April cabinet meeting, "If we opened up trade the whole population of China would benefit and might actually be induced to upset the ruling Communist clique." The cabinet acquiesced and in August 1954 agreed to allow Tokyo to expand its commerce with Beijing. The month before, to please West Europeans, including Britain, COCOM had agreed to revise the controls imposed upon the Soviet Union and Eastern Europe, reducing the list of sanctioned items by nearly 50 percent. Shortly thereafter, the U.S. modified its own list of goods embargoed to Russia. To placate the opposition in Congress, the White House argued that the revisions would allow U.S. businesses to export goods more easily to Western Europe. Furthermore, it got cooperation from its allies in expanding the controls aimed at the PRC. Realizing that lawmakers on Capitol Hill opposed a relaxation of the controls, COCOM agreed, albeit reluctantly, to add the 207 items removed from the European Soviet bloc control list to the China list, thus widening the differential.[30]

Did not permitting Tokyo to increase its trade with Beijing punch a hole in the policy of using economic pressure against China as a means of dividing the Sino-Soviet alliance? The answer is a qualified "yes." First, there were special reasons for giving Japan access to the China market, such as demands from U.S. industry to be free of competition from cheap Japanese products. Second, as Eisenhower suggested, allowing Tokyo to increase its trade with Beijing might create divisions between the PRC and Soviet Union by showing China what the West had to offer. Third, the United States still maintained its full-scale embargo against China. Fourth, the Eisenhower administration still sought to keep other nations, especially Britain, from increasing their trade with the PRC. As a January 1955 intelligence estimate pointed out, the United Kingdom "plays a major role in influencing the attitude of CHINCOM countries."[31] The Americans knew that if London were given the same kind of access to the China market that Tokyo had received, the entire trade controls system might come unglued.

Britain's ability to expand its trade with the Soviet Union did not mollify the U.K. business community. Contacts between Eden and Premier Zhou Enlai at Geneva helped open the door to an agreement to make regular exchanges of inventories of goods for sale. They also paved the way for a visit

30. Ibid., 125–26, 128; Minutes of the 193d Meeting of the NSC, Apr. 13, 1954, *FRUS, 1952–1954*, 14:410; memorandum, "History of COCOM/CHINCOM"; Førland, "'Selling Firearms to the Indians,'" 228–29; Michael Mastanduno, "Trade as a Strategic Weapon," 143, 146–48 and *Economic Containment: CoCom and the Politics of East-West Trade*, 98; Yuan, "Between Economic Warfare and Strategic Embargo," 87.

31. NIE 100–55, "Controls on Trade with Communist China," Jan. 11, 1955, *FRUS, 1955–1957*, 10:207.

by the Chinese vice minister for foreign trade to Britain in July and an invitation for a U.K. delegation of businesspeople to travel to the PRC. China seemed prepared to expand its trade with the West, and Beijing's expressed desire for more commerce with Britain created additional opposition in the United Kingdom toward the controls. Whitehall did not know how much its trade might increase with the PRC if the differential could be eliminated. But, as British Second Secretary of the Treasury Sir Leslie Rowan told Dulles, it "would be of some consequence." As an example of the possibilities for an expansion of Sino-British trade and the growing anger in the United Kingdom over the controls, Lloyd, in the same conversation, pointed to a recent layoff of workers at a British truck plant. "The factory could have sold trucks to Communist China," he explained, "which would have kept the employees working full time. The men were naturally asking why export orders could not be accepted which would give them full employment." To many British officials and businesspersons, it appeared unrealistic to ban items to Beijing that were being sent to the Soviet Union and routinely transshipped from there to China. Thus, in September, Peter Thorneycroft, the president of the British Board of Trade, told Dulles that Britain wanted to examine revision of the sanctions imposed against China.[32]

Once again, the Eisenhower administration was divided. The Defense and Commerce Departments wanted to fight any British attempt to revise the trade controls. The Pentagon argued that allowing Britain to ease the sanctions would increase the military potential of Beijing. Secretary of Commerce Sinclair Weeks declared that a relaxation of controls would set a dangerous precedent and undermine the entire sanctions program. Robertson joined Defense and Commerce in opposition. Dulles, though he also disliked the idea of allowing more trade with China, realized he had to adopt a more flexible position if he was to maintain any semblance of a controls system. The result was that the State and Treasury Departments called for maintaining the trade controls but argued that the United States should not exert its "influence in such a manner as would be seriously divisive or lead nations needing Chinese trade to accommodation with the Communist bloc."[33]

32. FO Minute by Wilson, Sept. 16, 1954, FO 371/110292, PRO; telegram, no. Dulte 16, Dulles to Department of State, Oct. 1, 1954, *FRUS, 1952–1954,* 14:671; memorandum of conversation, Jan. 31, 1956, *FRUS, 1955–1957,* 10:307–8; Foot, *Practice of Power,* 58–59; Michael Mastanduno, *Economic Containment: CoCom and the Politics of East-West Trade,* 98.

33. Minutes of 226th Meeting of the NSC, Dec. 1, 1954, *FRUS, 1952–1954,* 14:971–72; NSC 5429/3, "Current U.S. Policy toward the Far East," *FRUS, 1952–1954,* 12:979; memorandum to Dulles from Robertson, Oct. 5, 1954, RG 59, Records of the Bureau of Far Eastern Affairs Relating to Southeast Asia and the Geneva Conference, box 10, NA; Cohen and Iriye, eds., *Great Powers in East Asia,* 130.

Had the pressure become intense enough, it is likely that Churchill would have agreed to call for a revision of the trade controls against China. It is also likely, given his past statements and actions, that he agreed to examine the issue to mollify those in Britain calling for an expansion of trade, in the hope of putting off any final decision for as long as possible. As it turned out, he never would have to make such a decision. Despite Thorneycroft's comment, pressure within the United Kingdom for a second look at the sanctions against China actually *declined* from mid-1954 to mid-1955 because of the Quemoy-Matsu crisis.[34] Moreover, during the emergency in the Taiwan Strait, Churchill resigned, leaving Eden to determine the next steps.

As expected, the end of the offshore islands crisis, the return of relative stability to East Asia, and Eden's desire to adopt a China policy more independent of the United States revived the question of the trade sanctions. During the second half of 1955, Eisenhower administration officials heard from several individuals, including British Foreign Secretary Harold Macmillan, that the United Kingdom was under intense pressure to eliminate the differential. Dulles, hoping to obtain the release of American prisoners in China, urged Macmillan to delay action on the differential until the United States had an opportunity to use the sanctions as bargaining chips.[35]

In December, Eden decided he could wait no longer. British public opinion was putting intense pressure upon him. He also had no intention of indefinitely yielding to the Americans on the trade issue, as Churchill seemed to have done. Therefore, in December, Whitehall announced its intention to reduce unilaterally its controls on trade with China the next month. Britain's decision created a flurry in Washington. Dulles informed the NSC on December 8 that to prevent a complete collapse of the trade controls system, the United States probably would have to agree to some kind of relaxation while trying to keep as much of the differential as possible. Two weeks later, the NSC adopted this plan. In the meantime, the secretary of state warned Macmillan that unilateral action by Britain would create "a high degree of ill feeling" between the two allies. The foreign secretary could only reply that he would do his best to withhold his government from a final decision.[36]

---

34. Report by the Steering Committee of the Council on Foreign Economic Policy, CFEP 501/5, "Interim Report on Review of Economic Defense Policy," Mar. 24, 1955, *FRUS, 1955–1957*, 10:231.

35. Memorandum, Kalijarvi to Hoover, July 12, 1955, and telegrams, no. Secto 99, Delegation at the Foreign Ministers Meetings to the Department of State, Oct. 31, 1955, and no. Secto 335, Delegation at the Foreign Ministers Meetings to the Department of State, Nov. 16, 1955, *FRUS, 1955–1957*, 12:243, 266–67.

36. Telegrams, no. 2281, Aldrich to Department of State, Dec. 3, 1955, and no. 3258, Dulles to London, Dec. 10, 1955, *FRUS, 1955–1957*, 12:273–74, 277; memorandum to

In April, the White House finally made a proposal: eighty-one items would be removed from the CHINCOM controls. In return, Britain would agree to reverse a decision to remove copper wire from the COCOM list. Eden rejected the proposal. He later wrote, "There was no strong strategic argument in favour of this action, nor could we accept that copper wire was of direct military importance." Moreover, reinstating the controls on that item "would be most embarrassing . . . for our increased exports of copper wire were a principal ingredient of the recent expansion of Anglo-Soviet trade." Therefore, in mid-May, Lloyd, who had replaced Macmillan after the latter's short stint as foreign secretary, informed Eisenhower that the British government would employ wider use of a procedure in CHINCOM that allowed members to make "exceptions" to the controls list; under that procedure, the United Kingdom could freely ship such commodities as rubber, tractors, and tin to the PRC. Britain's decision angered both McCarthy and Defense Secretary Wilson. McCarthy submitted a provision that would suspend for a year U.S. assistance to any nation that shipped to communist nations goods embargoed by the United States. Wilson, for his part, urged Dulles to make a strong representation to Eden and inform him that "we may be forced to make a critical reappraisal of the whole structure of our relations." Dulles responded, "[M]aintaining an effective multilateral effort in the China trade control field is . . . a difficult and complex one, since it rests, and can only rest, on voluntary cooperation among the participating countries." To continue an effective system of controls required the United States to make some concessions. Republican Senator H. Alexander Smith of New Jersey used similar language to respond to McCarthy's proposed legislation. McCarthy's amendment, he said, "would have the effect of forbidding any country from receiving any aid if it shipped anything—even baby powder—to Communist China. . . . East-West trade controls depend on cooperation of our allies. Without such cooperation there can be no effective controls." Most of the upper house agreed and rejected the McCarthy amendment.[37]

Though Washington had acquiesced, albeit reluctantly, to expanded use

National Security Council from Lay, Feb. 6, 1953, *FRUS, 1952–1954,* 2:225–29; Minutes of 269th Meeting of the NSC, Dec. 8, 1955, and of the 271st Meeting of the NSC, Dec. 22, 1955, *FRUS, 1955–1957,* 3:209–14, 225–29.

37. Letters to Dulles from Wilson, June 22 and 26, 1956, RG 59, Records of the Deputy Assistant Secretary of State for Far East Economic Affairs (Baldwin and Jones), 1951–1957, box 2, NA; Minutes of 282d Meeting of the NSC, Apr. 26, 1956, and letters to Wilson from Dulles, June 26, 1956, and to Eisenhower from Dulles, May 14, 1956, *FRUS, 1955–1957,* 10:348–56, 363–64, 372–74; *Congressional Quarterly Almanac,* 84th Cong., 2d sess., 1956, 425, 426; Anthony Eden, *Full Circle,* 407–8; Wenguang Shao, *China, Britain, and Businessmen,* 109–10.

of the exceptions procedure, Britain still wanted CHINCOM to formally eliminate the differential. The Suez crisis of 1956, however, intervened, and in October, Lloyd convinced the cabinet that the time was not right to press for further revision of the controls system. The U.S. presidential elections were a month away, and the question of trade with China was a political hot potato in Washington. Moreover, wrote the foreign secretary, "Because of the Suez crisis and the fact that we have decided to appeal to the Americans for help if we have to buy dollar oil it is essential in my view that we should try to avoid creating new points of friction."[38] It was best to keep quiet pending the outcome of the 1956 elections and the Anglo-American dispute over Middle Eastern matters.

Tied in closely with the issue of Britain's trade with China was the Chinese Nationalist blockade of the mainland. The Nationalist government of Chiang Kai-shek declared in June 1949 that the entire coast from Fuzhou (Foochow) to the Liao River in Manchuria was off limits to foreign shipping, thereby covering all of the mainland's Communist-held ports, including Qingdao (Tsingtao), Shanghai, and Xiamen (Amoy). Whitehall considered Taipei's pronouncement an invalid "proclamation of blockade in international law" and refused to abide by it. British merchantmen thus continued to head to Communist ports; the Nationalist navy stopped and searched a number of these ships.[39] The British approached the United States in 1952 about interference with their shipping, but the negative American response led Whitehall to decide not to press the matter.

Nationalist obstruction of British shipping continued after the end of the Korean War. During the whole of 1953, the KMT intercepted forty-five U.K. merchantmen, including five in one four-day period, July 25 through 28. In August, S. P. Osmond of the Admiralty asked John McKenzie of the Foreign Office whether Whitehall should approach Washington about the KMT blockade. McKenzie felt an official approach would be a bad idea. "American public opinion is much inflamed against our trade with China," he said, "and the American Administration would certainly be hotly attacked if any of its

38. Telegram, no. CA-2286, Dulles to Certain Diplomatic Missions, Sept. 11, 1956, *FRUS, 1955–1957*, 10:394–96; memorandum by the Secretary of State for Foreign Affairs, C.P. (56) 221, "East/West Trade: China," Oct. 1, 1956, CAB 129/83; Minutes of Cabinet Meeting, C.M. 60 (56), Oct. 3, 1956, CAB 128/30, PRO.

39. Memorandum, "Chinese Nationalist Interference with British Shipping," Feb. 27, 1953, RG 59, Bureau of Far Eastern Affairs, Miscellaneous Subject Files for the Year 1953, box 3, NA; "Blockade of Reds in China Ordered," *New York Times*, June 21, 1949. For examples of Nationalist harassment of U.K. shipping, see "British Freighter Released," *London Times*, Jan. 8, 1952; "Ship Attacked Near Foochow," *London Times*, Oct. 27, 1952; "British Ship Attacked Off Foochow," *London Times*, Dec. 3, 1952.

departments did anything that could be construed as in any way aiding that trade." Furthermore, previous official requests for help from the United States had gotten nowhere, "and we are not anxious to be rebuffed again." He added, though, that informal approaches seemed to have "had some effect in curbing the Nationalists," and he noted that Whitehall had asked E. H. Jacobs-Larkcom, the consul in Taiwan, to continue informal discussions with U.S. officials on the island.[40]

In September, Jacobs-Larkcom approached U.S. Ambassador to Taiwan Karl Rankin about the interference with British shipping. Nutting and Alan Tindal Lennox-Boyd, the minister of transport and civil aviation, were skeptical that such informal, low-level approaches would have any effect and therefore suggested a direct, formal discussion with officials in Washington. Both Eden and Crowe recommended against it, pointing out, as had McKenzie, that previous approaches had gotten nowhere. They also noted the political difficulties the Eisenhower administration would face if it pressured the KMT to stop its actions against U.K. shipping. Finally, strong pressure upon the White House "would inevitably underline the divergences of Anglo-American policy in the Far East and embarrass the major lines of our policy in that area."[41] With such high-level opposition to formal discussions with the United States, it is not surprising that there were no such talks between the two Western allies during the remainder of 1953 or all of 1954 on the issue of KMT interference with British shipping.

The first offshore islands crisis changed matters. In September and November, respectively, the Nationalist government warned London not to send ships to the Chinese port of Xiamen and to keep British vessels out of the whole of the Taiwan Strait. Parliament regarded the warnings as further infringement on British shipping. The Churchill government, accordingly, came under additional pressure to act on the matter. Whereas Churchill was reluctant to tackle the subject of trade controls, he insisted the United States provide some assistance to stop the KMT's actions. Historians can only speculate on why he decided to lean on Washington when it came to the Nationalist blockade but not on the restrictions on commerce with the PRC. It is likely, however, that by answering calls to stop KMT harassment of U.K. shipping he could alleviate some of the pressure to expand trade with China yet

40. Enclosure to dispatch, no. 42, Tamsui to Foreign Office, June 24, 1954, FO 371/110194; telegram, no. NISUM 127, C.S.O. (I) F.E.S. to Admiralty, July 31, 1953, and letters to McKenzie from Osmond, Aug. 5, 1953, and McKenzie to Osmond, Sept. 2, 1953, FO 371/105286, PRO.

41. Telegram, no. 168, Jacobs-Larkcom to Foreign Office, Sept. 4, 1953, FO 371/105287; FO Minute by Crowe, Dec. 7, 1953, and letter to Secretary, Ministry of Transport and Civil Aviation from Crowe, Dec. 12, 1953, FO 371/105286, PRO.

avoid directly challenging the White House on a particularly sensitive subject. Whatever his reasoning, he gave Eden his approval to send out two telegrams on November 23. The first, to the new consul in Taiwan, A. H. B. Hermann, made clear that London would not abide by the Nationalist warning. The second, to Washington, asked for U.S. help in dealing with the KMT government. As an incentive, Eden warned that a lack of White House assistance would make Britain's "position more difficult" in dealing with a recently tabled Soviet resolution that accused the United States of staging provocative demonstrations off the PRC's coast. Eden's warning had the intended effect: on December 7, the State Department informed Makins that it had urged Taipei "to take great care to avoid incidents" and "promised to speak in the same sense to the [Nationalist] Chinese Minister in Washington." Hermann's replacement, A. A. E. Franklin, noted that the U.S.'s approach, as well as "the firm but tactful handling of the situation in the straits by British ships," led Taipei to realize that it "had more to lose than gain by interfering and attacking shipping." There were only three serious incidents involving British merchantmen during the whole of 1955.[42]

After 1955, Nationalist interference with British shipping continued to decline. During the 1958 Quemoy-Matsu crisis, the United States again urged Taiwan to show restraint. At the same time, the Nationalists sought to improve relations with Whitehall, which led them to act carefully with regard to U.K. merchantmen. Indeed, after 1959, there were no reports of incidents between British ships and the Nationalist navy.[43] Yet the end of Nationalist interference with U.K. shipping did not mean that the larger question of whether Britain would abide by the overall trade controls policy had been resolved.

42. Telegrams, nos. 101 and 128, Hermann to Foreign Office, Sept. 13 and Nov. 16, 1954; no. 105, Foreign Office to Tamsui, Nov. 23, 1954; and no. 5767, Foreign Office to Washington, Nov. 23, 1954, FO 371/110313; telegram, no. 2665, Makins to Foreign Office, Dec. 9, 1954, FO 371/110314; dispatch, no. 13, Franklin to Foreign Office, Mar. 20, 1956, FO 371/120864. For parliamentary statements regarding Nationalist harassment of U.K. shipping, see *Hansard Parliamentary Debates,* 5th ser., vol. 532, (1953–54), col. 91 and vol. 533, cols. 1230–32. For information on the Soviet resolution, see Kathleen Teltsch, "Soviets Ask U.N. to Denounce U.S. in China Attacks," *New York Times,* Oct. 16, 1954, and Evan Luard, *A History of the United Nations,* vol. 1, *The Years of Western Domination, 1945–1955,* 304–5.

43. Letter to Lloyd from Wright, Mar. 10, 1958, FO 371/133496; letter to Lloyd from Veitch, Mar. 23, 1959, FO 371/141369; letter to Lloyd from Veitch, FO 371/150529; telegrams, nos. 2147 and 466 Saving, Hood to Foreign Office, Aug. 4 and 15, 1958, FO 371/133551; letter to Franklin from Crowe, Oct. 22, 1956, FO 371/120928, PRO; dispatch, no. 10, Young to Foreign Office, Jan. 27, 1961, FO 371/158461, PRO. I found at the PRO no official reports of Nationalist interference with British shipping after 1959.

The American position on trade and the British position on Chinese representation in the UN handicapped the allies' ability to make headway in talks with CCP officials. Sino-American negotiations opened in Geneva a few months after the first offshore islands crisis ended. For Washington, the talks offered the opportunity to free American nationals imprisoned in China, as well as to obtain a promise from the PRC not to use force against Taiwan. Meanwhile, London was holding its own talks with CCP officials aimed at convincing China to agree to exchange ambassadors and to establish full diplomatic relations with Great Britain. Both Western allies found that getting what they wanted would take far longer than they had hoped.

The Sino-American ambassadorial talks, which opened in August 1955, had strong support in the United States. Democrat Walter George of Georgia, chairman of the Senate Foreign Relations Committee, believed the negotiations offered the opportunity to settle major outstanding issues between the two countries. Other Democrats, as well as twelve prominent Republicans, joined George, and polls showed that 70 percent of Americans were in favor of negotiations.[44]

Why such support for the negotiations when just a year earlier there had been such opposition to the Geneva Conference? First, in November 1954, the government in Beijing had imprisoned a number of Americans. And second, the two nations had nearly gone to war over Quemoy and Matsu. Even members of the China bloc could not fail to note the strong animosity among Americans toward the idea of fighting with the PRC over the two islands. The talks offered an opportunity to settle both concerns. The Sino-American joint announcement of July 25 declaring the opening of negotiations stated that the purpose of the discussions was "to aid in settling the matter of repatriation of civilians who desire to return to their respective countries and to facilitate further discussions and settlement of certain other practical matters now at issue between both sides." Dulles explained that of these "other practical matters," the most important was to convince China to renounce the use of force against Taiwan.[45] Achievement of this goal might prevent another crisis from erupting in the Taiwan Strait.

Moreover, unlike the meeting at Geneva the year before, these discussions were to be held between ambassadors, not foreign ministers. Robertson explained to both George and Representative James Richards (D-South Car-

44. William W. White, "Full U.S. Parley with China Seen," *New York Times*, July 27, 1955; Robert Accinelli, "Eisenhower, Congress, and the 1954–55 Offshore Island Crisis," 342.

45. Dana Adams Schmidt, "President Reports Gains for Peace, Says Geneva Proved All Desire It; U.S. and Red China Envoys to Meet," *New York Times*, July 26, 1955; "Dulles' Remarks on Red China and Big 4 Talks," *New York Times*, July 27, 1955.

olina), chairman of the Foreign Affairs Committee, that the White House had no intention of raising the level of the talks to that of foreign ministers. While Robertson did not say so, the White House believed that a higher level meeting would imply recognition of the government in Beijing. Ambassadorial talks did not connote the same degree of approval and thus would face less opposition within Congress. To cover its back, however, the administration publicly made clear that the talks did not in any way suggest the United States would recognize the government in Beijing.[46]

While the United States opposed talks at the foreign ministers' level, the possibility of a meeting between Zhou and Dulles was the primary reason China had first proposed the ambassadorial discussions. The negotiations at Geneva had clearly demonstrated that the United States recognized the PRC was a force with which it had to deal. A foreign ministers' meeting would make this all the clearer; it would also greatly enhance China's prestige. But Beijing had other reasons for desiring the talks. In particular, it wanted the United States to agree to relax the trade embargo, which would give China greater access to the goods it needed for its economic development.[47]

Once the discussions began, the two negotiators, Wang Bingnan for China and U. Alexis Johnson for the United States, focused on the question of prisoners. Wang accused the Eisenhower administration of holding Chinese nationals in the United States against their will, an allegation Robertson called "balderdash."[48] In an attempt to break the ensuing deadlock, Wang on August 11 proposed a formula by which the nationals of both the United States and China (each detained in the other country) could leave for home if they wished. The Chinese representative suggested that China use India and the United States use Britain as intermediaries. Dulles was not sure

46. Memoranda of conversation, Sept. 21 and 22, 1955, RG 59, General Subject Files Relating to the People's Republic of China, 1954–61, box 24, NA; Circular telegram, no. 163, Hoover to All Diplomatic and Consular Missions, Sept. 12, 1955, *FRUS, 1955–57,* 3:86–87; Dwight D. Eisenhower, *Public Papers of the Presidents of the United States: Dwight D. Eisenhower, 1953–1961,* 1955, 738, 765; Dulles, *American Policy toward Communist China,* 163–64.

47. "Chou Bids Chiang Confer on Ways to 'Free' Taiwan," *New York Times,* June 29, 1956; Johnson, *Right Hand of Power,* 248.

48. Telegram, no. 244, Johnson to Department of State, Aug. 2, 1955, and memorandum of conversation, Aug. 9, 1955, *FRUS, 1955–1957,* 3:7–10, 23. According to Trevelyan, China's accusation was not "balderdash." "Since the Korean War," the chargé pointed out, "the Americans had been preventing Chinese students with technical qualifications from leaving the United States, so that the Communists should not have the benefit of their special skills." See Humphrey Trevelyan, *Worlds Apart: China, 1953–5, Soviet Union, 1962–5,* 84. See also Yelong Han, "An Untold Story: American Policy toward Chinese Students in the United States, 1949–1955."

whether to accept Wang's proposal. It did not apply to American nationals who had charges pending against them or who were in jail. Since this was true of all U.S. citizens in China, he told Makins that Wang's offer was "empty." Yet making a concession to the PRC might convince it to make concessions of its own, such as releasing at least a few of the prisoners. And rejecting the offer could lead to a breakdown of the talks, with the United States to blame. Thus, despite his misgivings, the secretary of state finally instructed Johnson to accept Wang's suggestion. With agreement reached, the following month Wang and Johnson released a joint announcement, stating that their nations would "expeditiously" work to allow the nationals of the other country to leave if they wished; Chinese citizens believing they were being held against their will could turn to India for help, while Americans could look to Britain. During the next week, New Delhi and London agreed to act as functionaries.[49]

With that settled—or so it seemed—the two nations turned to other issues. A few days after the agreed announcement, Wang called for turning discussion to the embargo and a foreign ministers' meeting. The Eisenhower administration was not prepared to talk about either. "Our trade-economic pressures are the most effective weapon we have," Dulles told Robertson. "We ought to give them what they want when we get something we want." The State Department thus declared that it would not "enter into a discussion of trade restrictions with the Chinese Communists" as long as the PRC "refuse[d] to renounce the use of force in the Taiwan area and continue[d] to hold imprisoned American citizens as political hostages." A Dulles-Zhou meeting, meanwhile, would enhance China's prestige and anger Taiwan and the China bloc. Johnson informed Wang he would not discuss either subject until all Americans had been released by Beijing and proposed instead to center on a renunciation of force. Wang's response was two-fold: first, a renunciation of force "could be resolved only by [a] higher level meeting." Second, treatment of Taiwan was an internal matter. Putting the two together, Johnson concluded that the Communists would not agree to renounce the use of force "unless they get something they want very badly." He speculated a foreign ministers' conference fit into this category.[50] In sum, China wanted a

49. Telegram, no. 1921, Makins to Foreign Office, Aug. 18, 1955, FO 371/115010, PRO; telegrams, no. 402, Johnson to Department of State, Aug. 11, 1955, and nos. 495 and 745, Dulles to Geneva, Aug. 14 and Sept. 19, 1955; and "Agreed Announcement of the Ambassadors of the United States of American and the People's Republic of China," Sept. 10, 1955, FRUS, 1955–1957, 3:27–28, 38–39, 85–86, 93.

50. Telegrams, nos. 722 and 1051, Johnson to Department of State, Sept. 14 and Nov. 3, 1955, FRUS, 1952–1954, 3:89–90, 155–57; telephone conversation, Oct. 7, 1955, Papers of John Foster Dulles, Telephone Calls Series, box 4, DDEL; letter to Sebald from

Dulles-Zhou meeting before it would move on to other issues, while the United States wanted to move on to other issues before it would consider a Dulles-Zhou meeting.

Washington's determination to achieve a declaration rejecting the use of force greatly disturbed Taiwan. In January 1956, the State Department explained that such a declaration did not suggest that Taiwan or China had to give up "its objectives and policies in the region." Taipei's response was quick and strong. On January 26, it issued an aide memoire, declaring that a renunciation of force "would be tantamount to an admission by the US to equal responsibility for the existing situation in the Taiwan Strait, for which the Chinese Communists should and must be held solely responsible." Furthermore, the form of the U.S-proposed declaration would imply "de facto recognition of the Chinese Communist regime," thus weakening the resistance of the free people of Asia to communism. "It would also encourage those countries who are already inclined toward the idea of two Chinas"—Britain was undoubtedly on this list of nations—"to pursue their machinations with renewed and greater vigor."[51]

None of these arguments were new. As early as September 1955, Taiwanese Ambassador to the United States Wellington Koo had expressed his nation's opposition to a renunciation of force. He had also contended that the talks signified U.S. recognition of Beijing, which Robertson had assured him was not the case. The January aide memoire was far stronger in tone than Koo's previous approaches, yet it did not have the intended effect. The following month, the State Department explained that a renunciation of force, if accepted by the Chinese, "would make renewed aggression in defiance of their commitments more hazardous for them." If they refused, "their aggressive intent is revealed for all the world to see."[52] It was, the Americans felt, a win-win proposal.

Obviously, the KMT government regarded the talks as a serious threat. It did not want the United States to do anything that would enhance the pres-

Johnson, Nov. 11, 1955, RG 59, General Subject Files Relating to the People's Republic of China, 1954–61, box 24, NA; *Department of State Bulletin* (Oct. 8, 1956): 553. Qiang Zhai, "Dulles, Wedge, and the Sino-American Ambassadorial Talks, 1955–1957," 32–33.

51. *Department of State Bulletin* (Jan. 30, 1956): 164–67; telegram, no. 681, Rankin to Department of State, Jan. 26, 1956, *FRUS, 1955–1957*, 3:279–82.

52. Memorandum of conversation, Sept. 30, 1955, *Confidential U.S. State Department Central Files, China: Foreign Affairs, 1955–1959*; memoranda of conversation, Nov. 17 and Dec. 6, 1955, RG 59, General Subject Files Relating to the People's Republic of China, 1954–61, box 24, NA; memorandum of conversation, Feb. 1, 1956, and telegram, no. 481, Hoover to Department of State, Feb. 13, 1956, *FRUS, 1955–1957*, 3:295, 298, 307–8.

tige of the government in Beijing. Furthermore, if China agreed to renounce the use of force, then pressure would increase upon Taiwan to do the same, thereby destroying Chiang Kai-shek's hopes of returning to the mainland. At the very least, the United States would be unable to assist a Nationalist effort to return to the mainland; Chiang realized that a successful attack upon China would require U.S. logistical support.[53]

In fact, Chiang had little about which to worry. Beijing refused to consider any renunciation of force that included Taiwan. Although it had not made any serious effort to attack the island, the PRC considered Taiwan a part of China. Zhou declared in June 1956 that "the question as to what means will be used by China is entirely a matter of China's sovereignty and internal affairs, in which no outside interference will be tolerated. Therefore, a Sino-American announcement should in no way allow interference in this matter."[54] Beijing did not then, nor would it ever, renounce the use of force.

Things were not going well on the question of prisoners either. In November 1955, the British chargé in Beijing, Con O'Neill, prepared letters for the seventeen Americans still held in China—including the thirteen imprisoned the previous year—and enclosed with each a copy of the September announcement. The Communist government agreed to let him send the letters to the prisoners but placed stringent controls on O'Neill's ability to meet with them. The chargé, angered by these restrictions, wrote Macmillan that he believed the controls were designed to put pressure on the United States at Geneva. He added that he doubted the prisoners would receive his letters.[55]

In mid-November, China released three of the prisoners. Two weeks later, O'Neill received word that his letters had been delivered to the remaining fourteen. Zhou, though, refused to allow the chargé to see the Americans. Despite the contention by the Indian ambassador to the United States, Gaganvihari Mehta, that he faced no restrictions in meeting with Chinese in America, Zhou argued otherwise and refused to let O'Neill have access to the U.S. prisoners. When O'Neill expressed dissatisfaction with the implementation of the September announcement, the Chinese premier rebuffed him. Mac-

---

53. In April 1956, Chiang wrote Eisenhower that "Free China should be given an opportunity to establish beachheads on the coast, to encourage general revolt throughout [the PRC]. . . . Only logistical support from the United States would be required." Memorandum, Dulles to Eisenhower, Apr. 30, 1956, WHO-Office of the Staff Secretary, Subject Series, State Department Subseries, box 1, DDEL.

54. Memorandum to McConaughy from Jacobson, July 11, 1956, *Confidential U.S. State Department Central Files, China: Foreign Affairs, 1955–1959.*

55. Telegrams, nos. 1185 and 1186, Hoover to Geneva, Nov. 9, 1955, *Confidential U.S. State Department Central Files, China: Foreign Affairs, 1955–1959;* telegram, no. 1012, O'Neill to Foreign Office, Nov. 4, 1955, FO 371/115200.

millan concluded that O'Neill was unlikely to make any further progress and that it was up to Johnson at Geneva to voice American disapproval with the way in which China was interpreting the September agreement.[56]

Realizing that O'Neill was getting nowhere, the Eisenhower administration decided upon a new tactic. In June 1956, Makins informed Lloyd that the State Department intended to tell all Chinese criminals in U.S. prisons that they could apply for parole or commutation of their sentences so they could go home. Additionally Mehta could interview all of these prisoners to determine if they wanted to return to China. This new strategy, Dulles explained, was designed to achieve a psychological advantage over the PRC at Geneva. The initial response of Beijing, Makins reported the following week, was "confused." A few days later, though, Wang rejected the American offer. Johnson believed, probably accurately, that China did not want to have a repeat of what had occurred in Korea, when thousands of Chinese refused to return home. O'Neill concluded that Beijing would refuse to release any more prisoners until it got something in return, most likely a foreign ministers' meeting.[57] Ultimately, the PRC did not release the last American prisoners until after Richard Nixon's trip to China in 1972.

While the United States was having troubles with China at the Geneva talks, Britain was having its own problems with the PRC. From the time it recognized the Communist government in January 1950, London had hoped to exchange ambassadors with Beijing and establish full diplomatic relations. In March, China requested clarification of Britain's attitude on two issues before it would move forward on the question of exchanging ambassadors: PRC representation in the United Nations and Chinese property in Hong Kong. (The latter referred to some seventy Nationalist planes at Hong Kong, to which Beijing laid claim.) Later that month Britain explained that it would vote for China once there was a majority on the Security Council in its favor. It would also transfer the aircraft to the PRC if no other nation claimed them. The PRC considered Whitehall's answer unsatisfactory and asked for further clarification. In May 1950, London sent its reply but received no response.[58]

56. Telegrams, nos. 1069 and 1088, O'Neill to Foreign Office, Dec. 5 and 9, 1955; no. 1559, Foreign Office to Beijing, Dec. 12, 1955; and no. 5893, Foreign Office to Washington, Dec. 12, 1955, FO 371/115200, PRO; "Three More Americans Released by China," *London Times,* Nov. 18, 1955.

57. Telegrams, no. 1253 and no. 442 Saving, Makins to Foreign Office, May 31 and June 5, 1956, FO 371/120895; telegram, no. 346, O'Neill to Foreign Office, June 19, 1956, FO 371/121016, PRO; telegrams, no. 2022, Johnson to Secretary of State, June 8, 1956, and no. 2183, Dulles to Geneva, June 19, 1956, *Confidential U.S. State Department Files, China: Foreign Affairs, 1955–1959.*

58. Brief by Allen, "Geneva Conference: China: United Kingdom Recognition and Diplomatic Relations," Apr. 4, 1954, FO 471/110245, PRO; Tania Long, "Why Don't the Chinese Recognize Recognition?" *New York Times,* May 14, 1950.

During the Korean War, both sides considered it inappropriate to discuss establishing full diplomatic relations, but at the end of the conflict the issue arose again. Some progress did occur at the Geneva Conference. Up to the summit, Beijing had recognized Trevelyan not as chargé but as "head of the British delegation for negotiations of the establishment of diplomatic relations." The PRC was pleasantly surprised by Eden's attitude at Geneva and agreed to refer to Trevelyan as chargé. Moreover, it asked to put a diplomatic mission in London.[59]

The Chinese request created a stir in the U.K. capital. Trevelyan urged Whitehall to accept the proposal. "It answers the old American argument that we have made a gesture to the Chinese which has not been reciprocated," he argued, and would help Britain better protect its interests in China. Eden agreed but realized that the American reaction had to be taken into consideration. He believed, though, that Washington would not make a strong protest. "Now that our differences with United States policy in South-East Asia are narrowing and that we are known to be acting closely together [at Geneva]," stated the foreign secretary, "I do not think that any serious damage will be done, provided a proper explanation were given to the United States Government." Eden raised the matter with U.S. Undersecretary of State Walter Bedell Smith, who agreed that the American reaction would not be strong. With that, Eden recommended acceptance of the Chinese offer. The cabinet concurred but, to avoid angering the United States, decided to make it clear that "the establishment of formal diplomatic relations would remain a matter for negotiation between the two governments."[60] There is no evidence that London's decision led to any significant outburst within the United States, possibly because American attention was focused on the U.S. position and role at the Geneva summit.

Further movement proved impossible. In October 1955, Zhou informed O'Neill that his government disapproved of the British position on UN representation; therefore, an exchange of ambassadors and the achievement of full diplomatic relations could not occur. The Chinese also began to argue about the presence of a U.K. consul on Taiwan, which they contended symbolized British recognition of the Nationalist government.[61] Beijing continued after 1955 to use the issues of representation and Taiwan to justify its re-

59. Brief by Allen, "Geneva Conference"; FO Minute by Nutting, May 7, 1954, FO 371/110245, PRO; Zhai, *Dragon, the Lion, and the Eagle,* 146.

60. Telegrams, no. 592, Trevelyan to Foreign Office, June 4, 1954, and no. 658, Eden to Foreign Office, FO 371/110245; Minutes of Cabinet Meeting, C.C. 40 (54), June 15, 1954, CAB 128/27, PRO; Tang, *Britain's Encounter with Revolutionary China,* 122–23.

61. Telegram, no. 922, O'Neill to Foreign Office, Oct. 8, 1955, PREM 11/4673, PRO; Boardman, *Britain and the People's Republic of China,* 145, 148.

fusal to exchange ambassadors. Not until 1972 did the United Kingdom and the People's Republic establish full diplomatic relations.

In October 1956, the Suez crisis brought down the twenty-one-month-old British government. By that time, the allies' policies on China appeared to be on a collision course. Eden might have agreed with Churchill on the need to avoid another Korea and therefore stood united during the Indochina and Quemoy-Matsu crises; beyond that, the two men did not see eye-to-eye. It was not that Eden was less committed to containing communism than Churchill or more mindful of the United Kingdom's economic problems. Rather, it was more a question of personality. If war with the PRC was not at issue, Churchill intended to do everything possible to avoid creating tensions in the Anglo-American alliance. He refused to challenge the United States over China's representation. On the trade question, he did believe it was important for Britain to expand its commerce, and the Soviet Union no longer represented the danger that China did. Accordingly, he called for more trade with the Soviet Union and Eastern Europe. He also successfully pressured Washington to get Taipei to cease its harassment of U.K. shipping. But despite growing pressure for him to do so, he refused to take the additional step of seeking a relaxation of the controls against Beijing.

Eden's personal views were opposite those of his predecessor. He attached less weight to the Anglo-American alliance and consequently had fewer inhibitions about challenging the United States over policy toward the PRC. He was prepared to cooperate with Washington, particularly on the question of obtaining the release of American nationals held in China. But he was far more willing to tackle the questions of Chinese representation and trade. It must be kept in mind that his attitude on the latter subject was reinforced by public opinion: the expansion of commerce with the Soviet Union and Eastern Europe and the end of Nationalist harassment of U.K. shipping had not stopped calls at home for more trade with Beijing. Additionally, reducing the controls on trade with China could also serve to divide the Sino-Soviet alliance by giving the PRC direct access to Western goods. Yet given his attitude on the importance of the Anglo-American alliance and his opposition to constantly yielding to the United States, it is likely that even without public opinion, this subject would have become an area of contention. Taking into account Eden's views on China, his relationship with Dulles, and his unwillingness to follow the American lead, it is highly possible that had the Suez crisis and Eden's resignation not occurred, an Anglo-American schism still would have taken place, but over the PRC. At the same time, his resignation did not mean the slate was clean. In particular, Eden's successor would have to face up to calls in Britain for a relaxation of the trade controls against the PRC.

5

"OUR RELATIONSHIPS MUST BE RESTORED," 1957–1960

Never since the end of World War II had relations between the United States and Britain been as bad as after the Suez crisis.[1] The British believed that the Americans had ignored their interests when the United States had joined with, of all countries, the Soviet Union, in opposing the action taken by France, Israel, and Britain. At the same time, the crisis had demonstrated the extent to which Britain had failed to recover economically from World War II. American financial pressure, combined with Britain's fluid reserves, had forced London to back down. The British public felt angry at and betrayed by the United States. But the nation's uncertain economic health, combined with its need for American military support to deter the communist threat in Europe, required Whitehall to repair its relations with the United States as soon as possible. This job fell to the new prime minister, Harold Macmillan.

Mending the damage done to the alliance was not going to be easy, as China continued to pose serious problems. The prime minister was under intense pressure to eliminate the differential in trade with the People's Republic. Another crisis in the Taiwan Strait renewed fears of a conflict like that in Korea. And the question of China's representation in the UN remained unresolved. Macmillan trod cautiously, successfully eliminating the differential and making clear his concerns over the crisis in the Taiwan Strait; however, he did so in the manner least likely to create new tensions with his country's closest ally. Meanwhile, he followed the U.S. lead on China's representation, though by 1960 he had serious doubts how much longer the moratorium might last.

Macmillan had already had a long career in government, serving as Winston Churchill's liaison to Eisenhower during the campaign against Germany in North Africa in World War II and later as minister of housing and then defense in Churchill's postwar government. Under Anthony Eden, he had served a short stint as foreign secretary before being transferred to the Exchequer, where he was when Eden resigned.

1. Alistair Horne, *Harold Macmillan*, vol. 2, *1957–1986*, 21.

Like Churchill, Macmillan gave primacy to his nation's ties with the United States as opposed to those with members of the other two circles, Western Europe and the Commonwealth. In fact, he had no choice. Britain continued to rely upon America to support its military power and economic well-being, a fact underscored by the Suez crisis. As the Foreign Office stated in 1957, "We should pursue a policy in step with that of the US. We have no alternative." Consequently it is not surprising that he made improving Anglo-American relations his top priority. He wrote, "Somehow, without loss of dignity and as rapidly as possible, our relationships must be restored." His effort was facilitated by a longtime friendship with his American counterpart, Dwight D. Eisenhower.[2]

The United States also had reason to repair its relations with the United Kingdom. Whitehall still controlled large areas of the globe and was active in Europe, Africa, the Middle East, and the United Nations. Indeed, Washington took the initiative: on January 22, 1957, Eisenhower invited the prime minister to meet him in Bermuda. Macmillan accepted. The British ambassador in Washington, Sir Harold Caccia, wrote, "The Prime Minister's meeting with the President will provide the impetus needed to re-launch the alliance."[3]

Yet if Britain could expect to come out of the Bermuda Conference having improved relations with the United States, it could not anticipate a change in U.S. China policy. Caccia informed the Foreign Office that in preparation for the conference, it should know that officials in the State Department, including Secretary of State John Foster Dulles, considered U.S. policy toward the People's Republic to be proper. Eisenhower shared the view of many of his advisers that China was still under UN indictment as an aggressor nation. Additionally, the American public opposed a change in their nation's policy toward China. Lastly, with the congressional elections coming up the following year, the GOP wanted to avoid any decisions about the PRC that might split their ranks. London understood that Washington would remain intransigent on China. A. J. Mayall, the assistant in the Far

2. Charmley, *Churchill's Grand Alliance*, 301; W. Scott Lucas, "The Cost of Myth: Macmillan and the Illusion of the 'Special Relationship,'" in *Harold Macmillan: Aspects of a Political Life*, ed. Richard Aldous and Sabine Lee, 17, 19; John Dickie, *"Special" No More: Anglo-American Relations: Rhetoric and Reality*, 97; Harold Macmillan, *Riding the Storm, 1956–1959*, 199; When the two future leaders first met is unclear. Macmillan said Nov. 1942, Eisenhower 1943. Harold Macmillan, *Pointing the Way, 1959–1961*, 306; Dwight D. Eisenhower, *The White House Years: Waging Peace, 1956–1961*, 120.

3. Telegram, no. 309, Caccia to Foreign Office, Feb. 11, 1957, FO 371/126684, PRO; Shlaim, Jones, and Sainsbury, *British Foreign Secretaries*, 158; Macmillan, *Riding the Storm*, 240.

Eastern Department of the Foreign Office, wrote that Macmillan had been informed in his brief for the conference that "we will not be able to sell our case to the Americans in a single operation" when it came to Beijing.[4]

Indeed, when Eisenhower, Macmillan, Dulles, and British Foreign Secretary Selwyn Lloyd met at Bermuda in March, the Americans showed no willingness to reconsider their relations with the PRC. Both Eisenhower and Dulles noted the strong opposition in the United States to recognizing Beijing or allowing it into the United Nations. The president himself "felt that public opinion was more aroused about the casualties in Korea than about the far greater casualties in World War II." Dulles urged that Britain adopt the American position on nonrecognition and UN representation; he suggested that if Whitehall agreed to these two points, it would make it easier for Americans to accept London's desire to increase trade with the PRC. Macmillan said he might consider the secretary of state's proposal but soon was to reject it.[5]

If Britain and the United States remained divided over China, they found accord elsewhere. Given his nation's economy, Macmillan decided to cut the United Kingdom's conventional forces and, like Washington, place more emphasis on the nuclear deterrent. Britain's allies, including the United States, did not much care for Whitehall's decision, but Eisenhower agreed to give London sixty Thor missiles to add to its deterrent capabilities. Macmillan, meanwhile, got Eisenhower and Dulles to understand his country's position on the Middle East, which ultimately led to the "Eisenhower Doctrine" (under which Washington promised to extend military and economic aid to the Middle East and to use U.S. armed forces if necessary to protect any Middle Eastern nation from communist aggression). The Western leaders concurred that the meeting helped repair the damage to the relationship between their nations, Eisenhower commenting that Bermuda was "by far the most successful international conference that I have attended since the close of World War II." China, though, still remained an issue; no agreement had been reached on the question of the trade controls imposed against the PRC.[6] This subject would be the first of several to test the true success of Bermuda.

By the time Macmillan took office, Whitehall was under intense pressure to relax the controls on trade with Beijing. Led by the Labour Party, these in-

4. Telegram, no. 459, Caccia to Foreign Office, Feb. 26, 1957 and FO Minute by Mayall, Feb. 27, 1957, FO 371/127239, PRO.

5. Memorandum of conversation, Mar. 20, 1957, WHO-Office of the Staff Secretary: Records, 1952–1961, International Trips and Meetings Series, box 3, DDEL

6. Hoopes, *Devil and John Foster Dulles,* 410–11; Horne, *Harold Macmillan,* 2:27; Eisenhower, *Waging Peace,* 124; Macmillan, *Riding the Storm,* 259.

dividuals continued to argue that failure to act soon would allow other nations to capture more of the China market. They also increasingly attacked Whitehall for stalling rather than unilaterally eliminating the differential in trade with the communist bloc.[7] Macmillan knew that a decision was imperative. He wanted to avoid renewing tensions in his relationship with the United States, particularly over a sensitive issue such as trade with China. Still, he could not allow himself to continue to come under attack, especially when it was clear that the health of the U.K. economy remained tenuous. Caccia recommended that if the prime minister was going to act, 1957 was the year to do it. It was not an election year in the United States, and therefore such action would do less damage to the Eisenhower administration—and Anglo-American relations—than if Britain waited until 1958. Additionally, trade with the mainland was compatible with the containment strategy. In a 1958 letter to Dulles, the prime minister explained that the longer China was isolated from the West, the more likely it would join the Soviet bloc.[8] In short, like his predecessors, Macmillan contended that trade offered a means of driving wedges into the Sino-Soviet alliance and weakening the communist world.

As in 1956, the White House realized it had to make some concessions in hopes of maintaining as much of the embargo as possible. "The whole control system," wrote Clarence Randall, the head of the Council on Foreign Economic Policy, "is rapidly deteriorating because of wholesale evasion on the part of other nations with respect to th[e] differential." He added that this was "particularly true with Great Britain. Her economic situation is difficult, and she is reaching out insistently toward the more marginal markets." If the United States continued to refuse "to negotiate a narrowing of the China differential," it would "seriously damage the whole multilateral control organization, and might conceivably destroy it." Taking such warnings into account, the Eisenhower administration agreed in March to a liberalization of the trade controls with respect to China, but one that would maintain the differential. While the United States intended to sustain its position on the trade sanctions, it hoped that its demonstrated flexibility would appease Britain.[9]

7. For examples of the pressure Macmillan faced from Parliament to eliminate the differential, see *Hansard Parliamentary Debates,* 5th ser., vol. 563 (1956–57), cols. 670–72; vol. 564, cols. 902–3; vol. 568, cols. 26–27, 573–74, 1722–24, 1902–3; vol. 569, cols. 23–24.

8. Telegram, no. 310, Caccia to Foreign Office, Feb. 11, 1957, FO 371/126684; draft letter to Dulles from Macmillan, Mar. 17, 1958, FO 371/133369, PRO.

9. Memorandum to Parsons from Randall, Mar. 12, 1957, WHO-Office of the Staff Secretary: Records, 1952–1961, Subject Series, White House Subseries, box 5, DDEL.

The British, however, thought the White House had not gone far enough. The United Kingdom wanted not a smaller differential, but none at all. "It was becoming extremely difficult," Lloyd told Dulles, to justify the differential to the people of Britain and Parliament, who regarded "the Russians as their principal enemies rather than the Chinese." Like Dulles, he played "let's make a deal," suggesting that if the Americans acquiesced to the British on trade, Whitehall could more easily give in to the White House on Chinese representation.[10]

With the two sides far apart on the trade issue, the United States in April agreed to a meeting of a Consultative Group to discuss trade. It also proposed to relax further the controls by removing over two hundred items from the embargo, but this would still maintain a differential. In May, Lloyd rejected the proposal, saying it was "no good." Concerned, Dulles urged Eisenhower to tell Macmillan not to eliminate the differential. The president, who, as previously noted, saw more benefits than costs in relaxing the controls on trade, told his secretary of state that he agreed with London's position: "Communist China and Soviet Russia should be treated alike." Yet he still agreed to send a message to Macmillan, arguing that eliminating the differential would help China "build up the military potential which threatens us in this area and which we have the primary responsibility to resist." He pointed also to the opposition in Congress to the British position. Macmillan refused to budge. He responded that the U.S. offer did not go far enough. "I am very sorry to tell you that I shall have to stick to the line shared by that large number of countries, including the great majority in Europe, who want to bring the Russian and Chinese List together."[11]

Whitehall made its final decision at the end of May. At a cabinet meeting held on the twenty-ninth, Lloyd said that during 1956 and at the Bermuda Conference, Washington had received warnings that London could not maintain the differential much longer. He realized that eliminating it would anger Congress; he thus proposed that the Macmillan government say that while it was abolishing the differential, it would continue to cooperate in maintaining controls on trade with the Soviet Union and China. The cabinet concurred, adding that such an announcement would not do any lasting damage to Anglo-American relations. To wait any longer would increase dif-

10. Memorandum of conversation, Mar. 22, 1957, *FRUS, 1955–1957,* 10:434–36.
11. Circular telegram, no. CA 8615, Dulles to Certain Diplomatic Missions, Apr. 17, 1957; telegram, no. Dulte 6, Dulles to Department of State, May 3, 1957; telegram, no. 6179, Whitney to Department of State, May 14, 1957; memorandum to president from Dulles, May 16, 1957; telegram, no. 8070, Dulles to London, May 17, 1957; and letter to Macmillan from Eisenhower, May 21, 1957, *FRUS, 1955–1957,* 10:443–46, 450, 451–52, 455–57, 460–61.

ficulty with Parliament and British industry, and ongoing disagreement with the United States over particular cases was likely to prove more damaging in the long run to relations between the two allies. The same day, Macmillan informed Eisenhower of his government's decision: "I feel we cannot any longer maintain the existing differential between Russian and Chinese trade and we shall be making a statement to this effect in Parliament tomorrow."[12]

At the end of June, Ambassador Caccia reported that Britain's decision on trade with China represented "the first time since the Suez crisis" that it had "parted company from the United States in a sensitive area of policy." Even so, the reaction in the United States was relatively muted, possibly in part because of a statement given by Eisenhower at a press conference, which was designed to soothe public reaction to Britain's decision. Even the China bloc's reaction was relatively sedate. The bloc itself limited its retort to the form of a press statement and a full-page advertisement in the international edition of the *New York Times* opposing trade with China. Despite the relatively mild reaction, Caccia warned Whitehall, "We should beware of thinking that, because we have dealt successfully with the matter of China trade, we can move on with similar ease to the problem of the admission of the Peking Government to the United Nations."[13]

Caccia's warning was valid. In 1956 and again in 1957, Congress overwhelmingly declared its opposition to seating the PRC in the United Nations. Americans in general felt similarly, with an overwhelming majority against seeing China's entrance into the international body. Caccia felt that while the chances of the United States going through with its periodic threat to leave the UN if China were admitted were not as great as in the past, should the PRC be seated, Eisenhower's personal intervention would be required to mollify Congress's reaction.[14] And the American position at the Bermuda Conference had demonstrated no weakening of the U.S. position.

The White House continued to maintain that China's admission to the United Nations would have dire repercussions. Dulles explained in the middle of the year that if the PRC entered the UN, "it would appear as a striking

12. Minutes of Cabinet Meeting, C.C. 43 (57), May 29, 1957, CAB 128/31, PRO; letter to Eisenhower from Macmillan, May 29, 1957, *FRUS, 1955–1957*, 10:467–68.

13. Dispatch, no. 166, Caccia to Foreign Office, June 24, 1957, CAB 21/3275, PRO; letter to Eisenhower from Macmillan, June 12, 1957, AWF-International Series, box 23, DDEL; Dwight D. Eisenhower, *Public Papers of the Presidents of the United States: Dwight D. Eisenhower, 1953–1961, 1957*, 277–78; "China Trade Decision a 'Calculated Risk,'" *London Times*, June 1, 1957; Bachrack, *Committee of One Million*, 136.

14. *Congressional Quarterly Almanac*, 85th Cong., 1st sess., 1957, 611; Kusnitz, *Public Opinion and Foreign Policy*, 162; telegram, no. 459, Caccia to Foreign Office, Feb. 26, 1957, FO 371/127239, PRO.

Chinese Communist victory. Resistance to communism would be softened everywhere, morale in the only non-Communist nations of the Far East with significant military strength would suffer grievously and the penetration of Chinese Communist influence throughout the area would be immensely facilitated."[15]

In 1956, Britain voted for the yearly moratorium on discussion of the representation question but planned to demand a full hearing on the matter in return. But following Suez, and in light of American sensitivity to the subject of China's admission, Whitehall backtracked. In July 1957, Lloyd said that his government should soon make its position on representation public and argued in favor of continuing to support the United States. Furthermore, there was no longer a need to withhold Britain's support to obtain concessions on the embargo: "There is no longer reason to keep back from the Americans, for bargaining purposes, an official statement on our agreement again to support a 'moratorium' resolution at the next Session." A. C. Maby of the British embassy in Beijing added that he did not expect the PRC to respond angrily to London's position: China's reaction in 1956 was not very strong, Beijing still lacked support for its claim to Taiwan's seat, and the PRC showed little interest in being admitted. In September, the moratorium passed. As Maby had anticipated, China's response to the 1957 vote was mild.[16]

Significantly, the next month, Lloyd sent a memo to Dulles, saying that Britain would never, without prior agreement with the United States, seek or support China's representation in the United Nations.[17] Why the Macmillan government was prepared to commit itself to such an extent remains unclear. It is likely, however, that having achieved an end to the trade differential, London felt it could support the United States' position. Moreover, the Suez crisis, the ever-present Soviet threat, and China's mild reaction to Whitehall's support of the moratorium probably influenced Lloyd's memorandum. The British government clearly had decided to reject Anthony Eden's intention of challenging the United States on the admission of the PRC into the UN. Similarly, Macmillan proved highly cautious in his approaches to Washington when another crisis broke out over Quemoy and Matsu.

15. Circular telegram, no. CA-10548, Dulles to All American Diplomatic and Consular Posts, June 12, 1957, *Confidential U.S. State Department Central Files, China: Foreign Affairs, 1955–1959.*

16. Minutes of Cabinet Meeting, C.C. 57 (57), July 25, 1957, CAB 128/31; Circular telegram, no. 114, Commonwealth Relations Office to Commonwealth High Commissioners, Aug. 8, 1957; letter to Morland from Maby, Aug. 28, 1957; and telegram, no. 1496, Dixon to Foreign Office, Sept. 20, 1957, FO 371/127448, PRO; dispatch, no. 832, Martin to Department of State, Oct. 7, 1957, RG 59, Central Decimal File, 1955–1959, box 2609, NA.

17. Letter to Dulles from Lloyd, Oct. 25, 1957, *FRUS, 1955–1957,* 27:838.

Why Beijing decided to raise tensions in the Taiwan Strait beginning in late August 1958 is not completely clear. The available material, however, suggests several reasons. First, for nearly a decade, the United States had provided Taiwan and the Nationalist government of Chiang Kai-shek with large amounts of economic and military aid. In that time, Chiang had placed one-third of his army on the islands, conducted guerrilla operations against mainland China's coastline, and harassed Chinese shipping. To Mao, Chiang represented a thorn in the side that required removal. Wu Lengxi, a member of the CCP's Standing Committee, recalled that the Chinese leader justified his decision in part "to crack down on the Nationalist Army's frequent and reckless harassment along the Fujian coast across from Jinmen [Quemoy] and Mazu [Matsu]."[18]

Furthermore, reviewing 1957, Mao and his lieutenants concluded that communism was indeed superior to capitalism. The Soviet launching of *Sputnik* and the world's first intercontinental ballistic missile provided the proof. As Mao told the Supreme State Council in September 1958, "As far as the international situation is concerned, our view has always been optimistic, which can be summarized as the East Wind prevails over the West Wind."[19]

In addition, Mao wanted to increase support at home for his domestic policy. In 1958, the Chinese leader launched the Great Leap Forward, an economic program designed to propel China ahead of the Soviet Union and move it from socialism to communism. He urged all Chinese to work to "catch up" with the economic power of the United States. Promoting this effort required breaking down "the myth of American omnipotence by challenging the U.S. presence in the Taiwan Strait." As Mao declared in September, during the height of the crisis, "A tense situation can mobilize the population . . . and can therefore promote the Great Leap Forward in economic construction."[20]

Fourth, there was the widening rift between the Soviet Union and China. Soviet advances in missile and space technology led Soviet Premier Nikita Khrushchev to talk of his nation surpassing the West; however, this would be done economically and ideologically, not militarily. He thus spoke of "peaceful coexistence" with the West. In the nuclear age, war was something to be avoided. Mao, for his part, had, by the first offshore islands crisis, come to the conclusion that the United States did not want "peaceful coexistence." He also believed that a peaceful relationship with the West contradicted the argu-

18. Xiaobing Li, Jian Chen, and David L. Wilson, "Mao Zedong's Handling of the Taiwan Straits Crisis of 1958: Chinese Recollections and Documents," 209.

19. Ibid., 216.

20. Ibid., 271; Zhai, *Dragon, the Lion, and the Eagle*, 181.

ment that capitalism and communism were in a state of constant conflict. In short, according to Mao's doctor, Li Zhisui, the bombardment of the islands represented the Chinese leader's "challenge to Khrushchev's bid to reduce tensions between the Soviet Union and the United States."[21]

These differences between Beijing and Moscow were not new; as early as 1953, the Central Intelligence Agency had concluded that areas of disagreement existed between the two communist powers. But they had grown in the year or so prior to the outbreak of the second islands crisis. In 1956, Khrushchev denounced Josef Stalin; Mao regarded himself as "China's Stalin," and the Soviet leader's speech "forced Mao on the defensive." In early 1957, Chinese Premier Zhou Enlai had an "acrid exchange" with Khrushchev over the latter's "revisionist" policies, which supposedly led the Soviet leader to comment on Zhou's "bourgeois" background. In July 1958, Khrushchev and Mao held talks, during which the former attacked the Great Leap Forward and the Chinese leader's "bellicosity." At the same time, the Soviet leader offered to help set up nuclear installations in China, but with the catch that Russia's "finger [would] be on the nuclear button." Mao rejected the offer, declaring "we shall never be dictated to, by anyone." (The Soviet Union during 1958, however, did provide China with nuclear specialists, including two nuclear weapons designers.)[22]

The same month as Mao's meeting with Khrushchev, the United States and Britain sent military forces into Lebanon and Jordan, respectively, in response to a revolution in Iraq that toppled that nation's pro-Western government. Rather than respond militarily, the Kremlin, to Mao's anger, called for a summit and then for a meeting of the UN Security Council to deal with the crisis. The Chinese leader decided he had to show Moscow how communists should deal with the imperialist West. In so doing, he might also convince the Arabs to stand up for themselves.[23]

A variety of domestic and foreign policy interests played their part, therefore, in Mao's decision to begin bombarding the offshore islands in late August. The first offshore crisis had continued for eight months; this one lasted only two. But it raised many of the same issues between London and Washington as had the first one, especially the extent to which the latter in-

21. Li, *Private Life of Chairman Mao,* 270.

22. John Lewis Gaddis, *Russia, the Soviet Union, and the United States: An Interpretive History,* 222; Dick Wilson, *Zhou Enlai: A Biography,* 211–12; Han Suyin, *Eldest Son: Zhou Enlai and the Making of Modern China, 1898–1976,* 270; John Wilson Lewis and Xue Litai, *China Builds the Bomb,* 64.

23. Zhai, *Dragon, the Lion, and the Eagle,* 181; Xiaobing Li, "Making of Mao's Cold War: The Taiwan Straits Crises Revised," in *China and the United States,* ed. Xiaobing Li and Hongshan Li, 60.

tended to defend Quemoy and Matsu and whether such a commitment might mean another Korean-style conflict.

On July 17, Mao made the decision to shell Quemoy, but there were delays, and the first shot was not fired for another month. By that time, the Americans and British were aware that China was preparing for some kind of action. The British consul in Taiwan, Alan Veitch, reported that the siting of long-range guns on the mainland and troop concentrations opposite Quemoy had led Chiang to place his military forces on full combat readiness. U.S. naval forces in the region also were prepared for possible war.[24]

Responding to the growing tension, Eisenhower took the position that the islands should be abandoned, as he had in the first offshore crisis. Yet, as in the first crisis, he believed that forcing the Nationalists to give up the islands would cause severe repercussions. Compelling Chiang to abandon Quemoy and Matsu, he and Dulles felt, would signal other Asian nations that they had no hope of holding out against China and would destroy Taiwan's morale.[25]

On August 23, China began its bombardment of Quemoy and Matsu. Early on, it seemed Mao wanted to take the islands, if possible. He pointed out to his subordinates that the U.S.-Taiwan defense treaty "did not clearly indicate whether the U.S. defense perimeter included Jinmen and Mazu." He felt it was best to "wait and see what international response, especially American responses, there were to our shelling, and then we could decide on our next move." He strongly suggested if the United States did not want "to carry these two burdens on their backs," then he would take them.[26] This statement seems odd given that Mao had ended the first crisis just three years earlier partly out of fear that the Nationalists might agree to abandon them. In fact, as one scholar has noted, capturing the islands was not his primary goal. Mao never brought to bear the military power he needed—especially air power—to take the islands. Moreover, if the Nationalists left the islands, or if the communists captured them, "it would move the Civil War enemy much further (100 miles) from the mainland, making it harder to attack in the future."[27] Rather, Mao took a cautious approach. He wanted to raise tensions in the

24. Li, Chen, and Wilson, "Mao Zedong's Handling of the Taiwan Straits Crisis of 1958," 224–25 (notes 23–25); telegram, no. 65, Veitch to the Foreign Office, July 18, 1958, FO 371/133523, PRO.

25. Memoranda of conferences with the president, Aug. 12 and 14, 1958, AWF-DDE Diary Series, box 35, DDEL.

26. Li, Chen, and Wilson, "Mao Zedong's Handling of the Taiwan Straits Crisis of 1958," 209–10.

27. Thomas J. Christensen, *Useful Adversaries: Grand Strategy, Domestic Mobilization, and Sino-American Confrontation, 1947–1958,* 230–31.

strait but not to the point of provoking a Sino-American war or of forcing the KMT off Quemoy and Matsu.

As during the first offshore islands crisis, the United States' response was equivocal, designed to keep the Communists guessing. On the first day of the bombardment, Dulles, in a well-publicized letter to Representative Thomas Morgan (D-Pennsylvania), the acting chairman of the House Committee on Foreign Affairs, said that the interdependence of the islands and Taiwan had "increased" over the past four years. Any attempt to take the islands, he said, would constitute "a threat to the peace of the area." He left unclear to what extent the United States would commit itself; rather, Eisenhower would make that decision. Similarly, in a September 4 press conference, Dulles announced that if Beijing attempted to seize Quemoy and Matsu, the United States would regard it as a threat against Taiwan and the Far East in general. Alluding to the Formosa Resolution of 1955, Dulles said that "military dispositions have been made . . . so that a presidential determination, if made, would be followed by action both timely and effective."[28]

Chiang again wanted a clear commitment to the offshore islands. Two days after the publication of the letter to Morgan, the Taiwanese ambassador to the United States, Hollington Tong, pressed Acting Assistant Secretary of State for Far Eastern Affairs J. Graham Parsons for a clear statement of U.S. support.[29] The Eisenhower administration refused, for such a guarantee would undermine its flexibility. The same day as Tong's meeting with Parsons, the president met with several of his advisers, including Undersecretary of State Christian Herter. Eisenhower and Herter agreed that the United States had to avoid "a full commitment." In a racially charged comment, the president added, "The Orientals can be very devious; they would then call the tune . . . We should try to gain effect through a firm demeanor, but avoid making statements from which we might later back off." On August 27, however, he did order an aircraft carrier and four destroyers to the Taiwan Strait to beef up the U.S. naval presence in the region.[30]

Eisenhower also began to consider the nuclear option, though he clearly regarded it as a last resort. In an August 29 meeting, the president decided that if the Communists simply harassed the offshore islands, the United States would "try to stay out of the battle." But if the PRC tried to take the is-

28. Zhai, *Dragon, the Lion, and the Eagle,* 184. For Dulles's statement, see *Department of State Bulletin* (Sept. 22, 1958): 445–47.

29. Zhai, *Dragon, the Lion, and the Eagle,* 184–85.

30. Ibid., 186; memorandum of conference with the president, Aug. 25, 1958, AWF-DDE Diary Series, box 35, DDEL.

lands or Taiwan itself, then he would give serious consideration to using atomic weapons. At the same meeting, the administration decided to begin escorting Nationalist ships supplying the islands, though American vessels themselves would remain in international waters.[31]

At the end of the month, the U.S. ambassador to Taiwan, Everett F. Drumright, argued that, in his view, the Chinese planned to take the islands, unless they were stopped by the United States. "I believe," he said, "we should move ahead with preparations for localized retaliatory action designed to lift [the] interdiction of [Quemoy]." Drumright did not say if his proposal included tactical nuclear weapons. The White House had doubts that the situation was as serious as the ambassador suggested, or that it would reach a point where the use of atomic weapons might require serious consideration. Intelligence reports estimated that the Communists had no intention of attacking the islands.[32] Unquestionably, the Eisenhower administration—like its counterpart in Beijing—wanted to see how the situation developed before acting.

As with the first Quemoy-Matsu crisis, the British wanted a peaceful resolution. Once again, there was strong domestic opposition to the possibility of another Korea. U.S. Ambassador to Britain Jock Whitney reported that in the event of an American response, "even with conventional weapons," to a Communist assault, "we should presumably expect very strong criticism from [the] UK public, particularly Labour and Liberal elements. Embassy contacts furthermore estimate that even Conservatives might well find it difficult to support US military action, in view of [the] expected adverse general reaction in [the] UK." Whitney added that the "delicate British position in Hong Kong" further limited Macmillan's flexibility. Finally, he said, in light of the Suez crisis, "some Tories" might find it difficult to support American military action. Should the United States use nuclear weapons, the "public reaction in [the] UK would be much more adverse."[33]

Aside from public opinion in his own country, Macmillan could not ignore that throughout the Commonwealth. He told Dulles that India, Malaya, Ceylon, and Ghana would oppose "any action. I do not attach overwhelming importance to that, because they are always neutralist, but they have a considerable influence on Asiatic opinion at least." Australia "will be fearful

31. Memorandum of conference with the president, Aug. 29, 1958, AWF-DDE Diary Series, box 35, DDEL.

32. Telegram, no. 260, Drumright to Secretary of State, Aug. 30, 1958, AWF-International Series, box 1; Special Watch Report of the Intelligence Advisory Committee, no. 421-A, Aug. 29, 1958, AWF-Intelligence Series, box 11, DDEL; memorandum of conversation, Aug. 25, 1958.

33. Telegram, no. 1230, Whitney to Secretary of State, Aug. 29, 1958, AWF-International Series, box 11, DDEL.

of trouble which might involve them" and was "just approaching an election"; New Zealand "will tend to favour words rather than actions. South Africa will keep aloof."[34]

Yet Macmillan did not want to undermine the relationship with the United States he had worked so hard to rebuild. In a "Dear Friend" letter to Eisenhower, the prime minister stated that his "overriding concern is that our countries should not be divided or appear to be divided." But "if the worst should happen," he realized he might need to steer British public opinion "at very short notice." To prepare for that, he asked Dulles and Eisenhower how they viewed the situation.[35]

Dulles responded the next day. The United States preferred that Chiang remove his troops from the islands, but past attempts to convince the Nationalist leader to do so had failed. Washington refused to use coercion for fear of undermining the KMT government. The same outcome could be expected if the Chinese took the islands. Furthermore, Dulles said, if Chiang lost power, communism would take hold in Taiwan, thereby threatening the whole of Southeast Asia, the Western Pacific, Australia, and New Zealand. Finally, using words that greatly concerned Macmillan, Dulles noted:

> There is also a question as to whether if we did intervene we could do so effectively without at least some use of atomic weapons; I hope no more than small air bursts without fallout. That is of course an unpleasant prospect but one I think we must face up to because our entire military establishment assumes more and more that the use of nuclear weapons will become normal in the event of hostilities.

If the United States did not use nuclear weapons, "then we face a very grave situation indeed in the face of the massive manpower of the Sino-Soviet bloc." Dulles said that he and Eisenhower hoped that Macmillan would try to guide the British public to support the United States, even should the worst occur.[36]

The president remained reluctant to use atomic weapons, even small ones. In a September 4 meeting with Dulles and other advisers, Eisenhower argued that even if the United States limited a nuclear response to air bursts, Communist retaliation "might well be against Taiwan itself and beyond rather than directed simply at Quemoy." Yet the White House wanted to keep the Communists guessing in the hope of deterring an attack against the islands.

34. Letter to Dulles from Macmillan, undated, *FRUS, 1958–1960,* 19:139.
35. Macmillan, *Riding the Storm,* 543–44; letter to Eisenhower from Macmillan, Sept. 3, 1958, AWF-International Series, box 24, DDEL.
36. Letter to Macmillan from Dulles, Sept. 4, 1958, Papers of John Foster Dulles, Subject Series, box 11, DDEL; Macmillan, *Riding the Storm,* 546.

Consequently, the president approved the statement given by Dulles later that day. The secretary of state explained to Macmillan the purposeful ambiguity of his message, noting that it "does not involve any final commitment but does go far to indicate that the President would probably act if there were an effort to take Quemoy and Matsu." Macmillan, still concerned, made one more attempt, on September 5, to convince the United States to persuade Chiang to abandon the islands. The next day Eisenhower rejected the prime minister's plea; rather, he pointed to a statement Zhou Enlai had issued that day, calling for a resumption of the Geneva talks. (Mao had broken the talks off in January 1958 after the U.S. representative, U. Alexis Johnson, was reassigned and Washington failed to name someone of ambassadorial level to replace him.) The United States replied by indicating its willingness to resume the ambassadorial discussions, now to be held at Warsaw. The president told Macmillan that he hoped Zhou's offer "means that the immediate crisis will become less acute, at least temporarily."[37]

It seems that questionable Soviet support played a hand in Zhou's statement. On September 7, Khrushchev issued a public warning that any attack upon China would be regarded as an attack on the Soviet Union itself; two weeks later, the Kremlin announced that any nuclear bombardment of the PRC would lead to a similar response by Russia against the United States. There is strong reason to believe that the Soviets were not just blowing smoke. In mid-September, Khrushchev told Chinese Ambassador to the Soviet Union Liu Xiao that he hoped China would continue with its "decisive" action against the islands and Taiwan. Furthermore, in late September, the Central Committee of the Communist Party of the Soviet Union (CCPSU) sent a letter to the Central Committee of the CCP, declaring that if the United States used tactical nuclear weapons against China, Russia would not do anything. But if Washington began using thermonuclear weapons, then the Kremlin would involve itself.[38] In sum, rather than showing a lack of support for the Chinese, the Soviets were actually providing substantial backing to their allies.

37. Memorandum to Dulles from Boster, Sept. 5, 1958, Papers of John Foster Dulles, Special Assistants Chronological Series, box 1; letter to Dulles from Macmillan, Sept. 5, 1958, and telegram, no. 2532, Dulles to London, Sept. 6, 1958, AWF-International Series, box 24; memorandum of conversation, Sept. 4, 1958, Papers of John Foster Dulles, General Correspondence and Memoranda Series, box 1, DDEL; memorandum of conference with the president, Sept. 4, 1958, *FRUS, 1958–1960,* 19:130–31; Tillman Durdin, "Red China Spurns U.S. Negotiator," *New York Times,* Apr. 13, 1958.

38. Mark Kramer, "The Soviet Foreign Ministry Appraisal of Sino-Soviet Relations on the Eve of the Split," 174–75; Vladislav Zubok, "Khrushchev's Nuclear Promise to Beijing during the 1958 Crisis," 219, 226–27.

Mao and his subordinates saw things differently. The Soviets' hardened stance came *after* Zhou's offer to resume the ambassadorial talks. In short, felt Beijing, the Kremlin came to its defense "only when it was clear that there was no possibility that a nuclear war would break out and no need for the Soviet Union to support China with nuclear weapons." Additionally, the CCPSU offered assistance *only* if the United States used thermonuclear weapons against the PRC; Moscow would do nothing to prevent the carnage that might ensue if Washington limited itself to conventional or tactical atomic weapons. Finally, in light of Khrushchev's late July meeting with Mao, Beijing probably concluded that even if the Eisenhower administration used thermonuclear weapons against China, the Soviets would be the ones to determine when, where, and how to use their atomic response. Hence, it did not matter what offers Khrushchev made or what position he took; Mao considered the Soviets unreliable.[39]

While doubting Soviet support, the Chinese had to consider Dulles's September 4 statement, as well as Nationalist victories in battles against communist aircraft. In the first offshore islands crisis, the United States forced Taiwan to abandon the Tachen islands, and Mao likely hoped Washington could induce Chiang to pull back again. This time, however, the Eisenhower administration stood firm. It sent not only an aircraft carrier and destroyers to the region, but also a squadron of fighter aircraft. Meanwhile, its Nationalist ally bloodied the nose of the Chinese air force, shooting down seven Communist planes and losing none of its own in clashes on August 25 and September 8. The PRC leader admitted that he had misjudged the rapidity with which Taiwan might ask for help from the Americans, as well as the speed and strength of the U.S. response. On September 5, he told China's Supreme State Conference that he "simply had not anticipated how roiled and turbulent the world would become" if the PRC began firing upon the islands. The crisis for Mao posed benefits, both abroad and at home, but he clearly was unwilling to go the distance, particularly when the Americans' position remained unclear and when he could not trust his closest ally. Caution remained the keyword.[40]

39. Melvin Gurtov and Byong-Moo Hwang, *China under Threat: The Politics of Strategy and Diplomacy,* 90, 91.

40. Kramer, "The Soviet Foreign Ministry Appraisal of Sino-Soviet Relations on the Eve of the Split," 174. For the buildup of U.S. forces, see K.W. Kenworthy, "Eisenhower Sees Increased Need to Guard Quemoy," *New York Times,* Aug. 31, 1958, and Jack Raymond, "More U.S. Planes Sent to Far East to Assist Taiwan," *New York Times,* Aug. 31, 1958. For information on the air battles, see "Reds Lose Two Jets in Quemoy Clash; Shelling Goes On," *New York Times,* Aug. 26, 1958; "Quemoy Garrison Supplied under U.S. Fleet's Escort; Reds Charge an Intrusion," *New York Times,* Sept. 8, 1958; and Stolper, *China, Taiwan, and the Offshore Islands,* 127.

Though the Chinese call for a resumption of the ambassadorial talks did not end the bombardment of the islands, it did offer the United States a way of extricating itself from the situation. And Eisenhower wanted out. Aside from the fact that he did not want war, his blustering had roused public opinion: letters to the State Department were running 80 percent against the White House. In a meeting with Secretary of Defense Neil McElroy—who had replaced Charles Wilson in October 1957—and presidential aide Andrew Goodpaster, Eisenhower argued that the islands were militarily untenable and "should be vacated." He recognized the difficulties in getting Chiang off of them, but he hoped for some kind of negotiated agreement. Yet a quick settlement seemed unlikely. Despite the resumption of the talks at Warsaw, the United States and China quarreled over achieving a cease-fire in the Taiwan Strait, with Chinese Ambassador Wang Bingnan again contending that the "liberation" of the islands was an "internal affair."[41] Without a cease-fire or a further decline of tensions, the United States could not expect Taiwan to agree to abandon the islands or even to reduce its forces on them.

Although Macmillan stood by the Eisenhower administration, the Labour Party again turned up the pressure on him. On September 15, Hugh Gaitskell, the party's leader, wrote the prime minister, urging him to make clear to Eisenhower that if the United States got into a war over the islands, he could not expect British support. The prime minister retorted that he wanted a peaceful resolution to the crisis but was not about to create another schism with the United States. He explained that it would play into the hands of the Communists if Britain allowed itself "to take public attitudes on difficulties which we hoped jointly to overcome." Additionally, he pointed out that Lloyd was already on his way to Washington to discuss the matter with U.S. officials.[42]

Lloyd spent over a week in the United States, holding talks with Eisenhower and Dulles. The White House still had not discounted the possible use of nuclear arms. On September 16, Dulles told the foreign secretary that if China attacked the islands, the United States would first respond with conventional arms, followed by atomic weapons, if necessary. Eisenhower took a slightly different stand when Lloyd met him a few days later. If it came to

---

41. Memorandum of conference with the president, Sept. 11, 1958, AWF-DDE Diary Series, box 26, DDEL; telegram, no. 435, Beam to Department of State, Sept. 18, 1958, *FRUS, 1958–1960,* 19:209–16; George C. Eliades, "Once More unto the Breach: Eisenhower, Dulles, and Public Opinion during the Offshore Islands Crisis of 1958," 357; Yi Sun, "John Foster Dulles and the 1958 Taiwan Strait Crisis," in *China and the United States,* ed. Xiaobing Li and Hongshan Li, 84.

42. Letters to Macmillan from Gaitskell, Sept. 15, 1958, and to Gaitskell from Macmillan, Sept. 15, 1958, PREM 11/2300, PRO.

using nuclear weapons, "it would have to be an all-out effort rather than a local effort." The president thus was counting out the use of atomic weapons in the immediate area to defend the islands. Eisenhower's stance pleased Lloyd, who reported back to a relieved Macmillan.[43]

The reduction of the tensions in the Taiwan Strait, combined with the Eisenhower administration's desire to avoid war with China, led the White House to again seek a way to persuade Chiang to reduce his troop strength on the islands. American officials regarded the large presence as a military liability. If the KMT decreased the number of soldiers on Quemoy and Matsu, or pulled them off altogether, it would remove the islands as a potential source of conflict between Beijing and Taipei and increase international support for the Taiwanese government. Under pressure from the administration, Chiang agreed on September 29 that he would not use the islands as staging grounds for an attack against the mainland. The following day, Dulles declared at a press conference that if a "reasonably dependable" cease-fire were achieved, "I think it would be foolish to keep these forces on these islands." His statement infuriated Chiang; despite Dulles's attempts to convince the Nationalist leader that the statement did not represent a change of U.S. policy, Chiang refused to reduce the number of soldiers on Quemoy and Matsu.[44]

Dulles's statement also had an effect upon Beijing. One of the PRC's fears was that the United States wanted to achieve a "two Chinas" solution to the ongoing China-Taiwan conflict. In the first offshore islands crisis, Mao had worried that the United States might force Chiang off the offshore islands, thus cutting the link between Taiwan and the mainland. The Chinese leader and his subordinates believed that Dulles's statement represented a new attempt at such a settlement. According to Wu, on October 3 and 4, the Chinese Politburo's Standing Committee met to discuss the matter. The committee concluded that Dulles intended to achieve a "two Chinas" solution by getting the Nationalists off the islands. "Mao asked us," said Wu,

> about the proposal of leaving Jinmen and Mazu in the hands of Jiang Jeishi [Chiang Kai-shek]. The advantage of this policy was that we could maintain contact with the Nationalists through this channel since these islands were very

43. Memorandum of conversation, Sept. 21, 1958, *FRUS, 1958–1960,* 19:249–52; telegram, no. 1071, Dixon to Foreign Office, Sept. 21, 1958, FO 371/133532, PRO; Macmillan, *Riding the Storm,* 554–55; Zhai, *Dragon, the Lion, and the Eagle,* p. 193.

44. Telegram, no. 290, Dulles to Taipei, Oct. 1, 1958, *FRUS, 1958–1960,* 19:315–16; Dispatch, no. 172, Drumright to Department of State, Oct. 6, 1958, RG 59, Records of the Policy Planning Staff, 1957–1961, box 135, NA; *Department of State Bulletin* (Oct. 20, 1958): 602; Zhai, *Dragon, the Lion, and the Eagle,* 200; J. H. Kalicki, *The Pattern of Sino-American Crises: Political-Military Interactions in the 1950s,* 196.

close to the mainland. Whenever necessary, we could shell the Nationalists. Whenever we needed tension, we could pull the noose tighter. Whenever we wanted a relaxation, we could give the noose more slack.

Additionally, said the Chinese leader, the islands provided a "means to deal with the Americans." If the PRC took over Quemoy and Matsu, or if Chiang abandoned them, "we would lose a reliable means by which we can deal with the Americans and Jiang." Wu stated that "all the participants at the meeting agreed with Chairman Mao's proposal" to allow the Nationalists to stay on Quemoy and Matsu. Accordingly, on October 6, Chinese Defense Minister Peng Dehuai, citing the September 30 news conference, announced that the siege of the islands would end if the United States stopped convoying Nationalist ships.[45]

Aside from preventing a "two Chinas" settlement, China believed that ending the crisis might drive a wedge between the United States and Taiwan. In this, the PRC proved somewhat successful. A week after Beijing's announcement, the United States ceased its convoying operations, to the chagrin of the KMT government. Later that month Dulles traveled to Taiwan, hoping to convince Chiang to take measures designed to prevent a resurgence of tensions. While not demanding that the Nationalist leader abandon the islands, he did want Chiang to reduce the number of troops he had stationed on them and, more important, to agree to a renunciation of force. In his discussions, he explained his reasoning on the latter point. Despite the lack of armistices in divided countries such as Vietnam and Korea, both sides acquiesced to the situation as it stood. West Germany, for its part, announced in October 1954 that it would never use force to seek the reunification of Germany. To agree to a renunciation of force, stated Dulles, "does not involve a 'two China' policy any more than there are 'two Korea', 'two Vietnam' or 'two Germany' policies."[46]

Dulles achieved his goal. In the official communiqué, issued October 23, the two nations reaffirmed their "solidarity" in the face of the Communist threat. Furthermore, Chiang agreed that the "principal means" for achieving the reunification of China had to be peaceful. (Therefore, for the first time, the Nationalist president officially acknowledged he had no hope of forcefully retaking the mainland.) Finally, the KMT leader agreed to a reduction in the number of troops on the islands. When he returned home, Dulles re-

45. Li, Chen, and Wilson, "Mao Zedong's Handling of the Taiwan Straits Crisis of 1958," 212–13; Chang, *Friends and Enemies*, 197.

46. Memorandum of conversation by Dulles, Oct. 29, 1958, *FRUS, 1958–1960,* 19:468–69; Zhai, *Dragon, the Lion, and the Eagle,* 201–2; Hoopes, *Devil and John Foster Dulles,* 453–56.

ported that he felt Chiang's new stance eased the recurring problem of Quemoy and Matsu. The question remained where the PRC stood, but if Beijing stopped its bombardments, the possibility of getting Chiang to remove more troops from the islands or even demilitarize them would increase.[47]

The communiqué represented achievements for Beijing on two grounds. First, the United States was putting additional reins on Chiang, which might curtail Nationalist harassment of China. Second, there was no evidence that the Taiwanese leader intended to or was asked to abandon Quemoy and Matsu. With these two considerations in mind, Beijing announced on October 25 its decision to bombard the islands only on odd-numbered days, a policy it continued for another twenty years.[48]

After two months of tension, the second offshore islands crisis came to an end. This one raised many of the same issues and problems as the first crisis. The United States remained firmly wedded to Chiang, unwilling to force him off Quemoy and Matsu but just as unwilling to go to war over them. Britain strongly resisted any action that might mean another Korea. It faced strong pressure, not just from its own public but from the Commonwealth, not to support a conflict over the islands. If there was one significant difference, it was the current prime minister's refusal to challenge the Americans. During the 1954–1955 crisis, Eden had stalled on Operation Oracle because of the White House's decision to sign a defense treaty with Taiwan; he had also exhorted Washington to get Chiang to evacuate the islands. Macmillan easily could have adopted a similar stance, particularly with regard to trying to get the Eisenhower administration to force Chiang off Quemoy and Matsu. He did not. As he suggested to Gaitskell, he was not going to create another schism with his closest ally, especially after having worked so hard to repair the damage to the Anglo-American alliance. He had no intention of destroying the success he felt had been achieved at Bermuda.

Macmillan's refusal to put pressure on the United States also might have had an impact upon Taiwan. During the first crisis in the Taiwan Strait, Chiang was clearly aware of Anglo-American differences and drew the conclusion that the lack of an American commitment to defend the islands was

---

47. "Report by the Secretary of State on His Recent Visit to Taiwan," NSC Meeting, Oct. 30, 1958, AWF-NSC Series, box 10, DDEL; "Joint Statement by Dulles and Chiang," *New York Times,* Oct. 24, 1958; Zhai, *Dragon, the Lion, and the Eagle,* 203; Zhang, *Deterrence and Strategic Culture,* 264. It is important to note that "principal means" did not rule out the use of force. Indeed, as Ambassador Drumright explained to the State Department, the "GRC has interpreted this reformulation of its mission as subordinating, but not ruling out, the use of military force in recovery of the mainland." Telegram, no. 918, Drumright to Secretary of State, Feb. 11, 1959, *FRUS,* 1958–1960, 19:526.

48. Stolper, *China, Taiwan, and the Offshore Islands,* 119.

the work of Britain. He made no such accusations in 1958. It was true that he now had a mutual defense treaty. He also might have realized from past and present experience that the United States had no intention of making a commitment to Quemoy and Matsu. Yet it is notable that this time Chiang made no accusations regarding arm-twisting by London, possibly because he noted Macmillan's unwillingness to take on Washington.

Interestingly, though not surprisingly, it seems that China hoped to split the Anglo-American alliance during the crisis. Mao recognized the differences that had occurred between the United States and Britain during the Suez affair. He wrote in January 1957, "The U.S. is trying to manoeuvre Britain out of the Middle East. . . . The two camps of imperialism are fighting for colonies. . . . We can make use of their contradictions to accomplish our ends." He also seemed to realize that at least some portions of the government in London had serious concerns about where the islands crisis might lead, noting on September 8 that "Britain is a vacillating element." Comparing the reaction in 1956 to the current political climate in the United Kingdom, he probably concluded that by taking a less harsh tone with the British he could accomplish another White House–Whitehall split. Indeed, on August 18, Mao told Peng, "[We are] preparing to shell Jinmen, dealing with [Chiang Kai-shek] directly and the Americans indirectly. Therefore, do not conduct military maneuvers in Guangdong and Shengzhen, so that the British would not be scared."[49] By not provoking Whitehall, Mao may have believed that he could create new divisions between a Britain that wanted to avoid war and a United States that was threatening possible nuclear action. If this was his intention, he failed.

If the Anglo-American alliance held firm during the second offshore islands crisis, the same cannot be said about that of the Soviet Union and China. Ironically, according to archival information from Moscow, Zhou's offer to resume the talks on September 6 angered Khrushchev who, in light of subsequent events, stood behind his ally. Yet the Soviet leader waited until after the tensions in the strait had begun to calm before he hardened his position, thereby angering a Chinese government that already doubted his reliability. Indeed, it is possible that the Soviet leader purposely stalled until September 7 to take a firmer stance so that he could get the best of both worlds: maintain the Sino-Soviet alliance but avoid the possibility of war. If this is the case, Beijing viewed his offers of support as too little, too late. Afterward, the anger and differences between the two countries grew; by mid-1959, the polemics

49. Yitzhak Shichor, *The Middle East in China's Foreign Policy, 1949–1977*, 70–71; Li, Chen, and Wilson, "Mao Zedong's Handling of the Taiwan Straits Crisis of 1958," 216, 220.

between them had reached the point that the United States no longer considered the Chinese government a Soviet satellite. By the end of 1960, angered with the PRC, the Soviet Union had withdrawn all of its technical experts from China.[50]

Anglo-American relations concerning the PRC were far quieter during 1959 and 1960 than were those between Beijing and Moscow. The United Kingdom supported the United States on Chinese representation, though by 1960 it had begun to question how much longer the moratorium might survive. The trade embargo, meanwhile, had become almost a nonissue.

In both 1958 and 1959, Britain supported the moratorium. In the latter year, the White House raised some concerns about India putting the representation issue on the UN agenda and asked Whitehall to intervene. London refused, on the grounds that it would anger the Indian government and create unwanted tensions in British-Indian relations. The United States dropped the matter, and the moratorium passed.[51]

The 1960 session, though, raised questions in London about the viability of the moratorium. In April, Caccia warned D. F. MacDermot, the superintending undersecretary of the Foreign Office's Far Eastern Department, that because 1960 was an election year in the United States, it was not a good time to raise the subject of Chinese representation. As long as the moratorium was not in danger, he argued, it was best not to oppose Washington. Macmillan held a similar view. But in a talk with Secretary of State Herter—who had replaced a terminally ill Dulles in 1959—the prime minister cautioned, "Some day our two governments would be faced with this problem."[52]

Macmillan no doubt had in mind the likely request from a number of newly independent African countries for admission to the United Nations. In February, Francis Galbraith, the first secretary of the U.S. Embassy in London, explained to Deputy Assistant Secretary of State for Far Eastern Affairs John Steeves,

> With the possible erosion of our position in the UN on Chinese representation as a result of new African states coming into the UN this year and later on,

50. Kramer, "The Soviet Foreign Ministry Appraisal of Sino-Soviet Relations on the Eve of the Split," 174–75; Gaddis, *Russia, the Soviet Union, and the United States,* 222; Lewis and Xue, *China Builds the Bomb,* 72.

51. FO Minute by Millar, Feb. 16, 1959 and letter to Twist from Dalton, Mar. 13, 1959, FO 371/141365; letter to Trench from Storar, June 4, 1959, and telegram, no. 178 Saving, Beeley to Foreign Office, July 15, 1959, FO 371/141366; FO Minute by Dalton, July 31, 1959 and telegram, no. 487, Dixon to Foreign Office, Sept. 22, 1959, FO 371/141367, PRO.

52. Letter to MacDermot from Caccia, Apr. 2, 1960, FO 371/150409, PRO; memorandum of conversation, Mar. 28, 1960, Papers of Christian A. Herter, box 8, DDEL.

the Foreign Office appears to be, so far, both passive and pessimistic. This is perhaps one of the main reasons for what I gather is their view that the moratorium, while probably safe this year and perhaps somewhat longer, cannot be held indefinitely.[53]

On October 8, the General Assembly once again voted in favor of postponement. To London, however, the moratorium looked to be in trouble, and it seemed new tactics might be required the following year. On October 11, the new foreign secretary, Lord Home—Macmillan in 1960 had moved Lloyd to the Exchequer and named Alec Douglas-Home to replace him—told Whitney that "there was no hope" of maintaining the moratorium again in 1961; many of the new UN members had abstained in the October 8 vote "only because they were new members and were feeling their way" and "that there was no doubt that they would vote next year and against the moratorium." Herter was less certain that new tactics were required, but he informed Home that the United States would consider the matter.[54] It would be up to the new American administration, though, to make any final determination on how to approach the representation question.

Looking back at the 1960 UN session, Michael Stewart, the British chargé d'affaires in Beijing, informed Home, "[L]ast October for the first time since the 'moratorium' procedure for the Chinese seat at the United Nations was introduced we received a protest against our vote." (Actually, this was not the case; in 1954, Zhou Enlai had indicated that one of the reasons the PRC refused to an exchange of ambassadors with Britain was because of the latter's approval of the moratorium.) Yet Whitehall's support for postponement did not greatly impair Sino-British relations. Stewart added, "Our so-called subservience to the United States was tempered by recurring bursts of anti-Americanism" in Parliament and the U.K. press. Beijing took notice of opposition to America's China policy in a December 1960 debate in Parliament as well as the publicity given to a visit to the PRC by British Field Marshal Bernard Montgomery. Mao and his subordinates hoped that these events suggested not only a change in London's stance toward China, but also a split in the Anglo-American alliance over policy toward Beijing. "Short, therefore, of some offensive act by Her Majesty's Government which requires immediate response," concluded the chargé, "[the Chinese] no doubt calculate that they can best serve their own interests by leaving us alone."[55]

53. Letter to Steeves from Galbraith, Feb. 15, 1960, RG 59, Central Decimal File, 1960–1963, box 470, NA.

54. Telegram, no. 1043, Dean to Foreign Office, Oct. 8, 1960, FO 371/150526, PRO; telegrams, no. 1736, Whitney to Secretary of State, Oct. 11, 1960 and no. 3750, Herter to London, Nov. 2, 1960, RG 59, Central Decimal File, 1960–1963, box 473, NA.

55. Dispatch, no. 16, Stewart to Foreign Office, Jan. 28, 1961, FO 371/158384, PRO.

With Anglo-Chinese relations on a good footing, trade relations between them remained healthy. And the United Kingdom needed that trade. During the first half of 1957, Britain's economy remained unstable, culminating in the middle of the year with a run on the nation's gold reserves. But by early 1959, following the passage of a new budget, the country's economy had begun to recover. The prosperity that ensued played a major part in Macmillan's decision to call elections that year and in his successful bid for the prime ministership.[56]

Yet Britain's financial difficulties during the Suez crisis and the run on the gold reserves the following year demonstrated the fragility of the country's economic health. Expanding trade remained vital to Britain. In July 1959, Chen Ming of the Chinese Ministry of Foreign Trade told K. G. Ritchie of the British mission in Beijing that China saw no reason why trade between the two nations could not continue to develop. The Chinese vice minister of foreign trade, Lu Xuzhang, similarly explained to Stewart that he was anxious for an expansion of commerce. The problem, said the vice minister, was the economic embargo against the PRC, though he avoided mentioning details. Despite the vice minister's comment, Stewart reported in early 1961 that trade between the two nations had increased 50 percent between 1959 and 1960.[57]

While Britain was determined to increase trade, the United States was just as determined to maintain its embargo. In March 1960, Herter told Commerce Secretary Frederick Mueller that it was vital to kill a study being conducted by Warren Magnuson (D-Washington), the chairman of the Senate Commerce Committee, on developing trade with China, because "if word got out" about it, "it might frighten some of our friends in the Far East." It seems that Herter succeeded, as there is no record of publication of the report. Indeed, the Eisenhower administration refused to alter its hard-line stance toward China in any respect. The talks in Warsaw remained bogged down over the release of American prisoners and the renunciation of force in the PRC's effort to "liberate" Taiwan. Eisenhower was very upset with the lack of progress. In light of Beijing's attitude, he explained to Prime Minister Nobusuke Kishi of Japan in January 1960, "there is no need to consider a change in United States policy."[58]

Desirous to maintain strong Anglo-American relations and to avoid another Suez, Harold Macmillan, like Churchill, sought to avoid difficulties

56. Horne, *Harold Macmillan,* 2:63–64, 142–43, 152; John Turner, *Macmillan,* 252.

57. Letters to Mocatta from Ritchie, July 15, 1959, and to Dalton from Stewart, Nov. 21, 1959, FO 371/141287; dispatch, no. 16, Stewart to Foreign Office, Jan. 28, 1961.

58. Memoranda of telephone conversations, Feb. 19 and Mar. 11, 1960, Papers of Christian A. Herter, box 12, and memorandum of conversation, Jan. 19, 1960, AWF-DDE Diary Series, box 47, DDEL.

with the United States. He refused to challenge the United States over Chinese representation, though he expressed his concern in 1960 that the moratorium might not last much longer. Realizing he had to act on the question of trade with China, he took the advice of his subordinates to make a decision in 1957 to avoid getting dragged into the 1958 U.S. electoral climate. During the second Quemoy-Matsu crisis, he demonstrated his concerns for Commonwealth opinion and the possibility that the tensions in the Taiwan Strait could turn into full-scale combat; yet he made clear his concerns in such a way as to avoid any serious or open dispute with Washington over the two islands. Macmillan had help in that the United States needed Britain's support around the world and also wanted to prevent another rift in the Anglo-American alliance. A schism did occur during the period 1957 to 1960, but it was not between Washington and London; rather, it was between Moscow and Beijing.

In retrospect, the Bermuda Conference was a success. Both the United States and Britain still had matters with China to settle, such as U.S. prisoners incarcerated in the PRC and Britain's desire for full diplomatic relations. But the two allies had successfully tackled issues that could have erupted into another Anglo-American split. Macmillan's desire to prevent another schism, combined with new tensions in Europe, would continue to guide him in his relations with the new administration of John F. Kennedy.

6

WINDS OF CHANGE? 1961–1963

When Harold Macmillan became prime minister, he confronted an administration in Washington that strongly resisted changes in its own or the U.K.'s China policy. The election of John F. Kennedy to the presidency, though, inspired hope in Whitehall that the U.S. stance toward the People's Republic might shift to one more in line with that of Britain. The hoped-for changes did not occur. Macmillan found himself dealing with the same concerns he had faced with the Eisenhower administration. On the one hand was his desire to avoid another Anglo-American rift, increased all the more by tensions in Europe over Berlin. On the other was his awareness of the United Kingdom's need for trade and its intention to avoid getting dragged into another Korea, the latter of which seemed a possibility during another crisis in the Taiwan Strait. Indeed, the only topic on which the two allies wholeheartedly agreed was the necessity of preventing Beijing from obtaining nuclear weapons. The prime minister successfully walked the tightrope, but not without some difficulty.

Prime Minister Macmillan and his ambassador to the United States, Harold Caccia, had high hopes following the election of John F. Kennedy to the presidency. Macmillan had personally known Eisenhower but not the new American head of state. He wished to develop a close working relationship with the president-elect. In December 1960, he sent a letter to Kennedy, stating that he considered it vital for the two nations to remain vigilant against the communist threat. He also indicated his longing—which he had held since at least 1957—to achieve a ban on nuclear testing.[1]

Macmillan's position on China was less clear than those on containment and atomic testing. Shortly after the U.S. elections, the prime minister wrote his foreign secretary, Lord Home,

> As you know, I have been for some time thinking how we would handle the new American President if it should be Kennedy. . . . With President Eisenhower we have a long comradeship covering nearly twenty years of war and peace. We therefore could appeal to memories. With this new and young President we

---

1. Macmillan, *Pointing the Way,* 306, 309–12.

have nothing of the kind to draw on. We must therefore, I think, make our contacts in the realm of ideas. I must somehow convince him that I am worth consulting not as an old friend (as Eisenhower felt) but as a man who, although of advancing years, has young and fresh thoughts.[2]

Whether these "young and fresh thoughts" included a new American approach toward the PRC, Macmillan did not say. But Caccia certainly was thinking along these lines. As early as January 1960, the ambassador had explained to Home that 1961 would mark the beginning of a new administration, one that might be willing to make some fresh moves in terms of U.S. policy toward China; those in Washington who opposed changes were, if not weakening, less vocal. In particular, the 1958 departure of Republican Senator William Knowland of California, a staunch opponent of the PRC who gave up his seat to run for the governorship of California, left those antagonistic to an alteration in America's China policy without one of their leading proponents.[3]

After Kennedy's election, Caccia was even more hopeful of changes in U.S. China policy. Noting that the president-elect did not commit himself to a position on the matter of representation, the ambassador informed London in December 1960 that Kennedy might accept Beijing's admission to the United Nations. Furthermore, since 1961 was not an election year, it would be easier for Kennedy to make changes in America's China policy—in this case, on Chinese representation—than in 1962. Therefore, he recommended that Britain make clear to the United States that it not only believed another attempt at the moratorium would fail, but also thought it could not abstain on this issue. The American response, he argued, would indicate whether Washington might move closer to London's position.[4]

There were indeed signs that Kennedy might reconsider America's China policy. In 1957, he had written an article for the journal *Foreign Affairs* in which he declared that the Republicans' attitude toward Beijing had been overly rigid and militaristic. During the campaign, he had said that his first goal would be to bring the PRC into nuclear test–ban talks, then being held at Geneva. "If that contact proves fruitful, further cultural and economic contact should be tried," he added.[5]

Several individuals who became high-level members of the administra-

2. Ibid., 307–8.

3. Letter to Lloyd from Caccia, Jan. 18, 1960, FO 371/150452, PRO.

4. Telegram, no. 654 Saving, Caccia to Foreign Office, Dec. 8, 1960, FO 371/150528, PRO.

5. John F. Kennedy, "A Democrat Looks at Foreign Policy," 44–59; Russell Baker, "Kennedy Favors Peiping Contacts," *New York Times,* June 15, 1960.

tion were also on record as favoring a second look at Washington's relationship with Beijing. In 1960, Chester Bowles, whom Kennedy named as his undersecretary of state, declared in *Foreign Affairs* that he favored the representation of both China and Taiwan in the United Nations—the so-called "two Chinas" solution—on the grounds that it would protect the Nationalist government while providing some flexibility in dealing with China. Adlai Stevenson, who became Kennedy's ambassador to the United Nations, stated the same year that to achieve peace in East Asia, the United States would have to make concessions, which "would presumably include an end to the American embargo on China's admission to the United Nations." There were even reports that Dean Rusk, whom Kennedy designated as his secretary of state—and who had a reputation as a hard-liner when it came to China— might prove more flexible than his predecessors in dealing with Beijing.[6]

Caccia, however, misread the political climate in the United States, which checked Kennedy's options on China. Kennedy was the first Democrat to become president since Harry Truman. And it was Truman's administration that had been accused of being "soft" on communism and of "losing" China. The new president had to be careful to avoid similar charges.[7]

Moreover, Kennedy had won the election by only 113,000 votes, the slimmest margin in American history. Secretary of State-designate Rusk later wrote that Kennedy felt "he lacked a strong mandate from the American people. Consequently, he was very cautious about selecting issues on which to do battle. And any change in China policy would have been one hell of a battle." Indeed, polls showed that a growing number of Americans opposed Beijing's admission to the UN. Eisenhower himself had told Kennedy the day before the latter's inauguration that he would return to public life if it seemed the PRC was going to be admitted to the UN.[8] The new president, particularly in light of his thin victory and the state of public opinion, could not afford to have the former general opposing him.

Finally, aside from public opinion, there was China's response. Kennedy stated that he hoped for an improvement in Sino-American relations: "We desire peace and we desire to live in amity with the Chinese people." Yet, he noted, "it takes two to make peace." Rather than using his speech as an opening toward improved relations, the CCP continually assailed him. Theodore Sorensen, Kennedy's special counsel, later wrote that the new president came

6. Chester Bowles, "The 'China Problem' Reconsidered," 476–86; Adlai Stevenson, "Putting First Things First: A Democratic View," 203; Warren I. Cohen, *Dean Rusk*, 95.

7. James N. Giglio, *The Presidency of John F. Kennedy*, 45.

8. Dean Rusk, *As I Saw It: Dean Rusk as Told to Richard Rusk*, 283; Giglio, *Presidency of John F. Kennedy*, 238.

to see "no way of persuading [the PRC] to abandon [its] aggressive design short of a patient, persistent American presence in Asia." Furthermore, the president felt "any American initiative now toward negotiations, diplomatic recognition or UN admission would be regarded as rewarding aggression."[9] As a result, Kennedy continued his predecessors' policy of pressure against China. Such became clear early in his administration, when the perennial question of China's representation in the United Nations arose.

There was a general realization among Kennedy administration officials that the moratorium was in its death throes. Rusk, as the reports suggested, did indeed want to take another look at U.S. China policy. This might seem odd given his well-known hard-line attitude toward the PRC. It was true that Rusk strongly disliked Mao Zedong and the Chinese Communists. Yet he was also a realist: China was here to stay. He thus assumed what one of his biographers called "a dual soft and hard-line." He wanted to contain the threat posed by Communist China but believed the PRC had to be "treated as a legitimate power." Accordingly, while he opposed sending food to China because he felt it would not alter Mao's attitude, he believed Beijing deserved a seat in the United Nations. Accordingly, like Bowles, Rusk favored a "two Chinas" solution. Taiwan's leader, Chiang Kai-shek, immediately rejected any idea of "two Chinas," as it would undermine his claim to the mainland. Moreover, given the moratorium's past success, the Kuomintang head of state saw no reason to abandon it. With Chiang adamantly opposed to any change of tactics, U.S. Ambassador to Taiwan Everett F. Drumright urged the administration to drop any consideration of seating both China and Taiwan in the United Nations.[10]

The White House ignored Drumright's advice. In April, the administration considered a "successor state" solution, by which the General Assembly would affirm Taipei's membership while making room for Beijing. To Chiang, this was little different from "two-Chinas." Not only did he reject it, but in the process he argued—again demonstrating his distrust of London—that the British were "spearheading [the] drive for 'two Chinas' in [their] own selfish interests and without regard to free world security interests in East Asia." Congress also opposed it. Even without Knowland to lead the bloc, congressional opinion on the PRC remained volatile. In a unanimous vote,

9. John F. Kennedy, *Public Papers of the Presidents of the United States: John F. Kennedy, 1961–1963*, 1961, 436; Theodore C. Sorensen, *Kennedy*, 665.

10. Telegram, no. 571, Drumright to Secretary of State, Mar. 20, 1961, RG 59, Central Decimal File, 1960–1963, box 1309; telegram, no. 738, Drumright to the Secretary of State, May 25, 1961, RG 59, Central Decimal File, 1960–1963, box 474, NA; Thomas J. Schoenbaum, *Waging Peace and War: Dean Rusk in the Truman, Kennedy, and Johnson Years*, 387–88; Thomas W. Zeiler, *Dean Rusk: Defending the American Mission Abroad*, 99.

the Senate declared its unwillingness to accept of any form of "two-Chinas" for the United Nations.[11] With such opposition, Kennedy told Rusk, "I don't want to read in the *Washington Post* and *The New York Times* that the State Department is thinking about a change in China policy."[12]

Shot down again, the administration searched for a solution that would guarantee Beijing's exclusion from the UN. In late July, it decided upon calling the Chinese representation issue an "important question."[13] Under this strategy, the General Assembly would declare by a simple majority that the matter of whether Beijing or Taipei should represent China was an "important" one. Afterward, it would require a two-thirds vote to change the representation of China.

Obtaining support for this scheme, however, required assistance from both Taipei and London. Taiwan's support was linked with applications the United Nations received in 1961 from both Outer Mongolia and Mauritania for membership. The United States believed that it had to support Outer Mongolia's petition, even though it was ruled by a pro-Russian communist government. Voting against Mongolia would result in a Soviet veto of Mauritania's application. In turn, the new African nations in the General Assembly would likely vote against Taiwan.[14] As for Britain, officials in the Kennedy administration shared the belief of their predecessors that London's backing was needed to keep China out of the United Nations.[15] To make the United Kingdom more willing to back the "important question," Rusk decided to link it with a proposal to set up a commission that would study the issue of Chinese representation and report to the United Nations. The secretary of state believed that a study committee would rally public support behind an "important question" resolution. His strategy worked. Earlier, Lord Home had told Rusk that the "important question" was a transparent way of keeping China out of the United Nations. Yet, by linking it to a study commission, he felt Britain could support it, for the commission might recommend Beijing's admission, which London favored.[16]

11. Memorandum of conversation, Apr. 4, 1961, PREM 11/4673, PRO; memorandum of conversation, Apr. 5, 1961, RG 59, Central Decimal File, 1960–1963, box 473 and telegrams, nos. 639 and 5, Drumright to Secretary of State, Apr. 21 and July 2, 1961, in RG 59, Central Decimal File, 1960–1963, box 1309, NA; Foot, *Practice of Power,* 38–39.

12. Quoted in Schoenbaum, *Waging Peace and War,* 388.

13. Memorandum of conversation, July 28, 1961, NSF-Country Files, box 22, JFKL.

14. Memorandum to Bundy from Battle, Sept. 5, 1961, NSF-Country Files, box 22, JFKL.

15. In March, during U.S. discussion of a "two-Chinas" solution, A.J. de la Mare, the head of the Foreign Office's Far Eastern Department, noted, "We get the impression that the Americans believe that United Kingdom support for their package deal would be crucial." See FO Minute by de la Mare, Mar. 3, 1961, FO 371/158444, PRO.

16. Memoranda of conversation, Aug. 6 and 7, 1961, FO 371/158449, PRO.

Macmillan determined to support the American request. For one, he had become quite close to the American president. After Kennedy's difficult meeting with Soviet Premier Nikita Khrushchev in June 1961, a shaken president had stopped off in London. Kennedy and Macmillan had hit it off; the prime minister afterward called the meeting "a success from the point of view of our personal relations. He was kind, intelligent, and *very* friendly. I find my friendship beginning to grow into something like that which I got with Eisenhower after a few months at Algiers." The president later commented that he could share his "loneliness" with his British counterpart.[17] Not wanting to undermine a growing friendship that could further strengthen Anglo-American relations, Macmillan had good reason to support the American request.

But Britain's status as the junior partner in the alliance gave Macmillan additional reason to support the Americans. Rusk's tabling of the "important question"–study committee resolution came during a second crisis over Berlin. Khrushchev had demanded the withdrawal of Western military forces from the city. When Kennedy refused, the Soviet premier threatened to sign a separate agreement with East Germany by the end of 1961, which would mean that East Germany could then force the West out of the city. Recognizing his country's reliance on American power, Macmillan told Home that "we should not quarrel with the Americans on a subject on which they feel so deeply on the eve of great perils in Europe." After further consideration, the British cabinet on September 5 decided in favor of supporting the U.S. position.[18]

With Britain seemingly on board, attention turned to Taiwan. Because of Outer Mongolia's communist regime, Taipei strongly opposed its admission, and as a member of the Security Council, Taiwan could veto Mongolia's application. On August 15, Kennedy sent a letter to Chiang, urging him to stand alongside the United States. He noted the likely repercussions if the KMT government voted against Mongolia's petition. "I am sure you will agree with me," he wrote, "that neither the United States nor the Republic of China can afford a defeat on a question of such fundamental importance." Chiang remained adamant. Seating the communist state, he replied, would undermine the "national honor and self-respect" of the Taiwanese people. If Taiwan gave in to international blackmail and agreed to the admission of Mongolia, "the effect of this abandonment of her moral position would be such a fatal blow that it could not be compensated by her continued presence in the United Nations."[19]

Chiang no doubt frustrated Kennedy. The Nationalist leader had already rejected a "two Chinas" and "successor state" resolution to the subject of rep-

17. Horne, *Harold Macmillan*, 2:302–5.
18. Memorandum to Lord Home from Macmillan, Aug. 12, 1961, PREM 11/4673; Minutes of Cabinet Meeting, C.C. 49 (61), Sept. 5, 1961, CAB 128/35, PRO.
19. Draft letter to Chiang from Kennedy, Aug. 15, 1961, NSF-Country Files, box 22 and letter to Kennedy from Chiang, Sept. 10, 1961, POF-Countries, box 113a, JFKL.

resentation and now seemed determined to derail the "important question." Kennedy tried again in October to persuade Chiang to alter his position. He offered Chiang a private assurance that he would use America's veto power in the UN to prevent China's admission, if it became necessary. The Taiwanese leader saw an opportunity and was quick to seize it. Two days after Kennedy's offer, the KMT foreign minister, George Yeh, told Ray Cline, the deputy for intelligence of the CIA, that he felt Chiang might become more flexible if the president added to his private assurance a public statement in support of Taiwan's seat in the UN. Yeh argued that this would give the Nationalist government something to use to explain to its people its change of stance on Outer Mongolia. Kennedy agreed, and on October 25, Chiang stated that he would not veto Outer Mongolia's application.[20]

Just as the difficulties with Taiwan were being solved, new ones appeared with Britain, when the United States suddenly withdrew support from its study commission proposal. The White House based its decision on opposition from Taiwan and from the American public, both of which rejected the idea of Washington supporting a committee that might ultimately recommend China's admission and possibly Taiwan's ouster. Therefore, the White House looked for another nation to sponsor the resolution. Whitehall refused to consider sponsorship, arguing that to do so might anger China and strain Britain's relations with the PRC.[21]

During the next month, the United States searched fruitlessly for a sponsor for the study committee. Finally, on November 23, the U.S. ambassador to Britain, David Bruce, informed London of the White House's decision to drop completely the study committee proposal and to rely strictly on the "important question" resolution, for which it was assured support. The head of the Foreign Office's Far Eastern Department, A. J. de la Mare, was furious. He could not believe that only five days before the question of Chinese representation was to arise in the United Nations, the United States decided to inform Britain that it could not keep its agreement. He added that the White House's decision would anger the ministers in London.[22]

Indeed, at the end of the month, Bruce discussed the matter with Lord Home and de la Mare. Home expressed frustration with the change in the

20. Letter to Chiang from Kennedy, circa Oct. 5, 1961, NSF-McGeorge Bundy Correspondence Files, box 398a; memorandum to Cline from Bundy, Oct. 11, 1961, NSF-Country Files, box 22; cables to Bundy from Cline, Oct. 14 and 25, 1961, NSF-Country files, box 23, JFKL; telegram, no. 259, Rusk to Taipei, Oct. 16, 1961, FRUS, 1961–1963, 22:160.

21. Memorandum to Kellerman from Tyler, Oct. 30, 1961, RG 59, Central Decimal File, 1960–1963, box 470, NA; telegram, no. 2179, Dean to Foreign Office, Nov. 22, 1961, FO 371/158456, PRO.

22. Telegram, no. 2078, Bruce to Secretary of State, Nov. 24, 1961, RG 59, Central Decimal File, 1960–1963, box 477, NA.

American position and added that the United Kingdom could not sponsor the study committee resolution. Bruce responded that the United States believed it could win on the "important question" alone. De la Mare warned that if the "important question" failed, the only alternative was a Soviet resolution that called for ousting Taiwan in favor of China.[23]

In early December, Michael Stewart, London's chargé d'affaires in Beijing, suggested a way out: if Britain avoided sponsoring the study commission and voted for both the "important question" and the Soviet resolutions, its action would receive approval in Beijing.[24] Home accepted the advice and instructed the British delegation to take a position similar to that recommended by the chargé. He added, though, that he hoped the UN could vote on the Soviet resolution paragraph-by-paragraph; this would allow Britain to dissociate itself from the resolution's third paragraph, which stated that "representatives of the Chiang Kai-shek clique" were "unlawfully occupying" China's place at the UN.[25]

Rusk did not approve of these instructions when he learned of them. While visiting Paris for a NATO foreign ministers' meeting, the secretary of state informed Pierson Dixon, the British ambassador to France, that he wanted to avoid a vote on the Soviet resolution. He thus suggested that after a vote on the "important question," a motion be made to table further debate on China's representation. When informed of Rusk's idea, Home balked. The secretary of state's proposal, he said, was simply "the moratorium under another guise" and would face opposition from both Parliament and the British public. On December 15, the United Nations voted, passing the "important question" by nearly a two-to-one margin and defeating the Soviet resolution. The British had concerns that their vote in favor of the Soviet resolution would anger the United States, but there was no serious outcry. Nevertheless, David Ormsby-Gore, the U.K. ambassador in Washington, recommended that in the future when dealing with China's representation, London should not give the impression that it was deliberately challenging U.S. leadership or unmindful of the Kennedy administration's domestic problems.[26]

23. Telegram, no. 2116, Bruce to Secretary of State, Nov. 28, 1961, RG 59, Central Decimal File, 1960–1963, box 477, NA.

24. Telegram, no. 622, Stewart to Foreign Office, Dec. 4, 1961, FO 371/158457, PRO.

25. These instructions were sent in an original form on Dec. 5, but went through some changes before being finalized on Dec. 8. See telegram, no. 5417, Foreign Office to New York, Dec. 5, 1961; telegram, no. 3301, Ormsby-Gore to Foreign Office, Dec. 6, 1961; and telegram, no. 638, Stewart to Foreign Office, Dec. 8, 1961, FO 371/158458; telegram, no. 5516, Foreign Office to New York, Dec. 8, 1961, FO 371/158459; and Minutes of Cabinet Meeting, C.C. 67 (61), Dec. 5, 1961, CAB 128/35, PRO.

26. Telegrams, no. 748, Dixon to Foreign Office, Dec. 11, 1961, and no. 4777, Foreign Office to Paris, Dec. 12, 1961, FO 371/158459; dispatch, no. 33, Ormsby-Gore to Foreign Office, Jan. 31, 1962, FO 371/164593, PRO.

Whitehall apparently ignored Ormsby-Gore's advice. Two months after the UN vote, another controversy arose, this time over whether the subsidiary bodies of the United Nations could determine their own membership. Given the decision in 1961 to abandon the moratorium, de la Mare decided that the lower bodies of the United Nations had a right to decide which nations might join them. He argued that neither the moratorium nor the "important question" applied to these organizations.[27]

Rusk disagreed. He contended that if the United States acquiesced in the matter of the subsidiary bodies, it might enable the PRC to enter the General Assembly through a back door; he believed that the decision of the assembly to treat Chinese representation as an "important question" applied to these lesser organizations. He also repeated his threat from 1961: if the General Assembly seated China, it would have "profound repercussions" in the United States "and impact upon [the] American attitudes toward [the] UK and continuing support for US active participation in international organizations."[28]

Berlin no doubt remained a concern to Macmillan and his subordinates. Accordingly, Home promoted within the Foreign Office a proposal made by the United States in mid-April. Under this proposition, the subsidiary bodies would agree, in light of the General Assembly's decision in December 1961, to refrain from taking any action in opposition to that decision. After further discussion and some slight changes in the wording, the British cabinet accepted the proposal. With U.K. support, in October the General Assembly defeated a Soviet resolution calling for China's admission and passed the "important question."[29]

The United States had emerged victorious in the United Nations, but not without increasing tensions in its relationships with Taiwan and Britain. The former did not want to give up on the moratorium and only did so after public and private guarantees of support from Washington. The latter became upset with the U.S. decision to give up on the study committee. It also be-

27. Telegram, no. 3012, Bruce to Secretary of State, Feb. 14, 1962; telegram, no. 3145, Bruce to Secretary of State, Feb. 27, 1962, RG 59, Central Decimal File, 1960–1963, box 478, NA.

28. Telegram, no. 4671, Rusk to London, Mar. 3, 1961, RG 59, Central Decimal File, 1960–1963, box 478, NA.

29. Telegram, no. 5613, Rusk to London, Apr. 18, 1962, and telegram, no. SECTO 8, Rusk to Secretary of State, May 1, 1962, RG 59, Central Decimal File, 1960–1963, box 478, NA; memorandum by Secretary of State for Foreign Affairs, C (62) 70, "Chinese Representation in Competent United Nations Organisations," May 10, 1962, CAB 129/109; Minutes of Cabinet Meeting, C.C. 34 (62), May 17, 1962, CAB 128/36, PRO; Thomas J. Hamilton, "Zafrulla Khan Elected as Head of UN Assembly," *New York Times,* Sept. 19, 1962; Arnold J. Lubasch, "U.N. Again Bars Peking; Assembly Vote Is 56 to 42," *New York Times,* Oct. 31, 1962.

lieved that even with passage of the "important question" in 1961, the UN's subsidiary bodies had a right to choose their own membership. But Macmillan was not willing to let his feelings or those of his subordinates create another rift in the Anglo-American alliance. He had gone through a great deal healing the schism caused by the Suez crisis, and the situation in Europe made it vital to maintain unity with Britain's closest ally. Therefore, Whitehall agreed to support the "important question" (minus the study committee) in 1961 and to back down on the subsidiary bodies the following year; however, it was not to be so accommodating on the question of Anglo-Chinese trade.

After three years of relative calm between the United States and Britain over trade controls, the issue arose again in August 1960, when Stewart informed the Foreign Office that he had learned that China wanted to buy Viscount 810 aircraft from Vickers Company of England. First produced in 1956, the four-engine turboprop flew at about 350 miles per hour and had a range of 1,760 miles. According to the chargé, the Chinese had formerly bought IL 18 planes from the Soviet Union; Beijing, though, had concluded that the IL 18s cost more and performed less well than the Viscounts.[30]

Stewart's letter both excited and worried the Macmillan government. Trade offered a means of driving wedges into the Sino-Soviet alliance by giving China contact with the West, and it might also open the door to even larger transactions, such as orders for building entire power stations or industrial plants.[31] The prospect of such large contracts greatly attracted London, which continued to face a negative balance of trade and a subsequent run on the country's monetary reserves. (In March 1961 alone, Britain's reserves lost £187 million.) The prime minister suggested as much when he explained to Rusk in mid-1962 that Britain had to trade with China because its survival required overseas commerce.[32] Yet there remained the question of the embargo. Specifically at issue was whether selling the planes to the PRC would constitute breaking the embargo's policy of not providing Beijing with strategic equipment. In light of these conflicting concerns, on August 11, E.

---

30. Letter to Dalton from Stewart, Aug. 1, 1960, FO 371/150433, PRO.

31. In May 1962, Col. Harold Burris, Vice President Lyndon Johnson's military aide, told him that the Soviet Union had decided not to help China build a dam on the Sanmen River. The PRC had turned to help from Britain. London agreed to assist the Chinese not only for reasons of commerce, but because it "hope[d] that U.K.-Chinese economic cooperation will create a cleavage between China and the Soviet Union." See memorandum to vice president from Burris, May 10, 1962, VPSF, box 5, LBJL.

32. Telegram, no. 366, Rodgers to Foreign Office, Aug. 12, 1961, FO 371/158424, PRO; Nigel Fisher, *Harold Macmillan: A Biography,* 266–67; memorandum of conversation, June 24, 1962, PREM 11/3738, PRO.

Youde of the U.K. embassy in Beijing wrote N. C. C. Trench of the Far Eastern Department, stating that before Britain did anything, it should check with its embassy in Washington and the Ministry of Aviation to make sure the Viscounts were not on the embargo list.[33]

Within a month, the embassy had confirmed that the planes were not on the list. Therefore, Trench suggested that Vickers ask the Chinese government about the planes. He argued that since the embassy stated that the aircraft were not on the embargo list, and since the inquiry would come from Vickers rather than COCOM—the multination committee that controlled trade with communist nations—the White House would know nothing. It was vital to keep Washington in the dark, he said, for it was an election year in the United States. "This should lessen," he continued, "the risk of a violent explosion of opinion in the U.S." (He also realized that once word did get out, the White House would not be particularly pleased.) The Far Eastern Department accepted his recommendation.[34]

Negotiations with the Chinese continued well into 1961. In August, members of the Board of Trade, Treasury, Bank of England, Ministry of Aviation, and the Foreign Office gathered to discuss the PRC's request. They agreed that the sale of the planes could create new tensions in Anglo-American relations, but no items on the planes were subject to the embargo. Furthermore, they were not suitable as troop transports because, argued the meeting's participants, they could not be used on short runways; this meant that China could not use them, as the United States might argue, for spreading aggression into neighboring nations. London decided not to inform Washington until just before or just after the signing of a contract for the planes.[35]

Over the next two weeks the situation became more complicated. First, the Foreign Office learned that the Chinese wanted a type of radar installed in the planes that was still subject to the embargo. Then, in early September, the American embassy in London got wind of the Viscount deal and made inquiries to the Macmillan government. The Foreign Office denied any knowledge of the matter.[36]

In October, Britain finally admitted a sale had been proposed and asked

33. Letter to Trench from Youde, Aug. 11, 1960, FO 371/150433, PRO. Why Youde did not know whether the planes were on the embargo list is not clear. He may have not had available the technical information on the planes to know if they or the equipment on them were on the list.

34. Letters to Denson from Trench, Sept. 6, 1960, and to de la Mare from Ledward, Sept. 19, 1960, FO 371/150433, PRO.

35. Record of Meeting at Foreign Office, Aug. 16, 1961, FO 371/158424, PRO.

36. FO Minute by Peck, Aug. 22, 1961, and telegram, no. 6103, Foreign Office to Washington, Sept. 1, 1961, FO 371/158424, PRO.

the United States for its views. The State Department responded that it opposed the transaction because it included an embargoed instrument. Additionally, Washington felt compelled to deny a license for a British subsidiary of an American firm to supply the equipment. The State Department added that a sale of the embargoed goods would anger Congress and the American public. But since Britain could obtain the equipment elsewhere, neither American arguments nor action impeded the transaction.[37]

On December 1, London decided to proceed with the sale; that same day, it signed a contract with Beijing. In defending the transaction to Washington, the British argued that the radar equipment had little strategic value. Furthermore, not allowing the sale would greatly increase "domestic UK pressures against the entire strategic trade control program," which would do more harm to Anglo-American relations than any potential criticism of the deal in the United States. On December 4, at a COCOM meeting, the British announced that they had issued the export license for the Viscounts.[38]

Britain's decision angered some members of Congress, particularly Senators Kenneth Keating (R-New York) and Prescott Bush (R-Connecticut). Keating charged that the transaction represented a "dangerous" precedent, suggesting that it might lead to additional, larger sales of equipment with potential or actual military use. The White House considered taking punitive measures but then decided to turn a blind eye. In the mid-1950s, when Britain first began to look into eliminating the differential, Secretary of State John Foster Dulles had argued the importance of making some concessions to the United Kingdom so as to maintain as much of the multilateral trade control system as possible. Kennedy and his advisers likely recognized the value of that strategy. With the situation in Berlin still unresolved, they probably did not want to present to the Kremlin a disunited Anglo-American front. It is also likely that the president did not want to ruin his friendship with Macmillan by pressing an issue on which the British felt strongly, just as the prime minister had warned against pressing the Americans on representation. Accordingly, the White House successfully calmed lawmakers while accepting London's action. Defense Secretary Robert McNamara told the Senate Armed Services Committee that the Viscount transaction would

37. Background paper for Bermuda Conference, "British Sale of 'Viscount' Aircraft to Communist China," Dec. 16, 1961, RG 59, Bureau of Far Eastern Affairs, Subject, Personal Name, and Country Files, 1960–1963, box 9, NA; "U.S. Equipment for Viscount Banned," *London Times,* Jan. 16, 1962.

38. Background Paper, "British Sale of 'Viscount' Aircraft to Communist China"; "Peking Buys Six British Airliners," *London Times,* Dec. 5, 1961; telegram, no. 1930, Beam to Secretary of State, June 29, 1961, RG 59, Central Decimal File, 1960–1963, box 1309, NA.

not "substantially" strengthen the communist bloc. Meanwhile, Rusk, at a December 8 press conference, stated simply that he was not happy about the sale, "but this is one of those transactions in the commercial field which governments must decide for themselves. I think I might just let it rest at that."[39]

While Britain sold Viscounts to China, the Kennedy administration cautiously took a second look at its trade policy. Reports of food shortages caused by the Great Leap Forward—to be discussed more fully in chapter eight—led the administration to consider selling provisions to China. Several members of the administration, including Bowles and Assistant Secretary for Far Eastern Affairs Averell Harriman, urged Kennedy to approve such an offer.[40]

Kennedy proceeded cautiously. Reports of the problems facing China had also made their way into the press and public discourse. Americans were sympathetic, but they wanted to be sure that if the United States made an offer of food, it would go directly to the Chinese people. They did not want a government-to-government transfer of aid that the CCP could use as it chose; it might sell the food for money with which to buy arms. Accordingly, the White House made an offer in June 1961 via the Sino-American ambassadorial talks to provide private donations of food to the PRC. Wang Bingnan, the Chinese representative at Warsaw, rejected the proposal.[41]

As the number of reports about China's crisis increased during 1962, Kennedy began to consider a government-to-government offer of food.[42] No doubt, he was influenced by Harriman, who argued for such an offer and for whom he had developed a high regard as a result of the assistant secretary's

39. "British Airliner Sale Opposed," *London Times,* Dec. 8, 1961; "British Sales to China Attacked," *London Times,* Mar. 26, 1962; "Transcript of Rusk's News Conference on Congo, Vietnam and Other Foreign Issues," *New York Times,* Dec. 9, 1961; "British Sale of 'Viscount' Aircraft to Communist China."

40. Memoranda, to Rusk from Harriman, Apr. 13, 1962, and to the NSC Standing Group from Bowles, May 25, 1962, Papers of James C. Thomson, Jr., box 15, JFKL; memorandum to Kennedy from Bowles, May 23, 1962, Papers of Chester Bowles, Series I, box 297, SML.

41. Telegram, no. 1930, Beam to Secretary of State, June 29, 1961, RG 59, Central Decimal File, 1960–1963, box 1309, NA. For background information on the decision to offer private donations of food, see memorandum to Johnson from McConaughy, May 18, 1961, RG 59, Bureau of Far Eastern Affairs, Subject, Personal Name, and Country Files, 1960–1963, box 4, NA. For examples of reports in the United States regarding China's food crisis, see *Newsweek* (Mar. 27, 1961): 38; *Time* (May 26, 1961): 25–26 and (Sept. 16, 1961): 35–36; and *New Republic* (June 11, 1961): 8–9; Kusnitz, *Public Opinion and Foreign Policy,* 96–97 and 121 n 17.

42. See, for instance, *Nation* (June 9, 1962): 507; *U.S. News and World Report* (June 11, 1962): 48 and (July 9, 1962): 65–67.

success in achieving a settlement in Laos earlier that year. (Indeed, Harriman was to become the president's favorite troubleshooter.) An offer, of course, would require a revision of the U.S. embargo against China. The Policy Planning Council (PPC)—formerly the Policy Planning Staff—in October 1961 recommended the necessary alteration of the program of trade controls so as to permit the shipment of food and medicine to the PRC. Furthermore, in March 1962, Walt Rostow, the head of the PPC, provided the administration with a paper put together by several of the State Department's regional bureaus, which also suggested an offer of government aid. Kennedy refused to shut the door to providing foodstuffs; still, he remained cautious, as reflected in a statement made at a news conference held in late May 1962. When asked if he might approve a government-to-government offer of food, the president responded:

> Well, there's been no indication of any expression of interest or desire by the Chinese Communists to receive any food from us, as I said at the beginning, and we would certainly have to have some idea as to whether the food was needed and under what conditions it might be distributed. Up to the present we have no such indications.[43]

His comment aroused the anger of a large segment of the U.S. press and public. It was one thing to suggest private donations meant for the people of China. But it was quite another to offer aid to the government, which would only help the Communist regime. (Kennedy also received a rejection from Beijing, which did not want to find itself begging for help from the United States.)[44]

The administration's stance now hardened. In their March study, the regional bureaus argued, "If . . . [Beijing] persists in its personal attacks against President Kennedy, or takes provocative action in Southeast Asia or elsewhere, we should deny the balance of the grain requested."[45] Renewed tensions in the Taiwan Strait in mid-1962, combined with the PRC's attack upon India later in the year, moved the White House to adopt this very position.

Chiang Kai-shek had been inspired by news of the difficulties China faced as a result of the Great Leap Forward. As early as May 1959, the Taiwanese leader had expressed his opinion to U.S. officials that the food shortages and

43. Policy Planning Council Report, "US Policy toward China," Oct. 26, 1961, RG 59, Central Decimal File, 1960–1963, box 1309 and memorandum to Ball from Rostow, Mar. 16, 1962, RG 59, Records of the Policy Planning Staff, 1962, box 223, NA; Kennedy, *Public Papers*, 1962, 431; Walter Isaacson, *The Wise Men: Six Friends and the World They Made*, 630–31; Sorensen, *Kennedy*, 734.

44. Kusnitz, *Public Opinion and Foreign Policy*, 103–4. Kusnitz cited much of the press as arguing that Kennedy's idea amounted to "feeding the mouth that's biting you."

45. Memorandum to Ball from Rostow, Mar. 16, 1962.

other economic problems created on the mainland by the Communists offered opportunities. He explained that month to Deputy Assistant Secretary of State for Far Eastern Affairs J. Graham Parsons, "If at this critical juncture we fail to cooperate in measures of exploitation we will give the Communists a new lease of life. The consequences for [Taiwan] and the U.S. will be grave indeed." The Eisenhower administration refused to support any proposal for an invasion, arguing that the conditions on the mainland had yet to reach the point where such an attack would stand a chance of success.[46]

Chiang was undeterred and tried his hand with the new Kennedy administration. In May 1961, he told Vice President Lyndon Johnson, who was then visiting Taiwan, that the chaos created by the Great Leap would soon lead to an uprising in the PRC. He said that the time had come for the United States and Taiwan to begin preparations so they would be ready to take advantage of the uprising when it occurred and could help the Nationalists return to the mainland. Johnson was noncommital, but this did not dissuade the KMT leader.[47] During the remainder of 1961 and into 1962, he continued his preparations to attack the mainland and publicly declared on several occasions that his nation's military was ready to assist in an uprising in the PRC. Both Kennedy and Rusk opposed Chiang's statements, arguing that they suggested that the United States would help in an effort to return the Nationalists to China. The president did not want to risk another fiasco like the 1961 Bay of Pigs or, worse, war with the PRC and possibly the Soviet Union. At the same time, he did not want to destroy Chiang's hope of ever returning to the mainland. Consequently, Kennedy agreed to a proposal by the Nationalist leader to drop small commando teams into China to foment unrest, believing that such an operation would not require American assistance, but refused to support anything larger. As a further demonstration of his seriousness, the U.S. president sent Harriman and the State Department's director of intelligence, Roger Hilsman, to Taiwan to make it clear that Taipei was still bound by its mutual security treaty with Washington not to stage large-scale operations against Beijing without American approval.[48]

46. Memorandum of conversation, May 2, 1959, RG 59, Records of the Policy Planning Staff, 1957–61, box 135, NA; memorandum, "President's Far Eastern Trip, June 1960," June 6, 1960, WHCF-Confidential File, Subject Series, box 57, DDEL.

47. Transcript of Breakfast Conference, May 15, 1961, Personal Papers, Papers of Robert Waldron, AC 81–89, LBJL.

48. Memorandum to Director of the CIA Office of National Estimates from Kent, July 27, 1961, NSF-Country Files, box 22; memorandum to Johnson from Burris, Jan. 31, 1962, VPSF, box 5, LBJL; memorandum to Harriman from Kennedy, Mar. 9, 1962, NSF-Country Files, box 22; telegrams, no. 410, Rusk to Taipei, Jan. 8, 1962 and no. 569, Drumright to Secretary of State, Feb. 13, 1962, NSF-Country Files, box 23, JFKL; Roger Hilsman, *To Move a Nation: The Politics of Foreign Policy in the Administration of John F.*

Chiang's statements also concerned China. In the middle of June, U.S. intelligence reported a buildup of Communist forces opposite Quemoy, one even larger than in 1958. Washington was unsure at first if the PRC was taking a defensive measure or preparing for another assault on the offshore islands but soon concluded that the former was more likely. On June 24, Rusk explained Washington's conclusions to Macmillan. The prime minister "replied vehemently that he simply did not understand United States policy on China. We did not even admit that China existed. He wondered what our long-run policy was. He regarded it as indefensible by any logic." Rusk explained that the United States based its policy on the PRC's belligerent attitude. The two men then dropped the subject.[49]

Why Macmillan's sudden explosion? Neither his memoirs nor biographies on him provide any explanation. Some speculation, though, is possible. First, Macmillan had been foreign secretary at the end of the first crisis in the Taiwan Strait and was prime minister during the second crisis. He may have become fed up with American support for Chiang, who seemed too willing to provoke a conflict with the PRC that might turn into another Korean (or even larger) war. Furthermore, the last few weeks had been very bad for him. Talks in early June with French leader Charles DeGaulle on Britain's admission to the European Economic Community had not gone well; the conservatives had done poorly in a by-election in the middle of the month; Macmillan's personal popularity was on the decline as a result of the so-called pay pause—an imposition of controls on government workers over wage settlements—which he had imposed in response to Britain's economic troubles; and Selwyn Lloyd had proven himself unfit at the Exchequer.[50] Add to that the present crisis in the Taiwan Strait, and it became all too much, leading to Macmillan's outburst. The fact that he quickly dropped the subject, howev-

---

Kennedy, 310–14; "Chiang Urges Early Action," *New York Times,* Mar. 30, 1962; "Chiang Threatens Reds," *New York Times,* Apr. 23, 1962. The first mention of sending small commando teams into China was in a Sept. 21, 1961, conversation between Taiwan's defense minister, Chiang Ching-kuo, and an unnamed American "observer." See memorandum to McConaughy from Yager, Nov. 8, 1961, RG 59, Subject, Personal Name, and Country Files, 1960–1963, box 4, NA.

49. Telegram, no. 2136, Cabot to Secretary of State, June 23, 1962, RG 59, Central Decimal File, 1960–1963, box 1309, NA; memorandum to Bundy from Bowles, June 18, 1962, Papers of Chester Bowles, Series I, box 297, SML; memorandum to Rusk from Hilsman, June 18, 1962; memorandum of conversation, June 20, 1962; and memorandum to Harriman from Hilsman, June 22, 1962, Papers of Roger Hilsman, Countries, box 1, JFKL; memorandum of conversation, June 24, 1962, RG 59, Records of the Policy Planning Staff, 1962, box 216, NA; Max Frankel, "Red China Building Up Troops and Jet Units Opposite Quemoy," *New York Times,* June 21, 1962; Hilsman, *To Move a Nation,* 318.

50. Horne, *Harold Macmillan,* 2:339–40.

er, suggests that he was not about to let this latest imbroglio undermine his relationship with the United States.

The crisis itself still needed to be resolved lest it become something worse. Using its contact at Warsaw, as well as the British, the United States made it clear that it would oppose any attempt by the PRC to take the islands as well as any effort by Chiang to land forces on the mainland. Just in case the warning was not heeded, Kennedy ordered the reinforcing of the Seventh Fleet and publicly warned Beijing that "[t]he United States will take the action necessary to assure the defense of Formosa and the Pescadores." As with the first two offshore islands crises, the president did not state specifically what response he might employ or whether it would involve a defense of Quemoy.[51]

The scare in the Taiwan Strait died down almost as quickly as it had begun. Why is still not clear. It is possible that U.S. reassurances played their part. Unlike during the islands crises of 1954–1955 and 1958, Washington had direct contact with Beijing through Warsaw and may have been able to alleviate China's concerns about America's intentions and its willingness to control Chiang. The buildup also might have been part of a plan by Mao to improve his nation's security in its southern provinces. It is clear that the KMT leader was upset. He wrote Kennedy in March 1963, "It would be of interest to you that our armed forces and people are of the view that my government wasted a good opportunity when it failed to act last year."[52]

No matter what Chiang's culpability in the third Quemoy-Matsu crisis might have been, the PRC's response provided a clear indicator to U.S. policymakers that China remained a danger. That became even clearer later in the year when its troops attacked India. The dispute between the PRC and India dated back to 1959, when Beijing had claimed that the border between the two nations was not properly delineated. Between 1959 and 1962, Chinese troops staged small incursions into India, and in September 1962, China began a major invasion of eastern India.

Since achieving independence, India had maintained a neutral position between the West and the communist bloc. The United States hoped that the PRC's attack on India would lead the New Delhi government to join the

---

51. Telegram, no. 2136, Cabot to Secretary of State, June 23, 1962; memorandum to Kennedy from Ball, June 21, 1962, and memorandum to Ball from Bundy, June 22, 1962, RG 59, Bureau of Far Eastern Affairs, Subject, Personal Name, and Country Files, 1960–1963, box 11, NA; telegram, no. 1658, Ormsby-Gore to Foreign Office, June 22, 1962, and memorandum of conversation, June 25, 1962, PREM 11/3738; memorandum of conversation, July 23, 1962, FO 371/164909, PRO; Kennedy, *Public Papers,* 1962, 509–10; Hilsman, *To Move a Nation,* 319.

52. Dispatch, no. 1, Garvey to Foreign Office, Jan. 1, 1963, FO 371/170668, PRO; letter to Kennedy from Chiang, Mar. 15, 1963, POF-Countries, box 113a, JFKL.

Western nations. Britain sympathized with the plight of its former colony.[53] Both London and Washington thus offered military aid to New Delhi.

The British clearly worried that their decision to assist India would anger the Chinese and create problems for Sino-British relations. On October 24, however, the Chinese foreign minister, Chen Yi, assured Malcolm MacDonald, Britain's former commissioner-general for Southeast Asia, that, despite London's position in the dispute, relations between the two countries were quite friendly. Chen's mild reaction pleased British officials.[54]

The Chinese had halted their military incursion by year's end, and the situation in the border area stabilized. But China's aggression had several repercussions. First, public reaction in Britain to the invasion led to London's postponement of a planned visit by the Chinese vice minister for foreign trade, Lu Xuzhang. Second, it facilitated the defeat in October 1963 of a resolution favoring Beijing's entry into the UN and passage again of the "important question."[55] Finally, in combination with the recent heightening of tensions in the Taiwan Strait, it affected the American position on the trade embargo, including the sale of food, and revived the dispute between the United States and Britain over the latter's plan to sell the Viscount planes to China.

China's activities in East and South Asia hardened the position of the United States toward Beijing. A March 1963 poll found that a plurality of Americans regarded China as a greater threat than the Soviet Union.[56] The Kennedy administration's policy reflected this hostility. As noted, in their March 1962 study, the State Department's regional bureaus had argued against providing aid to China if it engaged in aggressive activity. A policy paper put together late that year reiterated that intent: "The US should avoid actions and decisions . . . that would have the effect of easing pressures on the communist regime as presently constituted and oriented." Referring to the difficulties China then faced as a result of the Great Leap Forward, the paper continued:

We should seek to develop a sober appreciation of the great advantages that the free world derives from even a temporary forced preoccupation of communist China with its internal problems, and of the possibility that prolonged failure of the regime to solve those problems can lead to a break of truly historical impor-

53. Horne, *Harold Macmillan*, 2:415–16.

54. Telegram, no. 508, Garvey to Foreign Office, Oct. 29, 1962, and FO Minute by McLaren, Nov. 6, 1962, FO 371/164915, PRO.

55. "Report on Visit to United Kingdom of Mr. Lu Hsu-Chang, Vice Minister of the Foreign Trade of the People's Republic of China, 21st Mar.–12th Apr. 1963," FO 371/170691; telegram, no. 1796, Dean to Foreign Office, Oct. 21, 1963, FO 371/170721, PRO.

56. Kusnitz, *Public Opinion and Foreign Policy*, 106.

tance for the free world cause. We should, in short, get across the great stakes that all western nations have in letting the failures of the communists run full course and hence the need for a common policy of denying to the regime any relief from our side.

Accordingly, "the desirability of limiting to the extent possible the inflow of goods into China is obvious." The paper thus recommended that the United States maintain the present level of economic sanctions against China, including the sale of food.[57] The White House followed this policy and did not again offer food to Beijing during the remainder of Kennedy's term in office.

The United States also took a second look at the Viscount sale. The PRC's aggression, particularly that against India, led the White House to oppose any action that might increase Beijing's military potential. In February 1963, Lord Home reported that Washington now argued that the planes "will be a substantial addition to Chinese airlift capacity and that supplying them is inconsistent with our sympathy and aid for India, particularly our plan to assist Indian air defense." The British were not moved. The American equipment for the planes already had been delivered to Vickers, and the aircraft were being built (to the surprise of the United States). Furthermore, the British continued to argue that they could export the equipment by way of the exceptions rule; therefore, COCOM restrictions were not at issue. Finally, Britain's continued economic problems—the nation's treasury lost £100 million in just two days in March—continued to make trade vital. But to minimize American criticism of the transaction, the British decided to postpone for as long as possible their notification to COCOM that they intended to use the exceptions provision. In early July, the first Viscount left for China. There was no strong protest from the White House or Congress. The former probably decided that it was best to accept the transaction and move on. Lawmakers were not happy with Britain's decision to press forward despite the Sino-Indian conflict.[58] Yet they also likely realized Britain's need for trade and did not want to bring pressure to bear on London to the point of unduly straining Anglo-American relations. Additionally, it was not an election year, thereby reducing the chances Whitehall's decision would influence the U.S. political climate.

The British and Americans might have disagreed on the impact the Vis-

---

57. S/P Paper, "A U.S. Policy toward Communist China," Nov. 15, 1962, RG 59, Records of the Policy Planning Staff, 1962, box 232, NA.

58. Memorandum by Secretary of State for Foreign Affairs, C (63) 13, "East-West Trade Differences with the Americans," Feb. 4, 1963, CAB 129/112; Brief for Board of Trade Meeting, Mar. 21, 1963, FO 371/170700; telegram, no. 717, Foreign Office to Peking, July 2, 1963, FO 371/170701, PRO; "Washington Rejects Moscow Pipeline Protest," *London Times*, Mar. 25, 1963, p. 8; Horne, *Harold Macmillan*, 2:470.

counts would have on China's military capabilities, but they did see eye-to-eye on the need to prevent the PRC from getting a weapon of far greater power: an atomic bomb. Indeed, Kennedy was concerned enough with this issue that he personally asked Harriman in mid-1963 to approach Soviet Premier Nikita Khrushchev about a possible joint attack on the PRC's nuclear installations. Khrushchev rejected the proposal, and the president did not pursue it.[59]

It is odd that Kennedy looked into a joint air assault against China when he had consistently rejected Chiang Kai-shek's requests for help to attack the mainland. Bombing the PRC's nuclear facilities, one historian noted, "would certainly have thrown Asia into greater turmoil than any other single act since the Korean War." So why the distinction? Clearly, Kennedy was greatly disturbed by a nuclear China. In July, he telegraphed Harriman, who was in Moscow as the president's special representative, "I remain convinced that [the] Chinese problem is more serious than Khrushchev['s] comments in [the] first meeting suggest, and believe [that] you should press [the] question in [a] private meeting with him."[60] The president, in short, seemed to give greater consideration and importance to an attack on the PRC's nuclear facilities than to a Nationalist assault that stood little chance of success.

Macmillan also was troubled by the idea of a nuclear China. There is no evidence that he knew about Kennedy's approach to Khrushchev—and no doubt would have strongly opposed it had he known because of the potential repercussions—but he did believe that it might be possible to put a halt to the PRC's nuclear weapons program through a nuclear test–ban treaty, assuming Beijing agreed to sign it. In January 1962, the prime minister wrote the president: "If the test programme of the Great Powers goes on there is no hope of dealing with what you call the *n*th country problem. Some countries will develop powerful systems, probably the Chinese and eventually the Germans—and, of course, the French. Nothing can stop them if the Great Powers go on."[61]

The Kennedy administration recognized early the "*n*th country problem." In April 1961, John Steeves, the deputy assistant secretary of state for Far Eastern Affairs, reported to Hilsman that new information "made clear the fact that it is no longer a question of whether Peking is engaged in a nuclear weapons program, but only when a detonation may be expected." And there were doubts about China signing a nuclear testing agreement. The same

---

59. For more on this subject, see Gordon Chang, "JFK, China, and the Bomb," and *Friends and Enemies,* chap. 8, and Michael R. Beschloss, *The Crisis Years: Kennedy and Khrushchev, 1960–1963,* 619–20.

60. Chang, *Friends and Enemies,* 252, and "JFK, China, and the Bomb," 1300.

61. Harold Macmillan, *At the End of the Day, 1961–1963,* 156.

month that Steeves wrote his memo, the CIA reported that China "knows that most major disarmament agreements could not be fully effective without [its] adherence" and that it would use "the resulting leverage to demand the return of Taiwan, diplomatic recognition, and perhaps admission to the UN."[62]

The United States refused to make such concessions. In April, Lord Home explained to Rusk his belief that the PRC would not agree to discuss nuclear disarmament or nuclear testing unless it received admission to the United Nations. Rusk responded that Taiwan would never agree to such an exchange, and if China alone were represented in the United Nations, then there would be strong pressure upon the United States to leave the international body. He added that it was a moot point, because "there was little prospect for disarmament anyway."[63]

Yet the White House remained convinced a nuclear test–ban treaty was vital to keep China from obtaining an atomic capability. In a January 1963 meeting of the National Security Council, the president stated,

> The test ban is important for one reason. Chicom. If the Soviets want this and if it can help in keeping the Chinese Communists from getting a full nuclear capacity, then it is worth it. [I] can't foresee what the world would be like with this. [The] Chinese Communists are a grave danger. [The b]an is good if it does prevent them from becoming a nuclear power.[64]

Macmillan agreed. In a March letter to Kennedy, he argued that while a nuclear test–ban treaty "might not stop the Chinese and French tests altogether, it would certainly drive them both underground, which is a good thing from this angle."[65]

Anxiety over China's nuclear potential was linked to the Sino-Soviet split; the rift between the two communist powers was a mixed blessing. After the second Quemoy-Matsu crisis, relations between the two communist states worsened, particularly as China increasingly directed polemics at Khrushchev, and the latter talked of "peaceful coexistence" and improving relations with the West. The Soviet leader himself had become concerned about China's possible acquisition of nuclear weapons in light of its attitude. Al-

---

62. Memorandum to Hilsman from Steeves, Apr. 12, 1961, RG 59, Bureau of Far Eastern Affairs, Subject, Personal Name, and Country Files, 1960–1963, box 4, NA; "The Sino-Soviet Dispute and Its Significance," Apr. 1, 1961, *CIA Research Reports: China, 1946–1976.*

63. Memorandum of conversation, Apr. 4, 1961, RG 59, Central Decimal File, 1960–1963, box 473, NA.

64. Memorandum by Hilsman, "Mr. Hilsman's Remarks at Directors' Meeting, Jan. 20, 1963, Papers of Roger Hilsman, Subjects, box 5, JFKL.

65. Macmillan, *At the End of the Day,* 460.

though Macmillan's memoirs give little information on his views of the split, Kennedy welcomed it, for it represented the culmination of a hope espoused by Washington since 1949.[66]

At the same time, the Sino-Soviet rift made it less likely that China would sign a nuclear test–ban treaty. In mid-1962, Kennedy wrote Rusk, saying that he hoped to sign a treaty by early 1963 with the Soviet Union. In the six months after the treaty, he foresaw the Soviets and the United States making "every effort" to persuade China and France, respectively, to sign the agreement. This hope dwindled, however, in 1963. In January, the CIA reported that the divergence of interests between the two communist powers "are already so fundamental that, for the most practical purposes, a 'split' between them has already occurred." In fact, in June, Kennedy told the chancellor of Germany, Konrad Adenauer, that "Khrushchev had a real problem with the Chinese and no way to bring them into a test ban."[67]

But 1963 was still down the road; as 1962 progressed, it seemed unlikely that even Washington and Moscow would agree to a test-ban treaty. The situation changed drastically in October when U.S.-Soviet tensions reached new levels during the Cuban missile crisis. For thirteen days, the world watched as the superpowers seemed to move closer toward open conflict. Yet, at the end of the month, they reached an agreement, ending the crisis and leading to a collective sigh of relief in the United States and Europe.

Awareness of how close to nuclear war their two nations had come inspired the Soviet and American leadership to work together to prevent another such crisis. Their mutual concern seems to have lessened the pressure on Berlin. And it definitely moved the superpowers toward a nuclear test–ban agreement. In April 1963, Kennedy and Macmillan proposed a tripartite conference to discuss a nuclear test–ban treaty. In June, Khrushchev responded affirmatively, thus opening the door to talks, which began the following month.

In July, Macmillan received word that the United States and the Soviet Union had reached an agreement on nuclear testing. He was thrilled. He wrote in his diary, "I had to go out of the room. I went to tell D. [Dorothy, his wife] and burst into tears. I had prayed for this, night after night."[68] In August, the two superpowers signed the Nuclear Test Ban Treaty.

66. Chang, *Friends and Enemies*, 240. Macmillan, for his part, said simply, "These developments made it clear to me even at the time [1961] that the old lessons of history were once again providing true. Ideological agreement led no more on the Communist side to automatic cooperation than it did among the nations of Europe in the sixteenth and seventeenth centuries." Macmillan, *At the End of the Day*, p. 223.

67. Memorandum to Rusk from Kennedy, undated, POF-Departments and Agencies, box 88, JFKL; memorandum by Cline, "Sino-Soviet Relations," Jan. 14, 1963, *CIA Research Reports, 1946–1976*; Chang, *Friends and Enemies*, 240.

68. Quoted in Horne, *Harold Macmillan*, 2:522.

Aside from banning above-ground nuclear tests, the treaty widened the Sino-Soviet rift. Prior to the accord's signing, the Chinese made clear to the Soviets that they would not take part in it and urged Moscow to withdraw its support. After the superpowers agreed to it, China bitterly denounced the treaty, as well as the Kremlin and the White House, and determined to press on with its own nuclear research. The following month, it lambasted the Soviet Union, charging Moscow with allying with Washington against it, and assailed the policy of peaceful coexistence.[69]

Unfortunately for Macmillan, the delight he felt with the signing of the Nuclear Test Ban Treaty could not offset his distress over matters on the home front. In 1959, the prime minister shifted then–Foreign Minister Selwyn Lloyd to the Treasury and appointed Lord Home as foreign minister. Although the economy showed signs of improvement during that year, it began to worsen afterward. By mid-1962, Macmillan had decided to fire Lloyd and to reshuffle his cabinet. He acted in July, and the Night of the Long Knives, as it came to be known, created a huge stir within England. Just before his action, polls had shown a plurality of citizens were happy with his leadership; afterward, a majority listed themselves as dissatisfied.[70]

Macmillan's political fortunes continued to suffer. In January 1963, France, which had opposed Britain's entrance into the European Economic Community from the beginning, vetoed its application. By March, the Conservative Party was running fifteen points behind Labour, the largest lead for the Labour Party in seventeen years. As a result of Macmillan's inability to control Britain's continued economic troubles, a poll that same month found that 62 percent of Britons felt he should resign.[71]

Shortly thereafter, the Profumo scandal erupted. In 1960, John Profumo had been appointed secretary of state for war. In March 1963, the press became aware of an affair involving Profumo and Christine Keeler, a prostitute who also had been involved with the naval attaché at the Soviet embassy in London. Questions arose about whether Profumo had provided any information to Keeler that she might have passed on to the Soviets. Later that month, before the House of Commons, Profumo denied any "impropriety." Yet, Harold Wilson, the leader of the Labour Party, continued to press the issue, forcing Macmillan to take the matter seriously and to refer it to British intelligence. Finally, in June, Profumo confessed to the affair and to lying to Parliament.

Macmillan attempted to defend his administration, but his standing in

---

69. Morton H. Halperin and Dwight H. Perkins, *Communist China and Arms Control,* 114–16; Harry Schwartz, "Peking Charges Soviet Violation of Amity Treaty," *New York Times,* Sept. 14, 1963.

70. Horne, *Harold Macmillan,* 2:350.

71. Ibid., 456, 470.

public opinion polls declined even further; only 23 percent of Britons now favored his staying on as prime minister.[72] Macmillan himself began to feel fatigued, having expended a great deal of energy in his quest for a nuclear test–ban treaty and his efforts to deflect criticism of his government. Even so, he was unsure whether he would throw in the towel. Finally, a prostate illness in October convinced him that he should not run again. He turned the reins over to Lord Home. Home's term in government lasted only a year; the following October brought an election victory for Wilson and his Labour Party, returning that party to power for the first time since 1951.

Kennedy's career ended much more suddenly and tragically. On November 22, a little more than a month after Macmillan decided to resign, the president was shot and killed. Macmillan was stunned. He called the president's death "a staggering blow." He later recorded that Kennedy was "one of the best-informed statesmen whom it has ever been my lot to meet, and he was altogether without pedantry or any trace of intellectual arrogance. . . . He was always ready to listen to and to be convinced by argument."[73]

Macmillan clearly had the same concerns from 1961 to 1963 that he had had from 1957 to 1960. Furthermore, these concerns echoed those of his predecessors. One was the need to avoid another schism with the United States, made all the more important in light of the tense situation in Europe. Additionally, he wanted to avoid another Korea or taking actions that could cause additional harm to the U.K. economy or create troubles within the Commonwealth. Hence, Macmillan demonstrated his frustrations with America's inability (or unwillingness) to rein in Chiang Kai-shek and refused to give in to U.S. pressure not to sell the Viscounts to China. He made sure, however, to address these issues in ways that would avoid presenting a disunited front to the Communists. He dropped the Taiwan Straits matter almost as soon as he raised it; similarly, his government took pains to present the Viscount deal in a nonelection year and at the last minute so that there would be little time for the White House or Congress to react. Washington's shared desire to avoid disunity, combined with the close friendship that developed between the two allied leaders, gave the prime minister some maneuvering room, seen most clearly when he refused to back down on selling the Viscounts to Beijing.

Where he could give way, Macmillan did so, especially on the question of China's representation. In 1957, Foreign Secretary Selwyn Lloyd had argued that there was no need to hold back on the representation issue because the United States had accepted Britain's decision to eliminate the differential in

72. Ibid., 484.
73. Ibid., quote, 574–75.

trade. As the Kennedy administration, like its predecessor, did not put un-bending pressure on Whitehall on either the military or economic front, it is probable that Macmillan had no reason to use representation as a bargain-ing chip. Furthermore, as the prime minister pointed out, he did not want representation to create another schism with Washington while tensions in Europe were so high.

If there was one subject on which the two allies during 1961 to 1963 agreed from the beginning, it was on the need to keep China from obtaining nuclear weapons. Here, though, they achieved only part of what they wanted. The Soviets signed a test–ban treaty, but the PRC refused.

In January 1964, Ormsby-Gore wrote that Kennedy "remained far ahead of the public and the Congress . . . on almost all matters of foreign policy." He noted, for instance, that through their common efforts, the United States and United Kingdom had succeeded in signing a nuclear test–ban treaty. He continued, "I have no doubt that the general thrust of American policy in East-West relations, as always with the exception of Communist China, would have continued in a direction welcome to Her Majesty's Govern-ment."[74] Whether Kennedy's successor would also accept changes in the U.S. stance toward the PRC remained to be seen.

74. Dispatch, no. 1, Ormsby-Gore to Foreign Office, Jan. 1, 1964, FO 371/174261, PRO.

7

LABOUR TO THE FORE, 1964–1966

The accession of Alec Douglas-Home and Lyndon Johnson to the highest positions in their respective countries' governments did not mean a change in their attitudes toward China. The Labour Party's return to power in 1964 suggested a possible alteration in the U.K. position, but the new prime minister, Harold Wilson, acted cautiously. He did not want to be constantly yielding to the Americans, which created difficulties in his personal relationship with Johnson. At the same time, he realized his nation relied heavily on U.S. military and financial power. As a result, he supported the United States on Chinese representation and trade. Only on the question of the U.K. presence in Southeast Asia did he disagree with the White House, and even here he held off from a final decision for as long as possible in the name of Anglo-American unity. Johnson faced more serious difficulties with Taiwan, especially on the questions of China's UN representation and Taipei's request for technical assistance so it could attack the PRC's nuclear facilities. Johnson gave in on the question of representation and was able to rein in Chiang when it came to an air strike. But he proved less able to convince Wilson to keep British soldiers in Southeast Asia.

Douglas-Home had no desire to become prime minister. When Macmillan first proposed that he take over the reins of power, the then–foreign secretary explained that he liked the Foreign Office and did not want to renounce his peerage in the House of Lords. But after getting a clean bill of health, support from Parliament, and a request from the queen to form a government, he agreed to take over the prime ministership.[1]

For Johnson, the accession to power was more sudden and tragic. The vice president had been in John F. Kennedy's motorcade on November 22 when the American leader was killed. Secret Service agents quickly whisked Johnson away to safety. He wrote later, following the news of the president's death, "I found it hard to believe that this nightmare had actually happened. The violence of the whole episode was unreal, shocking, and incredible."[2]

1. Alec Douglas-Home, *The Way the Wind Blows*, 182–85.
2. Lyndon Baines Johnson, *The Vantage Point: Perspectives of the Presidency, 1963–1969*, p. 10.

The working relationship between Johnson and Douglas-Home lasted only a year; in October 1964, elections in Britain led to the latter's defeat by the Labour Party candidate, Harold Wilson. During that year, however, Douglas-Home made clear that he would follow the China policy of his predecessor. Though the issue of Chinese representation was just coming to a head when Britain held its elections, Douglas-Home would have supported the United States so as to avoid another split with Washington over a matter of policy. Moreover, 1964 was an election year in the United States, and past prime ministers had demonstrated a reluctance to make any significant moves on China policy at such times because of the volatile political climate in Washington. Indeed, in response to a January 1964 parliamentary question concerning the possibility of his visiting China or inviting a high Communist official to Britain, the prime minister stated that "the timing of visits of this nature requires careful consideration. I do not consider an immediate meeting to be practical."[3]

At the same time, Douglas-Home planned to hold firm on the question of trade. The Foreign Office noted in February 1964 that some sections of the American public opposed the United Kingdom's trading with the PRC. The United States, however, needed to appreciate British public opinion, which ran strongly in favor of such commerce. The Foreign Office concluded, "This is a subject on which our two countries must surely try to agree to differ."[4] In short, London had no intention of bringing its trade policy more in line with that of Washington.

While maintaining contacts with China through trade and diplomatic relations—which would also serve the purpose of widening the Sino-Soviet rift—Douglas-Home, like those before him, would also seek to limit the threat it posed to countries on its periphery. The Foreign Office in early 1964 expressed this very intention: Britain would continue its commercial and diplomatic ties while at the same time taking economic and military measures to prevent communism from taking hold in countries on China's borders. The Foreign Office added that London had no objection to exploiting Beijing's desire to reduce its economic dependence on Moscow "by offering long term credits or other artificial inducements."[5]

Johnson similarly had no intention of changing U.S. China policy. For example, at a February 1964 press conference, a reporter asked whether the president foresaw any situation in the near future that might lead him to rec-

3. "Relations with China," *London Times*, Jan. 29, 1964.
4. Brief, "East-West Trade," undated (Feb. 1964), FO 371/174283, PRO.
5. Brief, "Policy toward Communist China," undated, FO 371/174283, PRO.

ommend the PRC's admission to the United Nations. Johnson's answer was to the point: "No, I do not."[6]

Several considerations guided the American leader's stance on China. First, World War II had taught him that one could not appease aggressors. He stated in the House of Representatives in 1947, "Human experience teaches me that if I let a bully or my community make me travel the back streets to avoid a fight, I merely postpone the evil day. Soon he will chase me out of my house."[7]

Furthermore, the new president had come into office without a mandate of his own. He had achieved power through Kennedy's death rather than an election. He therefore wanted to avoid rocking the boat until he himself had been elected. "Rocking the boat" tied in with a third reason. Johnson's concerns for the poor, the elderly, and for minorities made him determined to enact programs designed to aid these groups. Minority issues, particularly civil rights, however, were highly charged in the 1960s, and when tackling them, one ran the risk of endangering other initiatives. Johnson himself wrote,

> Civil rights was both an emotional and a moral issue. As an emotional issue, it contained the seeds of rebellion on Capitol Hill—not just over civil rights but over my entire legislative program. As a moral issue, however, it could not be avoided regardless of the outcome.[8]

To drastically alter America's China policy would no doubt anger those elements in Congress opposed to any such changes and, thus, threaten Johnson's domestic programs.[9]

Finally, there was the amorphous issue of public opinion. The China bloc was losing influence by 1964. It had lost a leader to retirement, Senator William Knowland (R-California), in 1958, and in 1962, another outspoken China bloc official, Representative Walter Judd (R-Minnesota), failed in a bid for reelection. He proved irreplaceable. Then there was the muted reaction to a major policy statement in December 1963, given by Assistant Secretary of State for Far Eastern Affairs Roger Hilsman. In his speech, Hilsman called for an improvement in Sino-American relations: "We should like to be less ignorant of them and for them to be less ignorant of us." While he made it clear that the United States would continue to contain China, and offered little in the way of specific new policies, he did state, "We are determined to

6. Lyndon Johnson, *Public Papers of the Presidents of the United States: Lyndon Johnson, 1963–1969*, 1963–1964, 1:256.

7. Quoted in Doris Kearns, *Lyndon Johnson and the American Dream*, 99–100.

8. Johnson, *Vantage Point*, 37.

9. H. W. Brands, *The Wages of Globalism: Lyndon Johnson and the Limits of American Power*, 28–29.

keep the door open to new possibility of change." The speech aroused little public or congressional opposition, suggesting that Americans were prepared for a more constructive Sino-American relationship. Yet a poll conducted around the same time found that a majority of Americans still regarded China as a greater threat than the Soviet Union, opposed its admission to the United Nations, and rejected the idea of selling wheat to Beijing to help it solve its continuing food crisis.[10]

The contradiction in public opinion helps explain Johnson's wariness, aside from the other considerations listed above. It is also important to note that Hilsman's speech, though it suggested forming a more constructive relationship with China, likely aroused little opposition because of its cautious tone: the assistant secretary gave no details as to what policies the United States might consider changing and at the same time made it plain that Washington would continue its containment of Beijing.

In short, therefore, the period from late 1963 to late 1964 saw nothing in the way of significant changes in terms of Anglo-American policy toward China. Both nations maintained their previous attitudes on the issue. The election of Harold Wilson, though, and the accession of the Labour Party to a position of power in Britain added a new element and raised new questions for the United States.

The Labour Party had not been in power in Britain since 1951, when Clement Attlee lost the prime ministership to Winston Churchill. During the next thirteen years, the party, especially its left wing, strongly opposed the Conservatives' support of America's China policy. Though the Tories adopted some positions in opposition to the United States—such as on the issue of the differential in trade—Labour argued more needed to be done.

In the few years prior to Wilson's election, evidence suggested that if it returned to power, the Labour Party might seek further changes in U.K. China policy. In June 1959, Francis Galbraith, the first secretary of the U.S. embassy in London, noted that the party's "opinion on the Far East is critical of US policies, critical indeed of present UK policies in that area, and must inevitably supply a weaker will to act in the face of Communist probes and pushes in the Far East than has been the case with the Conservatives." Among other things, "Labour would probably stand as one for admission of Red China to the U.N."[11]

10. Bachrack, *Committee of One Million*, 203; "Report on Changes in Public Attitudes toward Communist China by Samuel Lubell Associates," undated, NSF-Country File, box 237, LBJL; State Department History, "Communist China," undated, Administrative Histories-Department of State, box 3, LBJL. For the full text of Hilsman's speech, see *Department of State Bulletin* (Jan. 6, 1964): 11–17.

11. Dispatch, no. 3053, Galbraith to Department of State, June 23, 1959, RG 59, Central Decimal File, 1955–1959, box 2609, NA.

During the early 1960s, Labour intensified its attacks on the Conservative government's policy toward Beijing. Most notably, in February 1961, the party published a pamphlet entitled "China and the West," in which it called for a "thorough reappraisal" of Britain's stance toward the PRC. It demanded the neutralization of Taiwan, the shortening and eventual scrapping the trade controls imposed against China, and the ending of British "subservience" to the United States by voting in favor of Beijing's representation in the UN.[12]

Wilson himself shared these sentiments. In 1960, he united with Barbara Castle—a high-level member of Labour's left wing who later joined Wilson's cabinet—in lambasting the U.S. government for refusing to allow American firms with subsidiaries in Britain to trade with China. During a visit to the United States in 1963, he stated on the television show *Meet the Press* that he favored Beijing's admission to the United Nations. In light of his attitude, in October 1964, days before his election, the magazine *U.S. News and World Report* declared, "Mr. Wilson's views are known to be opposed to U.S. policy on several issues of key importance," including "Red China's place in the United Nations."[13]

Although the Sino-Indian conflict revealed continued divisions within Labour over some aspects of Britain's China policy, the party won the 1964 elections. Several issues played their part in Labour's victory. First, the appearance in 1957 of the Campaign for Nuclear Disarmament (CND) split Labour between Hugh Gaitskell, then leader of the party, and his supporters, and Labour's left wing, which demanded Britain's unilateral nuclear disarmament. These divisions within Labour, combined with an improving economy, helped Macmillan win the 1959 elections. By 1961, however, Gaitskell had defeated the challenge to his leadership. He was aided by the verbal excesses of the CND itself, which caused the movement to lose support rapidly. Thus, by the beginning of 1962, the CND no longer represented a dividing force within Labour. Second, an economic boom that had hit England in early 1964 began to lose power, raising questions about the Conservatives' ability to run the country. Finally, there was Quintin Hogg. Hogg, also known as Lord Hailsham, had been Macmillan's minister for science and became overlord for education and science under Douglas-Home. During one stop in his campaigning for the prime minister, Hogg faced repeated heckling on

12. Rowan, "A Foreign Policy in Opposition," 252–53; airgram, no. G-1008, Barbour to Secretary of State, Feb. 16, 1961, RG 59, Central Decimal File, 1960–1963, box 1334, NA.

13. *Hansard Parliamentary Debates* 5th ser., vol. 632 (1960–61), cols. 368–78; *U.S. News and World Report* (Apr. 15, 1963): 19 and (Oct. 12, 1964): 55. For more on Barbara Castle, see "Sketches of 16 Cabinet Ministers Named by New Government in Britain," *New York Times,* Oct. 18, 1964.

the Profumo scandal. Exasperated, the minister retaliated: "If you can tell me there are no adulterers on the Front Bench of the Labour Party, you can talk to me about Profumo. If you cannot tell me that, you had better not dabble your fingers in filth." His attack created an uproar in England and further damaged the Conservatives' political ambitions.[14] When the votes were tallied in October 1964, Harold Wilson and the Labour Party emerged as victors.

The relationship that developed between Wilson and Johnson proved to be nothing like that between Macmillan and Kennedy. Whereas the latter pair had developed a close friendship, the former pair never did. Wilson rapidly came to dislike the president's talking down to him and the U.S. leader's attempts to control him with the so-called "Johnson treatment." The growing American commitment to Vietnam and Johnson's efforts to get Britain to send troops to fight alongside the Americans added to Wilson's disenchantment with the president. Likewise, Johnson had troubles with Wilson. The president liked to be in control. Wilson, though, had no intention of letting Johnson dominate him, and his efforts to distance himself personally from his American counterpart did little to endear him to the president. Johnson also openly expressed his belief that British prime ministers used visits to Washington to boost their political standing at home, though it is not clear why Johnson found this distasteful. Wilson's refusal to send troops to Vietnam and his attempts to mediate between parties to bring an end to the war served to further anger the president. (In fact, Johnson was supposedly so fed up with Wilson at one point that he referred to him as a "little creep camping on my doorstep.") Given their personal and policy differences, it is not surprising that the new prime minister publicly declared during his first visit to Washington in December 1964 that his nation's relationship with the United States was a "close" as opposed to a "special" one. Johnson, for his part, never mentioned in his memoirs his meeting with Wilson in December 1964—or the five other summits he held with the British prime minister in Washington during his five years in office—thereby suggesting a lack of respect for the U.K. head of state.[15]

Although Wilson had little personal liking for Johnson, and would have

14. Horne, *Harold Macmillan*, 2:215, 253, 333; Kenneth Young, *Sir Alec Douglas-Home*, 172, 212, 214.

15. D. Cameron Watt, *Succeeding John Bull: America in Britain's Place, 1900–1975*, 145; Austen Morgan, *Harold Wilson*, 271; Robert M. Hathaway, *Great Britain and the United States: Special Relations since World War II*, 77; Johnson quote from John Dumbrell, "The Johnson Administration and the British Labour Government: Vietnam, the Pound and East of Suez," 117. Dumbrell notes that this quote "may be slightly apocryphal . . . but it does have a ring of authenticity."

preferred to keep his distance, he was well aware of how heavily Great Britain relied on the United States, both militarily and economically. For instance, he told members of the Conservative opposition that the British were "dependent" on U.S. deterrent capabilities.[16] They also drew from America's financial strength, a concern that tied in with his hedging on a final decision to remove British troops from East Asia.

In short, Wilson had good reason to avoid shaking up his government's relationship with Washington. Accordingly, he was unwilling to adopt policies toward China that would provoke strong opposition in the United States. Such was the case when the issue of China's representation in the United Nations once again reared its head.

In light of Labour's past position on Chinese representation and Wilson's statements on the issue, the Johnson administration wanted to bring the new U.K. government firmly in line with its own policy. Within two weeks after Labour's victory, U.S. Secretary of State Dean Rusk held talks with the new British foreign secretary, Patrick Gordon-Walker. Rusk explained that more than ever, the United States was concerned about the PRC. In January 1964, over American objections, France recognized the Chinese Communist government. Furthermore, during the year—and as a result of the Cuban missile crisis—Soviet leader Nikita Khrushchev—whom the PRC did not like because of his continued talk of "peaceful coexistence" with the West—found himself replaced by Leonid Brezhnev. These events, said Rusk, probably led the PRC to believe that its policies were paying off; allowing Beijing into the United Nations would only provide further proof of this. He therefore hoped that Whitehall would continue to support the "important question." Gordon-Walker refused to make any commitment. Rusk therefore pressed the matter again on October 28. That same day, Assistant Secretary of State for International Organization Harlan Cleveland told the North Atlantic Council that it was necessary to stand firm on the representation question; China would consider admission to the United Nations a reward for aggression and cause more trouble.[17]

The pressure upon the Wilson administration worked. The prime minister himself likely worried that taking a position in opposition to the United States would strain the Anglo-American relationship, something he wanted to avoid, particularly at a time when Britain increasingly needed U.S. financial support. Though Washington foresaw a close vote, it expected to prevent

16. Harold Wilson, *The Labour Government, 1964–1970: A Personal Record,* 56.

17. Memorandum of conversation, Oct. 26, 1964 and telegrams, nos. 1880, Foreign Office to Peking, Oct. 28, 1964 and 39 Saving, United Kingdom Permanent Delegation to NATO to the Foreign Office, Oct. 29, 1964, FO 371/175977, PRO.

China's admission. As it turned out, though, a crisis involving Article Nineteen of the UN Charter—which prevents a UN member from voting if it is in arrears in its financial payments to the international organization—led the General Assembly to shelve all controversial issues, including the vote on representation.[18]

As the 1965 vote approached, the White House again questioned Britain's position. In August, Michael Stewart, the minister of the British embassy in Washington, informed William Bundy, the new U.S. assistant secretary of state for Far Eastern Affairs, that Britain again would vote for the "important question." Reports during the next two months suggested that the United States would prevail on the representation issue.[19]

The final vote proved both a victory and a defeat. The "important question" passed, and a resolution sponsored by Albania that called for the expulsion of Taiwan and the admission of the PRC was rejected, but only by a 47-to-47 tie. The official State Department history for the Johnson years pointed out that this vote was "very disturbing to the supporters of [Taiwan] because it (1) reflected the steadily weakening support of [Taipei's] position and (2) more ominously, implied a possible defeat the following year." Furthermore, if Beijing's supporters achieved a simple majority in 1966, they might put "pressure on wavering states or those such as the UK, which recognize Peking but which have supported the important question principle," to vote in favor of the PRC.[20]

The close vote created a problem for the United States and increased tensions in U.S.-Taiwanese relations. William Bundy recollected that in early 1966, he and Johnson had been concerned enough about the possibility of losing the representation vote that they seriously considered a change of position. Indeed, based upon recommendations from Bundy, U.S. Ambassador to the United Nations Arthur Goldberg, Assistant Secretary to the UN Joseph Sisco, and Rusk, Johnson had approved a plan to approach Canada and ask it to submit a resolution calling for the admission of both Beijing and Taipei.[21] The United States, in short, was again looking into "two Chinas."

18. Position Paper, "Visit of Prime Minister Harold Wilson, Dec. 7–8, 1964" dated Dec. 4, 1964, NSF-Country File, box 213, LBJL; Max Harrelson, *Fires All around the Horizon: The U.N.'s Uphill Battle to Preserve the Peace,* 212.

19. Memorandum of conversation, Aug. 18, 1965, RG 59, Central Foreign Policy Files, 1964–1966, box 3329, NA; memorandum to Johnson from Thomson, Sept. 14, 1965, Papers of James C. Thomson, box 11; memorandum to Bundy from Ropa and Cooper, Oct. 14, 1965, Papers of James C. Thomson, box 13, JFKL.

20. State Department History, "Chinese Representation in the UN," undated, Administrative Histories-Department of State, box 4, LBJL.

21. Oral History of William P. Bundy, June 2, 1969, LBJL Oral History Project. Though

Washington, ironically, had rejected such an idea in 1961, because of the resistant attitude of both Congress and Taiwan. And, just it had in 1961, Taiwan would condemn such a proposal.

Taiwan's leader, Chiang Kai-shek, was already unhappy with Washington. Following China's successful testing of a nuclear device in October 1964, both Chiang and his wife had requested that the United States provide Taipei with "such material and technical aid as are necessary for destroying the Chinese Communist nuclear installations." Washington had refused. In a clear allusion to the war in Vietnam, Rusk argued that Beijing's "reaction would be violent and would result essentially in the employment of their principal weapon, their enormous manpower, in offensive retaliatory operations beyond their borders." Moreover, such an attack would lead "all the nations of the world, including those on the periphery of China" to condemn the United States "for starting a nuclear war."[22]

The American attitude on China's representation only increased the Taiwanese leader's concerns. On June 30, the U.S. ambassador to Taiwan, Walter McConaughy, explained to Chiang that while the United States would continue to support Taipei's holding of a seat in the United Nations, in light of the 1965 vote, Washington might have to use new tactics to keep Taiwan in and China out. There is no evidence that Chiang knew of the U.S. approach to Canada, but he realized that "new tactics" might refer to "two Chinas." He made clear to McConaughy that he would not accept such a resolution, and if the PRC received admission, Taiwan would leave the UN. Two days later, Nationalist Foreign Minister Wei Tao-ming repeated Chiang's threat and added that as far as Taiwan was concerned, new tactics were not needed. Rusk was less certain, noting that Canada and Italy were wavering on the issue. During the next two months, U.S. and Taiwanese officials expressed their differences on representation. In the meantime, Britain reaffirmed its support for the "important question."[23]

In September, probably again because of Taiwan's opposition to a "two

---

the houses of Congress did not pass resolutions declaring their opposition to the admission of China, 334 lawmakers signed a petition in late 1966 declaring their opposition to letting Beijing into the international body. See "114 Liberals Urge U.N. to Bar Peking," *New York Times*, Oct. 31, 1966.

22. Letter to Johnson from Chiang, Nov. 23, 1964, NSF-Country File, box 244 and memorandum of conversation, Sept. 20, 1965, NSF-Country File, box 238, LBJL.

23. Telegram, no. 42, McConaughy to Secretary of State, July 5, 1966, NSF-Country File, box 239, LBJL; telegram, no. 22, McConaughy to Secretary of State, July 1, 1966; memorandum of conversation, July 3, 1966; telegram, no. 26684, Rusk to New York, Aug. 12, 1966; and telegram, no. 36063, Rusk to London, Aug. 26, 1966, RG 59, Central Foreign Policy Files, 1964–1966, box 3329, NA.

Chinas" proposal, Rusk announced that Washington would adhere to the past tactic of opposing another Albanian-style resolution and supporting the "important question." The secretary of state reaffirmed the view that China's admission would disrupt the activities of the United Nations. He also noted the PRC's support for North Vietnam in its war with South Vietnam and the United States. Finally, he stated that activity within China caused by the Cultural Revolution—to be discussed in the following chapter—underscored the "militancy and unyielding mood of Peking's current leaders."[24]

On October 27, however, Italy created problems for the United States when it proposed the establishment of a study committee. As noted previously, the White House in 1961 had considered such a measure, only to reject it because of opposition from within the country and from Taiwan. Shortly thereafter, Canada introduced its "two Chinas" proposal. The United States, which originally had asked Canada to introduce such a motion, now rejected it in favor of the "important question." Requests that the Canadian government withdraw its proposal failed. Pushed into a corner, Washington decided to support, but not cosponsor, the Italian resolution while moving forward on the "important question."[25]

Neither Britain nor Taiwan supported the U.S. decision. On November 12, N. C. C. Trench, the counselor of the British embassy in Washington, stated that his government could not back the study committee proposal because to do so might anger China and harm Sino-British relations. He added that London would support the "important question" and oppose the Canadian resolution. Taiwan's reaction was even stronger. Fearing that the study committee might lead to "two Chinas," in several discussions, Taiwanese officials threatened to recall their representative from the United Nations if the Italian resolution passed. Rusk suggested on November 26 that Johnson send a personal message to Chiang, urging him not to withdraw from the UN if the General Assembly adopted the Italian proposal.[26]

Johnson's appeal to Chiang had the intended effect. On November 29, McConaughy informed Rusk that the Nationalist leader had agreed that Taiwan would not leave the United Nations but would "withdraw" temporarily from

24. Circular telegram from Rusk, no. 49274, Sept. 16, 1966, RG 59, Central Foreign Policy Files, 1964–1966, box 3329, NA.

25. Administrative History, "Chinese Representation in the UN," LBJL.

26. Telegram, no. 32736, Rusk to New York, Nov. 12, 1966, RG 59, Central Foreign Policy Files, 1964–1966, box 3332; telegram, no. 1542, McConaughy to Secretary of State, Nov. 25, 1966, RG 59, Central Foreign Policy Files, 1964–1966, box 3330, NA; telegram, unnumbered, White House Situation Room to the president, Nov. 26, 1966, NSF-Country File, box 240, LBJL; Administrative History, "Chinese Representation in the UN," LBJL.

the international body as a form of protest. Ultimately, Chiang never had to implement his threat, as the General Assembly rejected the study committee and Albanian-style resolutions and passed the "important question."[27]

Johnson's personal appeal to Chiang and Wilson's wariness about challenging the United States played their parts in keeping China out of the UN. Interestingly, Wilson's desire to avoid difficulties with Washington was felt as well on the trade front. Given his past comments, it seemed that the new prime minister would strongly resist the restrictions on trade with Beijing. The opposite proved to be true, no doubt because of his country's economic dependence on the United States.

Between 1964 and 1966, calls increased from within the Johnson administration for a relaxation of the embargo, more so than they had during the Kennedy years. In October 1964, a month before Johnson's election, James Thomson, a special assistant on Far Eastern affairs in the State Department —and someone who had favored a change in the U.S. position toward China as early as 1961—recommended to National Security Adviser McGeorge Bundy that Washington alter its policies toward Beijing. His suggestions included an end to the differential in trade with the PRC and Russia: "[W]e should move quietly to place our trade in non-strategic goods with Communist China on the same basis as our trade with the Soviet Union." Thomson was not alone. During the next two years, Hong Kong Consul General Edward Rice; Edward Komer, a member of the National Security Council staff; and a study conducted by members of the State and Defense Departments called for a reexamination of the trade embargo, particularly in terms of food and medicine. Each argued that relaxation might moderate Beijing's feelings toward Washington.[28]

Yet there was opposition within the administration to any suggestion of a change in policy. At a June 1965 cabinet meeting, Rusk argued that neither concessions nor an offer of diplomatic recognition by the United States would lead the PRC to alter its policies toward Washington. In May 1966, Undersecretary of State George Ball told the U.S. ambassador to the Warsaw talks, John Gronouski—who was about to appear on television—that he was

27. State Department History, "Republic of China," undated, Administrative Histories-Department of State, box 3; telegram, no. 1587, McConaughy to Secretary of State, Nov. 29, 1966, NSF, Country File, box 240, LBJL; Administrative History, "Chinese Representation in the UN," LBJL.

28. Memorandum to Bundy from Thomson, Oct. 28, 1964, NSF-Country File, box 238; airgram, no. A-309, Rice to Department of State, Nov. 6, 1964, NSF-Country File, box 238; Study, "Communist China—Long Range Study," June 1966, NSF-Country File, box 245; memorandum to Johnson from Komer, Mar. 2, 1966, NSF-Files of Robert Komer, box 1, LBJL.

not to discuss the matter of trade with China.[29] Ball's order again suggested that Washington intended to maintain a hard line when it came to trade with Beijing.

Johnson supported the latter group. Despite winning election in 1964, he remained cautious. In 1965, not only was the president guiding his domestic programs—the Great Society—toward passage, but he was sending U.S. ground troops into Vietnam to protect the South Vietnamese government from communism. By the end of the year, there were 184,000 U.S. soldiers fighting the Vietcong and North Vietnamese in South Vietnam, as compared to only 16,000 U.S. "advisers" in November 1963. To ease the trade sanctions against China, which was providing military support to North Vietnam, would seem highly contradictory and could create an uproar in Congress, thereby threatening the president's domestic programs.

As with Chinese representation, the new prime minister was careful to avoid angering the United States over the subject of trade with China. In December 1964, Gordon-Walker quashed a year-long discussion over whether to allow the company Hawker Siddeley to sell Comet airplanes to Beijing. Not only was the Comet superior to the Viscount aircraft, but the Royal Air Force used Comets for transport; it would be, he argued, difficult to deny, both to India and the United States, that the plane had no military value. He concluded that "it would certainly be well to warn Hawker Siddeley that they should not assume that Her Majesty's Government would necessarily allow such a contract to be fulfilled."[30]

Of further interest are discussions between Wilson and Soviet Premier Alexei Kosygin that took place in February 1967. During these talks, which dealt primarily with Vietnam, Wilson asked Kosygin "whether he would favour a separation of the lists for China and the Soviet Union, involving less stringent controls on the latter." In effect, this would amount to a return to the differential, which Britain had eliminated in 1957. Wilson did not say how Kosygin responded. But the prime minister added that the Soviet premier "took note that this was an idea we were considering."[31]

Why Wilson would suggest a return to the differential is unclear. He might

29. Minutes of Cabinet Meeting, June 18, 1965, Cabinet Papers, box 3; memorandum of telephone conversation, May 9, 1966, Papers of George W. Ball, Personal Papers, box 3, LBJL.

30. Letters to Peck from Greenhill, Sept. 23, 1963 and to Paren from De Zulueta, Oct. 4, 1963, FO 371/170702; telegram, no. 3647, Ormsby-Gore to Foreign Office, Nov. 22, 1963, FO 371/170703; FO Minute by MacLehose, Nov. 25, 1964, and letter to president, Board of Trade from Gordon-Walker, Dec. 15, 1964, FO 371/175946, PRO.

31. Wilson, *Labour Government,* 349.

have made his offer to Kosygin for several reasons: first, Britain needed the trade; second, with or without the Comet sale, there was little evidence that eliminating the controls on trade would lead to any significant expansion in commerce with China.[32] Finally, and most important, Wilson likely believed the United States would react less violently to a relaxation of the trade embargo against the Soviet Union than against China. In the 1950s, the United States had proved much more willing to accept a relaxation in the trade controls aimed at Moscow than those directed at Beijing. The prime minister may have concluded that Washington would not object strongly to a further relaxation. And an increase in trade with the Kremlin could provide a means to improve East-West relations.

Wilson's desire to avoid difficulties in his relationship with Washington also made itself felt through the presence of British troops in East Asia. Facing continued economic difficulties at home, the prime minister realized he had to cut spending, including that for the military. Unwilling to weaken Anglo-American ties, he hedged for as long as possible. Only when he decided he had no choice did he begin the removal of British soldiers from the region.

In 1964, the United Kingdom maintained a sizeable military presence in the so-called east of Suez region (referring, logically, to territories east of the Suez Canal). Two considerations underlay this commitment: Whitehall wanted to continue to play the role of great power, and it had to help its former colony of Malaya (now Malaysia) defend itself against attacks from Indonesia. Accordingly, it had stationed 54,000 troops in Malaysia.

To the United States, Britain's military presence not only provided an important supplement to Washington's own forces in Vietnam, but also contributed to the effort to contain Communist China. The official State Department history for the Johnson years explained that London's presence in East Asia "was of highly significant political value from the US viewpoint as an adjunct to our efforts to contain Chinese Communist expansionism. A substantial British cutback would create a vacuum which would be difficult and costly for the United States to fill."[33]

The problem was that the United Kingdom was experiencing increasing difficulty playing its part. When Wilson took office, he inherited a balance of payments deficit of £800 million. Complicating matters was Britain's financial health, which showed no signs of improvement during the first half of 1965. From January to April, the nation's average trade deficit was £17 mil-

32. Dispatch, no. 7, Garvey to Foreign Office, Feb. 3, 1965, FO 371/181006, PRO.
33. State Department History, "Great Britain," undated, Administrative Histories-Department of State, box 1, LBJL.

lion; this figure grew to £57 million in just the month of May. The fact that it cost Britain £360 million a year to maintain its forces in the east of Suez region only added to London's financial woes.[34] Speculation in the pound continued, placing additional pressure on Britain's reserves.

Wilson strongly opposed devaluing the pound as a means of solving his country's fiscal troubles, arguing that it would be seen as a political act and "would have plunged the world into monetary anarchy." The United States also opposed devaluation, as it would make the dollar unstable and force Washington to raise interest rates. The subsequent fall in revenue would require raising taxes to fund both Vietnam and the Great Society. The result "would be mounting public sentiment in favor of withdrawal [from Vietnam] that would become irresistible."[35] Consequently, with powerful American support, London borrowed $3 billion in short-term loans, helping temporarily to ease pressure on the pound and on Britain's reserves.

These two issues—the role British troops could play in helping the United States contain communism in East Asia and the United Kingdom's own economic difficulties—placed severe limits on Wilson's flexibility in his relationship with the United States. As one of the prime minister's biographers explained,

> The state of the domestic economy and Britain's foreign relations were not distinct. The decision not to devalue had been made partly to reassure international opinion. But it was on foreign support—especially American—that the Government's ability to defend and maintain confidence in the currency rested. American goodwill, in turn, depended on Britain's continuing ability to serve US foreign policy as a reliable ally, giving moral or, as the White House increasingly hoped, practical help in Vietnam, performing a peace-keeping role East of Suez, and exerting an influence within the Commonwealth.[36]

In his memoirs, Wilson denied that there was any link between Britain's need for financial support and his backing of the U.S. effort in Vietnam. This was not the case. In February 1966, he told his cabinet to remember that American monetary assistance "is not unrelated to the way we behave in the Far East: any announcement of our withdrawal, for example, could not fail to have a profound effect on my personal relations with LBJ and the way the Americans treat us." Similarly, when Minister of Technology Frank Cousins later that year asked why Wilson had not taken a firmer stand on Vietnam,

---

34. Wilson, *Labour Government,* 107; Alan Dobson, "The Years of Transition: Anglo-American Relations, 1961–1967," 250; H. G. Nicholas, *The United States and Britain,* 169.

35. Wilson, *Labour Government,* 6; Jeremy Fielding, "Coping with Decline: U.S. Policy toward the British Defense Reviews of 1966," 638.

36. Ben Pimlott, *Harold Wilson,* 365.

the prime minister sharply retorted, "Because we can't kick our creditors in the balls."[37] Clearly, while Wilson might have defined his relationship with Washington as "close" rather than "special," he, like his predecessors, felt obliged to adopt policies with an eye to maintaining American goodwill.

But prudence demanded an examination of where Whitehall might cut spending, if necessary. The result was the first indication that Britain might reduce its presence east of Suez. In late May 1965, Gordon-Walker warned that because of his nation's fiscal troubles, London was going to "gradually give up" its bases in Aden and Singapore and transfer the soldiers located there to islands in the Indian Ocean and Australia. The foreign secretary's statement of intent greatly worried America as well as Australia and New Zealand. At quadripartite talks held in September in London between the United States, Britain, Australia, and New Zealand, the American representative stated that Singapore was "essential" to the "Western effort to create stability in the area." If the British abandoned their base there, "it would have [the] most serious adverse consequences" throughout Southeast Asia and the western Pacific. The United States also warned that the U.S. effort "to relieve the sterling was inextricably related" to London's maintenance of "its commitments around the world." Wellington, Canberra, and Singapore added pressure of their own. Singapore's leader, Lee Kwan Yew, said a U.K. withdrawal would undermine his government. New Zealand believed Britain's plan would increase pressure on it to make a commitment to the area that it wanted to avoid. Australia was even more cautious because of tensions between the Philippines and Malaysia over the Malaysian state of Sabah.[38]

Wilson and his subordinates realized that Britain's allies did not approve of talk of withdrawing from east of Suez. They continued to indicate, though, that fiscal constraints required removing the U.K. presence from the region. The Johnson administration urged London to defer any final decision, arguing that withdrawal "would make our task of containing Communist China more rather than less difficult."[39]

Not only did Wilson refuse to guarantee a continued, large British presence in East Asia, but he further frustrated the Johnson administration by his attitude toward the Vietnam War. Wilson agreed that communism had to be

37. Wilson, *Labour Government,* 264; Richard Crossman. *The Diaries of a Cabinet Minister,* 1:456; Philip Ziegler, *Wilson: The Authorised Life of Lord Wilson of Rievaulx,* 228–29.

38. Airgram, no. A-3017, Bruce to Department of State, June 3, 1965, RG 59, Central Foreign Policy Files, 1964–66, box 2774, NA; telegrams, nos. 1024 and Secun 5, Bruce to Secretary of State, Sept. 7 and 9, 1965, NSF-Country File, box 208, LBJL; Ziegler, *Wilson,* 210–11; McKinnon, *Independence and Foreign Policy,* 169–70.

39. Wilson, *Labour Government,* 187; Administrative History, "Great Britain," LBJL; memorandum to Johnson from Rostow, Jan. 20, 1966, NSF-Country File, box 209, LBJL.

kept in check, and he clearly saw a link between his position on the war and U.S. financial assistance. Accordingly, and despite growing opposition in Britain to the war, the prime minister publicly supported the U.S. effort. Yet his backing was moral, not military. He consistently refused Johnson's requests to send British troops to Vietnam. Not only was it financially and politically imprudent to send troops to Vietnam, but he did not want to risk getting dragged into another Korean-style conflict. Johnson did not appreciate Wilson's continued refusals. The prime minister's decision to dissociate Britain in mid-1966 from the U.S. bombing of Hanoi and Haiphong further angered the president. *U.S. News* noted that the British stance had led White House officials increasingly to question their relationship with the United Kingdom and to wonder if the latter had the "ability to pull its weight with the U.S. in the affairs of the world."[40]

The president also disliked Britain's attempts to mediate an end to the war. Wilson supported the U.S. war effort, but his backing did not mean he wanted the fighting to continue indefinitely. He was facing intense pressure both from within his own party and from British students to stop supporting the Americans. Furthermore, the longer and larger the U.S. commitment, the fewer resources Washington would be able to provide in the future to what the United Kingdom considered more vital interests, such as Europe. Hence, between 1965 and 1967, he made several attempts to bring about an end to the war. Johnson saw Wilson's efforts as interference, which further strained the relationship between the two men. For instance, during a telephone call in January 1965, a frustrated president chastised Wilson: "[W]hy don't you run Malaysia and let me run Vietnam?" When the two leaders met in June 1967, their "personal relations were cooler" than in the past. When the president "appealed to Wilson to reconsider recently announced plans for a withdrawal from East of Suez," the British head of state "seemed embarrassed and evasive." One U.S. official stated after the June meeting, "I'm afraid on this occasion the two of them didn't interrelate at all. It wasn't a case of a special relationship, there was just no relationship."[41]

The "recently announced plans" that concerned Johnson dated back to that April. Facing continued economic problems—and with the Indonesia-

40. Watt, *Succeeding John Bull,* 148; Hathaway, *Great Britain and the United States,* 90; Dumbrell, "The Johnson Administration and the British Labour Government," 221; Lloyd C. Gardner, *Pay Any Price: Lyndon Johnson and the Wars for Vietnam,* 172; *U.S. News and World Report* (Aug. 1, 1966): 33.

41. Memorandum of telephone conversation, Feb. 10, 1965, *FRUS, 1964–1968,* 2:229–32; Watt, *Succeeding John Bull,* 147; George C. Herring, *America's Longest War: The United States and Vietnam, 1950–1975,* 2d ed, 168–69; Nichols, *The United States and Great Britain,* 167, 168; Pimlott, *Harold Wilson,* 459–60, 465; Ziegler, *Wilson,* 224.

Malaysia conflict having ended in August 1966—the British accelerated their planning for a possible withdrawal. Most significantly, the British decided to add Singapore to their list of base cuts, with the intention of reducing their strength in Singapore and Malaysia by one-half by 1970 or 1971. London also proposed removing all of its troops from mainland Asia (with the exception of Hong Kong) by the mid-1970s. Rusk, McNamara, and Johnson all tried to convince Wilson and his advisers to defer a final decision. Once again pointing to the impact a U.K. withdrawal from East Asia would have upon the containment of China, the secretary of state contended that London's action "would be viewed in Hanoi and Peking" as a "victory for them." The Australian government and a "fighting mad" Lee Kwan Yew also approached Whitehall. All failed to convince the Wilson administration to reconsider.[42]

It is interesting that the Wilson government's determination to leave Southeast Asia came when it did; during the first half of 1967, the economic situation in Britain actually improved. The trade figures looked promising, and the economy seemed to be picking up steam.[43] Despite the improvement, it is likely that Wilson realized that his country was not out of the woods yet, and saving was still required.

The second half of 1967 showed just how precarious Britain's financial status was. The Six-Day War of June led to a closure of the Suez Canal and cut Britain off from Middle Eastern oil. The canal's closure alone cost Britain £20 million a month. The inability to obtain petroleum from the Middle East forced London to get it from other, more expensive sources. Making matters worse was a dock strike in Liverpool that began in October; the effects of the work stoppage began to spread to the foreign exchange markets. Wilson realized he was being forced into a decision he did not want to make. On November 8, Chancellor of the Exchequer James Callaghan and he agreed to devalue the pound and informed the White House. Frightened by the possible repercussions, the United States worked to put together another international financial package designed to save the British currency. On November 13, Wilson, informed by his advisers that the new package would require Britain to impose rigid domestic restrictions, rejected it. The Americans said they had done all they could. On November 18, Britain announced a 14 percent devaluation of the pound, from $2.80 to $2.40.[44]

---

42. Telegram, no. 177203, Rusk to London, Apr. 18, 1967, NSF-Country File, box 210; telegram, no. 179522, Rusk to London, Apr. 20, 1967, NSF-Country File, box 211, LBJL; Administrative History, "Great Britain," LBJL; Denis Healey, *The Time of My Life,* 289, 290, 292; Bruce Reed and Geoffrey Williams, *Denis Healey and the Policies of Power,* 204; Ziegler, *Wilson,* 331.

43. Wilson, *Labour Government,* 373.

44. Ibid., 209–10, 400, 440, 451–54; Childs, *Britain since 1939,* 134; British Petroleum reported in August 1967 that it expected to pay an extra £100 million by the end of

Therefore, during the second half of 1967, the British economy was again in severe trouble, and savings were needed. Following devaluation, Whitehall completed plans for cutting its forces east of Suez. In January 1968, Foreign Secretary George Brown informed the Johnson administration of Britain's formal decision to remove all its forces from East Asia—again, with the exception of Hong Kong—by March 13, 1971. The foreign secretary explained that this was necessary "to help achieve" one billion pounds "in overall budget savings in order to make devaluation work and to restore the strength of the sterling." Rusk expressed his disappointment and his feeling that Britain's decision would have a negative effect on American public opinion and on the willingness of the United States to maintain a presence in the region. He added that Washington could not fill the vacuum left by Britain. Johnson called it "a heavy blow." Even Wilson seemed to recognize the extent to which his decision downgraded his nation in the eyes of Washington when "he quoted lines from Kipling's 'Recessional' in the House of Commons." On January 18, the British government announced its decision.[45]

Despite Labour's accession to the prime ministership in 1964, British policy toward China followed that of Harold Wilson's Conservative Party predecessors. Like Harold Macmillan, Wilson did not want to create a schism with the United States, particularly when his country relied on Washington for military and financial support. He also believed in the importance of containing communism. Consequently, he supported the United States on the "important question," despite his comments as opposition leader, and refused to challenge the White House with regard to trade with Beijing.

Johnson could be pleased that Wilson demonstrated a reluctance to fight the United States on representation and commerce. But Vietnam got in the way of any improvement in their never-close relationship. Wilson's talk of removing the U.K. military presence from the east of Suez region was seen as a threat to the U.S. effort to wage war in Vietnam and to contain China. Realizing the link between Britain's financial health and the maintenance of American goodwill, the prime minister hedged on withdrawing British troops from East Asia and gave moral support to the war effort. But he refused to go further: fearful of another Korea, he rejected Johnson's request for combat troops and attempted to end that conflict. And, when he realized he had no choice, he began the process of withdrawing U.K. forces from East

---

the year as a result of increased transportation costs. Combined, the major British oil companies expected to spend an additional £350 million. See "BP Hardest Hit by Suez Ban," *London Times*, Aug. 31, 1967.

45. Administrative History, "Great Britain," LBJL; Hathaway, *Great Britain and the United States*, 84; Dickie, *"Special" No More*, 143.

Asia. Wilson's decision vis-à-vis Vietnam and east of Suez, combined with Johnson's attitude on those same issues, served not only to strain the chilly relationship between the two men, but also to devalue in American eyes the "special relationship" between the two countries.

8

"A POSTURE OF QUIET REASONABLENESS," 1966–1968

On May 26, 1966, the U.S. consulate in Hong Kong reported, "Since February, [the] weight of [China's] media has been increasingly directed toward internal events." Foreign events received little attention. Indeed, said the consulate, Chinese Foreign Minister Chen Yi recently had told journalists from Asia and Africa that "China's major enemies at present are internal ones, and that these enemies are now [a] much greater threat than external enemies." The telegram concluded, "We do not know precisely what is happening on [the] mainland and what it means."[1]

What the consulate was reporting were the opening salvos of what became known as the Great Proletarian Cultural Revolution. Like the Great Leap Forward, the Cultural Revolution created chaos in the PRC, but the American response was different. John F. Kennedy had continued the hard-line policy of his predecessors, despite the turmoil in China caused by the Great Leap. Lyndon Johnson did not, even though he too faced an intransigent Beijing. Changes in U.S. public opinion, the war in Vietnam, and the chaos within China caused by the Cultural Revolution led the Johnson administration to adopt a more flexible, conciliatory attitude, which it called a "posture of quiet reasonableness." Through this policy, the White House implemented, or considered implementing, a variety of measures designed to demonstrate its desire for an improvement of Sino-American relations. The importance of Washington's response to the Cultural Revolution was two-fold: first, while it did not eliminate areas of divergence in policy between the United States and Britain over China, it did represent the beginning of a process by which Washington's China policy came more in line with that of London. Second, it opened the door to the Sino-American rapprochement of 1972.

The Cultural Revolution had originated in the failure of the Great Leap Forward. Chinese leader Mao Zedong had hoped that the Great Leap, which

1. Telegram, no. 2152, Hong Kong to Secretary of State, May 26, 1966, RG 59, Central Foreign Policy Files, 1964–1966, box 2006, NA. This telegram was signed "Armstrong." There were, however, two people with the last name of Armstrong at the U.S. consulate in Hong Kong at this time. As it is not clear which one signed the telegram, I am crediting it to the consulate in general.

he initiated in 1958, would allow him to win the race with the Soviet Union to achieve communism and, at the same time, to expand China's economy. Instead, it created serious economic disruption. One major program of the Great Leap was to increase industrial production, particularly that of steel. Peasants were therefore asked to set up private steel furnaces on their land. By late 1958, some 40 percent of the nation's workforce was working on expanding the nation's industry, most of it in terms of smelting iron; peasants spent many hours at the furnaces, rather than in the fields. Those left tending crops had to work harder and longer hours, which proved more than they could endure. Food production fell, and famine spread. Crime increased as some people resorted to stealing food; others engaged in black market activities, taking advantage of those in need. In short, rather than creating the necessary foundation for the achievement of communism, the Great Leap was eroding it.[2]

In mid-1959, Mao finally became aware that the Great Leap was creating economic problems for his country. But he did not realize the seriousness of the situation. Others did. In July 1959, Defense Minister Peng Dehuai, in a letter to Mao, criticized the intiatives of the Great Leap Forward. The Chinese leader took it as a personal insult and had Peng purged. He replaced Peng with Lin Biao, the head of one of China's field armies and a staunch supporter of Mao's policies. Peng, though, was not alone. Liu Shaoqi, whom Mao had determined in 1945 would succeed him, came out against the Great Leap Forward in 1962. Though Mao was angered, Liu's view was shared by many others within the CCP and indicated how divided the party had become over government policy.[3]

Opposition to government policy, however, did not appear simply within the ranks of the CCP. There was growing dissatisfaction among the general population, reflected particularly in literature and scholarly discourse. Works critical of the Great Leap increasingly appeared, some of which called for the incorporation of capitalist ideals in the economy. Others supported unorthodox interpretations of Marxism or criticized the government's po-

2. Li, *Private Life of Chairman Mao*, 282–83; Stanley Karnow, *Mao and China: A Legacy of Turmoil*, 96–99; Roderick MacFarquhar, *The Origins of the Cultural Revolution*, vol. 2, *The Great Leap Forward*, 119. MacFarquhar's book is a must-read for those wanting to learn more about the Great Leap Forward. Also useful are Jasper Becker, *Hungry Ghosts: Mao's Secret Famine;* Xizhe Peng, "Demographic Consequences of the Great Leap Forward in China's Provinces"; and Penny Kane, *Famine in China, 1959–61: Demographic and Social Implications.*

3. Li, *Private Life of Chairman Mao*, 303–4, 310, 313–21, 385–86; John King Fairbank, *The Great Chinese Revolution: 1800–1985*, 304, 306, 321; Barbara Barnouin and Yu Changgen, *Ten Years of Turbulence: The Chinese Cultural Revolution*, 32–33, 37.

litical decision making. Most famous was a play by the vice mayor of Beijing, Wu Han, entitled *Hai Rui Dismissed from Office,* about the unfair dismissal of a Ming dynasty official by his emperor. Mao took the play as an attack upon his decision to fire Peng Dehuai and publicly rebuked the vice mayor.[4]

These attacks upon Mao's policies made the Chinese leader increasingly suspicious of those around him. His personal doctor, Li Zhisui, wrote that, as early as 1958, Mao believed that his opponents wanted to kill him. This fear "was tightening its grip" by the mid-1960s, making it increasingly difficult for the Chinese leader to trust people, including his doctor. By mid-1967, during the height of the Cultural Revolution, stated Li, Mao, "was suspicious of everyone and interpreted my reluctance to get politically involved as a sign of less than total loyalty to him. One did not need to side with the opposition to make Mao suspicious. Staying on the political sidelines roused his suspicions, too."[5]

During 1965, the debate gradually polarized the CCP. On the one hand were the "leftists" or "Maoists," who included Mao Zedong and Lin Biao. On the other were the "revisionists"—whom the U.S. media and government came to refer to as the "moderates" or "conservatives"—led by Liu Shaoqi. Mao disliked Liu and his supporters for two reasons. First, as far as Mao was concerned, they were inspired by the "revisionist" Marxism practiced by the Soviet Union, which preached peaceful coexistence. Second, they took the wrong attitude toward the growing U.S. threat in Vietnam.

The American escalation in Vietnam worried Mao. He was now threatened on both flanks: the Soviet Union to the north, and the United States to the south. Whereas Russia was the home of "revisionist" Marxism, the United States was the leader of the world anticommunist movement. As in Korea, Mao considered it important to help fellow communists, but Vietnam provided a possible route for a U.S. invasion of China itself. The Chinese leader did not want war with America, but he also did not favor peaceful coexistence. To deal with the U.S. threat, Mao began preparations for possible war with the United States, sent warnings to Washington not to invade North Vietnam, and provided massive amounts of aid—including 320,000 ground troops—to help Hanoi's war effort.

As far as Mao was concerned, the "revisionists" favored a different set of policies. If they took power, he feared, they would work to improve relations with the Soviet Union; abandon national liberation movements, such as that

4. Li, *Private Life of Chairman Mao,* 440–42, 447–48, 454; Barnouin and Changgen, *Ten Years of Turbulence,* 12–22.
5. Li, *Private Life of Chairman Mao,* 233–34, 443, 488.

in Vietnam; and seek a rapprochement with the United States. Removing the "revisionists" from positions of power—or eliminating them—would thus serve several purposes: the threat to Mao's very life would be removed, support for national liberation movements would continue, and tensions with Moscow and Washington would remain high. Indeed, keeping these tensions high would serve one other purpose. Just as Mao saw using the second Quemoy-Matsu crisis as a way to drum up support for the Great Leap Forward, so might using the fear of war with the United States help mobilize the Chinese people against the "revisionists."[6]

By the end of 1965, Mao was ready to implement what would become the Cultural Revolution. He was determined to eliminate Liu, Liu's supporters, and the general "revisionist" Marxist threat he felt was infecting China. He began a systematic process of expanding criticism against Liu, keeping secret from the "revisionist" leader his ultimate goal. In May 1966, Mao drafted the "May 16th Circular," which officially declared the beginning of the Cultural Revolution. But how to put it into effect remained unclear, a fact Mao used to his advantage. When questions arose over how to implement the Cultural Revolution at universities, Liu and other party leaders favored the sending of work teams. They were not certain if Mao would favor such an idea; therefore, Liu and another "revisionist," Deng Xiaoping, traveled to Hangzhou, where Mao was in "retirement." The Chinese leader used this opportunity to draw Liu out, giving an ambivalent response to his subordinate's recommendation. When he returned to Beijing, Liu ordered the sending of work teams to the universities. Mao now struck. He returned to the capital in July and denounced the work teams. The following month he demoted Liu and replaced him with Lin Biao.[7]

Mao next quickened the pace. He began rallying student support behind him, which took the form of the Red Guard movement. Millions of Red Guards traveled to assemblies to hear Mao speak, clogging the national transportation system. By August 1966, some ten million tons of goods and materials had piled up, leaving many Chinese short of food.[8] To make matters worse, the Red Guards, though organized to deal with "bourgeois" elements in China, soon began to go after "revisionist" party members, including Liu and Deng. The CCP leaders who found themselves under attack responded in kind, forming their own Red Guard groups.

6. For this paragraph and the previous one, see Zhai, *China and the Vietnam Wars,* esp. chap. 6.

7. Ibid., 140–41; Barnouin and Changgen, *Ten Years of Turbulence,* 71–78.

8. Hiroyuki Nagahashi, "China's Food Crises and Its U.S. Policy Change, 1965–1972," 14–16.

The situation grew more confused during 1967. The Red Guards at times attacked army installations; the army could not respond, as it had been ordered to stay out of the conflict. This changed in January, when the army received instructions to help the Left in the struggle against the "revisionists." The problem was that all of the mass organizations that had sprung up since the Cultural Revolution began swearing loyalty to Mao and claimed they sought to oust Liu. It therefore became impossible to determine who made up "the Left." Furthermore, in part because of Red Guard attacks upon their installations, the regional army commanders did not much care for the student radicals and began fighting them. In March and April, the government issued orders to restrain the regional armies, but with the effect that the Red Guards were able to intensify their attacks upon the military.[9] China appeared headed toward civil war.

After September 1967, the attacks on the regional commands by the Red Guards began to subside. Yet factionalism began to infect the army itself, leading to friction between regional and main-force units. Though Beijing again ordered the military to stay out of the conflict, it did not stop the factionalism, which soon appeared in the main-force units themselves. Mao realized that if this continued, his "last card would have been played and he would have lost control of the situation completely." Accordingly, in July 1968, he ordered the disbanding of the Red Guards and commanded the army to undergo political training. Furthermore, by this time, Mao had purged many of those individuals whom he perceived as threats. In fact, noted one historian of the Cultural Revolution,

> By 1969, seven of the seventeen members of the Politburo had been deprived of office and declared enemies of the party. Fifty-three of the ninety-seven members of the Chinese Communist Central Committee had been purged, as had four of the six regional first party secretaries and twenty-three of the twenty-nine provincial first party secretaries.

Among those individuals successfully purged was Liu Shaoqi. With the threat to his power largely removed, Mao began in September 1968 a process that officially brought an end to the Cultural Revolution, but not before tens of millions had been executed or died from starvation, lack of medical treatment, or even the cannibalization of those considered enemies of the state.[10]

The Cultural Revolution played an important part in America's reconsid-

9. Karnow, *Mao and China,* 134–43

10. Fairbank, *Great Chinese Revolution,* 330; Anne F. Thurston, *Enemies of the People,* 108, 124, 132–53; Barnouin and Changgen, *Ten Years of Turbulence,* 115; For incidents of cannibalism during the Cultural Revolution, see Yi Zheng, *Scarlet Memorial: Tales of Cannibalism in Modern China.*

eration of its China policy. Up to early 1966, the Johnson White House had given little sign that it was prepared to make concessions to the PRC, despite a growing clamor from within the administration for some significant indication of a willingness to improve relations. The White House's stance began to change, however, beginning in 1966. One reason had to do with trends among the general public. Although a majority of Americans remained opposed to or concerned about China, they were coming to regard Beijing, and not Taipei, as representing the majority of Chinese. For instance, possibly because of the war in Vietnam, the number of Americans opposed to the U.S.-Taiwan defense treaty rose from 6 to nearly 20 percent between 1966 and 1969. Moreover, while most Americans were still unwilling to see Beijing admitted to the UN, a larger number than before was prepared to accept such an eventuality. Indeed, a growing number of Americans wanted to learn more about the PRC itself. Such interest no doubt was facilitated in part by the activities of the chairman of the Senate Foreign Relations Committee, J. William Fulbright (D-Arkansas), who in March 1966 held a series of well-publicized hearings in which he criticized U.S. policy toward Beijing. In the meantime, the China bloc continued to suffer. For example, in early 1965, the bloc attempted to fund a documentary film explaining why the United States should remain hostile toward Beijing, but it could not raise the fourteen thousand dollars needed to produce it. Public requests to the State Department for speakers on China increased between 1966 and 1968 until they were second only to those for speakers on Vietnam.[11]

A change in public opinion, however, was not the only reason behind the Johnson administration's growing interest in improving relations with China. The expanding commitment in Vietnam also had an effect. The PRC's reaction to the American escalation of the war prompted the U.S. intelligence community to warn of possible Chinese intervention in the conflict if the United States sent ground troops into North Vietnam, or if it seemed the Hanoi government was about to fall. In addition, U.S. officials, including Rusk, Secretary of Defense Robert S. McNamara, and U.S. Consul General to Hong Kong Edward Rice, expressed their concern that if the United States overstepped certain limits—such as intensifying the bombing of North Vietnam—then it ran the risk of drawing China into the war.[12] These warnings had a powerful impact upon Johnson. He remembered Beijing's intervention

11. Kusnitz, *Public Opinion and Foreign Policy,* 115–18; Administrative History, "Communist China," undated, Department of State-Administrative Histories, box 3, LBJL. For the further decline of the China bloc, see Bachrack, *Committee of One Million,* chap. 10.

12. See, for instance, telegram, no. 7581, Rice to Secretary of State, May 1, 1967, NSF-Country File, box 241; memorandum to president from Rusk, Feb. 2, 1968, NSF-Country File, box 243; memorandum to president from McNamara, Oct. 14, 1966, NSF-NSC Meetings File, box 2; memorandum to president from Rostow, Apr. 27, 1967,

in the Korean War and did not want to face a similar situation in Vietnam.[13] As he said in his memoirs, "When a president faces a decision involving war or peace, he draws back and thinks of the past and of the future in the widest possible terms." Another Korea greatly concerned him. He told Senator Richard Russell (D-Georgia) in late May, 1964:

> I spend all my days with Rusk and McNamara and [National Security Adviser McGeorge] Bundy and [Special Adviser Averell] Harriman and [Deputy Secretary of Defense Cyrus] Vance and all those folks that are dealing with it and I would say that it pretty well adds up to them now that we've got to show some power and some force, that they do not believe—they're kinda like [UN Commander Douglas] MacArthur in Korea—they don't believe that the Chinese Communists will come into this thing. But they don't know and nobody can really be sure.

Similarly, he told reporters the month after the Gulf of Tonkin incident that he had received suggestions regarding an offensive against North Vietnam. "As far as I am concerned, I want to be very cautious and careful, and use it only as a last resort, when I start dropping bombs around that are likely to involve American boys in a war in Asia with 700 million Chinese."[14] An improvement in Sino-American relations could help guarantee that Beijing would stay out of the conflict.

The start of the Cultural Revolution added a final element. U.S. officials realized that there was a struggle within China, one that they correctly perceived as an effort by Mao to eliminate his rivals. They understood that there were two major groups in this struggle, with Liu Shaoqi leading one side and Mao and Lin Biao heading the other. Beyond that little was clear, as the situation remained very fluid. It was therefore impossible to determine who might win the struggle or how Sino-American relations might be affected.[15]

Yet it was important to hold out to both sides in the struggle the possibil-

---

NSF-Memos to the President, box 15; notes of president's meeting, Aug. 24 and Dec. 5, 1967, Tom Johnson's notes of meetings, box 1, LBJL

13. For two excellent studies of the Johnson administration's fear of another Korea, see Yuen Foong Khong, *Analogies at War: Korea, Munich, Dien Bien Phu, and the Vietnam Decisions of 1965;* and Jong Chul Park, "The China Factor in United States Decision-making toward Vietnam, 1945–1965."

14. Johnson, *Vantage Point,* 151; Michael R. Beschloss, ed., *Taking Charge: The Johnson White House Tapes, 1963–1964,* 364–65; Lyndon Johnson, *Public Papers of the Presidents of the United States: Lyndon Johnson, 1961–1969,* 1963–1964, 2:1164.

15. Memorandum, "The Leadership Upheaval in Communist China," June 17, 1966; telegram, no. 2327, Rice to State Department, June 25, 1966; and memorandum to Director, CIA Office of National Estimates, July 15, 1966, NSF-Country File, box 239; memorandum to Jenkins from Rostow, Dec. 22, 1966, and memorandum to Rostow from Jenkins, Feb. 3, 1967, NSF-Country File, box 240; memorandum to Rostow from Jenkins, June 1, 1967, NSF-Country File, box 241; memoranda, to Rostow from Jenk-

ity of improved relations. Consequently, the White House adopted its "posture of quiet reasonableness," so named by Alfred Jenkins—the Johnson administration's China watcher. The official State Department history of the Johnson administration explained that this policy had evolved from a belief that the Cultural Revolution might lead to the coming to power of "pragmatic leaders willing to reappraise China's relationship with the United States." In turn, while Washington would avoid "involvement in Chinese internal struggles," it would "make clear to the contenders that the option of better relations with the United States was open to them."[16] It is therefore not surprising that Johnson, during the last two years of his presidency, continued to call for an improvement in Sino-American relations.[17]

Though the White House sought to maintain a "posture of quiet reasonableness" and to stay out of China's internal affairs, there were officials in the administration who called upon the president to choose sides. Most of them favored the "revisionists." In September 1966, the U.S. ambassador to Yugoslavia, C. Burke Elbrick, sent a telegram to National Security Adviser Walt Rostow, saying that a "knowledgeable Yugoslav" had argued that if Lin Biao came to power, he might provoke a U.S. attack upon the PRC so as to obtain for the leftists more backing within China. Elbrick urged the United States to ease its pressure on Hanoi so as to give Lin less opportunity to provoke such an attack; he said that this would give the "revisionists" an opportunity to take power. The following month, the CIA backed the ambassador's argument. The agency stated that "visitors to Communist China have the impression that the accession of Lin will mean war between Communist China and the United States of America."[18]

The most persistent arguments against Lin, however, came from Consul

---

ins, Sept. 13 and Nov. 21, 1967, and CIA Intelligence Information Cable, "Apparent Chinese Intention to Restore Normalcy in Its Foreign Relations, as Reflected in Confidential Remarks by Chou-En-lai to Afro-Asia Conference," Jan. 15, 1968, NSF-Country File, box 242; memorandum to Rostow from Jenkins, Aug. 21, 1968, NSF-Country File, box 243; memorandum to president from Rostow, Jan. 9, 1967, NSF-Memos to the President, box 12; memorandum to president from Rostow, Feb. 20, 1967, NSF-Memos to the President, box 13; memorandum to Rostow from Jenkins, Apr. 21, 1967, NSF-Memos to the President, box 16; and memorandum to Jenkins from Rostow, July 2, 1968, NSF-Memos to the President, box 37, LBJL.

16. Memorandum to Rostow from Jenkins, Feb. 3, 1967, NSF-Country File, box 240, LBJL; Administrative History, "Communist China," LBJL.

17. See Johnson, *Public Papers,* 1966, vol. 2:930, 936, 998, 1222–23; 1967, vol. 1:13, 546; 1967, vol. 2:704, 1171–72; 1968–69, vol. 1:26.

18. Telegram, no. 1016, Elbrick to Rostow, Sept. 28, 1966 and CIA Intelligence Information Cable, "Chinese Communist Military and Economic Preparations to aid North Vietnam," Oct. 28, 1966, NSF-Country File, box 240, LBJL.

General Rice. At the end of August, taking note that the army commander now seemed to be Mao's heir-apparent, Rice told the State Department, "Lin's greater power hardly augurs well for us." Rice added, "If he wields power after Mao goes, he is likely to prove a thorough Communist, xenophobic in his nationalism, and lacking in true appreciation of the outside world." The consul's telegram shook Rostow so much that he forwarded it to President Johnson with a note saying that if Lin consolidated his position, he was "bad news."[19]

Such warnings influenced Rusk. In April 1967, he sent a telegram to Rice, asking about speculation that an escalation of the American attacks in North Vietnam would strengthen the position of the Maoists and, in turn, undermine the possibility of a "pragmatic regime in China." Rice responded three days later. "It is obvious," he said,

> that the need to prepare for war can be used to justify and secure popular acceptance of austerity measures and personal sacrifices which regime imposes for multiple purposes of which war preparation is only one. . . . Even Mao's purge of his opponents is being justified on grounds which include allegations [that his opponents] have already engaged in traitorous activity or are persons who would do so if foreign invasion afforded them the opportunity to turn against Mao's communist state.[20]

Rice's concerns about the Maoists did not mean that he regarded the moderates as the best solution for China but that he saw them as a lesser evil. As he stated in another telegram to the secretary of state in September 1967:

> it is the Maoists, urging opposite everything we support and support for everything we oppose, who are our most bitter enemies. It does not follow that Mao's enemies would be our friends. But they include the advocates of more moderate policies towards the outside world; they also include the pragmatists whose policies have given Communist China its periods of progress and internal stability.

Yet despite his favoring of the "revisionists," Rice, like Jenkins, felt it was best to keep quiet. "I think there is little benefit to be derived and some danger to our own interests involved in arguing [in favor of the "revisionists"] in public or international forums." The United States had only a very limited ability to influence conditions in China. Furthermore, it would anger U.S. allies to suggest that Washington favored continued anarchy in the PRC. Once again, when he received this telegram, Rostow forwarded it to Johnson. The

19. Telegram, no. 1392, Rice to State Department, Aug. 30, 1966, and memorandum, Rostow to the president, Aug. 30, 1966, NSF-Memos to the President, box 10, LBJL.

20. Telegrams, no. 184833, Rusk to Hong Kong, Apr. 28, 1967 and no. 7581, Rice to Secretary of State, May 1, 1967, NSF-Country File, box 241, LBJL.

president sent no response, but he clearly favored the "posture of quiet reasonableness." James Thomson, who represented the White House in a July 1966 conversation with State Department officials, noted that the president "wanted to keep a high degree of flexibility in the matter of reconciliation with Communist China."[21]

If most of those officials in the Johnson administration who expressed opinions of the situation in China favored the "revisionists," at least one person, John Roche of the White House staff, supported the Maoists. In early 1967, U. Alexis Johnson, the U.S. ambassador to Japan, publicly declared his support for the "moderates." Johnson's comment infuriated Roche, who penned a harsh memo to the president. He stated that he personally favored the pro-Maoist faction on the grounds that a victory for the "revisionists" would probably lead to a Sino-Soviet reconciliation, which would prove detrimental to America's interests. He concluded, however, "I would suggest that the Secretary of State issue firm instructions to our missions not to dabble in the religious wars of the Communist world."[22] Roche apparently was persuasive for he never again complained about Ambassador Johnson or any other U.S. official.

Yet the pressure upon the White House to take a stand on the turmoil in China came from outside the administration as well. Despite his promise in 1958 not to seek to return to the mainland by force, Chiang Kai-shek remained determined to reestablish himself in China. Between 1959 and 1963, he argued that the famine and economic problems created by the Great Leap Forward provided an opportunity for him to attack the mainland. Presidents Dwight D. Eisenhower and John F. Kennedy had refused to give Chiang the support he needed.

But the Kuomintang leader continued to look for opportunities to return to the mainland. In September 1966, the CIA reported that Chiang wanted to exploit the turmoil in China, but was frustrated by domestic problems, particularly a political "malaise" caused by "discouragement and apprehension with regard to U.S. policies and support." This concern was related first to a U.S. decision to terminate its economic aid to Taiwan. Washington believed that Taiwan's economy was strong and wanted to use its economic assistance elsewhere. Nationalist officials felt America's action came too soon

21. Telegram, no. 7581, Rice to Secretary of State, May 1, 1967, NSF-Country File, box 241, LBJL; telegram, no. 1876, Rice to State Department, Sept. 21, 1967, and memorandum to president from Rostow, Sept. 25, 1967, NSF-Memos to the President, box 23, LBJL; memorandum of conversation, July 21, 1966, Papers of W. Averell Harriman, box 442, Library of Congress, Washington, D.C..

22. Memorandum to president from Roche, Feb. 15, 1967, NSF-Name File, box 5, LBJL.

and too quickly. Chiang was further upset by his lack of adequate military forces to stage an attack on the mainland. Accordingly, the agency expected the KMT leader in the near future to ask for U.S. assistance.[23]

Indeed, just over a week after the CIA's report, Taiwanese Defense Minister Chiang Ching-kuo met with U.S. Ambassador to Taiwan Walter McConaughy and asked for U.S. help so that Chiang could attack the mainland. He said that since the beginning of the Cultural Revolution there had been a further deterioration in Sino-Soviet relations and increased turmoil in China. McConaughy replied that U.S. policy was not to use force against the PRC. Furthermore, if the United States supported Chiang's effort to return to the mainland, it would destroy opportunities provided to the United States by the Cultural Revolution.[24]

Chiang, though, continued to press his case. In March 1967, U.S. Ambassador to the United Nations Arthur Goldberg reported that during a trip to Asia—which included a stop in Taiwan—the Nationalist president had told him that in light of the Sino-Soviet split, "the drain of Vietnam on Peking's resources, and the serious turmoil on the mainland itself," now was the time to strike. All he asked for was U.S. logistical support. Goldberg said he avoided a substantive response, but he felt that Johnson should reject Chiang's request.[25]

The president did just that. In May, the CIA reported that Taiwan had no plans "in the near future" to stage an invasion of China. Recognizing his dependence upon the United States and not wanting to anger Washington, the KMT head of state backed down.[26] The United States had forced Chiang to accept its "posture of quiet reasonableness."

Britain adopted its own policy of "quiet reasonableness" in response to the Cultural Revolution. For London, the Cultural Revolution's effects were first felt in its colony at Hong Kong. For nearly a decade, Britain had had few concerns about the colony, despite attempts by Taiwan to use it for sabotage operations against China. Officials in London and Hong Kong Governor Sir Robert Black believed that Mao had no intention of putting pressure on the colony.[27]

23. CIA Intelligence Information Cable, Sept. 12, 1966, NSF-Country File, box 240, LBJL; Tucker, *Taiwan, Hong Kong, and the United States,* 62.

24. Telegram, no. 901, McConaughy to Secretary of State, Sept. 20, 1966, NSF-Country File, box 240, LBJL.

25. Memorandum of conversation, Mar. 1, 1967, NSF-Country File, box 241, and memorandum to president from Goldberg, Mar. 9, 1967, NSF-Memos to the President, box 14, LBJL.

26. CIA Intelligence Information Cable, May 8, 1967, NSF-Country File, box 241, LBJL.

27. Telegram, no. 311, Caccia to Foreign Office, Feb. 3, 1959, FO 371/141217; letters to Dalton from Stewart, May 10, 1960, to Stewart from MacLehose, May 21, 1960, and to

Though Hong Kong in 1966 felt some reverberations from the Cultural Revolution, the main impact occurred the following year. In May 1967, riots broke out over a wage dispute at a factory in Kowloon. Colonial police arrested and imprisoned a large number of rioters. On May 15, China responded by calling upon Britain to accept all of the workers' demands, to end "all fascist measures" in Hong Kong, and to apologize to and compensate those incarcerated. Beijing also placed a ban on travel by the British chargé d'affaires to China, Donald Hopson.[28]

The United States had some concerns that China's response to the rioting in Hong Kong would lead it to take strong measures against the colony. After the PRC issued its demands, Rusk wrote both Rice and U.S. Ambassador to Britain David Bruce. The secretary of state said that he did not believe Beijing would try to force the British out of Hong Kong, as it would hurt China economically. (In 1965 alone, China obtained about 40 percent of its exchange earnings through Hong Kong.) Nor did he expect the British to request U.S. support in defending the colony. But to play it safe, he ordered the two American officials not to indicate any U.S. willingness to defend Hong Kong. Washington already had an enormous military commitment in Vietnam and could not afford to help the British. Additionally, since Whitehall had proven unwilling to support the U.S. effort in Vietnam, there was no reason for the White House to assist British efforts to defend its colony.[29]

There is no evidence that Britain ever approached the United States for help in defending the colony, probably because U.K. officials did not see Hong Kong as seriously threatened. The United States, for its part, continued to show little concern about a possible Chinese attack on Hong Kong. A November intelligence report stated, "It has become apparent . . . that mainland China does not now wish to take over the colony." Rather, Beijing had consistently argued that "primary responsibility for the anti-British struggle lies with the leftists in Hong Kong and portray[s] the confrontation as a long-term affair." As long as there was no sign of an attack from China itself, Britain intended to stand firm in its opposition to communist activity in the colony.[30]

Stewart from Dalton, Aug. 8, 1960, FO 371/150433; Dispatch, no. 762, Governor of Hong Kong (Black) to Secretary of State for the Colonies, Mar. 16, 1964. FO 371/175888, PRO.

28. "Chinese Demands over Hong Kong," *London Times,* May 16, 1967; Background Paper, "Visit of Prime Minister Harold Wilson, June 1967," May 31, 1967, NSF-Country File, box 216, LBJL.

29. Telegram, no. 197313, Rusk to Hong Kong, May 18, 1967, NSF-Country File, box 241, LBJL; Tucker, *Taiwan, Hong Kong, and the United States,* 213–14.

30. "Peace is Uncertain on Hong Kong Line," *New York Times,* Aug. 5, 1967; memorandum to Rusk from Hughes, Nov. 16, 1967, NSF-Country File, box 242, LBJL.

If Beijing gave little indication of direct action against Hong Kong, the same cannot be said for British interests and nationals in China itself. Shortly after the PRC placed a travel ban on Hopson, Red Guards broke into the house of British diplomat Peter Hewitt, ransacked it, and frog-marched Hewitt—literally marched him about with his hands pinned behind his back—for several hours. Four days later, Beijing ordered Hewitt to leave Shanghai, where he had been stationed, and demanded that London close its post there. On their way to Shanghai airport, Hewitt and another British official, Raymond Whitney, were kicked and smeared with glue. Chinese demonstrators and Red Guards also forced their way into the British mission in Beijing and assaulted Britain's two first secretaries stationed there. In July, in retaliation for arrests in Hong Kong of communist activists, the PRC placed Reuters correspondent Anthony Grey under house arrest. The following month, demonstrators overran the British mission in the capital and set part of it on fire.[31]

It was in response to these attacks on its people and facilities that the government of Prime Minister Harold Wilson adopted it own form of "quiet reasonableness." London matched public clamor for the release of Grey— and some thirteen other Britons detained by the Chinese Communists— with continual representations to Beijing. Whitehall also placed restrictions that ultimately lasted three months on the travel of Chinese officials in Britain. But the Wilson government avoided taking stronger action that might further upset Sino-British relations. In July 1967, Alec Douglas-Home, speaking for the opposition, asked that the Wilson administration consider removing Britain's representation from China if Beijing refused to meet London's demands to release the Britons it was holding. William Rodgers, the undersecretary for foreign affairs, responded that this was a possibility. But, he added, "In some respects what we must seek to do is to follow the example of our staffs in protesting very strongly, but making the most of a difficult situation if we believe that it is in our long-term interests to do so." Hopson, who finally returned to Britain in August 1968, shared Rodgers's viewpoint. He contended that relations with China were still worthwhile: "It was the most populous country in the world and on the way to becoming a nuclear power." Furthermore, as Wilson pointed out at the end of 1968, taking strong action against China would only make it more difficult to secure

---

31. "Briton Refuses to Bow to Mao," *London Times,* May 19, 1967; A. M. Rendel, "China Expels Envoy from Shanghai," *London Times,* May 23, 1967; Anthony Grey, "Red Guards Kick British Envoys," *London Times,* May 25, 1967; "Peking's Mob Attack," *London Times,* June 8, 1967; "Peking Demonstrators Set Fire to British Embassy Buildings," *London Times,* Aug. 23, 1967; Boardman, *Britain and the People's Republic of China,* 138.

the release of Grey and other Britons held by the PRC.[32] Hence, despite calls for action, the Wilson government calmly protested the Chinese government's treatment of British nationals or interests in China, but it refused to take stronger measures that could create additional difficulties for Sino-British relations.

Yet the "posture of quiet reasonableness" involved more than just words. Since the Communist victory in China, Britain had sought to maintain contacts with the PRC, particularly through trade. Contacts, the British hoped, would prevent Beijing's isolation, moderate its attitude toward the West, and split the Sino-Soviet alliance. U.S. policy had tended toward the opposite pole—that the best way to deal with the Chinese Communists and divide Beijing and Moscow was through a policy of pressure. Even after it became clear in the early 1960s that the Sino-Soviet alliance had cracks, the United States maintained its policy of pressure. During the Cultural Revolution, however, the Johnson administration began to change this stance. It took some small steps toward the U.K. position that contacts might make the CCP more willing to seek better relations with the West.

The ever-contentious issue of Chinese representation remained off limits. Though Americans were less opposed to Beijing's admission to the United Nations than in previous years, a majority still did not want China represented. Therefore, in both 1967 and 1968, and over Taiwan's objections, the White House supported a study committee resolution so as to garner support for the "important question." The negative effect of the Cultural Revolution on world opinion and cool Soviet support for the PRC assisted the American effort to keep Beijing out of the international body. In both years—and both times with British support—the "important question" passed.[33]

---

32. "Angry Protest to China Envoy," *London Times*, May 20, 1967; Edward Cowan, "London Restricts Chinese," *New York Times*, Aug. 23, 1967; "Restrictions on Chinese Relaxed," *London Times*, Nov. 22, 1967; "Three More Britons Held by Chinese," *London Times*, Sept. 7, 1968; "China Urged to Release Britons," *London Times*, Oct. 18, 1968; "Britain Plans Strong Appeal for the Release of Grey," *London Times*, Nov. 28, 1968; *Hansard Parliamentary Debates*, 5th ser., vol. 750 (1966–67), col. 1533; Boardman, *Britain and the People's Republic of China*, 137–39; "China Frees British Envoy," *London Times*, Aug. 13, 1968; "Sir Donald Hopson Home," *London Times*, Aug. 20, 1968; "Securing the Release of Mr. Grey," *London Times*, Dec. 20, 1968, p. 6.

33. Kusnitz, *Public Opinion and Foreign Policy*, 164; Drew Middleton, "U.N. Bars Peking by Decisive Vote," *New York Times*, Nov. 29, 1967; Juan de Onis, "U.N. Again Rejects Seating of Peking" and "U.N. Roll-Call on Red China Issue," *New York Times*, Nov. 20, 1968; Administrative History, "Republic of China," undated, Department of State-Administrative Histories, box 3; Administrative History, "Chinese Representation in the UN," undated, Department of State-Administrative Histories, box 4, LBJL.

But the Johnson administration took other initiatives. Rusk did not like the incumbent Chinese leadership; accordingly, he could not ignore the possibility of a less belligerent regime taking power. Therefore, beginning in September 1966, he authorized the State Department's officers abroad to establish informal, private contacts with Chinese officials. Though the United States had a line of communication with China through the ambassadorial talks at Warsaw, it represented only a single route of intercourse and one that remained bogged down on issues such as how to deal with Taiwan. By expanding the number of contacts, Washington hoped to learn more about the attitudes of individual Chinese officers; to "help lessen the 'devil image' of the United States" in China; and to provide intelligence. Unfortunately, this effort at wider communication with Beijing largely failed. Some U.S. officers argued that their host government would disapprove of them contacting Chinese officials. Most, however, reported that the Cultural Revolution made Beijing unwilling to talk with them.[34]

A month after changing its policy on official contacts, the Johnson administration altered its general passport policy. In 1952, the U.S. government had banned the travel of its citizens to the PRC, on the grounds that the Communists were holding Americans prisoner. Under the new regulations, anyone with a reason to go to China (with the exception of tourism) could travel there. Some administration officials, including Assistant Secretary for East Asian and Pacific Affairs William Bundy and Acting Administrator of the Bureau of Security and Consular Affairs Philip Heymann, called for lifting all travel restrictions, but the growing turmoil in China made an end to the limitations on travel seem ill-advised.[35]

At the end of 1967, the federal courts stepped into the picture. In the case of *Lynd v. Rusk,* the United States Court of Appeals for the District of Columbia declared that any American who wished to travel to a restricted area could do so if they agreed not to use or take their passports to their destination. This was an important decision, for the U.S. government no longer had the right to deny American citizens, including tourists, the right to travel to China if they wished. The president and Rusk both expressed their willingness to abide by this decision. Indeed, the secretary of state again demonstrated his flexibility by arguing in favor of revising the administration's passport policy so that anyone who wanted to go to China could get a passport. No action was taken, however, before the end of Johnson's term in office. One possible reason for the lack of action was Beijing's continued hostility toward

---

34. Administrative History, "Communist China," LBJL.

35. Ibid.; Circular telegram, no. CA-13890, Herter to All American Diplomatic and Consular Posts, Aug. 10, 1960, RG 59, Central Decimal File, 1960–63, box 1308, NA.

the idea of Americans traveling to China. Though the State Department by mid-1968 had validated over three hundred passports for travel to the PRC, only a handful of travelers received permission from Beijing.[36] Nor would further revisions in passport policy guarantee that the PRC would admit more Americans. A second possible explanation was that it was not long after the appeals court decision that the Tet Offensive demonstrated that the United States was losing the Vietnam War. The public clamor that ensued and the administration's negotiations with the government in Hanoi to end the war may have drawn Americans' attention away from issues such as travel to China. Even so, the fact that the administration encouraged a liberalized travel policy demonstrated an important shift in thinking on China.

These changes in travel policy raised no outcry from the weakened China bloc, leading the administration to look into some other initiatives. In April 1967, the White House licensed for sale to China pharmaceuticals and medical supplies following reports of epidemics in the PRC created by the turmoil of the Cultural Revolution. Beijing rejected the offer, stating that it was a "dirty trick" and that there were no epidemics in China.[37]

Despite China's rebuff, administration officials continued to call for a relaxation of the trade embargo against the PRC. In February 1968, Rusk said he favored some additional, though minimal, steps that would allow for the shipment of food to China. He argued that with the United States embroiled in Vietnam, taking larger steps would be "misunderstood in key quarters," including Congress. Citing Rusk's memo, William Bundy and Assistant Secretary for Economic Affairs Anthony Solomon argued in favor of more significant changes, including an elimination of the differential. A Policy Planning Council report issued in December echoed the call from Bundy and Solomon. While the administration implemented none of these recommendations, the fact that high-level officials, including Rusk, were suggesting modification of the trade embargo represented steps forward.[38]

These changes, actual or contemplated, received some public exposure. Magazines ranging from *U.S. News and World Report* to the *Bulletin of the*

36. Administrative History, "Communist China," LBJL; Johnson, *Public Papers,* 1968–1969, vol. 1:26; memorandum to president from Rusk, Feb. 22, 1968, NSF-Country File, box 243, LBJL. For background of *Lynd* case, see Fred P. Graham, "Passport Denial Curbed by Court," *New York Times,* Dec. 21, 1967.

37. *Atlantic Monthly* (Oct. 1966): 8; Administrative History, "Communist China," LBJL.

38. Memorandum to Johnson from Rusk, Feb. 22, 1968 and memorandum to Rusk from Bundy and Solomon, undated, NSF-Country File, box 243; Policy Planning Council Report, "U.S. Policy toward Communist China," Dec. 1968, NSF-Subject File, box 50, LBJL.

Atomic Scientists noted the White House initiatives, particularly those on travel policy.[39] Yet there was not as much publicity as might have been expected. There seem to be at least two reasons. First, the decline in power of the China bloc meant less attention was drawn to changes in policy toward the PRC and less debate took place. Second, and more important, Americans directed most of their attention to other concerns, including civil rights, the Great Society, and, of course, Vietnam.

In short, the United States was taking some small, but important, steps toward modifying its China policy, a fact not lost on Britain. Yet there was no concerted Anglo-American approach. In light of past Sino-American relations, there was skepticism within the British government about the possibility of the United States achieving rapprochement.[40] Furthermore, there was little the White House could do to assist Whitehall's efforts to free its nationals from China. And though London could provide indications to Beijing of Washington's desire for improved relations, the present status of Sino-British relations and Mao's fear of, and hostility toward, the United States (at least through late 1968) likely would have made such approaches unsuccessful, if not impossible.

It is interesting to note the changed attitude of the United States toward China from the Great Leap Forward to the Cultural Revolution. Both created severe chaos in China and resulted in millions of deaths. During both, Washington understood the severity of the problems in the PRC. Yet the Kennedy administration had refused to use the chaos caused by the Great Leap Forward to try to improve relations with China, while the Johnson administration recognized the Cultural Revolution could provide an opportunity. The question, therefore, is why.

First, there was U.S. involvement in Vietnam. Under Kennedy, the American presence in Vietnam increased, but it was not until 1965 that a large-scale U.S. intervention with ground troops began. Given the PRC's warnings that it might also become involved militarily, as well as Johnson's fear of another Korea, it was important to convey that the United States was not a threat to China. Johnson clearly remembered that statements of intent with regard to the war had failed to keep Beijing from taking part in Korea; small concessions, such as alterations in the trade sanctions policy, would help emphasize that the United States did not pose a threat.

Second was public opinion. In the early 1960s, Americans had been

39. *Atlantic Monthly* (Oct. 1966): 4–12; *U.S. News and World Report* (Apr. 25, 1966): 16; *Bulletin of the Atomic Scientists* (June 1966): 93–96; *Saturday Review* (Aug. 9, 1966): 10; *Commonweal* (May 20, 1966): 252–53.

40. Boardman, *Britain and the People's Republic of China*, 144.

strongly opposed to improving relations with Beijing. By the mid-1960s, however, they wanted to learn more about the PRC, and the China bloc was no longer the opposition force it once had been. While the shift in public opinion did not mean Americans favored a Sino-American rapprochement —Americans, for instance, still resisted letting Beijing represent China in the United Nations—it did suggest a willingness to expand contacts between the two countries. The Johnson administration therefore could make some changes in U.S. China policy without facing the backlash that would have occurred a few years earlier.

Finally, there was the nature of the chaos in China. The Great Leap Forward was an economic program. It created severe problems for the PRC, but the United States did not see anything to suggest that the chaos on the mainland might lead to a change of leadership. The same was not true for the Cultural Revolution; it was a political battle, and the winners would lead China's government. It was in the interest of the United States to hold out the possibility for better relations should the victors of the Cultural Revolution seek it.

The fact was that Mao, by the end of 1968, wanted better relations with the United States. By September of that year, he had decided it was time to end the Cultural Revolution. During a conference that began that month, several high-level government officials, including Mao's wife, Jiang Qing, and Chinese Premier Zhou Enlai, gave speeches designed to convince the population that the Cultural Revolution was over in all but name. In April 1969, at the Ninth Party Congress, Mao officially declared an end to the Cultural Revolution, though its aftereffects lasted until his death in 1976.[41]

By the time of the Ninth Party Congress, China had begun to come out of its self-imposed isolation. During 1968 and 1969, Hong Kong released many of the Chinese it had put in jail. Public pressure in Britain for China to release Grey mounted, and in the fall of 1969, Beijing freed first the correspondent, then other Britons. Though there would be further arrests (and releases), U.K. officials increasingly saw a softening in the PRC's foreign policy.[42]

More important, China began altering its position toward the United

41. Clare Hollingsworth, *Mao*, 182; Fairbank, *Great Chinese Revolution*, 330–31, 333.

42. Boardman, *Britain and the People's Republic of China*, 139–43; "Freed Grey Inquires about Golf Clubs," *London Times*, Oct. 6, 1969; Peter Hazelhurst, "Grey Toasts Freedom in Champagne," *London Times*, Oct. 10, 1969. For examples of Britons freed or arrested, see: "Another Correspondent Is Freed by Red China," *New York Times*, Oct. 12, 1969; "Briton Held 3 Years is Free, Peking Says," *New York Times*, July 31, 1970; "Chinese Free Briton Held 3 Years as Spy," *New York Times*, Aug. 2, 1970; Tillman Durdin, "Chinese Release Another Briton," *New York Times*, Oct. 25, 1970.

States. Tense Sino-Soviet relations grew even more strained in July 1968, when Soviet leader Leonid Brezhnev declared his Brezhnev Doctrine, which justified intervention by the Soviet Union in other socialist nations. The following month, the Kremlin ordered the Red Army into Czechoslovakia to put down an attempt by that country to move out of the Soviet orbit. The PRC became concerned that it might be next, leading it to look for support from other nations, including the United States. With both sides interested in improved relations, the door was open to the Sino-American rapprochement of 1972.

Yet the United States easily could have misplayed its cards and delayed indefinitely an improvement in Sino-American relations. Li Zhisui pointed to Mao's growing fears in the decade or so before the Cultural Revolution. Not only did the Chinese leader believe that he had enemies around him, but also, as Rice suggested, that those enemies would join with the Americans if the United States attacked China. And there was clearly a belief among the Maoists that a Sino-American war would occur. Mao himself told a group of Japanese Communist officials in early 1966 that a war with the United States was inevitable and would occur "within two years at the latest." Foreign Minister Chen Yi carried this supposition a step further. In September 1966, he told Japanese officials that the Cultural Revolution "is [an] inevitable thing for us. It is part of preparation for war. It is so that no back-stabbers emerge when America comes to attack China, or if there are back-stabbers, they will be kept to [a] minimum." He added later in the conversation that the "direct effect of [the] Great Cultural Revolution is to eliminate forces which would cooperate with [the] US if [the] latter came to attack China."[43]

In light of such statements, the Johnson administration deserves credit for maintaining its "posture of quiet reasonableness." Any American statements opposing the Maoists easily could have fed Mao's paranoia to the point that he and his supporters were indeed a target of Washington. In turn, they might have been reluctant to improve relations with the United States, even after the Soviet invasion of Czechoslovakia. Though unlikely, the Maoists could have felt so threatened by Washington that they even might have sought to mend relations with the Kremlin. By keeping quiet, the Johnson administration gave the Chinese the option of improving relations with the United States, one which they grabbed.

The credit for the Sino-American rapprochement of 1972 has been given to Richard Nixon, for it occurred during his administration. Indeed, Nixon

43. Dick Wilson, *The People's Emperor, Mao: A Biography of Mao Tse-tung,* 429; telegram, no. 2072, Emmerson to Secretary of State, Sept. 17, 1966, NSF-Memos to the President, box 10, LBJL.

and his counterparts in Beijing took a number of important steps that would make an improvement in relations between their nations possible. At the same time, U.S. policy toward China finally came in line with that of Britain.

But acknowledgment must be given to the Johnson administration for facilitating Nixon's effort. Had administration officials favored the losing side in China's internal struggle, or even gone so far as to give support to Chiang Kai-shek's bid to return to the mainland, the possibility for a rapprochement could have been postponed indefinitely. Instead, the White House's reasonable posture and its silence on the factional struggles within China made possible an improvement in relations. Beijing rejected some of Washington's signals; others received stronger consideration at higher levels than in the past. Yet there was clearly greater flexibility shown by the United States, and at higher levels, than in previous years.

These moves understandably were made without the pushing or prodding of the United Kingdom. During this period of turmoil, Washington and London were more concerned about their own interests relative to, or within, China, than with how the other country was approaching the PRC. The United States wanted to improve its contacts and relations with Beijing; the United Kingdom wanted to maintain the contacts it already had and to protect its facilities and nationals within the PRC. Both approached Beijing from different directions without their respective policies intersecting. Still, these unilateral moves did not remove the possibility for an Anglo-American dispute over the PRC. The United States still had not eliminated the differential in trade, and the issue of China's representation in the United Nations remained unresolved. The latter in particular would open the door to a new dispute between the two allies.

9

"THE WEEK THAT CHANGED THE WORLD,"
1969–1972

In January 1969, Republican Richard Nixon became the new president of the United States. At first glance, Nixon seemed likely to halt or even reverse the moves made by the administration of Lyndon Johnson in favor of improving relations with China. The president-elect's anticommunist credentials and opposition to Beijing were well known. He had led the charge against Alger Hiss in the late 1940s, accused the Truman administration of being soft on communism and of "losing" China, staunchly supported Eisenhower's efforts to deter Beijing during the two Quemoy-Matsu crises, and, as late as 1964, attacked Senator J. William Fulbright's (D-Arkansas) appeal for a review of U.S. China policy, calling it "naive wooly-headed thinking."[1] Yet Nixon would unfailingly push to expand and accelerate the process begun by Johnson to better relations with the PRC, culminating in the Sino-American rapprochement of 1972.

In his efforts to improve relations with China, Nixon cut out the United Kingdom, a fact that did not please London officials; Taiwan was also concerned by his actions. Additionally, both allies had difficulties with Washington's change of tactics to save Taipei's UN seat. Between the time the United Nations made its decision on representation and Nixon's own trip to Beijing four months later, U.S. China policy had all but been brought in line with that of Great Britain.

Given his anticommunist credentials, Richard Nixon seemed like the last person who would want to improve relations with China. Yet his credentials made the new president the perfect individual to establish rapprochement with the Communist government in Beijing. He could not be accused of being "soft" on communism or of being a member of the "who lost China" club. And there was evidence, despite his past actions and statements, that he was prepared to consider improved relations with the PRC. In November 1953 then–Vice President Nixon met with British Commissioner General for

---

1. Quote from Stephen Ambrose, *Nixon*, vol. 2, *The Triumph of a Politician, 1962–1972*, 44.

Southeast Asia Malcolm MacDonald. MacDonald reported that the vice president "acknowledged that Chiang Kai-shek was a fading force." Nixon even said that if China "became more reasonable about the Korean political talks, we should seek to help them further. It might be possible to contemplate their entry into the United Nations Organisation, although American public opinion would make this difficult." He also talked of increasing trade with Beijing. This report represented the first indication that Nixon was prepared to keep an open mind on China.[2]

Nixon continued to demonstrate open-mindedness. In 1967, he told U.S. Ambassador to India Chester Bowles that it was vital to improve relations with China. In fact, in April of that year, he traveled to Asia to evaluate the situation in Vietnam and to learn more about how Asians viewed China. He found

> a growing concern about Communist China. Some who had adamantly opposed any change of American policy toward China had come around to the view that some new and direct relationship was essential if there were to be any chance at all after the Vietnam war was over to build a lasting peace in Asia in which free nations would have a chance to survive.[3]

Later in the year, Nixon explained in an article in *Foreign Affairs* the lessons he had learned from his trip. "Any American policy toward Asia," he said, "must come to grips with the reality of China." The PRC could not forever remain "outside the family of nations, there to nurture its fantasies, cherish its hates, and threaten its neighbors." This new American policy did not require "rushing to grant recognition to Peking, to admit it to the United Nations, or to ply it with offers of trade—all of which would serve to confirm its rulers in their present course." Rather, it meant "distinguishing carefully between long-range and short-range policies, and fashioning short-range programs so as to advance our long-range goals."[4]

During the 1968 presidential campaign, Nixon rarely discussed foreign policy, except as it concerned Vietnam, and mentioned China only once, in an interview with Harrison Salisbury, the assistant managing editor of the *New York Times*. But he again displayed his determination to improve relations with Beijing. Nixon told Salisbury he was "looking forward in his Administration in the White House to the inevitable negotiations with China. The China problem cannot be indefinitely swept under the table. This country must prepare to cope with it."[5]

2. Jonathan Aitken, *Nixon: A Life*, 227.

3. Richard Nixon, *The Memoirs of Richard Nixon*, 1:348–49.

4. James Mann, *About Face*, 17–18; Richard M. Nixon, "Asia after Viet Nam," 121.

5. Ambrose, *Nixon*, 2:191; Harrison Salisbury, "Nixon: Then and Now," *New York Times*, Sept. 16, 1968.

In the process of achieving rapprochement with the PRC, Nixon determined to cut the State Department out of the decision-making process. His national security adviser, Henry Kissinger, stated that the president-elect "had very little confidence in the State Department. Its personnel had no loyalty to him; the Foreign Service had disdained him as Vice President and ignored him the moment he was out of office. He was determined to run foreign policy from the White House." To keep State out of the loop, Nixon named a lawyer and old friend, William Rogers, as secretary of state; since Rogers had little familiarity with foreign policy, the president could keep the running of foreign affairs in the White House. Rogers realized Nixon's reason for appointing him, but he accepted his backseat position.[6]

While decreasing State's role in foreign policy, Nixon increased that of the National Security Council (NSC). Like Nixon, Kissinger by 1969 had come to regard a new policy toward China as both possible and essential. For the NSC–adviser-designate, "power, geography, economics, and military might took precedence" over ideology. Modern international relations, he contended, "were an intricate web rather than a fight between good and evil."[7]

These views appeared in the 1968 presidential campaign. During the contest for the GOP nomination, Kissinger supported the Republican governor of New York, Nelson Rockefeller. In May 1968, Kissinger wrote a speech for the candidate, in which Rockefeller declared, "In a subtle triangle with communist China and the Soviet Union, we can ultimately improve our relations with each—as we test the will for peace of both." One of Kissinger's biographers noted, "The voice was Rockefeller, but the ideas were those of Kissinger."[8]

The triangular relationship about which Kissinger wrote and Rockefeller spoke represented part of a sophisticated worldview that Kissinger and Nixon shared. It was obvious by this time that the Sino-Soviet alliance had torn at the seams. If the United States could bring China out of its isolation, Beijing could provide a challenge to Moscow's control over international communism. But there were additional reasons for improving relations with the People's Republic. Doing so would take attention away from the Vietnam War and place U.S. foreign policy in a more positive light. If he could achieve rapprochement with the Chinese Communists, Nixon could leave a strong mark on U.S. history. Finally, and most important, if the United States could achieve détente with not just the PRC, but also the Soviet Union, it could use the influence of the two communist powers in Hanoi to bring the war in Viet-

6. Henry A. Kissinger, *White House Years,* 11; Seymour M. Hersh, *The Price of Power: Kissinger in the Nixon White House,* 32.

7. Robert D. Schulzinger, *Henry Kissinger: Doctor of Diplomacy,* 77–78.

8. Walter Isaacson, *Kissinger: A Biography,* 125–26.

nam to an end (or so the administration hoped). As Raymond Garthoff explained, "[T]he dominant foreign policy preoccupation of Nixon and Kissinger in 1969, and indeed for the period through 1972, was not a détente summit meeting with Moscow, but finding an honorable exit from Vietnam." Improving relations with the two communist powers "were at that time seen as much as means to that end as they were ends in themselves."[9]

This worldview went far beyond anything expressed by the Johnson administration. Johnson and his advisers realized during the Cultural Revolution that combining their "posture of quiet reasonableness" with some minimal concessions might lead to improved Sino-American relations once the turmoil in China ended. Yet there is no evidence that they thought in terms of triangular relationships or of using improved relations with China as a means to end the Vietnam War. Indeed, it seems they were more interested in trying to convince Beijing that it should not intervene than they were in using the PRC's help to end the conflict.

But this triangular relationship expressed by Nixon and Kissinger was only part of an even larger proposal for a pentagonal world system, with the United States, China, the Soviet Union, Europe, and Japan each helping achieve a balance. Moscow's power by 1969 had reached the point where it was simply too expensive for Washington to fend it off alone. America needed its allies to play larger roles. Such a multipolar system, Kissinger had argued before he became NSC adviser, would not "guarantee stability," but it "would provide greater opportunities for working out a shared concept of international order."[10]

Achieving this world order, however, would require more than just Nixon's desire, and here a meeting of additional forces made such a vision possible. One was the state of public opinion. The China bloc was virtually dead. The *New York Times* reported in April 1970, "Organized pressure on behalf of Nationalist China, which once exerted a powerful influence on American politics and the direction of United States policy, appears moribund, a victim of old age and lack of interest." Americans, in fact, continued to demonstrate a desire to improve Sino-American relations. Even opinion on Beijing's admission to the United Nations showed some signs of change. One 1969 poll found that most Americans still opposed China's entrance into the international body. Yet another that same year established that a majority of

9. Gaddis, *Strategies of Containment*, 282; Marshall Green, John H. Holdridge, and William N. Stokes, *War and Peace with China: First-Hand Experiences in the Foreign Service of the United States*, 179–80; Raymond L. Garthoff, *Détente and Confrontation: American-Soviet Relations from Nixon to Reagan*, 77–78.

10. Richard C. Thornton, *The Nixon-Kissinger Years: Reshaping America's Foreign Policy*, 145–46; Gaddis, *Strategies of Containment*, 282.

Americans believed the United States should support Beijing's admission if a majority of UN members agreed to it.[11]

Moreover, China showed an interest in improving relations. The Brezhnev Doctrine and the Soviet invasion of Czechoslovakia in July and August 1968, respectively, frightened the PRC and led Beijing to realign its policy toward the United States. "The United States and the Soviet Union are different," Chinese leader Mao Zedong explained to his doctor, Li Zhisui. "The United States never occupied Chinese territory. America's new president, Richard Nixon, is a longtime rightist, a leader of the anti-communists there. I like to deal with rightists. They say what they really think—not like the leftists, who say one thing and mean another." It was ironic that Mao declared his favoritism toward "rightists" when it was those opposed to the Left that he perceived as a threat during the Cultural Revolution. Mao had clearly changed his thinking. In fact, with the Chinese leader's approval, Prime Minister Zhou Enlai personally instructed his subordinates to carefully monitor U.S. China policy and to inform him "continuously of all aspects of the American attitude towards China."[12]

In sum, forces were coming together that would make possible the Sino-American rapprochement of 1972: Nixon and Kissinger favored such an improvement, which fit in with their multipolar worldview; American public opinion showed increasing support for a change in U.S. China policy; and Beijing itself was realigning its position in favor of the United States. For Britain, the question would be what role, if any, it would play in trying to bring Washington and Beijing together.

To the chagrin of officials in London, Britain played no role in Nixon's effort to improve Sino-American relations. Nixon was known for maintaining a distance from those persons he did not trust or who treated him cooly. Just as the president kept a list of correspondents he liked and those he did not—oftentimes demanding that the latter group be cut off from all sources at the White House—he seemed to favor certain foreign leaders.[13] (Limiting those nations involved in his efforts to improve relations with the PRC served the additional benefit of keeping policy-making centralized in the White House and reduced the chance of leaks.)

In the process of developing lines of communication with China, Nixon used several nations, including Romania, France, and Pakistan, that had links

11. "'China Lobby,' Once Powerful Factor in U.S. Politics, Appears Victim of Lack of Interest," *New York Times*, Apr. 25, 1970; Kusnitz, *Public Opinion and Foreign Policy*, 164, 167.

12. Li, *Private Life of Chairman Mao*, 514; Barbara Barnouin and Yu Changgen, *Chinese Foreign Policy during the Cultural Revolution*, 99.

13. Aitken, *Nixon*, 376.

to Beijing and whose leaders had personal ties to the president. During his world trip of 1967, Nixon stopped in Romania, where he received a warm welcome, and met with President Nicolae Ceausescu. One of Nixon's biographers wrote that Nixon "never forgot that, when others turned their backs on him, Ceausescu and the Romanians treated him royally." He also developed a close friendship with France's leader, Charles de Gaulle, whom he had first met in 1963. Nixon's relationship with Pakistan dated back to 1952. He became good friends with that nation's leader, Marshal Mohammad Ayub Khan. Though Ayub was overthrown in March 1969, Nixon and Kissinger realized that Pakistan's ties with China could prove useful; therefore, they were quick to work with the new government of General Agha Mohammed Yahya Khan.[14]

Yet London had diplomats in China. Why did Nixon not use them as well? One likely reason is that Kissinger did not give much weight to the "special relationship." He therefore had no reason to accord the United Kingdom exceptional status when it came to opening relations with the PRC. Nixon, though, did believe in the "special relationship," and it therefore seems odd that he would agree with Kissinger in cutting Britain out of the loop. The fact that he omitted London seems to be more a case of his not getting along well with Britain's leaders. His relationship with Prime Minister Harold Wilson had gotten off to a rocky start when Wilson refused to reconsider appointing John Freeman as ambassador to the United States. In 1962, in the *New Statesman,* Freeman had called Nixon "a man of no principle whatsoever except a willingness to sacrifice everything in the cause of Dick Nixon." The new president also did not trust the prime minister's smooth talk and gave Wilson "a fishy-eyed stare" when his British counterpart suggested that they get on a first-name basis.[15] In short, at the very time that Nixon was making breakthroughs in his China policy, his relationship with Wilson was equivocal.

If Nixon's treatment of Wilson was at best cool, the president had high hopes for developing a close friendship with Edward Heath. By 1970, the British economy had shown signs of improvement, but a sudden economic downturn just before the elections held in June that year led to a victory for Heath and his Conservative Party. "There was no foreign leader," wrote Kissinger, "for whom Nixon had a higher regard, especially in combination with Sir Alec Douglas-Home, Heath's Foreign Secretary, whom Nixon pos-

---

14. Ibid., 318–19, 381; Ambrose, *Nixon,* 2:107–8; Shirin Tahir-Kheli, *The United States and Pakistan: The Evolution of an Influence Relationship,* 30–31.

15. Dickie, *"Special" No More,* 143; Renwick, *Fighting with Allies,* 292–93; Aitken, *Nixon,* 380–81; Ambrose, *Nixon,* 2:255.

itively revered." But "the relationship never flourished. Like a couple who have been told by everyone that they should be in love and who try mightily but futilely to justify these expectations, Heath and Nixon never managed to establish the personal rapport for which Nixon, at least, longed in the beginning."[16]

The main problem for Nixon was that Heath, even more so than Wilson, downgraded the "special relationship." This is not to say that he was anti-American. He did favor close Anglo-American relations. He told the National Press Club in 1973 that while he wanted détente, "until [it] has been achieved it would be foolish for the Western powers to weaken the solidarity or power of our alliance." He also warned against the United States staging an early withdrawal from Vietnam and allowed Washington to use London's military facilities at Diego Garcia. Even so, Heath saw Britain's future aligned with Europe's, not with that of the United States. The United Kingdom's entry into the European Economic Community became his first and overriding priority. Accordingly, he had to downgrade the "special relationship." Heath knew that France feared Britain would act as a "Trojan Horse" for the White House, "providing a surrogate veto for a US Administration over European attempts to develop external policies of their own." For Kissinger, it was an interesting paradox: "Wilson, whom Nixon distrusted, had reached for an easier and more personal relationship than did Heath, whom Nixon greatly admired."[17] Unwilling or unable to establish close relations with Wilson or Heath, the president excluded them from his plans for China.

Nixon's efforts to improve relations with the PRC began even before he took the oath of office. With the Cultural Revolution approaching an official end, Beijing decided to test the Johnson administration's signals that it wanted to improve Sino-American relations. Therefore, in November 1968, Beijing offered to resume the Warsaw talks, which had broken off earlier in the year. The Johnson administration, with Nixon's approval, accepted.[18]

Following his inauguration, Nixon not only picked up where Johnson left off, he determined to increase and speed up his predecessor's use of signals

16. Malcolm Pearce and Geoffrey Stewart, *British Political History, 1867–1995: Democracy and Decline,* 491–92; Kissinger, *White House Years,* 932–33.

17. Heath quoted in John Baylis, ed., *Anglo-American Relations since 1939: The Enduring Alliance,* 184; Kissinger, *White House Years,* 933–34; John Campbell, *Edward Heath: A Biography,* 336, 337; Christopher Hill and Christopher Lord, "The Foreign Policy of the Heath Government," in *The Heath Government, 1970–1974: A Reappraisal,* ed. Stuart Ball and Anthony Seldon, 306, 307.

18. Memorandum to Rostow from Jenkins, Dec. 2, 1968, NSF-Country File, box 243, LBJL; Kissinger, *White House Years,* 167.

and concessionary measures to indicate a desire for improved relations. On February 1, 1969, he ordered Kissinger to explore "possibilities of rapprochement with the Chinese." He added, "This, of course, should be done privately and should under no circumstances get into the public prints from this direction." Accordingly, Kissinger ordered the preparation of a study on U.S. China policy. In March, the NSC adviser called for a review of American trade policy toward communist nations, including the PRC.[19]

The Nixon-Kissinger initiative temporarily ran into trouble. Just two days before the Warsaw talks were to begin, Beijing canceled them, arguing that the United States was behind the defection of Liao Heshu, China's senior diplomat in the Netherlands. Nixon's call for building an antiballistic missile system to protect America from "a potential Chinese threat" had further upset the Communists. But Sino-Soviet military clashes over claims to the Ussuri River changed matters. Tensions became severe enough that the Soviets—in an ironic and, to Washington, surprising twist—asked the United States whether it would sympathize with a preemptive strike by Moscow against the PRC. The White House made it clear that it would not. The Soviets, however, did implement in June a diplomatic offensive to try to isolate China, which included sending out feelers to Taiwan. In light of Moscow's moves, Kissinger wrote Nixon that "the Soviets may become more flexible in dealing with East West issues. . . . Thus, Soviet concern may have finally reached the point that it can be turned to our advantage." Alluding to the triangular relationship, Nixon responded, "This is our goal."[20]

The Chinese also seemed willing to play ball. Despite Nixon's comment on the antiballistic missile system, Beijing remained seriously concerned about the state of its relations with Moscow. In April, Lin Biao, Mao's heir-apparent, declared, "We must on no account relax our revolutionary vigilance because of victory and on no account ignore the danger of U.S. imperialism and Soviet revisionism launching a large-scale war of aggression." Kissinger took note of Lin's statement: "It listed the Soviet Union and United States as equal threats to the People's Republic, fulfilling one of the preconditions of triangular diplomacy, that the United States should not be the principal enemy."[21]

19. Kissinger, *White House Years,* 169–70, 173; memorandum to Kissinger from Nixon, Feb. 1, 1969, WHCF-Subject Files, box 17, NPMP; memoranda, to Secretaries of State and Defense and Director for Central Intelligence from Kissinger, Feb. 5, 1969, and to Secretaries of State, Defense, Commerce, Treasury, and Agriculture, and the Special Representative for Trade Negotiations, Director of Central Intelligence, and President of Export Import-Bank from Kissinger, Mar. 28, 1969, *Documents of the NSC: Fourth Supplement.*

20. *Newsweek* (Mar. 3, 1969): 42; Kissinger, *White House Years,* 170–71, 178–79; Chang, *Friends and Enemies,* 285–86.

21. Kissinger, *White House Years,* 176.

With America's past adversaries now in conflict with each other—and both sending signals that they no longer regarded the United States as their main adversary—it became possible for Nixon to reduce U.S. commitments abroad. In July, the president declared what became known as the "Nixon Doctrine": the United States would continue to abide by its treaties and to provide a nuclear umbrella to its allies. But if one of its allies were attacked, that nation would have primary responsibility for protecting itself. The Nixon Doctrine represented a vital point of the administration's vision for its pentagonal world system, with America's friends playing a larger role.[22]

The president's policy of "Vietnamization" was the clearest manifestation of the Nixon Doctrine. By increasingly turning the war effort over to South Vietnam, Washington could curtail the enormous resources it was pouring into the war effort and help bring the unpopular conflict to an end. But there also was a China component to Vietnamization. By pulling U.S. soldiers out of Vietnam, America could reduce Beijing's concerns about a U.S. threat and make the PRC more willing to improve relations. Indeed, as 1969 progressed and Washington started removing troops from South Vietnam, the PRC began withdrawing soldiers it had stationed along the Sino-Vietnamese border and moving them northward. Simultaneously, there was a marked increase in Chinese polemics aimed at the Soviet Union.[23]

In the meantime, the administration looked for a way to respond to Lin's signal. The same month as the declaration of the "Nixon Doctrine," the United States announced a reduction of its trade sanctions against Beijing—allowing China for the first time to buy grain from the United States—and further eased (but did not terminate) restrictions on travel to the PRC. In response, on July 24, Beijing released two Americans whose boat had capsized a few days earlier and whose life raft had drifted into Chinese waters.[24]

The White House regarded the PRC's act of reciprocity as promising further movement forward. At the time China released the two Americans, Nixon was on a round-the-world trip that included stops in both Pakistan and Romania. The president told both Yahya Khan and Ceausescu that China could no longer remain isolated and that Washington would oppose any effort to keep it so. He asked the Pakistani and Romanian leaders to pass his comments on to the PRC. The administration also continued publicly to express its desire for improved relations, as in an August 8 speech by Secretary Rogers: "We recognize, of course, that the Republic of China on Taiwan and Communist China on the mainland are facts of life." This speech was par-

22. Franz Schurmann, *The Foreign Politics of Richard Nixon: The Grand Design*, 37.
23. Thornton, *Nixon-Kissinger Years*, 20–21.
24. Kissinger, *White House Years*, 180.

ticularly significant, for it implied recognition of the Communist government. The *New York Times* noted that it "abandons the long-held concept that the Nationalist regime of President Chiang Kai-shek on Taiwan is the true [Chinese] government, though dispossessed, of all China."[25]

Despite its signals, both overt and covert, the administration felt things were not progressing fast enough. Therefore, in September, Nixon and Kissinger ordered the U.S. ambassador to Poland, Walter Stoessel, Jr., to contact secretly the Chinese ambassador in Warsaw and ask him to reestablish the ambassadorial talks. Not until December was Stoessel able to get in touch with the Chinese chargé d'affaires, Lei Yang, whom he literally had to chase down. When Mao learned of the approach, he was excited. "We have been talking without saying anything for eleven years. Now we can start over again and talk seriously. Nixon must be sincere when he sends word that he is interested in talking with us." Two days later, the Chinese embassy called Stoessel; the two sides agreed to resume the meetings in January 1970.[26]

The first of a series of breakthroughs came at the talks. In January, following instructions, Stoessel said that the White House was prepared to send a high-level representative to Beijing. Furthermore—and this represented a major concession—the United States was willing to reduce its forces on Taiwan; this did not meet China's long-held demand for an end of the U.S. "occupation" of the island, but it was a step in that direction. At a second meeting in February, Lei accepted the U.S. offer to send a representative to Beijing. Stoessel, for his part, further shifted the American position on Taiwan, declaring Washington's willingness to reduce its facilities on the island "as tensions in the area diminish."[27]

The acceptance of the U.S. offer to send a representative to Beijing led to a dispute between the State Department and the national security adviser. State wanted to move slowly on making concessions to the PRC for fear that it would upset America's Asian allies, but Kissinger favored speed. Unfortunately for the NSC adviser, the U.S. invasion of Cambodia in April 1970 led Beijing to cancel the Warsaw meeting planned for the following month.[28]

In mid-June, with the tensions surrounding the Cambodia bombing eas-

25. Ibid., 180–81; Robert Trumbull, "2 ANZUS Partners Back U.S. on China," *New York Times*, Aug. 9, 1969.

26. Hersh, *Price of Power*, 359–60; memorandum of conversation, Sept. 9, 1960, RG 59, Central Foreign Policy Files, 1967–1969, Political and Defense, box 1843, NA; Mao quote from Li, *Private Life of Chairman Mao*, 515.

27. Kissinger, *White House Years*, 360–61; telegram, no. 1118, Stoessel to Secretary of State, Jan. 20, 1970, RG 59, Subject Numeric Files, 1970–73, box 2187, NA.

28. Kissinger, *White House Years*, 690–92; William Bundy, *A Tangled Web: The Making of Foreign Policy in the Nixon Presidency*, 107–9.

ing, the administration attempted to renew its contact with Chinese officials. But China was in the midst of a debate between Mao and Zhou Enlai, who supported improving relations with the United States, and Lin Biao, who was frightened of Washington. Relations among the three men soured, and Lin was killed in September 1971, when he attempted to flee China.[29]

Not until July did Beijing give another sign of its serious interest in improving relations. That month, it released an American missionary, Bishop James Walsh, who had been arrested in 1958 for espionage. The administration appreciated this gesture. But, Kissinger recalled, "both Nixon and I were convinced that the overriding necessity was to establish a confidential means of communication, unencumbered by bureaucratic interests and the traditional liturgy, which could be trusted by both sides."[30]

Nixon again used the Yahya Khan and Ceausescu back channels. In October, both leaders visited the United States. Nixon asked Yahya Khan to send word to Beijing that Washington considered good Sino-American relations "essential" and that the United States "would never join in a condominium against China." He repeated to Ceausescu his interest in friendly relations; moreover, Nixon during the talk referred to China as "the People's Republic of China." This was the first time an American president had referred to China by its official name, and it represented a further signal of American interest in rapprochement.[31]

Though Nixon kept his back-channel connections to China a secret, he knew that both Taiwan and the Soviet Union had their eyes on the public moves he was making. He therefore sought to allay any concerns they might have over his policy. In response to a personal request from Chiang, Nixon declared in January 1969 that he would continue to oppose China's admission to the United Nations. In August 1969, Rogers, who was on a tour of Asian Pacific nations, declared during his stop in Taipei that the United States intended to maintain its treaty obligations to Taiwan. He also discounted the changes in travel and trade policy with the PRC; he noted, for instance—in a likely reference to *Lynd v. Rusk*—that the ban on travel would not hold up in court, and therefore even without action by the White House, there would have been an easing of restrictions on travel to China. In December, Vice President Spiro Agnew began a multination tour of his own. Nixon personally asked him to reassure Chiang that the American stance toward the Na-

29. For more information on the Mao-Lin conflict, see Barnouin and Changgen, *Ten Years of Turbulence,* 199–246; Karnow, *Mao and China,* 428–32; Ross Terrill, *Mao: A Biography,* 359–69; and Li, *Private Life of Chairman Mao,* 517–19, 531–41.

30. Kissinger, *White House Years,* 697, 698.

31. Ibid., 699; Ambrose, *Nixon,* 2:400.

tionalist government was unchanged. During 1970, the American president continued his effort to quell any concerns in Taipei, telling both Defense Minister Chiang Ching-kuo and Premier C. K. Yen that Washington would not "sell [Taiwan] down the river."[32]

Nixon did not completely assuage the fears of the Nationalist government. In December 1969, the White House further relaxed the embargo against China. Taiwan responded angrily, charging that America's "action would further aggravate tensions in the region." The following month, Rogers refused to state that the United States regarded the Nationalist government as "the government of all China, including the mainland." "The result," reported Terence Smith of the New York Times, "was to leave the inference that a change in the traditional posture might be in the offing." Finally, on March 13, Senator Charles Mathias (R-Maryland) proposed an amendment that would repeal the Formosa Resolution of 1955. The State Department declared that it would not oppose the amendment's passage. Although the full Senate later the following year rejected the Mathias amendment, State's refusal to combat the Maryland senator's proposal greatly upset Taipei. One Nationalist official stated that put together, the actions of the White House looked "like a trend away from support for us. . . . We wonder where it will all end. Something the United States Government never tells us is just how far it is going to go in the direction of making up to the Chinese Communists."[33]

Nixon also tried to reassure the third point in his "triangle," the Soviet Union. In October 1969, Soviet Ambassador to the United States Anatoly Dobrynin expressed his government's anxieties about Nixon's moves toward the PRC. The president responded, "Anything we have done or are doing with respect to China is in no sense designed to embarrass the Soviet Union. . . .

32. Telegrams, no. 246, McConaughy to Secretary of State, Jan. 26, 1969, and no. 307, Jan. 31, 1969, RG 59, Central Foreign Policy Files, 1967–1969, Political and Defense, box 1854; memorandum of conversation, Aug. 3, 1969, RG 59, Central Foreign Policy Files, 1967–1969, Political and Defense, box 1855, NA; Richard M. Nixon, Public Papers of the Presidents of the United States: Richard Nixon, 1969–74, 1969, 16; Samuel Kim, "Rogers Assures Seoul of Help in Case of Attack," New York Times, Aug. 2, 1969; "Rogers Assures Taipei of U.S. Policy," New York Times, Aug. 3, 1969; James N. Naughton, "A 10-Nation Tour Begun by Agnew," New York Times, Dec. 27, 1969; Tad Szulc, "Foreign Leaders Meet with Nixon," New York Times, Oct. 26, 1970; Tucker, Taiwan, Hong Kong, and the United States, 104.

33. James N. Naughton, "Agnew Supports U.S.-Peking Talks; Calls on Chiang," New York Times, Jan. 3, 1970; Terence Smith, "Rogers Says U.S. Might Aid a Drive by Saigon in Laos," New York Times, Jan. 30, 1970; "State Department Now Neutral on Repeal of Tonkin Resolution," New York Times, Mar. 13, 1970; Tillman Durdin, "Taipei is Worried by U.S. Shift on Chinese Reds," New York Times, Mar. 19, 1970; John W. Finney, "Senate, 47–44, Kills Fund Curb on Vietnam War," New York Times, Oct. 29, 1971.

Within ten years, China will be a nuclear power capable of terrorizing many other countries. The time is running out when the Soviet Union and the United States can build a different kind of world." Administration officials publicly repeated these private statements. In January 1970, Rogers explained that the resumption of the Warsaw talks and U.S. contacts with China were not designed to exploit the Sino-Soviet quarrel. The Kremlin refused to allow Nixon's moves to upset an improvement in U.S.-Soviet relations, but Washington's actions were a cause for concern.[34]

At the end of 1970, the contacts with China achieved a second breakthrough. In December, Yahya Khan informed the White House that Beijing would accept a visit by a special U.S. envoy to discuss the issue of Taiwan. The White House responded that it was prepared to talk about Taiwan, as well as "a broad range of [other] issues." The following month, the Romanian government passed word that the PRC was prepared to have Nixon himself visit, thus broaching the idea of a presidential trip for the first time.[35]

This latest achievement excited the Nixon administration. In February, however, the effort at rapprochement briefly received another setback when the United States and South Vietnam launched an attack into Laos to destroy Vietcong bases and lines of communication. Beijing responded angrily, calling Washington's action a "grave provocation." The president had to engage in damage control, stating at a February 17 news conference that his target was only North Vietnam. "This action is not directed against Communist China. . . . I do not believe that the Communist Chinese have any reason to interpret this as a threat against them or any reason therefore to react to it." Nixon also did not let Beijing's response undermine continued signals of a desire for improved relations. At the end of the month, the president submitted a foreign policy report to Congress, in which he stated his desire "for contacts between the Chinese and American peoples." In March, the administration sent another signal when it ended all restrictions on travel to China (to the displeasure of Taiwan).[36]

In April, the efforts at rapprochement took an unexpected and, for the president, welcome turn of events. That month, both the U.S. and Chinese ping-pong teams participated in the World Table Tennis Championship, held in Japan. During the meet, a member of the American squad exchanged gifts with the captain of the Chinese team. Two days later, on April 6, Beijing for-

34. Nixon, *Memoirs,* 1:502; "Assurance to Russia over China Talks," *London Times,* Jan. 17, 1970; Garthoff, *Détente and Confrontation,* 270.

35. Kissinger, *White House Years,* 700–703.

36. Telegram, no. 1150, McConaughy to Secretary of State, Mar. 17, 1971, RG 59, Subject Numeric File, 1970–73, box 2205, NA; "China Charges Provocation," *New York Times,* Feb. 9, 1971; Nixon, *Public Papers,* 1971, 160; Ambrose, *Nixon,* 2:428.

mally invited the American team to China. Nixon recalled, "I was as surprised as I was pleased by this news. I had never expected that the China initiative would come to fruition in the form of a Ping-Pong team. We immediately approved the acceptance of the invitation."[37]

The American athletes received a dazzling reception from the Chinese people. Furthermore, "ping-pong diplomacy," as it came to be called, offered the administration an opportunity to demonstrate again its desire for improving relations. During 1969, the United States had eased its trade restrictions against China; but the invitation and treatment of the table tennis team provided a justification for a further relaxation. On April 14, Nixon announced the removal of several trade controls, relaxed others, and called for a review of remaining controls on nonstrategic items. Following the review, the administration on June 10 announced that it was reducing significantly the number of goods still under embargo and would permit Chinese commercial imports.[38]

Two weeks after Nixon's announcement, the final breakthrough came, when the administration received a formal invitation for a high-level emissary to travel to Beijing. Nixon chose Kissinger for this role. In July, the NSC adviser left on his secret trip, about which Rogers was not informed until after Kissinger was on his way.[39]

During their talks, Kissinger and Zhou Enlai agreed to eventual withdrawal of all U.S. military forces from Taiwan. The NSC adviser also asked for China's help in ending the Vietnam War. It is now known as well that Kissinger provided ultrasensitive intelligence regarding Russian military activities along the Sino-Soviet border.[40] When news of the visit was announced by the White House, it surprised Britain and angered Taiwan.

Britain, in fact, had kept close track of the public announcements made by the United States as it moved toward improving relations with China. Both the Wilson and Heath governments clearly understood that Nixon wanted to achieve rapprochement, though they were skeptical of his chances

---

37. Kissinger, *White House Years*, 709; Nixon, *Memoirs*, 2:12.

38. Terence Smith, "U.S.-Chinese Thaw Remains Distant," *New York Times*, Nov. 13, 1970; Fred Emery, "Mr. Nixon Opens the Way for Trade with China after Peking's Table Tennis Gesture," *London Times*, Apr. 15, 1971; Tad Szulc, "U.S. Weighs Policy on Chinese Trade," *New York Times*, May 6, 1971; Kissinger, *White House Years*, 712, 723, 732; Ambrose, *Nixon*, 2:451.

39. Rogers was informed on July 8. At the time, Kissinger was in Pakistan, the last of several stops before he traveled to Beijing. Kissinger, *White House Years*, 738–39.

40. Hersh, *Price of Power*, 374–76. See also Garthoff, *Détente and Confrontation*, 264 n 117. The Nixon administration continued to provide information on the disposition of Soviet troops after the Kissinger-Zhou meeting. See William Burr, ed., *The Kissinger Transcripts: The Top Secret Talks with Beijing and Moscow*, 50–51.

of success. They did not know of Nixon's secret maneuverings. Ironically, the *New York Times* reported in late June 1971 that the White House would neither confirm nor deny stories that Nixon had asked Beijing some months earlier if it might invite him or a representative to China in early 1972.[41] If Whitehall noticed this article, it did not follow up on it, as suggested by the shock exhibited in London when Nixon told the world of Kissinger's secret trip to Beijing.

London's primary task during this period was to return Sino-British relations to their pre–Cultural Revolution footing. Signals from Beijing suggested that China wanted to achieve the same goal. The release of communist activists arrested in Hong Kong during the Cultural Revolution led the PRC in October 1969 to free Reuters correspondent Anthony Grey, who had been under house arrest since 1967. Though the Communists would arrest (and later release) other Britons, British officials continued to see evidence of softening on China's part. Foreign Secretary Michael Stewart in April 1970 expressed such a perception when he noted "a decided improvement in economic relations [with China]. We find political relations on a more satisfactory basis than before."[42]

Amelioration of relations continued during 1971. In February, British officials moved back into the U.K. mission in Beijing, which they had abandoned in 1967 after it was sacked and partly burned by Chinese radicals. The following month, Zhou Enlai apologized for the attack on the mission and promised to meet the cost of rebuilding it. In early April, and for the first time, Beijing provided information on four Britons it still held. London took such acts as further evidence of interest in improving relations. In the middle of the month, Acting British Chargé d'Affaires to China Richard Samuel commented that relations between Britain and the PRC were "in a very happy phase."[43]

One British goal, though, remained unfulfilled: raising Anglo-Chinese relations to the ambassadorial level. Beginning in 1950, Britain sought to elevate the relations between the two nations from that of chargé d'affaires to ambassador, but this effort stalled over two issues. The first was Britain's sup-

41. Terence Smith, "Washington Speculates on Ambassadorial Transfer Soon," *New York Times*, June 28, 1971.

42. Boardman, *Britain and the People's Republic of China*, 137, 143; "Stewart Says China Seems More Friendly," *London Times*, Apr. 20, 1970.

43. "British in Peking Back in Offices Gutted in 1967," *New York Times*, Feb. 16, 1971; "Razing of British Office Brings a Chou Apology," *New York Times*, Mar. 20, 1971; A. M. Rendel, "China to Pay for Sacking of British Mission," *London Times*, Mar. 23, 1971; "Britons Held by China Are in Good Health," *London Times*, Apr. 14, 1971; Relations with China in a Happy Phase, Envoy Says," *London Times*, Apr. 17, 1971.

port for the United States on the question of Chinese representation in the United Nations. The other was London's maintenance of a consulate in Taiwan. London wanted to meet China's demands, but doing so opened the door to another dispute with Washington.

Once again, the controversy surrounded China's representation in the United Nations. In 1970 the PRC was serious about entering the international body. Although China in previous years had indicated a desire to obtain admission, it was now determined to do so. First, Beijing's activities during the Cultural Revolution had led it into disputes with over thirty of the approximately forty nations with which it had diplomatic relations, including Indonesia, India, Burma, Nepal, Mongolia, Kenya, Tunisia, France, and Great Britain.[44] The PRC wanted to regain respectability in the eyes of the world, and admission to the United Nations would be proof of success. Second, given its rapidly deteriorating relations with the Soviet Union, Beijing wanted new connections so it would not find itself isolated.

When he took office, Nixon had adopted the position of his predecessors that the representation issue was an "important question." Despite continued misgivings about preventing Beijing's admission, London followed Washington's lead. Efforts by the United States to keep China out succeeded in 1969, but continued success was not certain. Therefore, by the time of the 1970 vote, there was a marked shift in American strategy in favor of a "two Chinas" solution: rather than trying to keep the communists out, the White House would seek to keep the Nationalists in. The Nixon administration realized neither Taiwan nor China would easily accept such a solution, but considered it the best possible resolution to the issue.[45]

The British government also shifted its position. Beijing's desire to enhance its standing in the world was expressed through clear signals that it was prepared to exchange ambassadors. In November 1970, the Chinese Communist chargé in London, Ma Jiachun, told the head of the Foreign Office's Far East Department, John Morgan, that Beijing wanted to tear down its embassy and erect a new one "capable of accommodating an ambassador." In March 1971, Zhou Enlai met with the U.K. chargé in Beijing, John Denson. Not only was this the first time since 1949 that a Chinese Communist prime

---

44. See Barnouin and Changgen, *Chinese Foreign Policy during the Cultural Revolution,* chap. 3.

45. Henry Tanner, "U.N. Vote Refuses a Seat for Peking for the 20th Year," *New York Times,* Nov. 12, 1969; "U.S. Eases Stand in Debate at U.N. on Seating Peking," *New York Times,* Nov. 13, 1970; James M. Naughton, "White House Says U.S. Still Opposes Peking U.N. Seat," *New York Times,* Nov. 14, 1970; Robert Trumbull, "Rogers is Ending his Pacific Tour," *New York Times,* Aug. 11, 1969; "Both Chinas Oppose Plan," *New York Times,* Nov. 19, 1970.

minister had asked to meet with the U.K. representative, but it was during these talks that Zhou offered to rebuild the British embassy in China. Given the PRC's desire for better relations, as well as the 1970 UN vote, the British minister in Washington, Guy Millard, explained in January 1971 that the "important question" was "a rapidly sinking ship" and that Britain could support neither a "two Chinas" formula nor any tactic designed to further delay Beijing's entrance into the UN.[46]

Britain's sudden decision worried U.S. officials. They too realized that the "important question" was unlikely to last, and that there was strong support for giving Beijing China's seats in the General Assembly and the Security Council; they thus decided in May upon a two-stage strategy to deal with the representation issue. First, U.S. allies would propose a dual representation formula that would not mention the Security Council seat and that would require a two-thirds vote to expel Taiwan. Then the United States would put forward a separate resolution that also called for dual representation but would offer the Security Council seat to Beijing. The White House believed the PRC would refused to sit alongside Taiwan, making the question of the Security Council seat moot. The Chiang government, despite some qualms, agreed to support this formula. Britain was another story. Its attitude when it came to voting was vitally important. As Undersecretary of State Marshall Green and Assistant Secretary of State for International Organizations Samuel De Palma explained to Rogers, "While we have never assumed that we could persuade the British to work actively for dual representation, we could be hurt if they chose to work in opposition to it. An early, frank exchange of views is needed."[47]

This "frank exchange of views" failed to move the British. Douglas-Home explained to U.S. Ambassador to Britain Walter Annenberg that if Taiwan were willing to sit as Taiwan in the general assembly, with its status to be determined by Beijing and Taipei, then London might reconsider. "Failing that, however, the British position was firmly to support [the] PRC's entry as [the] sole representative of China." He added, though, that London would do all it could to avoid making the U.S. position more difficult.[48]

46. Memoranda of conversation, Nov. 13, 1970 and Jan. 20, 1971, RG 59, Subject Numeric Files, 1970–73, box 3209; telegram, no. 3552, Annenberg to Secretary of State, Mar. 8, 1971, RG 59, Subject Numeric Files, 1970–73, box 3210, NA.

47. Memorandum of conversation, May 28, 1971, and memorandum from Green and De Palma to Secretary of State, Mar. 23, 1971, RG 59, Subject Numeric Files, 1970–73, box 3210; memorandum to the president from Rogers, Sept. 5, 1971, RG 59, Subject Numeric Files, 1970–73, box 3212, NA.

48. Telegram, no. 6685, Annenberg to Secretary of State, July 20, 1971, and letter to Rogers from Douglas-Home, Aug. 4, 1971, RG 59, Subject Numeric Files, 1970–73, box 3211, NA.

Taiwan was also being problematic. In July, Taipei had accepted the U.S. dual representation formula following Japan's agreement to act as a cosponsor. It soon became clear, however, that several key countries in addition to the United Kingdom would not support the two-stage proposal. Accordingly, the Nixon administration decided to support a one-stage formula by which the U.S. would propose a resolution offering the Security Council seat to China. Taiwanese Foreign Minister Chow Shu-kai reacted angrily, charging that it would violate Article Twenty-three of the UN Charter, which declared that the membership of the Security Council would include the "Republic of China." The U.S. ambassador to Taiwan, Walter McConaughy, explained that while the Nationalists might have a good legal case, "a great number of UN members in these times make their decisions and cast their votes without particular regard for Charter restraints or legal niceties." Possibly with Britain in the back of his mind, he added that these countries based their votes "on their conception of immediate national interest . . . without great regard for moral or legal considerations." Pressure from McConaughy and Kissinger forced the Chiang government to reluctantly accept the new formula.[49]

Therefore, by mid-1971, both the United States and Britain wanted to improve relations with China. Indeed, Nixon supported initiatives that were gradually moving America's China policy more in line with that of Whitehall. But the representation issue continued to cause problems, not only in U.S.-U.K. relations, but also in America's relationship with Taiwan. The president's surprise announcement of July 1971 would further stretch America's ties with these two allies.

On July 15, Nixon shocked the world when he announced that Kissinger had made a secret trip to China and that he himself had accepted an invitation by Zhou Enlai to travel to Beijing. "I have taken this action," he declared, "because of my profound conviction that all nations will gain from a reduction of tensions and a better relationship between the United States and the People's Republic of China."[50]

A variety of responses met Nixon's announcement. U.S. congressional

49. Telegrams, nos. 3078 and 3239, McConaughy to Secretary of State, July 7 and 24, 1971, RG 59, Subject Numeric Files, 1970–73, box 3211; telegrams, no. 3688, McConaughy to Secretary of State, Sept. 10, 1971 and no. 3735, Gleysteen to Secretary of State, Sept. 16, 1971, RG 59, Subject Numeric Files, 1970–73, box 3213, NA; memorandum, the president from Rogers, Sept. 5, 1971; Patrick Tyler, *A Great Wall: Six Presidents and China: An Investigative History,* 112–13; Tucker, *Taiwan, Hong Kong, and the United States,* 104.

50. Richard M. Nixon, *Public Papers,* 1971, 819–20.

opinion—with the exception of that expressed by what remained of the China bloc—largely favored his action. Democratic Senator Mike Mansfield of Montana, the Senate majority leader, declared that he was "flabbergasted, delighted, and happy," and that he was "looking forward to a new day." The Republican leader in the Senate, Hugh Scott, also expressed his support, calling Nixon's move "an extremely important step in producing world peace." The public remained more skeptical, with a slight majority still distrustful of China.[51]

Other countries responded to the announcement with embarrassment or anger. When he took office, Nixon had promised to consult Japan in advance if he changed U.S. policy toward China. His sudden announcement, of which Tokyo had received no warning, shocked and embarrassed Japan, which had supported America's China policy. Taiwan, not surprisingly, lodged a strong protest, believing it had been double-crossed by the United States. Yen charged that Nixon's decision "could lead to a tragedy far more serious than that involved in the fall of the Chinese mainland" to communism in 1949. The Soviet Union questioned "whether Nixon is really undertaking his voyage in the name of peace" and accused China of making "a secret deal with imperialism." But the announcement did not undermine Nixon's hope of achieving détente with Moscow, and there is evidence that it actually made the Kremlin even more willing to improve relations with the United States.[52]

Reaction in Britain was mixed. The *London Times* declared that Nixon's action did not guarantee Sino-American friendship, "but it [will] at any rate provide the possibility of inquiry and explanation between the two sides, and that could be the beginning of progress." Publicly, Heath declared his support, calling Nixon's planned visit an "important initiative." Privately, though, the Heath government was not pleased with the lack of consultation. The U.S. initiative vis-à-vis China, wrote Annenberg, was "taken unilaterally and without advance consultation." The British, he continued, were "startled," and were now having "long second thoughts about the 'special relationship.'" The ambassador added that the China initiative, as well as other unilateral American moves, had led Heath "to assess future relationships dif-

---

51. John W. Finney, "Congress Chiefs Pleased; Taiwan Lodges a Protest," *New York Times,* July 16, 1971; Bachrack, *Committee of One Million,* 268–69; Kusnitz, *Public Opinion and Foreign Policy,* 138.

52. "Nixon Visit Infuriates Formosa, Embarrasses Japan, and Makes UN Changes Likely," *London Times,* July 17, 1971; Leo Goodstadt, "Hanoi Bitter about Nixon Visit," *London Times,* July 20, 1971; David Bonavia, "China Accused of Secret Deal with Imperialism," *London Times,* July 22, 1971; Joan Hoff, *Nixon Reconsidered,* 201; LaFeber, *Clash,* 354–55.

ferently and consequential on new patterns of power evolution as between the US, the USSR, China, Japan, and the European Community."[53] Prior to Nixon's announcement, Heath was already reconsidering his relationship with the United States, but Annenberg's telegram pointed to the frustration felt in the Heath government over Nixon's refusal to consult with it on his moves toward China.

Following the announcement, the possibility of the PRC entering the United Nations increased; nations once reluctant to vote for Beijing now seemed more willing to do so. But what may have had the biggest impact was Henry Kissinger's trip to China in October 1971. Designed to prepare further for Nixon's trip the following year to the Chinese capital, the NSC adviser's junket coincided, without his realizing it, with the UN vote on Chinese representation. He explained in December 1971,

> Originally, we tried to set the second trip at the end of September, but that came too close to the Chinese celebrations on October 1st [the date the Chinese communists declared a government in 1949]. In any event, of course, we subsequently found that China was in domestic upheaval at that time; so the end of September would not have worked out in any case. During the first week of October, Haile Selassie [the leader of Ethiopia] was in China. Following his visit, we were already in the middle of October. The fact of the matter is that *we* actually picked the date (the 18th) for the second trip.

"We did this," he continued, "after looking at the prior history of the China voting in the United Nations. If you will look at the record you will find that the vote in the United Nations on China representation has never taken place before the 15th of November. We thought we could go to China [and] return" before the United Nations voted.[54]

Despite the coincidental dates of his trip and the UN vote, Kissinger argued that the former did not affect the latter. "I cannot find the vote of a single country which I believe would have been different if we hadn't gone to China." In fact, his trip gave the impression that the United States wanted Beijing in and Taipei out, a feeling shared by both Taiwan and Japan. One Latin American diplomat commented, "It is strange how the United States wants us to vote to keep Taiwan in at the very time when President Nixon is sending an emissary to Peking to improve his relations with the Chinese." He added, "It is unrealistic for the Americans to leave us holding the bag to save

53. Telegram, no. 11176, Annenberg to Secretary of State, Dec. 8, 1971, WHSF-WHCF, Subject Files, Oversize Attachments, box 9, NPMP; "President Nixon's Journey," *London Times,* July 17, 1971; Marcel Berlins, "Mr. Heath Assures the U.S. on Europe Unity," *London Times,* July 20, 1971.

54. Memorandum of conversation, Dec. 17, 1971, WHSF-Alexander M. Haig Files, box 49, NPMP.

Taiwan." Indeed, when the United Nations voted on October 25, the General Assembly, by a 76-to-35 vote—more than the two-thirds required—determined that the Communist government should represent China in the international body, and it expelled Taiwan. Britain voted in favor of the PRC but, as it had vowed, did not support the U.S.-sponsored "important question" resolution designed to maintain Taiwan's membership. The Nationalist reaction was strong. The *United Daily News,* Taipei's largest newspaper, blamed the United States for the Nationalists' ouster. Taiwan responded skeptically to the White House's reassurances that it would not let the UN vote alter its military commitment to the KMT government. The U.S. response was more muted, with the *New York Times* reporting that "most knowledgeable officials [in Washington] had concluded in the last 48 hours that the weeks of arm twisting and private pressure in foreign capitals would fail to save Taiwan's seat and were therefore not surprised by the outcome."[55] After twenty-two years, Taipei no longer represented China.

The White House spent the next few months after Kissinger's journey on preparations for Nixon's trip, planned for February 1972. The administration made a final gesture three days before Nixon's departure: on February 14, the United States eliminated the remainder of the trade differential. Traveling via Hawaii, the president arrived in Shanghai on February 21. Zhou Enlai greeted the president at the airport; Nixon took care to shake the Chinese premier's hand. "I knew that [Z]hou had been deeply insulted by [former Secretary of State John] Foster Dulles's refusal to shake hands with him at the Geneva Conference in 1954." When he made this gesture, added the president, "One era ended and another began."[56]

Nixon spent a week in China, where he covered a wide range of issues with Mao and Zhou, including Vietnam, Sino-Soviet relations, and Taiwan. Nixon made it clear to Zhou that the United States would gradually withdraw its military forces from Taiwan and that, as far as the White House was concerned, "There is one China, and Taiwan is a part of China." He added that he hoped to achieve a normalization of U.S.-PRC relations, though he understood that Taiwan posed a barrier to reaching that goal.[57]

55. Ibid.; memorandum of conversation, Oct. 7, 1971, RG 59, Subject Numeric Files, 1970–73, box 3214, NA; Tad Szulc, "U.N. Debate on China Expected to Open Thursday, Four Days Early," *New York Times,* Oct. 7, 1971; "U.N. Seats Peking and Expels Taipei; Nationalists Walk Out before Vote; U.S. Defeated on Two Key Questions," *New York Times,* Oct. 26, 1971; Tillman Durdin, "Taipei: Chiang Says Vote in Assembly Was Illegal," *New York Times,* Oct. 27, 1971; Tillman Durdin, "Taipei Hopes to Continue Active International Role," *New York Times,* Oct. 28, 1971; Isaacson, *Kissinger,* 352.

56. Kissinger, *White House Years,* 1055; Nixon, *Memoirs,* 2:26.

57. Memorandum of conversation, Feb. 22, 1972, NSA.

Taiwan also posed a problem in the joint communiqué that would be released to the public. Nixon explained to the Chinese prime minister that it was important for him to "be able to go back to Washington and say that no secret deals have been made between [us] on Taiwan. So what I must do is have what we would call 'running room' which the communique language I hope will provide." Otherwise, Nixon later wrote, he could find himself under attack from "the various pro-Taiwan, anti-Nixon, and anti-P.R.C. lobbies and interest groups at home," who might succeed in turning his China initiative "into a partisan issue. . . . Then, if I lost the election, whether because of this particular factor or not, my successor might not be able to continue developing the relationship between Washington and Peking." The final formula, therefore, was to agree to disagree. Beijing reasserted its claim to represent all Chinese and repeated its demand that the United States withdraw from Taiwan. Washington acknowledged, for the first time, that Taiwan was a part of China and that the China-Taiwan issue had to be settled peacefully by the Chinese people themselves, and promised that Washington would reduce its military presence on Taiwan "as the tension in the area diminishes."[58]

On February 27, the Chinese government held a farewell dinner for Nixon. In his toast, the president reflected on all that had been accomplished, and hinted at the possibilities for the future: "This magnificent banquet marks the end of our stay in the People's Republic of China. We have been here a week. This was the week that changed the world."[59]

Nixon did more than achieve rapprochement with Beijing. He also brought U.S. China policy in line with that of the United Kingdom (though, of course, this was not his goal). In 1948 and 1949, at least on paper, U.S. and British policies toward the PRC were quite similar. Both desired to remain flexible and keep their options open pending a resolution to the civil war in China. But Communist gains on the mainland during 1949, the Korean War, and Beijing's intervention in that war led to the United States adopting the use of pressure against China while Britain favored maintaining contacts. Under Johnson, the United States began to adopt policies more in line with those of London, and Nixon completed this process.

Although Nixon cut the British out of his efforts to achieve rapprochement with Beijing, it does not mean the United Kingdom had suddenly become unimportant to him. Its position in world affairs, including the issue of Chinese representation, remained important. Whitehall, though, had no

58. Memorandum of conversation, Feb. 24, 1972, NSA; Nixon, *Memoirs*, 2:40–41; Nixon, *Public Papers*, 1972, 378.
59. Nixon, *Memoirs*, 2:379–80.

intention of kowtowing any longer to the White House on this subject, and the fact that the Nixon administration shared Britain's desire to improve relations gave the Heath government additional freedom to maneuver. Lack of support from the United Kingdom required the United States to change tactics, to the chagrin of Taiwan, which had long had concerns over the Nixon administration's attitude toward the PRC.

By the time Nixon arrived in China, the United States had ended restrictions on travel to the mainland, eliminated the trade differential, and accepted the right of Beijing to represent China in the United Nations. Though the United States would not formally recognize the Communist government until 1979, the Nixon administration, through its statements and the president's trip to Beijing, implied informal recognition. In 1972, therefore, the circle was nearly complete.

CONFRONTING COMMUNISM

In early 1951, a dying British Foreign Secretary Ernest Bevin explained to his country's cabinet that Great Britain needed to maintain close ties to the United States. He added, though, that London had to "exert sufficient control over the policy of the well-intentioned but inexperienced colossus on whose cooperation our safety depends."[1] Bevin's comment is most telling: on the one hand, he realized that the United Kingdom's survival rested on the economic and military might of the United States; on the other, he hoped that Whitehall could influence the direction of American policy. Given the former, achieving the latter would prove no easy task.

The fact of the matter was that Britain was a power on the decline. Financially drained by World War II and threatened by the specter of communism, Whitehall had little choice but to turn to the United States. In February 1949, the Permanent Under-Secretary's Committee concluded that "neither the Commonwealth alone, nor Western Europe alone, nor even the Commonwealth plus Western Europe would be strong enough, either economically or militarily" to resist the Soviet Union without "the full participation of the United States." Along similar lines, one Conservative Member of Parliament commented that the Suez crisis "proved that without American support we could not sustain the most tin-pot of campaigns for more than three days."[2]

British reliance upon the United States might not have been so troubling had the two allies seen eye-to-eye on every issue, but such was not the case. The Suez crisis is one example. To the United Kingdom, the rise of Arab nationalism in the 1950s threatened its interests in the region. Following Gamal Abdel Nasser's nationalization of the Suez Canal, Whitehall decided it had no choice but to act to protect its interests.

The United States saw things differently. Britain's refusal to accept the growth of Arab nationalism promoted anti-Western feeling in the Middle East. Continued hostility toward the Arabs would benefit the Soviet Union, allowing it to expand its influence in one of the most strategically important parts of the world. Washington's success in using financial pressure to get

1. Quoted in Ritchie Ovendale, *Anglo-American Relations in the Twentieth Century,* 61.
2. Ibid.; Hathaway, *Great Britain and the United States,* 51.

London to remove its military presence from the canal region provided strong evidence of how much Whitehall depended on the United States for support and the difficulties it faced in trying to move in a different direction.

Vietnam posed problems for the two allies as well. U.S. officials regarded the fight in Vietnam as part of the larger struggle to combat Soviet-style communism. Their counterparts in the United Kingdom agreed on the need to contain communism, but they feared being dragged into the conflict, which could then become another Korean-style war. At the same time, there was a realization in Whitehall that maintaining American goodwill required at the very least moral support for the U.S. war effort. Accordingly, Prime Minister Harold Wilson continually made clear that the United Kingdom stood behind its closest ally. He refused, though, to go the extra step of sending ground troops to Vietnam, despite American urging that he do so, and made unwelcome attempts to peacefully end the conflict. He also decided, after some hedging, to remove the U.K. military presence from Southeast Asia, in the face of American opposition to the plan.

The Suez crisis, Vietnam, and the removal of British troops from the east of Suez region provide insights into the ways in which the United States and United Kingdom approached China. During the Cold War, U.S. officials had a tendency to view events abroad within the larger framework of the struggle against Soviet communism. Concerns over Arab nationalism in the Middle East and Vietnam in Southeast Asia are two examples from a much longer list. Americans felt that resisting communism required the real or threatened use of force, be it military, economic, or political in nature. Failing to issue credible threats, backed up, if necessary, by action, would undermine American credibility and weaken resistance to communism elsewhere. "There comes a point," President Dwight D. Eisenhower wrote Prime Minister Winston Churchill during the first Quemoy Matsu crisis, "where constantly giving in only encourages further belligerency."[3]

The British tended to take a different position. They did not like communism and wanted to prevent its spread. But the United States too often responded to communism in emotional and ideological terms whether or not Western interests were seriously affected. If they were, as the British felt was the case in Suez, then action was necessary. If not, then other means should be used. Unfortunately, U.K. policymakers felt, Washington was too willing to threaten rather than to negotiate or compromise, which could achieve the same goals. As Prime Minister Harold Macmillan explained to Secretary of

---

3. Telegram, no. 4266, Dulles to London, Feb. 18, 1955, *FRUS, 1955–1957*, 2:294. See also Robert J. McMahon, "Credibility and World Power: Exploring the Psychological Dimension in Postwar American Diplomacy."

State John Foster Dulles in March 1958, London's decision to recognize the PRC was beneficial: not only did it help promote trade relations—which would aid the British economy—but if there ever "was a crack in the present monolithic fabric of Chinese Communism, we should be in a better position to put our wedge in because we had a Mission on the spot and officials trained in the country." The hard-nosed U.S. attitude not only was having the opposite impact, but it also was allowing the PRC to play the role of "innocent victim," thereby winning sympathy from other countries.[4]

At issue, therefore, was not the goal of containing China, but the best method of achieving it. Throughout the period in question, 1948 to 1972, British policy toward China was consistent, following the line espoused by Macmillan: negotiate and compromise with the Communists so as to protect and enhance Britain's interests in the region, and foster a Sino-Soviet split. American policy, however, gravitated in the opposite direction. At first, officials in the Harry S. Truman administration sounded a lot like their British counterparts (at least on paper): maintaining contacts with the CCP represented the best method of separating it from Moscow and tempering its feelings toward the West. But fears regarding the spread of communist power, Chinese Communist actions against U.S. interests and personnel, and domestic political constraints moved the Truman government toward a harder position. Washington cut most of its communications with the CCP and imposed controls on trade. Still, the White House contended, this new policy would drive wedges.

Following China's intervention in the Korean War, policy changed again. To demonstrate to Americans and to America's allies that it was determined to stop communism's expansion and punish the PRC, the White House adopted a policy based solely on pressure. The United States greatly increased the amount of military and economic assistance it provided to East Asia and, in the case of Korea, engaged in actual warfare. It also imposed a full-scale embargo against the Mao Zedong government. Any talk of political contacts ended. Rather, the United States now argued that recognizing the PRC or permitting its entrance into the United Nations would symbolize a reward for aggression. Again, though, the Truman administration argued that such a stance would split the Sino-Soviet alliance and ultimately force the CCP to seek Western assistance. This policy of pressure continued throughout the 1950s and well into the 1960s, despite the clear emergence of cracks in the relationship between Beijing and Moscow.

What irked officials in the United Kingdom was not simply the fact that

4. Zhai, *Dragon, the Lion, and the Eagle,* 212–13; draft letter to Dulles from Macmillan, Mar. 17, 1958, FO 371/133369.

the United States was adopting what it saw as an unrealistic policy toward China but that Washington wanted it to go along. American foreign policy in the Cold War was predicated upon the idea of developing a world opinion—defined as European opinion—that would cooperate to contain communism without actually going to war.[5] The United States valued Britain's attitude above those of all other nations. Accordingly, time and again, American officials made clear that U.K. backing was vital to an effective policy of pressure.

Here was the rub. The United Kingdom was dependent on the United States. A failure to follow the American lead on China could result in cuts in much-needed U.S. assistance—a threat that was, in fact, verbalized repeatedly by American policymakers—and expose to the communist world a rift in the Western alliance. The best Britain could do was to accept the American position as much as possible without undermining its own vital interests, while, as Bevin suggested, trying to influence the directions American China policy took.

Exerting that influence was difficult, for undergirding the power relationship between the United States and Britain and their disagreements over the best method by which to contain the PRC were a variety of political and cultural considerations. One was public opinion. Britons simply did not share Americans' sentimentality toward China. To most people in the United Kingdom, inside and outside the government, the main concern was protecting and expanding British trading interests on the mainland. No matter who the leadership in Beijing, London had no choice but to accept reality and move on.

The fact that the Chinese had rejected liberal U.S. values for communism galled Americans. Still, the anticommunist government on Taiwan had Westernized leaders—personified by Madame Chiang Kai-shek—wedded to the United States. As a result, much of the U.S. public and Congress opposed measures that might weaken efforts to contain the PRC or threaten the survival of the Nationalist government. China's intervention in Korea, its imprisoning of U.S. nationals, its aggressiveness in the Taiwan Strait and against India, and its polemics aimed at the United States all served to reinforce Americans' anti-Beijing mind-set. Not until the late 1960s, with the wasting away of the China bloc and the activities of lawmakers such as J. William Fulbright, was there a reconsideration of this attitude, thereby helping make possible the initiatives of Lyndon Johnson and Richard Nixon.

Allies outside the Anglo-American relationship also had an impact on the China policy of Washington and London. Whitehall had to compete against

5. See Frank Ninkovich, *Modernity and Power: A History of the Domino Theory in the Twentieth Century.*

a Nationalist government whose leader, Chiang Kai-shek, was a clever manipulator of American politics. Despite British pressure upon Washington, Chiang got from the United States a defense treaty and the Eisenhower administration's reluctant agreement to let him maintain a military presence on Quemoy and Matsu. He also obtained from Washington a promise to use its veto to protect his seat in the United Nations and killed discussion in 1961 of replacing the moratorium with a "two Chinas" solution.

Adding to Britain's difficulties was its role as leader of the Commonwealth. Having assumed that position, Whitehall could not ignore the attitude of its members, particularly India, New Zealand, and Australia, each of which had interests in East Asia. At times, such as during discussion of United Action, the U.K. government found unanimous support from these countries, which gave it some additional leeway in trying to move U.S. China policy in directions it favored. At other times, though, such as in the case of the Southeast Asia defense pact, it faced a divided Commonwealth, which placed additional restraints on its efforts to influence the United States.

China's attitude also played a role. The CCP leadership was much more suspicious of, and hostile toward, Washington than London. The United States was the rising power that refused to recognize the PRC or vote for its admission to the United Nations—thereby placing major roadblocks to Beijing's achievement of international legitimacy—and gave large-scale assistance to the Nationalists. Of course, there was a tactical side to taking a more hostile attitude toward the United States than toward Great Britain: it would, hoped Mao and his lieutenants, split the Anglo-American alliance. While this effort never succeeded, it did further anger a U.S. public already furious over China's rejection of American values. In turn, it became even more difficult for Britain to budge U.S. policy.

Thus, issues of power, culture, and politics made it very difficult for the United Kingdom to convince the United States that the latter's methods of containing China were wrong. Indeed, with their influence limited, and with their heavy reliance upon the United States, British officials more often than not found themselves forced to accept the American policy of pressure. They did not turn over the China National Aviation Corporation and Central Air Transport Corporation aircraft to Beijing. They backed away from pressing the United States on aid to Taiwan and Douglas MacArthur's leadership during the Korean War, branded China an aggressor, sent troops to Korea and issued the warning statement after that conflict ended, agreed to impose additional controls on trade with the PRC, and followed the U.S. lead on Chinese representation.

Whitehall reserved what influence it did have for use on two issues. The first focused on policies that would jeopardize Britain's financial well-being.

The second was the possible expansion of the conflict in Korea and, after that war, any situation that could open the door to another such conflagration. In both cases, however, London acted most cautiously.

With Britain's economy weak after World War II, Whitehall adamantly opposed a full-scale embargo against China. But under intense pressure from the United States, especially after November 1950, to at least place additional controls on commerce with the PRC, the U.K. government relented. Following the war, increasingly loud voices in Britain called for relaxing those controls and eliminating the differential in trade. Not wanting to anger the United States, Winston Churchill only went so far as to push for ending Nationalist harassment of British shipping. When Macmillan finally eliminated the differential, he did so only after a great deal of hedging, and he made sure to act in a nonelection year. Similarly, when his government determined to sell the Viscount aircraft to China, pains were taken to inform Washington only at the last minute. The fact that the decision on the Viscounts was also made in a nonelection year helped as well. Finally, Wilson's determination to remove Britain's military presence from the east of Suez region came only after years of stalling and a realization that to wait any longer would seriously impair the U.K. economy.

The British also wanted to keep Korea, as well as later crises, from turning into another world war. Clement Attlee made clear to Truman in 1950 his nation's concerns over talk of using nuclear weapons in Korea. Likewise, Churchill informed Arthur Ringwalt that Britain disapproved of United Action. Churchill, Eden, and Macmillan expressed their opposition to U.S. support for Chiang Kai-shek during the three Taiwan Strait crises, while Wilson rejected American requests that he send ground troops to Vietnam.

Again, though, the British generally proceeded cautiously. When Truman refused to grant Attlee a written statement that he would not use nuclear weapons in Korea, Attlee relented. Wilson, as noted, mixed his refusal to send U.S. ground troops to Vietnam with public support for the American war effort there. Churchill, Eden, and Macmillan disliked American support for Chiang Kai-shek, but they realized that pushing Washington too hard risked exposing a rift in the Anglo-American alliance. This caution was seen most clearly in Macmillan, who time and again worried that if he did not act carefully, he might open the door to another Suez.

On these two topics—Britain's financial well-being and Korea—the British were able to maintain some semblance of independence, or even to guide U.S. policy in directions they favored. One reason was America's desire to develop a world opinion opposed to communism. No matter how much U.S. presidents and their secretaries of state disapproved of the government in Beijing, they were not prepared to force their counterparts in the United

Kingdom to accept America's China policy initiative-for-initiative if it meant placing the solidity of the Anglo-American alliance in peril. Thus, when Macmillan explained why he had no choice but to eliminate the differential on trade and why selling the Viscounts was so important to his country, Washington accepted those actions rather than face the destruction of the trade controls system altogether.

Second, while the Commonwealth at times could place limits on Britain's ability to influence the United States, it could also help. Here, the British used America's desire to develop a world opinion opposed to communism against Washington. A good example is the crisis in Indochina. Even though Australia and New Zealand backed the U.S. position on a Southeast Asia defense pact, India did not. Accordingly, Britain could argue—and did—that the American stance would mean losing support in Asia. When Whitehall enjoyed Commonwealth support, as in the case of United Action, it had even greater leeway in how far it would go to please the United States.

American public and governmental opinion helped as well. Although Washington officials distrusted and most Americans feared or even hated the PRC, it did not mean they wanted to see an expansion of the war in Korea or, after Korea, another such conflict. The response to crises in Indochina and the Taiwan Strait provide excellent examples of such sentiment. Such feeling enhanced Britain's freedom of action or its ability to move U.S. China policy. Furthermore, as Americans became more interested in the PRC, and as the U.S. leadership demonstrated a greater willingness to develop ties with the Communist government, so too could Britain seek greater independence of action.

Finally, one cannot ignore personalities. The friendship between Eisenhower and Churchill and Macmillan and the close ties that developed between Macmillan and Kennedy no doubt facilitated Britain's efforts to explain and defend their positions to Washington. Even when personalities clashed, as in the case of Johnson and Wilson, things did not deteriorate to the point that either country was prepared to break up the alliance. Two individuals were exceptions to the rule. Anthony Eden wanted to downgrade the Anglo-American relationship and to challenge the U.S. policy of pressure. Given his willingness to openly contest the United States' views on topics the White House considered particularly sensitive and his generally poor relationship with members of the Eisenhower administration (especially Dulles), it is likely that, had Eden not resigned in 1956, a schism in the Anglo-American alliance still would have occurred, but over China. Edward Heath, like Eden, wanted to downgrade the Anglo-American alliance; and, like Eden and Dulles, Heath's relationship with Nixon was, at best, cool. Unlike Eden, though, Heath had an advantage in that U.S. China policy was changing as well, allowing him greater freedom of action without fear of repercussions.

In short, the British did not completely follow the American line toward China. Still, the fact was that during much of the period in question, the United Kingdom found it impossible to fully adopt the policy of conciliation and negotiation it favored. British officials realized that they were the junior partners in the Anglo-American relationship and had to adopt many facets of a policy toward China they did not favor, saving their influence for those matters they considered most important. (And even then, they proceeded most carefully.) The extent to which they succeeded in using that influence varied. As U.S. policy toward Beijing changed, and as Britain in the early 1970s reassessed its ties to America, Whitehall began returning to its original approach with the PRC. It had been, however, no easy road.

BIBLIOGRAPHY

Primary Sources

Manuscript Collections

Butler Library, Columbia University, New York, N.Y.
    Papers of Wellington Koo
Dwight D. Eisenhower Library, Abilene, Kan.
    Ann Whitman File
    White House Central Files
    Papers of the U.S. President's Commission on Foreign Economic Policy
    Papers of the White House Office, Office of the Staff Secretary
    Papers of John Foster Dulles
    Papers of James C. Hagerty
    Papers of Christian A. Herter
Gelman Library, George Washington University, Washington, D.C.
    National Security Archive
Lyndon B. Johnson Library, Austin, Tex.
    Cabinet Papers
    National Security File
    State Department Administrative Histories
    Tom Johnson's Notes of Meetings
    Vice Presidential Security File
    Papers of George W. Ball
John F. Kennedy Library, Boston, Mass.
    National Security File
    President's Office File
    Papers of Roger Hilsman
    Papers of James C. Thomson
Library of Congress, Washington, D.C.
    Papers of W. Averell Harriman
Mudd Library, Princeton University, Princeton, N.J.
    Papers of John Foster Dulles
    Papers of George F. Kennan
Preston Library, Virginia Military Institute, Lexingon, Va.
    Marshall Foundation National Archives Project

Sterling Memorial Library, Yale University, New Haven, Conn.
  Papers of Chester Bowles
Harry S. Truman Library, Independence, Mo.
  President's Secretary's File
  Selected Records Relating to the Korean War
  Papers of Dean Acheson
  Papers of Clark Clifford
  Papers of George Elsey

Government Archives

National Archives of the United States, Washington, D.C. Record Group 59,
  General Records of the Department of State
Richard Nixon Presidential Materials Project
Public Record Office, Kew, London, United Kingdom
  Cabinet Records
  Foreign Office Records
  Prime Minister's Office Records

Published Governmental and Archival Documents

Documents on British Policy Overseas. Series 2, Vol. 4. (London: Her Majesty's
  Stationery Office, 1984–).
Foreign Relations of the United States. (Washington, D.C.: Government Print
  ing Office, 1948–).
  1948, Vol. 3.
  1949, Vols. 8 and 9.
  1950, Vols. 2, 6, and 7.
  1951, Vols. 2, 6, and 7.
  1952–1954, Vols. 2, 3, 6, 12, 13, 14, 15, and 16.
  1955–1957, Vols. 2, 3, 10, 11, and 27.
  1958–1960, Vol. 19.
  1961–1963, Vol. 22.
  1964–1968, Vol. 2.
United Kingdom, Parliament. *Hansard Parliamentary Debates.*
U.S. Department of State. *Department of State Bulletin.*
U.S. President. *Public Papers of the Presidents of the United States.*
University Publications of America. *CIA Research Reports, 1946–1976.* Frederick, Md.: 1982. Microfilm, 6 reels.
  ———. *Confidential U.S. State Department Central Files, China: Foreign Affairs, 1950–1954.* Frederick, Md.: 1985. Microfilm, 6 reels.
  ———. *Confidential U.S. State Department Central Files, China: Foreign Af-
  fairs, 1955–1959.* Frederick, Md.: 1987. Microfilm, 10 reels.

———. *Confidential U.S. State Department Central Files: United States-Chinese Relations, 1940–1949*. Frederick, Md.: 1984. Microfilm, 7 reels.

———. *Documents of the National Security Council, 4th supplement*. Frederick, Md.: 1987. Microfilm, 7 reels.

Contemporary Periodicals

Atlantic Monthly
Bulletin of the Atomic Scientists
Commonweal
Congressional Quarterly Almanac
London Times
Nation
New Republic
New York Times
Newsweek
Saturday Review
Time
U.S. News and World Report

Oral Histories

Aldrich, Winthrop. Dwight D. Eisenhower Library.
Bundy, William P. Lyndon B. Johnson Library.
Ringwalt, Arthur. Harry S. Truman Library.

Secondary Sources

Articles

Accinelli, Robert. "Eisenhower, Congress, and the 1954–55 Offshore Islands Crisis." *Presidential Studies Quarterly* 20 (spring 1990): 329–48.

Attlee, Clement R. "Britain and America: Common Aims, Different Opinions." *Foreign Affairs* 32 (January 1954): 190–202.

Belmonte, Laura. "Anglo-American Relations and the Dismissal of MacArthur." *Diplomatic History* 19 (fall 1995): 641–67.

Bowles, Chester. "The 'China Problem' Reconsidered." *Foreign Affairs* 38 (April 1960): 476–86.

Brands, H. W., Jr. "Testing Massive Retaliation: Credibility and Crisis in the Taiwan Strait." *International Security* 12 (spring 1988): 124–51.

Buhite, Russell D. "Missed Opportunities? American Policy and the Chinese Communists, 1949." *Mid-America* 61 (October 1979): 179–88.

Calingaert, Daniel. "Nuclear Weapons and the Korean War." *Journal of Strategic Studies* 11 (1988): 177–202.

Chang, Gordon. "JFK, China, and the Bomb." *Journal of American History* 74 (March 1988): 1287–1310.

Chang, Gordon, and He Di, "The Absence of War in the U.S.-China Confrontation over Quemoy and Matsu in 1954–1955: Contingency, Luck, Deterrence?" *American Historical Review* 98 (December 1993): 1500–24.

Chen, Jian. "China and the First Indo-China War, 1950–54." *China Quarterly* no. 133 (March 1993): 85–110.

———. "The Myth of America's 'Lost Chance' in China: A Chinese Perspective in Light of New Evidence." *Diplomatic History* 21 (winter 1997): 77–86

———. "The Ward Case and the Emergence of Sino-American Confrontation, 1948–1950." *Australian Journal of Chinese Affairs* no. 30 (July 1993): 149–70.

Dingman, Roger. "Atomic Diplomacy during the Korean War." *International Security* 13 (winter 1988/89): 50–91.

Dobson, Alan. "The Years of Transition: Anglo-American Relations, 1961–1967." *International Studies* 16 (1990): 239–58.

Dockrill, M. L. "The Foreign Office, Anglo-American Relations and the Korean War, June 1950–June 1951." *International Affairs* 62 (summer 1986): 459–76.

Dumbrell, John. "The Johnson Administration and the British Labour Government: Vietnam, the Pound and East of Suez." *Journal of American Studies* 30 (1996): 211–31.

Eliades, George C. "Once More unto the Breach: Eisenhower, Dulles, and Public Opinion during the Offshore Islands Crisis of 1958." *Journal of American–East Asian Relations* 2 (winter 1993): 343–67.

Farrar, Peter N. "Britain's Proposal for a Buffer Zone South of the Yalu in November 1950: Was It a Neglected Opportunity to End the Fighting in Korea?" *Journal of Contemporary History* 18 (April 1983): 327–51.

Fielding, Jeremy. "Coping with Decline: U.S. Policy toward the British Defense Reviews of 1966." *Diplomatic History* 23 (fall 1999): 633–56.

Foot, Rosemary. "Anglo-American Relations in the Korean Crisis: The British Effort to Avert an Expanded War, December 1950–January 1951." *Diplomatic History* 10 (winter 1986): 43–57.

———. "Nuclear Coercion and the Ending of the Korean Conflict." *International Security* 13 (winter 1988–1989): 92–112.

Førland, Tor Egil. "'Selling Firearms to the Indians': Eisenhower's Export Control Policy, 1953–54." *Diplomatic History* 15 (spring 1991): 221–44.

Garver, John W. "Little Chance." *Diplomatic History* 21 (winter 1997): 87–94.

Han, Yelong. "An Untold Story: American Policy toward Chinese Students in the United States, 1949–1955." *Journal of America–East Asian Relations* 1 (spring 1993): 77–99.

Hao Yufan, and Zhai Zhihai, "China's Decision to Enter the Korean War: History Revisited." *China Quarterly* no. 121 (March 1990): 94–115.

Hosoya, Chihiro. "Japan, China, the United States, and the United Kingdom, 1951–2: The Case of the 'Yoshida Letter,'" *International Affairs* 60 (spring 1984): 247–59.

Immerman, Richard H. "The United States and the Geneva Conference of 1954: A New Look." *Diplomatic History* 14 (winter 1990): 43–66.

Kennedy, John F. "A Democrat Looks at Foreign Policy." *Foreign Affairs* 36 (October 1957): 44–59.

Kramer, Mark. "The Soviet Foreign Ministry Appraisal of Sino-Soviet Relations on the Eve of the Split." *Cold War International History Project Bulletin* 6–7 (winter 1995/1996): 170–85.

Kuehl, Daniel T. "Airpower vs. Electricity: Electric Power as a Target for Strategic Air Operations." *Journal of Strategic Studies* 18 (1995): 237–66.

Lee, David. "Australia and Anglo-American Disagreement over the Quemoy-Matsu Crisis, 1954–55." *Journal of Imperial and Commonwealth History* 23 (January 1995): 105–28.

Li, Xiaobing, Jian Chen, and David L. Wilson. "Mao Zedong's Handling of the Taiwan Straits Crisis of 1958: Chinese Recollections and Documents." *Cold War International History Project Bulletin* 6–7 (winter 1995/1996): 208–26.

McMahon, Robert J. "Credibility and World Power: Exploring the Psychological Dimension in Postwar American Diplomacy." *Diplomatic History* 15 (fall 1991): 455–71.

Mastanduno, Michael. "Trade as a Strategic Weapon: American and Alliance Export Control Policy in the Early Postwar Period." *International Organization* 42 (winter 1988): 121–50.

Matray, James I. "Truman's Plan for Victory: National Self-Determination and the Thirty-Eighth Parallel Decision in Korea." *Journal of American History* 66 (September 1979): 314–33.

Nixon, Richard M. "Asia after Viet Nam." *Foreign Affairs* 46 (October 1967): 111–25.

Ovendale, R[itchie]. "Britain, the United States, and the Recognition of Communist China." *Historical Journal* 26 (March 1983): 139–58.

Pemberton, Gregory James. "Australia, the United States, and the Indochina Crisis of 1954." *Diplomatic History* 13 (winter 1989): 45–66.

Peng, Xizhe. "Demographic Consequences of the Great Leap Forward in China's Provinces." *Population and Development Review* 13 (December 1987): 639–70.

Rossi, John P. "The British Reaction to McCarthyism, 1950–54." *Mid-America* 70 (January 1988): 5–18.

Rushkoff, Bennett C. "Eisenhower, Dulles and the Quemoy-Matsu Crisis, 1954–1955." *Political Science Quarterly* 96 (fall 1981): 465–80.

Schonberger, Howard. "Peacemaking in Asia: The United States, Great Britain, and the Japanese Decision to Recognize Nationalist China, 1951–52." *Diplomatic History* 10 (winter 1986): 59–73.

Sheng, Michael. "The Triumph of Internationalism: CCP-Moscow Relations before 1949." *Diplomatic History* 21 (winter 1997): 95–104.

Smith, Raymond, and John Zametica. "The Cold Warrior: Clement Attlee Reconsidered." *International Affairs* 2 (spring 1985): 237–52.

Stevenson, Adlai. "Putting First Things First: A Democratic View." *Foreign Affairs* 38 (January 1960): 191–208.

Stueck, William W. [Jr.]. "The Limits of Influence: British Policy and American Expansion of the War in Korea." *Pacific Historical Review* 55 (February 1986): 65–95.

Warner, Geoffrey. "The Anglo-American Special Relationship." *Diplomatic History* 13 (fall 1989): 479–99.

Weathersby, Kathryn. "New Findings on the Korean War." *Cold War International History Project Bulletin* 3 (fall 1993): 1, 14–18.

———. "The Soviet Role in the Early Phase of the Korean War: New Documentary Evidence." *Journal of American–East Asian Relations* 2 (winter 1993): 425–58.

Wested, Odd Arne. "Losses, Chances, and Myths: The United States and the Creation of the Sino-Soviet Alliance, 1945–1950." *Diplomatic History* 21 (winter 1997): 105–15.

Wolf, David C. "'To Secure a Convenience': Britain Recognizes China— 1950." *Journal of Contemporary History* 18 (April 1983): 299–326.

Woodard, Gary. "Australian Foreign Policy on the Offshore Islands Crisis of 1954–5 and Recognition of China." *Australian Journal of International Affairs* 45 (1991): 242–63.

Wright, Nancy Allison. "Claire Chennault and China's 'Airline Affair.'" *Journal of the American Aviation Historical Society* 41 (1996): 300–311.

Xiang, Lanxin. "The Recognition Controversy: Anglo-American Relations in China, 1949." *Journal of Contemporary History* 27 (April 1992): 319–43.

Yasuhara, Yoko. "Japan, Communist China, and Export Controls in Asia, 1948–52." *Diplomatic History* 10 (winter 1986): 75–89.

Yuan, Jing-dong. "Between Economic Warfare and Strategic Embargo: U.S.–U.K. Conflicts over Export Controls on the PRC, 1949–57." *Issues & Studies* 30 (March 1994): 67–96.

Zhai, Qiang. "China and the Geneva Conference of 1954." *China Quarterly* no. 129 (March 1992): 103–22.

———. "Dulles, Wedge, and the Sino-American Ambassadorial Talks, 1955–1957." *Chinese Historians* 2 (June 1989): 29–44.

Zubok, Vladislav M. "Khrushchev's Nuclear Promise to Beijing during the 1958 Crisis." *Cold War International History Project Bulletin* 6–7 (winter 1995–1996): 219, 226–27.

Books

Accinelli, Robert. *Crisis and Commitment: United States Policy toward Taiwan, 1950–1955*. Chapel Hill: University of North Carolina Press, 1996.

Acheson, Dean. *Present at the Creation: My Years in the State Department*. New York: W. W. Norton, 1969.

Aitken, Jonathan. *Nixon: A Life*. Washington: Regnery, 1993.

Aldous, Richard, and Sabine Lee, eds. *Harold Macmillan: Aspects of a Political Life*. New York: St. Martin's Press, 1999.

Alexander, Bevin. *The Strange Connection: U.S. Intervention in China, 1944–1972*. New York: Greenwood, 1992.

Ambrose, Stephen E. *Eisenhower*, vol. 2, *The President, 1952–1969*. New York: Simon & Schuster, 1984.

———. *Nixon*, vol. 2, *The Triumph of a Politician, 1962–1972*. New York: Simon & Schuster, 1989.

Appleman, Roy E. *Disaster in Korea: The Chinese Confront MacArthur*. College Station: Texas A&M University Press, 1989.

Bachrack, Stanley D. *The Committee of One Million: "China Lobby" Politics, 1953–1971*. New York: Columbia University Press, 1976.

Ball, Stuart and Anthony Seldon, eds. *The Heath Government, 1970–1974: A Reappraisal*. London: Longman, 1996.

Barnouin, Barbara, and Yu Changgen. *Chinese Foreign Policy during the Cultural Revolution*. London: Kegan Paul International, 1998.

———. *Ten Years of Turbulence: The Chinese Cultural Revolution*. London: Kegan Paul International, 1993.

Bartlett, C. J. *British Foreign Policy in the Twentieth Century*. New York: St. Martin's, 1989.

———. *A History of Postwar Britain, 1945–1974*. London: Longman, 1977.

Baylis, John, ed. *Anglo-American Relations since 1939: The Enduring Alliance*. Manchester, U.K.: Manchester University Press, 1997.

Beaverbrook, Lord. *The Decline and Fall of Lloyd George*. New York: Duell, Sloan and Pearce, 1963.

Becker, Jasper. *Hungry Ghosts: Mao's Secret Famine*. New York: Free Press, 1996.

Bennett, Edward M. *Recognition of Russia: An American Foreign Policy Dilemma*. Waltham, Mass.: Blaidsell Publishing Co., 1970.

Beschloss, Michael R. *The Crisis Years: Kennedy and Khrushchev, 1960–1963.* New York: Edward Burlingame, 1991.

Beschloss, Michael R., ed. *Taking Charge: The Johnson White House Tapes, 1963–1964.* New York: Simon & Schuster, 1997.

Blum, Robert M. *Drawing the Line: The Origin of the American Containment Policy in East Asia.* New York: W. W. Norton, 1982.

Boardman, Robert. *Britain and the People's Republic of China, 1949–74.* London: Macmillan, 1976.

Bohlen, Charles. *Witness to History, 1929–1969.* New York: W. W. Norton, 1973.

Boorman, Howard L. *Biographical Dictionary of Republican China,* 5 vols. New York: Columbia University Press, 1970.

Borg, Dorothy, and Waldo Heinrichs, eds., *Uncertain Years: Chinese-American Relations, 1947–1950.* New York: Columbia University Press, 1980.

Brands, H. W. *The Wages of Globalism: Lyndon Johnson and the Limits of American Power.* New York: Oxford University Press, 1995.

Brecher, Michael. *India and World Politics: Krishna Menon's View of the World.* London: Oxford University Press, 1968.

Brendon, Piers. *Ike: His Life and Times.* New York: Harper & Row, 1986.

Brinkley, Douglas, ed. *Dean Acheson and the Making of U.S. Foreign Policy.* New York: St. Martin's, 1993.

Brookshire, Jerry H. *Clement Attlee.* Manchester, U.K.: Manchester University Press, 1995.

Bullock, Alan. *Ernest Bevin: Foreign Secretary, 1945–1951.* London: Heinemann, 1983.

Bundy, William. *A Tangled Web: The Making of Foreign Policy in the Nixon Presidency.* New York: Hill & Wang, 1998.

Burr, William, ed. *The Kissinger Transcripts: The Top Secret Talks with Beijing and Moscow.* New York: New Press, 1998.

Campbell, John. *Edward Heath: A Biography.* London: Jonathan Cape, 1993.

Chang, Gordon H. *Friends and Enemies: The United States, China, and the Soviet Union, 1948–1972.* Stanford: Stanford University Press, 1990.

Charmley, John. *Churchill's Grand Alliance: The Anglo-American Special Relationship, 1940–57.* London: Hodder & Stoughton, 1985.

Chen, Jian. *China's Road to the Korean War: The Making of the Sino-American Confrontation.* New York: Columbia University Press, 1994.

Childs, David. *Britain since 1939: Progress and Decline.* New York: St. Martin's, 1995.

Christensen, Thomas J. *Useful Adversaries: Grand Strategy, Domestic Mobilization, and Sino-American Conflict, 1949–1958.* Princeton: Princeton University Press, 1996.

Clayton, David. *Imperialism Revisited: Political and Economic Relations between Britain and China, 1940–54*. New York: St. Martin's, 1997.

Cohen, Warren I. *Dean Rusk*. Totowa, N.J.: Cooper Square Publishers, 1980.

Cohen, Warren I., and Akira Iriye, eds. *The Great Powers in East Asia, 1953–1960*. New York: Columbia University Press, 1990.

Colville, Sir John R. *The Fringes of Power: 10 Downing Street Diaries, 1939–1955*. New York: W. W. Norton, 1985.

Cray, Ed. *General of the Army: George C. Marshall, Soldier and Statesman*. New York: W. W. Norton, 1990.

Crossman, Richard. *The Diaries of a Cabinet Minister*, vol. 1. London: Hamilton, 1975.

Cumings, Bruce. *Origins of the Korean War*, vol. 2, *The Roaring of the Cataract, 1947–1950*. Princeton: Princeton University Press, 1990.

Cumings, Bruce, ed. *Child of Conflict: The Korean-American Relationship, 1943–1953*. Seattle: University of Washington Press, 1983.

Danchev, Alex. *Oliver Franks: Founding Father*. Oxford: Clarendon, 1993.

Davies, John Paton. *Dragon by the Tail: American, British, Japanese, and Russian Encounters with China and One Another*. New York: W. W. Norton, 1972.

Dickie, John. *"Special" No More: Anglo-American Relations, Rhetoric and Reality*. London: Weidenfeld & Nicolson, 1984.

Dobbs, Charles. *The United States and East Asia since 1945*. Lewiston, N.Y.: Edwin Mellen, 1990.

Dockrill, Michael and John W. Young, eds. *British Foreign Policy, 1945–56*. New York: St. Martin's, 1989.

Douglas-Home, Alec. *The Way the Wind Blows*. London: Collins, 1976.

Dower, John. *War without Mercy: Race and Power in the Pacific War*. New York: Pantheon Books, 1986.

Dulles, Foster Rhea. *American Policy toward Communist China: The Historical Record, 1949–1979*. New York: Thomas Y. Crowell, 1972.

Dutton, David. *Anthony Eden: A Life and Reputation*. London: Arnold, 1997.

Eden, Anthony. *Full Circle*. Boston: Houghton Mifflin, 1960.

Edwards, Lee. *Missionary for Freedom: The Life and Times of Walter Judd*. New York: Paragon House, 1990.

Eisenhower, Dwight D. *The White House Years: Mandate for Change, 1953–1956*. Garden City, N.Y.: Doubleday, 1962.

———. *The White House Years: Waging Peace, 1956–1961*. Garden City, N.Y.: Doubleday, 1965.

Fairbank, John King. *The Great Chinese Revolution: 1800–1985*. New York: Harper & Row, 1986.

Feng, Zhong-ping. *The British Government's China Policy, 1945–1950*. Keele, U.K.: Ryburn Publishing, 1994.

Finkelstein, David M. *Washington's Taiwan Dilemma, 1949–1950: From Abandonment to Salvation.* Fairfax, Va.: George Mason University Press, 1993.

Fisher, Nigel. *Harold Macmillan: A Biography.* London: Weidenfeld & Nicolson, 1982.

Foot, Rosemary. *The Practice of Power: U.S. Relations with China since 1949.* Oxford, U.K.: Clarendon, 1995.

———. *A Substitute for Victory: The Politics of Peacemaking at the Korean Armistice Talks.* Ithaca, N.Y.: Cornell University Press, 1990.

———. *The Wrong War: American Policy and the Dimensions of the Korean Conflict, 1950–1953.* Ithaca, N.Y.: Cornell University Press, 1985.

Freiberger, Steven Z. *Dawn over Suez: The Rise of American Power in the Middle East, 1953–1957.* Chicago: Ivan R. Dee, 1992.

Gaddis, John Lewis. *The Long Peace: Inquiries into the History of the Cold War.* New York: Oxford University Press, 1987.

———. *Russia, the Soviet Union, and the United States: An Interpretive History.* New York: Wiley, 1978.

———. *Strategies of Containment: A Critical Appraisal of Postwar American National Security Policy.* New York: Oxford University Press, 1982.

———. *The United States and the End of the Cold War: Implications, Reconsiderations, Provocations.* New York: Oxford University Press, 1992.

———. *We Now Know: Rethinking Cold War History.* Oxford, U.K.: Clarendon, 1997.

Gallicchio, Marc S. *The Cold War Begins in Asia: American East Asian Policy and the Fall of the Japanese Empire.* New York: Columbia University Press, 1988.

The Gallup Poll: Public Opinion, 1935–1971, vol. 2. New York: Random House, 1972.

Gardner, Lloyd C. *Pay Any Price: Lyndon Johnson and the Wars for Vietnam.* Chicago: Ivan Dee, 1995.

———. *Safe for Democracy: The Anglo-American Response to Revolution, 1913–1923.* New York: Oxford University Press, 1984.

Garthoff, Raymond L. *Détente and Confrontation: American-Soviet Relations from Nixon to Reagan,* revised ed. Washington, D.C.: Brookings Institution, 1994.

Gati, Charles, ed. *Caging the Bear: Containment and the Cold War.* Indianapolis: Bobbs-Merrill, 1974.

Giglio, James N. *The Presidency of John F. Kennedy.* Lawrence: University Press of Kansas, 1991.

Gilbert, Martin. *Winston S. Churchill,* vol. 8, *"Never Despair," 1945–1965.* Boston: Houghton Mifflin, 1988.

Goncharov, Sergei N., John W. Lewis, and Xue Litai. *Uncertain Partners: Stalin, Mao, and the Korean War.* Stanford: Stanford University Press, 1993.

Grasso, June M. *Truman's Two-China Policy, 1948–1950.* Armonk, N.Y.: M. E. Sharpe, 1987.

Green, Marshall, John H. Holdridge, and William N. Stokes. *War and Peace with China: First-Hand Experiences in the Foreign Service of the United States.* Bethesda, Md.: Dacor Press, 1994.

Gurtov, Melvin, and Byong-Moo Hwang. *China under Threat: The Politics of Strategy and Diplomacy.* Baltimore: Johns Hopkins University Press, 1980.

Hahn, Emily. *The Soong Sisters.* Garden City, N.Y.: Doubleday, 1942.

Halperin, Morton H., and Dwight H. Perkins. *Communist China and Arms Control.* New York: Frederick A. Praeger, 1965.

Hamby, Alonzo L. *Man of the People: A Life of Harry S. Truman.* New York: Oxford University Press, 1995.

Harding, Harry, and Yuan Ming, eds. *Sino-American Relations, 1945–1955: A Joint Reassessment of a Critical Decade.* Wilmington, Del.: Scholarly Resources, 1989.

Harrelson, Max. *Fires All around the Horizon: The U.N.'s Uphill Battle to Preserve the Peace.* New York: Praeger, 1989.

Harris, Kenneth. *Attlee,* revised ed. London: Weidenfeld & Nicolson, 1995.

Hathaway, Robert M. *Great Britain and the United States: Special Relations since World War II.* Boston: Twayne, 1990.

Head, William P. *America's China Sojourn: America's Foreign Policy and Its Effects on Sino-American Relations, 1942–1948.* Lanham, Md.: University Press of America, 1983.

Healey, Denis. *The Time of My Life.* New York: W.W. Norton, 1989.

Herring, George C. *America's Longest War: The United States and Vietnam, 1950–1975;* 2d ed. Philadelphia: Temple University Press, 1986.

Hersh, Seymour M. *The Price of Power: Kissinger in the Nixon White House.* New York: Summit, 1983.

Herzstein, Robert E. *Henry R. Luce: A Political Portrait of the Man Who Created the American Century.* New York: Charles Scribner's, 1994.

Hilsman, Roger. *To Move a Nation: The Politics of Foreign Policy in the Administration of John F. Kennedy.* Garden City, N.Y.: Doubleday, 1967.

Hoff, Joan. *Nixon Reconsidered.* New York: Basic Books, 1994.

Hollingsworth, Clare. *Mao.* London: Triad Paladin, 1985.

Hoopes, Townsend. *The Devil and John Foster Dulles.* Boston: Little, Brown, & Co., 1973.

Horne, Alistair. *Harold Macmillan,* vol. 2, *1957–1986.* London: Macmillan, 1989.

Hunt, Michael H. *The Genesis of Chinese Communist Foreign Policy.* New York: Columbia University Press, 1996.

———. *The Making of a Special Relationship: The United States and China to 1914.* New York: Columbia University Press, 1983.

Hunter, Jane. *The Gospel of Gentility: American Women Missionaries in Turn-of-the-Century China.* New Haven: Yale University Press, 1984.

Immerman, Richard H., ed., *John Foster Dulles and the Diplomacy of the Cold War: A Reappraisal.* Princeton: Princeton University Press, 1990.

Isaacson, Walter. *Kissinger: A Biography.* New York: Simon & Schuster, 1992.

———. *The Wise Men: Six Friends and the World They Made.* New York: Simon & Schuster, 1986.

Jenkins, Roy. *Truman.* London: Collins, 1986.

Jespersen, T. Christopher. *American Images of China, 1931–1949.* Stanford: Stanford University Press, 1996.

Johnson, Lyndon Baines. *The Vantage Point: Perspectives of the Presidency, 1963–1969.* New York: Holt, Rinehart & Winston, 1971.

Johnson, U. Alexis. *The Right Hand of Power.* Englewood Cliffs, N.J.: Prentice-Hall, 1984.

Jones, Peter. *America and the British Labour Party: The "Special Relationship" at Work.* London: I. B. Tauris, 1997

Kalicki, J. H. *The Pattern of Sino-American Crises: Political-Military Interactions in the 1950s.* London: Cambridge University Press, 1975.

Kane, Penny. *Famine in China, 1959–61: Demographic and Social Implications.* New York: St. Martin's, 1988.

Kaplan, Lawrence S., Denise Artaud, and Mark Rubin, eds. *Dien Bien Phu and the Crisis of Franco-American Relations, 1945–1955.* Wilmington, Del.: Scholarly Resources, 1990.

Karnow, Stanley. *Mao and China: A Legacy of Turmoil,* 3d ed. New York: Penguin, 1990.

Kaufman, Burton I. *The Arab Middle East and the United States: Inter-Arab Rivalry and Superpower Diplomacy.* New York: Twayne, 1995.

———. *The Korean War: Challenges in Crisis, Credibility, and Command.* Philadelphia: Temple University Press, 1986 and 2d ed. New York: McGraw-Hill, 1997.

Kearns, Doris. *Lyndon Johnson and the American Dream.* New York: Signet, 1976.

Keith, Ronald C. *The Diplomacy of Zhou Enlai.* New York: St. Martin's, 1989.

Kennan, George. *Memoirs: 1950–1963.* Boston: Little, Brown, & Co., 1972.

Khong, Yuen Foong. *Analogies at War: Korea, Munich, Dien Bien Phu, and the Vietnam Decisions of 1965.* Princeton: Princeton University Press, 1992.

Khrushchev, Nikita. *Khrushchev Remembers.* Translated and edited by Strobe Talbott. Boston: Little, Brown, & Co., 1970.

―――. *Khrushchev Remembers: The Glastnost Tapes.* Translated and edited by Jerrold L. Schecter with Vyacheslav V. Luchkow. Boston: Little, Brown, & Co., 1990.

Kim, Gye-Dong. *Foreign Intervention in Korea.* Aldershort, U.K.: Dartmouth, 1993.

Kissinger, Henry A. *White House Years.* Boston: Little, Brown, & Co., 1979.

Koen, Ross Y. *The China Lobby in American Politics.* New York: Harper & Row, 1974.

Kusnitz, Leonard A. *Public Opinion and Foreign Policy: America's China Policy, 1949–1979.* Westport, Conn.: Greenwood, 1984.

LaFeber, Walter. *The Clash: A History of U.S.-Japan Relations.* New York: W. W. Norton, 1997.

Leary, William M. *Perilous Missions: Civil Air Transport and CIA Covert Operations in Asia.* Tuscaloosa: University of Alabama Press, 1984.

Lee, Steven Hugh. *Outposts of Empire: Korea, Vietnam, and the Origins of the Cold War in Asia, 1949–1954.* Montreal: McGill-Queen's University Press, 1995.

Leffler, Melvyn P. *A Preponderance of Power: National Security, the Truman Administration, and the Cold War.* Stanford: Stanford University Press, 1992.

Levin, N. Gordon. *Woodrow Wilson and World Politics: America's Response to War and Revolution.* New York: Oxford University Press, 1968.

Levine, Steven I. *Anvil of Victory: The Communist Revolution in Manchuria, 1945–1948.* New York: Columbia University Press, 1987.

Lewis, John Wilson, and Xue Litai. *China Builds the Bomb.* Stanford: Stanford University Press, 1988.

Li, Xiaobing, and Hongshan Li, eds. *China and the United States: A New Cold War History.* Lanham, Md.: University Press of America, 1998.

Li, Zhisui. *The Private Life of Chairman Mao.* New York: Random House, 1994.

Louis, William Roger, and Hedley Bull, eds. *The "Special Relationship": Anglo-American Relations since 1945.* Oxford: Clarendon, 1986.

Luard, Evan. *A History of the United Nations,* vol. 1, *The Years of Western Domination, 1945–1955.* New York: St. Martin's, 1982.

MacArthur, Douglas. *Reminiscences.* New York: McGraw-Hill, 1964.

McCoy, Donald R. *The Presidency of Harry S. Truman.* Lawrence: University Press of Kansas, 1984.

MacDonald, Callum. *Britain and the Korean War.* Oxford: Basil Blackwell, 1990.

MacFarquhar, Roderick. *The Origins of the Cultural Revolution*, vol. 2, *The Great Leap Forward*. London: Columbia University Press, 1983.

McKinnon, Malcolm. *Independence and Foreign Policy: New Zealand in the World since 1935*. Auckland: Auckland University Press, 1993.

McLellan, David S. and David C. Anderson. *Among Friends: Personal Letters of Dean Acheson*. New York: Dodd, Mead, & Co., 1980.

Macmillan, Harold. *At the End of the Day, 1961–1963*. New York: Harper & Row, 1973.

———. *Pointing the Way, 1959–1961*. New York: Harper & Row, 1972.

———. *Riding the Storm, 1956–1959*. New York: Harper & Row, 1971.

Marks, Frederick W., III. *Power and Peace: The Diplomacy of John Foster Dulles*. Westport, Conn.: Praeger, 1993.

Martin, Edwin W. *Divided Counsel: The Anglo-American Response to Communist Victory in China*. Lexington: University Press of Kentucky, 1986.

Mastanduno, Michael. *Economic Containment: CoCom and the Politics of East-West Trade*. Ithaca, N.Y.: Cornell University Press, 1992.

Mayers, David Allan. *Cracking the Monolith: U.S. Policy against the Sino-Soviet Alliance, 1949–1955*. Baton Rouge: Louisiana State University Press, 1986.

———. *George Kennan and the Dilemmas of U.S. Foreign Policy*. New York: Oxford University Press, 1988.

Melanson, Richard, and David Mayers. *Reevaluating Eisenhower: American Foreign Policy in the 1950s*. Urbana: University of Illinois Press, 1987.

Morgan, Austen. *Harold Wilson*. London: Pluto, 1992.

Mosley, Leonard. *Dulles: A Biography of Eleanor, Allen, and John Foster Dulles and Their Family Network*. New York: Dial Press, 1978.

Nagai, Yonosuke, and Akira Iriye, eds. *The Origins of the Cold War in Asia*. New York: Columbia University Press, 1977.

Neils, Patricia. *China Images in the Life and Times of Henry Luce*. Savage, Md: Rowman & Littlefield, 1990.

Neils, Patricia, ed. *United States Attitudes and Policies toward China: The Impact of American Missionaries*. Armonk, N.Y.: M. E. Sharpe, 1990.

Nicholas, H. G. *The United States and Britain*. Chicago: University of Chicago Press, 1975.

Ninkovich, Frank. *Modernity and Power: A History of the Domino Theory in the Twentieth Century*. Chicago: University of Chicago Press, 1994.

Nixon, Richard. *The Memoirs of Richard Nixon*, 2 vols. New York: Warner, 1978.

Nogee, Joseph L., and Robert H. Donaldson. *Soviet Foreign Policy since World War II*. New York: Pergamon, 1981.

Ovendale, Ritchie. *Anglo-American Relations in the Twentieth Century*. New York: St. Martin's, 1998.

Pach, Chester J., Jr. *Arming the Free World: The Origins of the United States Military Assistance Program, 1945–1950.* Chapel Hill: University of North Carolina Press, 1991.

Pach, Chester J., Jr., and Elmo Richardson. *The Presidency of Dwight D. Eisenhower,* revised ed. Lawrence: University Press of Kansas, 1991.

Panikkar, K. M. *In Two Chinas: Memoirs of a Diplomat.* London: Allen & Unwin, 1955.

Patterson, James T. *Grand Expectations: The United States, 1945–1974.* New York: Oxford University Press, 1996.

Pearce, Malcolm, and Geoffrey Stewart. *British Political History, 1867–1995: Democracy and Decline,* 2d ed. London: Routledge, 1996.

Pearce, Robert D. *Attlee's Labour Governments, 1945–51.* London: Routledge, 1994.

Pimlott, Ben. *Harold Wilson.* London: Harper Collins, 1992.

Pruessen, Ronald W. *John Foster Dulles: The Road to Power.* New York: Free Press, 1982.

Purifoy, Lewis McCarroll. *Harry Truman's China Policy: McCarthyism and the Diplomacy of Hysteria, 1947–1951.* New York: New Viewpoints, 1976.

Randle, Robert F. *Geneva 1954: The Settlement of the Indochinese War.* Princeton: Princeton University Press, 1969.

Rankin, Karl Lott. *China Assignment.* Seattle: University of Washington Press, 1964.

Reed, Bruce, and Geoffrey Williams. *Denis Healey and the Policies of Power.* London: Sidgwick & Jackson, 1971.

Reese, Trevor R. *Australia, New Zealand, and the United States: A Survey of International Relations, 1941–1968.* London: Oxford University Press, 1969.

Renwick, Sir Robin. *Fighting with Allies: America and Britain in Peace and at War.* New York: Times Books, 1996.

Reynolds, David. *Britannia Overruled: British Policy and World Peace in the Twentieth Century.* London: Longman, 1991.

Rusk, Dean. *As I Saw It: Dean Rusk as Told to Richard Rusk.* Edited by Daniel S. Papp. New York: W. W. Norton, 1990.

Ryan, Mark A. *Chinese Attitudes toward Nuclear Weapons: China and the United States during the Korean War.* Armonk, N.Y.: M. E. Sharpe, 1989.

Schaller, Michael. *Altered States: The United States and Japan since the Occupation.* New York: Oxford University Press, 1997.

———. *The American Occupation of Japan: The Origins of the Cold War in Asia.* New York: Oxford University Press, 1985.

———. *The United States and China in the Twentieth Century.* New York: Oxford, 1979.

Schoenbaum, Thomas J. *Waging Peace and War: Dean Rusk in the Truman, Kennedy, and Johnson Years.* New York: Simon & Schuster, 1988.

Schonberger, Howard B. *Aftermath of War: Americans and the Remaking of Japan, 1945–1952.* Kent, Ohio: Kent State University Press, 1989.

Schulzinger, Robert D. *Henry Kissinger: Doctor of Diplomacy.* New York: Columbia University Press, 1989.

Schurmann, Franz. *The Foreign Politics of Richard Nixon: The Grand Design.* Berkeley: University of California Press, 1987.

Seagrave, Sterling. *The Soong Dynasty.* New York: Harper & Row, 1985.

Shao, Wenguang. *China, Britain, and Businessmen: Political and Commercial Relations, 1949–57.* London: Macmillan, 1991.

Shaw, Yu-ming. *An American Missionary in China: John Leighton Stuart and Chinese-American Relations.* Cambridge, Mass.: Council on East Asian Studies, 1992.

Sheng, Michael. *Battling Western Imperialism: Mao, Stalin, and the United States.* Princeton: Princeton University Press, 1997.

Shichor, Yitzhak. *The Middle East in China's Foreign Policy, 1949–1977.* Cambridge: Cambridge University Press, 1979.

Shlaim, Avi, Peter Jones, and Keith Sainsbury. *British Foreign Secretaries since 1945.* London: David & Charles, 1977.

Shuckburgh, Evelyn. *Descent to Suez: Diaries, 1951–56.* New York: W. W. Norton, 1986.

Smith, Felix. *China Pilot: Flying for Chiang and Chennault.* Washington: Brassey's, 1995.

Sorensen, Theodore C. *Kennedy.* New York: Harper & Row, 1965.

Stevenson, Richard W. *The Rise and Fall of Détente: Relaxations of Tension in U.S.-Soviet Relations, 1953–84.* London: Macmillan, 1985.

Stoler, Mark A. *George C. Marshall: Soldier-Statesman of the American Century.* Boston: Twayne, 1989.

Stolper, Thomas E. *China, Taiwan, and the Offshore Islands: Together with an Implication for Outer Mongolia and Sino-Soviet Relations.* Armonk, N.Y.: M. E. Sharpe, 1985.

Stueck, William [Whitney, Jr.]. *The Korean War: An International History.* Princeton: Princeton University Press, 1995.

———. *The Road to Confrontation: American Policy toward China and Korea, 1947–1950.* Chapel Hill: University of North Carolina Press, 1981.

Suyin, Han. *Eldest Son: Zhou Enlai and the Making of Modern China, 1898–1976.* New York: Hill and Wang, 1994.

Tahir-Kheli, Shirin. *The United States and Pakistan: The Evolution of an Influence Relationship.* New York: Praeger, 1982.

Tang, James Tuck-Hong. *Britain's Encounter with Revolutionary China, 1949–54*. New York: St. Martin's, 1992.

Terrill, Ross. *Mao: A Biography*. New York: Harper & Row, 1980.

Thornton, Richard C. *The Nixon-Kissinger Years: Reshaping America's Foreign Policy*. New York: Paragon House, 1989.

Thurston, Anne F. *Enemies of the People*. New York: Alfred A. Knopf, 1987.

Trevelyan, Humphrey. *Worlds Apart: China, 1953–5, Soviet Union 1962–5*. London: Macmillan, 1971.

Truman, Harry S. *Memoirs*, vol. 2, *Years of Trial and Hope*. Garden City, N.Y.: Doubleday, 1956.

Tucker, Nancy Bernkopf. *Patterns in the Dust: Chinese-American Relations and the Recognition Controversy, 1949–1950*. New York: Columbia University Press, 1983.

———. *Taiwan, Hong Kong, and the United States, 1945–1992: Uncertain Friendships*. New York: Twayne, 1994.

Turner, John. *Macmillan*. London: Longman, 1994.

Tyler, Patrick. *A Great Wall: Six Presidents and China: An Investigative History*. New York: Public Affairs, 1999.

Watt, D. Cameron. *Succeeding John Bull: America in Britain's Place, 1900–1975*. Cambridge: Cambridge University Press, 1984.

Weiler, Peter. *Ernest Bevin*. Manchester, U.K.: Manchester University Press, 1993.

Wilbur, C. Martin, and Julie Lien-ying How. *Missionaries of Revolution: Soviet Advisers and Nationalist China, 1920–1927*. Cambridge: Harvard University Press, 1989.

Williams, Francis. *Twilight of Empire: Memoirs of Prime Minister Clement Attlee*. Westport, Conn.: Greenwood, 1961.

Wilson, Dick. *The People's Emperor, Mao: A Biography of Mao Tse-tung*. Garden City, N.Y.: Doubleday, 1980.

———. *Zhou Enlai: A Biography*. New York: Viking, 1984.

Wilson, Harold. *The Labour Government, 1964–1970: A Personal Record*. London: Weidenfeld & Nicolson, 1971.

Xiang, Lanxin. *Recasting the Imperial Far East: Britain and America in China, 1945–1950*. Armonk, N.Y.: M. E. Sharpe, 1995.

Young, John W., ed. *The Foreign Policy of Churchill's Peacetime Administration, 1951–1955*. Leicester, U.K.: Leicester University Press, 1988.

Young, Kenneth. *Sir Alec Douglas-Home*. London: J. M. Dent & Sons, 1970.

Zeiler, Thomas W. *Dean Rusk: Defending the American Mission Abroad*. Wilmington, Del.: Scholarly Resources, 2000.

Zhai, Qiang. *China and the Vietnam Wars, 1950–1975*. Chapel Hill: University of North Carolina Press, 2000.

————. *The Dragon, the Lion, and the Eagle: Chinese-British-American Relations, 1949–1958*. Kent, Ohio: Kent State University Press, 1994.

Zhang, Shu Guang. *Deterrence and Strategic Culture: Chinese-American Confrontations, 1949–1958*. Ithaca, N.Y.: Cornell University Press, 1992.

————. *Mao's Military Romanticism: China and the Korean War, 1950–1953*. Lawrence: University Press of Kansas, 1995.

Zheng, Yi. *Scarlet Memorial: Tales of Cannibalism in Modern China*. Boulder, Colo.: Westview, 1996.

Ziegler, Philip. *Wilson: The Authorised Life of Lord Wilson of Rievaulx*. London: Weidenfeld & Nicolson, 1993.

Unpublished Materials

Nagahashi, Hiroyuki. "China's Food Crises and Its U.S. Policy Change, 1965–1972." Master's thesis, California State University at Long Beach, 1994.

Park, Jong Chul. "The China Factor in United States Decision-making toward Vietnam, 1945–1965." Ph.D. diss., University of Connecticut, 1990.

Rowan, Randy. "A Foreign Policy in Opposition: The British Labour Party and the Far East, 1951–1964." Ph.D. diss., Texas Tech University, 1992.

INDEX

Acheson, Dean: background of, 5; and support for Kuomintang, 5, 19; and "wedge" strategy, 8; and Anglo-American "special relationship," 14, 14n35; and economic sanctions against China, 18, 23, 48, 49, 50–51; and CATC-CNAC controversy, 21; and recognition of PRC, 24–25; and Korean War, 31–35 passim, 39, 40, 41, 45–53 passim, 56, 57, 59; and Chinese representation in UN, 34, 52–53; mentioned, 99

Addis, John, 58

Adenauer, Konrad, 168

Agnew, Spiro, 221–22

Aldrich, Winthrop, 61, 99

Allison, John, 39

Amethyst, 18

Anglo-American relations: and Chinese civil war, 1–3, 8; and inconsistency in U.S. China policy, 7, 13; and economic sanctions against China, 13, 16–18, 29, 30, 31, 42, 43, 47–51, 64, 97, 102–12, 117, 122–28 passim, 156–60, 164–65, 170–71, 175, 176, 182–84, 206, 219, 221, 222, 224, 231, 233; and recognition of PRC, 14, 23–27, 51; and "special relationship," 14–15, 53, 54–55, 124, 126, 135, 138, 141, 145–46, 152, 156, 158, 162–63, 170–71, 177, 187, 190, 216–17; and CATC-CNAC controversy, 20–23, 56, 56n67; and U.S. support for Taiwan, 20, 30, 33, 43, 61–62, 64, 85–86, 176, 238, 239; and Chinese representation in UN, 28, 29, 31, 33, 34, 42, 51–53, 64, 98–102, 122, 123, 128–29, 143–44, 145, 148–56 passim, 175–82 passim, 204, 214–15, 226–28, 230–33, 238; and Korean War, 31–35 passim, 39–64 passim, 238; and KMT harassment of British shipping, 43–44,

97, 112–14, 122, 239; and Japanese peace treaty, 44–45, 57–58; and United Action, 66–68, 72, 74, 78–79; and Southeast Asia defense pact, 67–76 passim, 240; and Geneva Conference, 72–79 passim; and Quemoy-Matsu crises, 81–95 passim, 123, 131–43 passim, 146, 162–63, 170, 236, 239; and economic sanctions against Soviet Union, 105–6, 108, 122, 183–84, 236, 238–39, 240; and U.S. prisoners held by PRC, 115–20 passim; and U.K. exchange of ambassadors with PRC, 121, 122; and Bermuda Conference (1957), 124–25; and Berlin crisis (1961–1962), 147; and relaxation in U.S. China policy, 148–49, 171; and Nuclear Test Ban Treaty, 166–68, 170; and east of Suez, 184–90, 235; and Vietnam War, 184–89 passim, 235; and Sino-American rapprochement, 207, 215–17, 224–25, 229–30

Annenberg, Walter, 227, 229–30

Attlee, Clement: background of, 3–4; and CATC-CNAC controversy, 22; and recognition of PRC, 25, 175, 239; and Korean War, 32–33, 39, 42–46 passim, 50, 57, 64; and economic sanctions against China, 43, 50; mentioned, 6, 15

Austin, Warren, 48

Australia: and U.K. recognition of PRC, 26; and Korean War, 49, 59, 238; and Southeast Asia defense pact, 67, 70, 75, 240; and United Action, 68, 74; and Quemoy-Matsu crises, 83, 91, 134–35; and east of Suez, 186, 188

Ayub Khan, Mohammad, 216

Ball, George, 182–83

Bandung Conference, 92, 94